Iranian Literature after the Islamic Revolution

To Ambroise, Casarie, Octavie and Prudence

Iranian Literature after the Islamic Revolution

Production and Circulation in Iran and the World

Laetitia Nanquette

EDINBURGH
University Press

Edinburgh University Press is one of the leading university presses in the UK. We publish academic books and journals in our selected subject areas across the humanities and social sciences, combining cutting-edge scholarship with high editorial and production values to produce academic works of lasting importance. For more information visit our website: edinburghuniversitypress.com

© Laetitia Nanquette, 2021, 2023

Edinburgh University Press Ltd
The Tun – Holyrood Road
12 (2f) Jackson's Entry
Edinburgh EH8 8PJ

First published in hardback by Edinburgh University Press 2021

Typeset in 11/15 Adobe Garamond by
Servis Filmsetting Ltd, Stockport, Cheshire

A CIP record for this book is available from the British Library

ISBN 978 1 4744 8637 8 (hardback)
ISBN 978 1 4744 8638 5 (paperback)
ISBN 978 1 4744 8640 8 (webready PDF)
ISBN 978 1 4744 8639 2 (epub)

The right of Laetitia Nanquette to be identified as author of this work has been asserted in accordance with the Copyright, Designs and Patents Act 1988 and the Copyright and Related Rights Regulations 2003 (SI No. 2498).

Contents

List of Illustrations	vii
Acknowledgements	ix
Note on Permissions	xi
Note on Translation and Transliteration	xiii
Introduction	1

Part 1 The Literary Field within Iran

1	Forms and Genres in Contemporary Iranian Literature	23
2	Digital Literature: The Importance of the Medium	45
3	The Iranian Literary Field: An Overview	72
4	Book Production within Iran: A Look at the Numbers	113
5	Iranian Children's Literature: A Success Story Nationally and Globally	138

Part 2 The Literary Field in the Diaspora

6	Iran and the Diaspora: Irreconcilable Divisions?	155
7	Translation and Reception in the US and France	180
8	Iranian Writers in Australia	207
9	Post-revolutionary Iranian Literature in the World and in the Persian Cultural System	229

Afterword 255

References 259
Index 287

Illustrations

Figures

1.1	Book cover of a popular novel	23
1.2	Book covers of highbrow novels	24
2.1	Internet censorship in Iran	50
2.2	Fatemeh Ekhtesari's she'rgraphy on Instagram	70
4.1	Market volume, from data extracted from the Iran Book House report and the Small Media report	119
4.2	Number of book titles produced per year according to Small Media, from data extracted from the Small Media report	122
4.3	Number of titles produced per year according to Iran Book House, from data extracted from the Iran Book House report	123
4.4	Average number of copies produced per book title per year, from data extracted from the Iran Book House report	124
4.5	Number of book titles produced per year per type, from data extracted from the Iran Book House report	128
4.6	Number of book titles produced per year per production location, from data extracted from the Iran Book House report	131
4.7	Number of publishers per type, from data extracted from the Iran Book House report	134
5.1	The Book Garden in Tehran, Children's literature section	139
7.1	Ethnic origin of translators	187
7.2	Primary activity of translators	188
7.3	Proportion of publishers by activity	189

7.4 Location of publishers by region   191
7.5 Number of texts translated per author   193
7.6 Translated genres   196
8.1 Religious affiliation of Iranians in Australia   211

Tables

1.1 Percentage of book publications according to genres, from data extracted from the Iran Book House website as of July 2019   25
4.1 Number of books published per city for the year 2012, from data extracted from the Iran Book House report   132
9.1 Reviews of *Censoring an Iranian Love Story, Reading Lolita in Tehran* and *The Book of Fate* online, as of August 2019   232

Map

8.1 The number of people who speak Persian (excluding Dari) at home in the Sydney area   212

Acknowledgements

I am grateful to each and every one of the people I have talked to in Iran and in the Iranian diaspora over the years that it took to complete this book: without your generosity in sharing your time and knowledge, this project would not have been possible. There are too many of you to name individually, but I hope each of you will recognise your valued contribution in the pages that follow. I also hope the circulation of this book, as well as its Persian translation, might act as a token of my appreciation for the work that you do.

To my colleagues at UNSW in the English programme and beyond, thank you for your support. I would particularly like to acknowledge the members of the Iranian Studies Network at UNSW for their help in developing this project in its different stages, including Behnam Fomeshi and Adineh Khojastehpour. I also wish to express my gratitude to Elham Naeej and Setayesh Nooraninejad for being stellar research assistants and essential readers at different points of this project. I am grateful to my Persian teacher and colleague Fatemeh Shams for discussing this book in Persian with me.

Several friends, colleagues and students were kind enough to read working drafts of this book, contributing to the development of some of its ideas. It gives me immense pleasure to thank them here: Bill Ashcroft, Omid Azadibougar, Max Bledstein, Rasha Chatta, Michelle Langford, Mazda Moradabbasi, Amin Palangi, and Mahsa Salamati – I sincerely appreciate your feedback, and all that I have learnt from you. I hope we will have many more years of exchanging ideas.

The initial idea for this book came to me during my Fulbright visiting fellowship at Harvard University, and I am grateful to the Department of Comparative Literature for hosting me and giving me the impulse to start this project. I am also grateful to the institutions that funded my fellowship: Fulbright commission (US), Arthur Sachs Foundation (France), Roshan Cultural Heritage Institute (US) and Fondation de France (France). This book has been researched and written during my time at UNSW, first as a Vice-Chancellor's Postdoctoral Fellow, then as a Fellow of the Australian Research Council (ARC), as well as in the role of lecturer. I want to express sincere thanks to the ARC for giving me the space and time to research and write this book through a Discovery Early Career Researcher Award (DE150100329). This research was carried out with approval from the UNSW Human Research Ethics Advisory Panel B: Arts, Humanities and Law HC15288, and in accordance with the appropriate research ethics guidelines.

Various parts of this book were shared at conferences and seminars, and I am appreciative of the audiences at these events for raising important questions and helping me to refine my ideas.

Finally, I am thankful to my family. Thanks to my mother for supporting my love of books. My husband Ambroise has been with me through many years and in many places: thank you for sharing your life with me. To our three daughters, Casarie, Octavie and Prudence: I am forever happy, proud and grateful to be your mother.

Note on Permissions

Parts of Chapters 7 and 9 contain material from my article 'The Translations of Modern Persian Literature in the United States: 1979–2011', published in *The Translator* on 22 September 2016, available online at https://www.tandfonline.com/doi/abs/10.1080/13556509.2016.1227530?journalCode=rtrn20.

Parts of Chapters 6 and 7 have been published in my chapter in *The Iranian Diaspora: Challenges, Negotiations, and Transformations* 'Diaspora and Literary Production. Iranians in France', Mohsen Mostafavi Mobasher ed., University of Texas Press, 2018: 178–95.

Parts of Chapter 9 are derived from my article 'The Global Circulation of an Iranian Bestseller', published in *Interventions: International Journal of Postcolonial Studies*, 19:1, 2017, copyright Taylor & Francis, available online at https://www.tandfonline.com/doi/full/10.1080/1369801X.2016.1191960.

Chapter 6 contains material from my article 'The Circulation of Iranian Texts around the World: The Appearance of a Transnational Iranian Publishing Industry?', *Australian Humanities Review*, 62, November 2017: 157–69.

Parts of Chapters 2 and 6 are using my chapter published in *The Edinburgh Companion to the Postcolonial Middle East* 'Towards a globalization of contemporary Iranian literature? Iranian literary blogs and the evolution of the literary field', Anna Ball and Karim Mattar eds, Edinburgh University Press, 2019: 383–406. 'Reproduced with permission of The Licensor through PLSclear.'

Chapter 8 contains material from 'Refugee Life Writing in Australia: Testimonios by Iranians', published in *Postcolonial Text*, 9: 2, 2014.

Chapter 4 is derived from 'Contemporary Persian Literature and Digital Humanities', published in *Persian Literature as World Literature*, Mostafa Abedinifard, Omid Azadibougar and Amirhossein Vafa eds, Bloomsbury, forthcoming in 2021.

All are reproduced with permission. For permission to republish, I thank the editors, journals and presses.

Note on Translation and Transliteration

For transliterations, I have followed the *Iranian Studies* journal system. I employ the most commonly used anglicised forms of Persian words and names and all Persian words are italicised. Translations are my own unless otherwise indicated.

Introduction

Close to the University of Tehran, Revolution Square (Meydan-e enqelab) is the epicentre of the world of the book – lined with bookstores, publishers, street book vendors, and institutions like the Iran Book House (Khaneh-ye ketab). Vendors sell banned books in broad daylight on the pavement along Revolution Street and adjacent streets in central Tehran. Government publishers like Sureh Mehr are right next to underground presses and to the independent Union of Tehran Publishers and Booksellers. The area around Revolution Square embodies the paradoxes and the multiple layers of the literary world in post-revolutionary Iran.

Culture in general and literature specifically have been central to the foundation of the Islamic Republic of Iran and have remained so since: culture is essential to the ways it defines itself and to the defence of its ideas. Gholam Khiabany argues that:

> The Islamic state, which came to power after 1979, more than anything else defined itself in a 'cultural' sense. The two aims of the cultural policy of the new state were based on destruction of an imposed 'western' and 'alien' culture, and the replacing of it with a dignified, indigenous, and authentic Islamic culture which had declined under the previous regime. (2010: 139)

After forty years of the Islamic Republic, this centrality of culture to the upkeep of the regime is even more pronounced. Indeed, Fahrad Khosrokhavar and Olivier Roy in the context of post-war Iran (1980–8) argue that culture is what remains when utopia has disappeared (Khosrokhavar and Roy

1999: back cover). The examples of Sacred Defence literature, which the regime heavily finances and which portrays the literature of the war, and of the poetry nights organised by the Supreme Leader Ali Khamenei (Shams 2015b), testify to this importance of maintaining the culture of the Islamic Republic in the struggle to preserve its rule. Whilst many Iranians, including those who support the Islamic Republic and the war veterans considered to be the guardians of the revolution, are disillusioned with the regime, it is critical to study the way culture is used to bridge the gap between it and the people. The fight over culture is also at the centre of debates between the Iranian diaspora and Iranians from within. 'Soft war' (*Jang-e narm*) is felt as a very real threat by all echelons of the state, and the nation's current Supreme Leader Khamenei often mentions it in his speeches and refers to it on his website. Narges Bajoghli defines soft war as 'a term that is used loosely by Iranian officials to refer to the ways in which the United States, European powers, and Israel influence Iranian politics with the soft power of culture' (2019: 39). The diaspora is often considered to be playing a key role in this soft war.

In quantitative terms too, culture, and especially the publication of books, is critical. Iran is one of the countries that publishes most in the world. In 2016 the Spectator Index put Iran ninth on the list, with 72,871 books published per year, just after France and before Italy. Even if we consider the fact that print runs are low and have been decreasing drastically over the last forty years, the high number of titles published testify to an intense book culture, which is an integral part of the Islamic Republic's ideology on the culture industry. There are other signs of this intensity, like the existence of the Iran Book News Agency, a governmental organisation linked to the Iran Book House, dedicated to reporting news about the book industry.

Understanding Contemporary Iran through its Literary Field

This book aims to show what literature can tell us about post-revolutionary Iran and to profile the Iranian literary field in all its complexity, its variations, its disjuncture, by insisting on its polyvocality. It narrates several different aspects of the story of contemporary literature: within Iran and in the diaspora; the independent and the governmental fields; canonical literature (defined as the texts recognised by literary institutions and the texts perceived as worthy of reading and interpretation), as well as popular and children's literatures; the local, the national and the global levels and all the informal connections in between. All these voices and strands need to be understood in their relations to one another, in order to analyse the state of contemporary Iranian literature. Despite, or maybe because of, censorship, sanctions, strong nationalism and exile, contemporary Iranian literature is complex, as so many factors add layers to its understanding. This book takes a broad scope in order to show its richness.

In the pages below, I define the scope and perimeter of the research, explain my methodology, as well as the main theoretical framework used. I also give a detailed synopsis of the chapters.

My main audience is English-speaking and based in western countries, which is why I make frequent references to western literary markets and traditions as elements of comparison. I wish to dispel western assumptions about contemporary Iranian culture and bring the complexity of the Iranian literary field to a wider audience. Later, I hope this book will be translated into Persian to continue the dialogue with colleagues and readers in Iran.

Scope and Perimeter

My analysis focuses on the last four decades since the Islamic Revolution (1979–2019). The revolution was not only a regime change; it radically modified all areas of society including culture, and it has to be understood as a rupture in the literary field too, although it is also important to look at the continuities. Therefore, I mostly use the term 'post-revolutionary' to define the period I study, where the revolution and its ideas are still at the centre of the debates.

The book focuses on Iran and on the Persian language for several reasons. Although Persian is the official language, other languages like Azeri, Kurdish and Arabic are used in Iran. However, Persian is the only official common language and it is where the bulk of literary production and exchanges happen. Here it is important to underline that the Islamic Republic implements a strict language policy and limits the possibility of using other languages. This hegemony of the Persian language has an impact on the structure of the literary field, which is dominated by Persian language texts. There is little room for texts in minorities languages to circulate in

Iran. I also restrict my analysis to Persian because this is the language that I speak and read. I only refer to the Iranian space, although Persian is the common language of Afghanistan and Tajikistan, because I am looking at the conditions of production, distribution and reception of literature, and these appear to be very different in those three countries and in their respective diasporas. For example, although Afghans, an important community in Australia, are also Persian speakers, there is a strong divide along national lines and therefore scant literary engagement between Iranian and Afghan writers based in Australia, as I develop in Chapter 8. While I will not discuss this at length, it is important to have in mind that

> the Persian language's stance is a double and contradictory one, which owes mostly to its particular history: in spite of its internationally peripheral position, it imagines itself as a universal language and is loaded with such assumptions. So, it fails to see its new position in the world and, at the same time, conveniently disallows the representation of specific linguistic, religious, etc. categories at the national level. (Azadibougar 2014: 97)

This is critical when we discuss issues of globalisation, as the Persian language is nowadays a peripheral one that scarcely circulates, yet it has a tradition of being a language of culture, a lingua franca from the fifteenth to the nineteenth century across Asia. This movement of the language informs the reflections of some of the writers and publishers involved, and even the state, which does not resign to its peripherality.

Although there are signs that we might be moving to language-based literatures, with corpuses of Francophone literature or Arabic literature, as Alexander Beecroft has argued, the structures are still national. Our world literature system is based on national literatures, as institutional structures of literature 'operate on national assumptions' (Beecroft 2015: 239). Despite the importance of the postcolonial paradigm to reflect on the power relations between Iran and the rest of the world, as well as on its relations with the diaspora, its argument for transnational border-crossing mostly does not apply to my analysis of the contemporary Iranian literary field. Indeed, for the diaspora, as I will show later, the nation and a form of nationalism that excludes the other are an essential part of the cement between Iranians, even with the advent of new technologies. Niki Akhavan argues: 'the internet has been used to straighten – rather than to challenge – nationalism and other exclusionary ideologies' (2013: 3). She adds:

> Ironically, the transnational connections the Internet makes possible do not necessarily translate to a transcending of national boundaries; in fact, they often work to entrench them. And while the Internet may facilitate the coming together of geographically dispersed individuals, nationalism is often the glue that precipitates and maintains such transnational connections. (Akhavan 2013: 17)

The move to a diaspora that is largely digitally connected has not changed the form of nationalism that bounds Iranians, which is indeed strong. Iran is both diasporic and patriotic. In this book, I refer to Iranian's imagined community, an identity and a sense of belonging, but patriotism is the political term for this. In 2011, a poll by the World Values Survey stated that Iranians ranked number 1 in the world when it came to nationalism, with 92 per cent of Iranians claiming to be 'very proud' of their nationality, compared to 72 per cent of Americans, and less than 50 per cent of French and British people.

Iran is not only a nation state but also an identity and a belonging space, what Benedict Anderson calls an 'imagined community' (1983). Therefore, I include the Iranian diaspora in my analysis, especially works written by Iranians outside of Iran in other languages than Persian. Some of these texts could be studied within their national framework, as American or French literature, but since Iran remains a referent for Iranian writers, it is important to study them in addition as a group belonging also to Iranian literature. The implications of categorising them as such means that I focus on the common Iranian referent and see their links and differences through the Iranian lens. They belong to two cultural traditions at the same time and my book studies these influences side by side. This approach of understanding texts within two different traditions is common in the study of pre-modern Persian literature, through the idea of 'Persianate literature'. Marshall Hodgson studied works in Turkish, Urdu and Chagatai as Persianate literatures, 'we may call all these cultural traditions carried in Persian or reflecting Persian inspiration "Persianate"' (1977: 293). More recent scholarship uses the term Persianate to refer to the influence of Persian culture and the Persian language in a vast region ranging from Turkey across Central Asia to India (Amanat and

Ashraf 2018; Green 2019). Persian was a lingua franca from the fifteenth century until the end of the nineteenth century. The connotations of the term 'Persianate' are mostly to pre-modern Iran and are linked to the language, whereas I am interested in the Iranian space as an identity and a space of belonging, beyond the use of Persian. The term 'Iranian literature' thus encompasses literatures published outside of the Iranian nation state. This means that the association of Iran and the subject of Iranian literature with the current geographical borders of Iran does not work anymore. What we see happening throughout the twentieth century but mostly after the revolution, the period I study in this book, is that the focus on the language is replaced by an insistence on Iran as an imagined community, a space of belonging which goes beyond Persian. Literatures from Iranians across the world thus produce small clusters of Iran outside its borders, either in Persian or in the local languages.

In this book, I touch upon different literary genres as elements of comparison, especially in the second chapter on digital literature that discusses poetry, but I otherwise restrict my analysis to prose fiction. This is firstly because of the essential link between novels, and by extension fiction, and nations, especially in authoritarian contexts where the state has a high stake in literary products. Prose fiction emphasises national elements more than poetry, which is more attentive to form and language in contemporary Persian texts. Benedict Anderson argued that the novel is linked to the emergence of nation states and I believe there is a crucial relation between novel and nation (Anderson 1983). The relationship between nation and novel has been studied in literary fields like the English one (Parrinder 2008). Because my focus is on Iran as an imagined community in the national context, the novel is naturally my preferred genre of study. Here it is important to note that the distinction between genres in Iran is perhaps not as clear cut as in other literary fields: as novels, novellas and short stories have loose definitions, it is usually best to speak about 'prose fiction' rather than specific genres. The second reason of my focus on prose fiction is that genres like drama or essays are published in small numbers and mostly belong to the independent field, so they influence the field only in one way. As for poetry, its place is predominant in the Persian cultural system, although it is shifting, as I demonstrate in my last chapter. Poetry's dynamics are different from fiction and deserve a specific study. I analyse poetry's mechanisms only in the specific instance of digital literature since the digital space brings it closer to the way prose fiction functions. Books like the one by Shams on state-sanctioned poets of the post-revolutionary period will complement my book (Shams 2020).

My understanding of what constitutes a literary text is broad; it is 'any text that in a given community has been imbued with cultural value and that allows for high levels of complexity and significance in the way it is constructed' (Snir 2018: 8). This means that I include not only prose texts published by independent publishers, but also popular texts since there are no classics without popular literature, as well as children's literary fiction and texts that could be called propagandist, but that are defined as literary by the governmental institutions. While most of my study focuses on print texts, Chapter 2 studies literary blogs and literary Instagram. In Chapter 1, I discuss processes of canonisation and define the criteria used to determine popularity and reception.

Here it is important to define two terms that I use throughout the book to refer to institutions in the literary field. 'Governmental' is used to define publishers (and institutions or persons) who are primarily funded by the government and/or the state. The state is directly linked to the Supreme Leader, while the government changes with each new president of the Islamic Republic, so they are not equivalent. However, I talk about governmental and state institutions and publishers as one entity under the term 'governmental' in this book for the sake of simplicity and because it is difficult to have access to the main funding source. The content of governmental publishers' publications can be aligned entirely with the discourse of the Islamic Republic, like that of the publisher Sureh Mehr; or not, like the publisher Amir Kabir. In general, though, it is aligned in terms of thematic and stylistic content, and recognisable for literary practitioners within Iran. I use the term 'governmental' because it is the closest to what the publishers in this field call themselves in Persian (*nasher-e dowlati*). However, there is no mention of the state (*hokumat*) in the term 'governmental publisher'. This choice (*dowlati* over *hokumati*) should be kept in mind and seen as a way for the state to hide itself behind the term governmental. Fatemeh Shams has done an analysis of the governmental literary field for poetry and calls it 'official', insisting on its formal relation with state power (2015b: 14). I prefer to use a term closer to the Persian, hence my choice of 'governmental'.

The second key term, 'independent', refers to publishers whose main source of funding is private. In Persian, the term is private publisher (*nasher-e khosusi*). I have chosen the term independent because it resonates more with western readers. The content of their publications is not necessarily in opposition to the discourse of the Islamic Republic, although some of the well-known independent publishers like Cheshmeh have a reputation for also being radical, that is, pushing the boundaries of the state discourse, in their publications. A lot of independent publishers produce textbooks, self-help books and children's books, where the ideological content and alignment with Islamic Republic discourse is not a key issue, since they mainly do not engage with potentially problematic topics. All publishers, to the exception of underground publishers but even the independent ones, still get some help from the government at some point. During some periods, as I show in Chapter 3, most publishers received their paper supplies from the government, which was an important financial contribution. It is also common for independent publishers to receive direct funding from the government occasionally; however, this issue is difficult to investigate, as an independent publisher, which builds its credentials on its independence from the government and gains prestige from being termed independent, would not want such help to be known. Being independent often comes as a badge of honour.

Therefore, it is crucial not to draw a strict line between the two categories: all publishers in Iran, except the underground ones, have to stay in line with the government demands and all have to go through the censorship process. Even in western literary fields, it is important not to divide too strictly between the market and the government, since the market is not devoid of governance, for example through the role of international organisations like UNESCO (Brouillette 2014). While such organisations do not play a major role in Iran, it is critical to not draw a sharp distinction between the two segments.

Methodology

The book uses a mixed methodology: I bring together close readings, interviews done during fieldwork, sociological methods inspired by the

Bourdieusian model of cultural production, as well as digital humanities approaches using a large amount of data. I strongly believe close reading and distant reading should be practised together and the use of Bourdieu is important to overcome the dichotomy between them. The fact that the book focuses on the contemporary period also demands such a back and forth between literary texts and the attention to their material conditions.

Society is composed of a plurality of fields: economic, cultural, political. They are autonomous spaces structured along relations of domination and with stakes specific to them. This book thus analyses these relations in Iranian society and how they come into being: 'literature is never simply a given, but is always performatively and materially instituted by translators, publishers, academies and academics, critics, and readers, as well as authors themselves' (Helgesson and Vermeulen 2016). Like Sarah Brouillette, I believe it is important to 'encourage more analyses of the relationships between literature, politics, and economics, and therefore more interaction between humanities and social sciences approaches to cultural production' (2007: 176). It is important to adapt the Bourdieusian concepts to the Iranian field and the contemporary period: there are not only pure art and commercial art, autonomous and heteronomous, and what Bourdieu defines as 'social art' is indeed a main component of the Iranian literary field. 'Marked as "completely ambiguous", as an anomaly, at least in this respect, social art is consequently disregarded in Bourdieu's modelling of literary production, bracketed as a scholarly afterthought rather than explicitly theorized' (Zimbler 2009: 601). More than anything else, I will show the differences between Iran and other fields, where governmental literature, or 'social art' as Bourdieu calls it, that carries a political message is more than an afterthought and a vestige of the past. The division that Bourdieu makes between the pole of large-scale production driven by short-term profitability and the pole of small-scale production is not relevant either to the Iranian literary field (Bourdieu and Johnson 1993). The tension is mainly between the autonomous principle of literary value and the heteronomous principle of political usefulness, whereas in the case of most contemporary western fields, the heteronomous principle is economics. Zuzanna Olszewska argues on this that 'arguments about the necessity for artistic and literary autonomy in contemporary Iran are inherently political and ethical statements' (2015: 114). Social art, which speaks 'on behalf of the disempowered, seeks neither temporal reward nor artistic purity' (Zimbler 2009: 60), has to be integrated into the analysis.

Fieldwork in the authoritarian context of Iran requires a specific approach. First, the data used in distant reading methods should be taken with caution and further explained, since access in Iran is difficult and reliability is an issue. For example, it is not always clear when the first date of publication is, even for recent publications. Second, the data collected is different from other fields which are more open. Because of the politicisation of fieldwork in Iran, some interviewees are also anonymous. The constraints of fieldwork in Iran and the necessity to compromise are many. In a special issue of *Iranian Studies* in 2004, scholars of both Iranian and non-Iranian origin like myself, reflected on this issue (Friedl and Hegland 2004). The conditions have deteriorated since, and it is a challenge and sometimes a safety issue to do fieldwork in Iran. However, it is also important not to think that everything about doing fieldwork in Iran is extraordinary. Shervin Malekzadeh rightfully notes that it is important to blend in, and that mostly, Iranians are living ordinary lives. This frame of mind, which I have tried to have during my stays in Iran, allows the researcher doing fieldwork to blend in and to see what is really exceptional in the findings (Malekzadeh 2016).

The data for this book was partly collected through my personal involvement with the Iranian literary and cultural community inside Iran and in France, the UK, the US and Australia between 2005 and 2019. I interviewed, in various formats including formal and informal discussions and in open-ended discussions, dozens of Iranians working largely in the field of culture. They were primarily writers, translators, civil servants of cultural institutions, academics, publishers, readers and bookstore owners. Some of them will not be identified. I have interviewed literary practitioners prominent in their respective area: for example, the writer Amir Hossein Khorshidfar; the publisher Afshin Shahneh Tabar from Candle & Fog and a past president of the Union of Tehran Publishers and Booksellers;[1] the director of international affairs of the Saadi Foundation, Mohammad Reza Darbandi; the literary agent Lili Hayeri Yazdi; writers in the diaspora like Peyman Esmaili in Australia and Shahriar Mandanipour in the US. I was also a participant

---

[1] Most publishers also sell their own books, and sometimes are general booksellers.

observer at cultural events in all these countries, such as the Tehran Book Fair, literary readings and talks, and an active participant in some projects, such as the Persian Publishers Network through the International Alliance of Independent Publishers in France.[2]

To finish on the methodology, since there is no reliable data on reception, no large-scale study of reading practices for example, I only touch upon the issue of reception with anecdotes, fieldwork experiences and comments on sites like Goodreads, which was a very important site among Iranians for discussing books until it was sanctioned in 2019. It is typically a site that complexifies the boundaries between reception, promotion and socialisation, so it can be used as an indicator of trends. We do have literacy rates, which are very high. In 2016, the overall adult male (15+) literacy rate of Iran was recorded by the UNESCO Institute for Statistics as 90.35 per cent while that of adult females was 80.79 per cent. In the 15–24 years old group, the male literacy rate is 98.27 and the female 97.93, so the gap between females and males has clearly closed in the last decade. Enrolment in tertiary education in 2016 was 71.96 per cent of the male population, and 65.52 per cent of the female.[3]

Contribution to Theoretical Debates

The book contributes to the study of complex and shifting global literary networks. It shows how global literary exchanges happen even in a 'closed' country like Iran and what these exchanges tell us about the different forms globalisation takes. World literature debates are useful to study Iranian literature beyond the national level, in terms of its interaction with the world.

---

[2] One aspect of the Iranian literary field which did not make it into this book are literary associations. I comment briefly on literary workshops in Chapter 1 and on *dowrehs* (circles) in Chapter 3. The Ministry of Culture and Islamic Guidance stated that in a space of two years only, in 2018 and 2019, 782 literary associations (*anjoman-ha-ye adabi*) had submitted claims for registrations across the country (Ministry of Culture and Islamic Guidance 2019). Literary associations often run *dowrehs* or literary workshops (*kargah-ha-ye adabi*) and there are plenty of unofficial literary groups that run *dowrehs*, for example *Shahnameh khani* (Reading of the *Shahnameh*) or *Mowlana khani* (Reading of Rumi). I aim to do further research on this in my next project.

[3] UNESCO, Education in Islamic Republic of Iran 2016.

My understanding is not of world literature as the globalisation of the world. Indeed, the facts are that there do not exist many interdependencies nor deterritorialisations of the literary exchanges in Iran, as I will develop. This book combines the centre–periphery model of Immanuel Wallerstein (1974) and the circulation model of David Damrosch (2003), as this combination works best in the post-revolutionary Iranian context.

Iran is a significant country for such a study for two reasons. First, Iran possesses a rich culture at the crossroads of civilisations. Second, the Islamic Revolution of 1979 and the war with Iraq have constrained local cultural production, without extinguishing it. Consequently, Iranian culture has become decentralised and developed in its diaspora from several locations, making it an important site for understanding the circulation of literature today. The market within Iran is not regulated by supply and demand, but by a complicated mix of state intervention, censorship and readers' expectations. For example, contrary to most western countries where the visibility of the writer on the cultural scene is often linked to the number of books she/he sells, many writers of Iranian bestsellers are invisible on the national cultural scene. Fattaneh Haj Seyed Javadi, the author of one of the most famous romance bestsellers in the last two decades, has only given two interviews to newspapers and has never appeared on TV or radio (Haj Seyed Javadi 1995). Given these unique factors, a methodology appropriate to the Iranian context and a thorough investigation of the Iranian literary field both within Iran and globally are necessary to accurately analyse what Iranian literature is and does in a global world.

I use globalisation in a general sense as 'the movement of objects, signs and people across regions and intercontinental space. The globalization of culture entails the movement of all three' (Held 1999: 329). The political sciences scholar David Held adds that there is globalisation when there are 'infrastructures and institutions of cultural transmission, reproduction and reception on a global – transregional or transcontinental – scale' (1999: 330). Iran's globalisation after the revolution has happened on a smaller scale than many other countries at similar development stages due to its political isolation.

It is also the case that in the Islamic Republic, the market and globalisation often appear as modes of resistance against the authoritarian state.

The literary people opposed to the state are often the same ones asking for a freer market. This is not specific to Iran, and as I show throughout the book, the functioning of culture in authoritarian states bears similarities, despite the wide diversity of ideological approaches. In Iran, the positive results of commercialisation – the selling of romances for example – seem to outweigh the negative, in that it leads to a more vibrant and more open literary scene. However, I am not proposing that Iranian literature be read as global. The constraints are too many, as I explain throughout the book. What I am proposing is to read the production and circulation of Iranian literary products and persons globally by looking at several national contexts. In this, seeing the links or understanding the absence of links between Iran and its diaspora will be critical, and this forms the second part of my book. It appears that post-revolutionary Iranian literature is on the margins of the world system and not global as such, but perhaps at the centre of several national systems, not only the Iranian one, because it speaks forcefully to several national literary contexts.

This book shows that there is plenty of disjuncture in global cultural exchanges. As I have argued elsewhere, the stories of the routes that cultural products take are not always determined by a well-defined law of networks, but by encounters between those who happen to be there at the right moment (Nanquette 2017b). This element of chance is evident in stories of migration itself, as we can see in the narratives of asylum seekers who rely on people they encounter at various points in their journeys. Shahram Khosravi describes these stories of border-crossing (Khosravi 2010), while Fariba Adelkhah describes the specific case of Iranian transnational trade and exchange and their entanglement with family (Adelkhah 2016). The same happens in the circulation of cultural products, whose circulation relies on chance encounters.

Diaspora theories have been powerful in recent decades to explain some of the phenomena encountered by Iranians. It is now accepted to use the term diaspora for expatriate minorities like Iranians (Safran 1991). I prefer it to the use of exile, as it is more encompassing but it is important to note that the term diaspora as such does not exist in Persian. *Mohajerat* is migration, and has a religious connotation since it evokes the flight of Muhammad from Mecca to Medina; while *ghorbat* and *tab'id* translate as exile with the latter term having a political connotation. The general term 'outside of the country' (*kharej az keshvar*) is a paraphrase to refer to the Iranians living outside of the country.

There is a long tradition of Iranian culture being in exile. During the Constitutional Revolution of 1907, translators, intellectuals and politicians were often living outside of Iran. Politicians have often been exiled throughout Iran's history and the example of Ayatollah Khomeini living in Iraq for decades and in France for a few months, before coming back to Iran in 1979, is only a more recent example of it. With this context in mind, it is important not to think of post-revolutionary Iran as exceptional and to understand it in the framework of diaspora theories. My understanding is loosely based on Robin Cohen's, who defines five types of 'diaspora' (1997: 178): 'victim', 'imperial', 'labour', 'trade' and 'deterritorialized'. While Cohen does not study the Iranian diaspora itself, his framework helps us to analyse its general social and political characteristics. The Iranian diaspora reflects many of the features defined by Cohen (although not all of them), one of which is 'the possibility of a distinctive creative, enriching life in tolerant host countries' (1997: 187). This has proven to be true of the Iranian diaspora around the world: as Iranians adapt to the norms and expectations of each host society, their cultural production differs accordingly. Cohen rightly reminds us that 'constructing a taxonomy of diasporas is a highly inexact science, partly because the taxa concerned are overlapping or change over time' (1997: 179). In the Iranian case, the categories of 'victim', 'labour' or 'deterritorialized' diaspora overlap and vary according to various periods of time. In many respects, the Iranian diaspora is a victim diaspora because, after the Islamic Revolution, there was a period of forced migration by those opposed to the Islamic Republic regime. They may have fought against the Shah, but expected a more pluralistic regime to be established. In 1980, the war with Iraq also prompted many people to leave. In 2009, after the contested presidential elections in Iran, there was a further wave of forced migration linked to politics. Nonetheless, over time, the Iranian diaspora has become increasingly labour-oriented, although it should be acknowledged that the reasons for leaving are always multiple. With economic issues and a desire for more freedom often combining to drive migration, it now occurs across all segments of Iranian society and draws people from throughout the country, including the provinces. What is particularly important in adapting Cohen's analysis is the engagement with tropes about Iran and nostalgia for the country, its past, its classical literature, and the Persian language, as well as stories of the journey to leave Iran. This nostalgia exists not only for the first generation of Iranian migrants but also for the later generations, who might never have been to the country. Marianne Hirsch refers to this construction of the lost homeland as 'postmemory':

> 'Postmemory' describes the relationship that the 'generation after' bears to the personal, collective, and cultural trauma of those who came before – to experiences they 'remember' only by means of the stories, images, and behaviors among which they grew up. But these experiences were transmitted to them so deeply and affectively as to seem to constitute memories in their own right. Postmemory's connection to the past is thus actually mediated not by recall but by imaginative investment, projection, and creation. (Hirsch 2012: 5)

This postmemory exists even in the third and fourth generations of the Iranian diaspora. On the other hand, in the construction of this postmemory, the fraught relationships between Iran and many of the countries where Iranians are living are an additional factor. The fact that the Iranian state sometimes blocks the return of its diaspora, takes it hostage in certain circumstances, and has an ontological opposition to the west and its returnees increases the divides that exist between Iran and its diaspora.

While I want to break the divide that exists between the studies of the Iranian diaspora and the study of Iran, with often different academics working on these topics, my findings reveal this divide in concrete ways. We cannot get away from the fact that this divide is essential for understanding the exchanges between Iran and the rest of the world, including the Iranian diaspora. When I started working on this project, my premise was that literary texts and practitioners exchanged a lot. This was based on what I had experienced about exchanges between the Iranian diaspora and Iran in general, and in culture, in Iranian cinema as well as Iranian music. Farzaneh Hemmasi in her book on music shows the interactions between Iran and the diaspora when it comes to pop music (Hemmasi 2020). However, the more I researched this topic, the more I discovered that such interactions do not take place on the same scale and level in literature, as I detail in the second part of the book. As I detail in Chapters 6 to 8, writers, translators, publishers and other literary practitioners make literary exchanges happen despite all odds but they are the exception rather than the rule.

Structure of the Book

The book is divided into two parts. The first part focuses on post-revolutionary Iranian literature within Iran, while the second part analyses post-revolutionary Iranian literature globally and the nation's relations with the diaspora. The first section takes up the first five chapters. Chapter 1 defines the genres existing in contemporary Persian literature today. It explains the scarcity of western-style genre fictions such as horror or fantasy, and focuses on the genres of the crime novel and the romance. It argues that the production of the crime novel is particularly constrained by the structures of the literary field and censorship, which does not allow alternative visions of justice to exist, while romances are booming and being supported, maybe paradoxically, by the Islamic literary production system. This first chapter also studies the political genres that are specific to Iran, giving representative micro-readings of the literature of the 'Sacred Defence' (the Iran–Iraq War), as well as the literary texts devoted to the imams and the Supreme Leader, published mostly by governmental publishers.

Chapter 2 explains the forms literature takes in new media. It analyses the importance of digital literature in the field. After literary blogs, which in the early 2000s were crucial in redefining the field and introducing new forms of literature, especially short forms, Instagram and Twitter are now sites of literary innovation, especially in terms of genres. This chapter studies the impact of the digital medium on the evolutions of contemporary Iranian literature through case studies and close readings of literary blogs (between around 2002 and 2009), especially the reformist blog/website *Khabgard*, the blog of the conservative writer Abdul Jabbar Kakaei, and Instagram (from around 2014). This chapter engages with both prose fiction and poetry, which functions in similar ways to prose in the digital space and does not need a separate study.

Chapter 3 examines first the polarisation of the independent and government sectors according to political orientation and explains the history of this division in the Iranian literary field. There is a great deal of heteronomy in the field, which is heavily governed by the Iranian state, but the Iranian literary field is also increasingly shaped by free-market forces. This section describes in concrete ways how the polarisation works at the micro and macro levels, and the recent evolutions that have occurred. The chapter then takes into consideration the restrictions of the market, those internal to Iran (from censorship to material constraints on paper supplies) as well as external to Iran (sanctions, lack of copyright agreements). Finally, I analyse two institutions that represent how the field works: the Saadi Foundation, a recently founded cultural institution focused on Persian language, and the Union of Tehran Publishers and Booksellers. They are both examples of the struggle for cultural power, the overlapping of cultural institutions and the polarisation of the field that is happening in Iran.

Chapter 4 uses the database from Iran Book House to visualise the production and distribution of literary texts within Iran since the 1979 revolution. It provides new findings based on quantitative data on places of publication, and the evolution of the publications according to politics, categories of publishers and categories of texts. The analysis of this database allows me to give precise figures on phenomena that have only been sketched out previously, due to the inaccessibility of the data. It confirms some ideas, for example the ebb and flow of publications according to politics, and contradicts others, for example that governmental publishers publish higher quantities of texts than independent ones.

Chapter 5 makes a junction between the two parts of the book, by discussing both production within Iran and circulation outside of the country. It studies the governmental policies about and institutions of children's literature to understand how this specific sub-field has functioned in the last forty years and why it has been relatively successful nationally and internationally, as opposed to adult fiction. It argues that the field has been heavily invested in by the government, as children's literature was seen as a way to implement the 'Neither Western nor Eastern' directive and to give new meanings to the idea of the child and the development of a new Islamic man and woman. This was done mainly through institutions that helped built a professional children's literature field. In this sense, children's literature is like post-revolutionary

Iranian cinema, which has benefited from various forms of support and been recognised internationally for a long time.

I then move to the second part of the book on the circulation of contemporary Iranian literature globally and within the Iranian diaspora. The Iranian diaspora is spread widely and is well-connected otherwise, but not when it comes to global literary exchanges. Chapter 6 reflects on the divide that exists between literary practitioners who leave Iran and those who stay, rather than close reading texts published by diaspora writers, like the memoir *Reading Lolita in Tehran* by Azar Nafisi or the graphic novel *Persepolis* by Marjane Satrapi, as they have been extensively studied. I argue that diaspora writers deal with a crisis of legitimacy within Iran. Although this is starting to change, mistrust between Iranians from within and in the diaspora is still prevalent, due to historical and political grudges. The fact that books by Iranians published abroad are banned in Iran or cannot be easily bought increases these grudges. The divide is visible in the gap between the market within and outside Iran and cooperation is only occurring on a small scale. I study such examples of cooperation, such as through the publisher Candle & Fog, based in both Tehran and London, as well as the obstacles to cooperation, based on interviews and case studies with literary practitioners from the US, the UK, Iran, France and Australia.

Because there is no exhaustive database grouping Iranian publishers in the diaspora, Chapter 7 uses qualitative data to analyse translations and reception from modern Persian literature primarily in two countries critical for the Iranian diaspora: France and the US. In these countries, highbrow texts and poetry in Persian are translated, with little attention paid to a wider market or to bestsellers. The chapter draws on a database of publications of translations from Persian into English that I have compiled over the years, as well as interviews with publishers and translators like Sara Khalili. It compares the circulation of Persian literature in France and the US, with analogies to countries like Germany and the UK.

Chapter 8 argues that Australia exhibits some particularities in the reception of Persian literature due to a different history of migration: the Iranian migration is more recent and less upper and middle class than in Europe and North America. Australia is a literary field where Iranian literature has evolved due to the demands of the Australian reader, especially due to the demand for refugee stories, which are prevalent in Australia, while rare in Europe and America. Refugee stories have been at the forefront of book publications and have won literary prizes, in the context of a country where the discourse on refugees is crucial to politics. This chapter analyses the field of Iranian-Australian writings and compares it to the countries of western Europe and North America analysed earlier. It brings in a picture of Iranian writers in that country that differs from the one generally shared of Iranians in other diasporic places.

In Chapter 9, I reflect more broadly on the place of contemporary Persian literature in the Persian cultural system. I argue that the literary is slowly being replaced by the visual, which partly accounts for the challenges faced by Persian texts. I also make a comparison with Iranian cinema and visual arts. Iranian cinema has given Iranian culture a specific global force, with arthouse films specially produced for festivals and an important body of scholarship focusing on its various aspects. The chapter compares the production of literature to Iranian visual arts, which, more recently, have become prominent on the international art scene. While the success of Iranian films is partly linked to state cultural film policies, equivalents do not yet exist in the literary field and are only starting to appear in the visual arts. With the exception of children's literature, Iranian literature lacks such support.

PART I
THE LITERARY FIELD WITHIN IRAN

1

Forms and Genres in Contemporary Iranian Literature

When browsing the fiction section of bookshops in Iran, two categories stand out for the differences in their covers: the voluminous romances, with cover pictures of candles, hearts, flowers and women (veiled of course), while the others, literary fiction, are short novels, or more what we would call novellas in western literary fields, with simple cover pictures that do not have much on them, and a couple of paragraphs from the book quoted on the back cover. Most of the fiction published in post-revolutionary Iran fits into these two broad categories, as I elaborate in this chapter.

Figure 1.1 Book cover of a popular novel.

Figure 1.2 Book covers of highbrow novels.

In this chapter, I discuss the formal and generic characteristics of contemporary Iranian literature, with a focus on prose fiction. Whereas other chapters in this book are largely concerned with the politics and sociology of the literary field as a whole, here I give an overview of contemporary Iranian literature. My guiding question is: What are its main genres and forms?

I focus on prose fiction, firstly because of the essential link, discussed in the introduction, between novels and nations – especially in authoritarian contexts where the state has a large stake in literary products – and secondly because other genres like drama or literary criticism are published in very small numbers and influence only the independent fields to which they belong. They do not have much of an impact on the wider field.[1] The following table, based on the analysis of the Dewey categories of the Iran Book House (*Khaneh-ye ketab*), shows the percentage of publications in each category over the years from 1980 to 2018. It features the three main genres

---

[1] I have explained in the introduction why I largely exclude poetry from my analysis in this book.

Table 1.1 Percentage of book publications according to genre, from data extracted from the Iran Book House website as of July 2019.

	Poetry	Fiction	Drama	Literary techniques (books about teaching) literature)
1980	21	62	0.5	9
1990	37	35	0.9	3
2000	50	33	1.7	7
2010	50	32	2.0	8
2018	41	44	2.5	5

relevant to western readers – fiction, poetry and drama – plus the category of books on teaching literature, as it is a non-negligible percentage. There is also a small group of around 5–10 per cent comprising genres like critical analysis, letters and uncategorised.

While poetry composed around 20 per cent of the production in 1980, it has increased over the years and is composing close to half of the market in 2018. On the other hand, fiction's place was 62 per cent in 1980 and has decreased to 44 per cent in 2018. The evolution of drama, although increasing, is difficult to analyse since we are dealing with very small numbers, at a maximum of 2.5 per cent. As I mentioned in the introduction, because poetry has different dynamics, it needs a separate study, which Shams has initiated (2015b). I only study poetry when I look at digital literature in Chapter 2.

Compared to western book markets where genre fiction is the biggest seller, there is little science-fiction, horror, fantasy or crime fiction in Iran as I detail further. Romances however are extremely successful. There are also entire genres defined by politics and religion which depend on a separate literary circuit linked to the government. Here I explain these differences from western literary traditions and book markets, and look at the political genres that are specific to Iran, focusing on the literature of the Iran–Iraq war known as 'Sacred Defence' literature (*Adabiyyat-e moqavemat* or *Adabiyyat-e defa'-e moqaddas*), as well as the literature devoted to religious figures (*Adabiyyat-e mazhabi*). I see literature as being composed of not only highbrow, canonical literature, but also popular literature, and – in the case of authoritarian governments like Iran – governmental literature. Ignoring one of these three kinds of literature would mean giving a truncated analysis of the literary field. For this reason, the present chapter offers an encompassing view of the literary texts published in Iran after the revolution by paying close attention to the category of genres and forms. Definition of the canon is always a contentious issue but more so in the Iranian literary field because at least three types of canons exist: the one in the diaspora; the one defined by the government that is taught in schools and universities, which includes texts imbued with the Islamic Republic ideology; and the one recognised by the independent field, which includes writers who do not fit with the ideology. Examples would be Sadegh Hedayat, recognised as canonical and the father of the modern Persian novel in most literary history scholarships (Mirabeidini 2007), whose books are still banned in Iran, but nonetheless circulate relatively freely. When discussing canonical texts, I will need to refer to these three sets of canons, which are sometimes antithetical. As for determining popularity, the term 'popular' in Persian – appealing to the mass (*ammeh pasand*) – is vague. Like 'literature that everyone reads' (*adabiyyat-e hamehkhun*), most terms used to describe popular literature are pejorative. 'Genre literature' (*adabiyyat-e zhanr*), is only used by literary critics and does not resonate with a broader readership.[2]

Does popular refer to the number of copies and/or the total number of books printed? A highbrow canonical writer like Simin Daneshvar with *Savushun* could be included since it has been printed in 500,000 copies (Daneshvar 1969). Does it refer to the aesthetic content of the book? In this case, popular would apply to genre fiction texts, especially romances, and defined in opposition to highbrow literature. But it would not include a popular text promoted by the government, *Da*, which is a memoir on the Iran–Iraq war (Nanquette 2013b). There needs to be a compromise between these two elements and I will use 'popular' for texts that have a high number of prints or copies, and that are defined by practitioners in the field as such. There will be some contradictions and tensions depending on where practitioners belong in the field. I will discuss the number of prints and copies

---

[2] Contrary to the US where many critics hold academic positions and where the university and the literary fields are linked, literary critics and the university in Iran do not interact much. The US is quite unique in this regard. France also has literary critics that are mostly moving in different circles to those of the university.

in Chapter 3 when I go into the details of data for publication. They are unreliable and they do not tell the whole story, but we still need to use them to have an idea of general reading trends.

Much like critics such as Northrop Frye and Alastair Fowler, I believe genres are important categories to understand literary phenomena. Genres are flexible and need to be understood historically and geographically, as well as in relation to one another. As John Frow argues, 'genres are not fixed and pre-given forms' and texts are better understood as 'performances of genre rather than reproductions of a class to which they belong' (2014: 3). He adds that 'no text is ever unframed, even if it is the case that the act of citation or of translation or merely survival from one moment in time to another all alter the generic framework within which texts are read' (Frow 2014: 30).

Genres need to be rethought in this book not only because of the specificities of post-revolutionary Iran, but because of the ways they are used by authors in Iran. It is also necessary to compare Iranian genres with their more familiar western counterparts, since traditional European genres have been an important influence on modern Persian literature. Scholars like Mehdi Khorrami have argued that one problem with the scholarship on Persian literature is that it is too focused on politics, and does not pay sufficient attention to aesthetics and criticism (Khorrami 2003). Additionally, with exceptions like Omid Azadibougar (2014) and Jamal Mirsadeghi (2008), scholars writing on Persian literature have tended to discuss genre in relation to classical works. My main aim in this chapter is thus to contextualise modern Persian literature and criticism within existing theory on genres, focusing on those that are specific to the post-revolutionary context. As in many western literary fields, there is a large variety of texts and genres, ranging from post-modern stories to magical realist stories to intergenerational novels. I do not get into the detail of all of them, for example there are a lot of historical novels, as well as novels that develop a story over several generations. These do not differ widely from western historical novels in terms of form, content or production so I do not analyse them. What I am interested in are the texts that do not have equivalents in western literary fields, or whose dynamics of production are distinct.

Genre Fiction in Iran

A striking characteristic of bookshops in Iran is the overwhelming presence of romances despite the quasi absence of other genre fictions. Where is all the horror, crime, fantasy and science fiction that fill the western book markets? Some of these genre fictions are read directly in English by the younger generation of readers, however this only applies to those who have an adequate level of education in English. So, whilst texts like the *Assassin's Creed* series (based on the famous video games of the same title) are popular with a small number of readers, they are not circulated widely.

Genre fiction is used here to describe texts that are recognisable in terms of style, form and content, and that fit neatly into particular categories, which are often subdivided into sub-genres. It describes texts that are written, marketed and consumed generically. The reception aspect is crucial to distinguishing such works from other texts. Broadly speaking, in most of the western literary traditions, one can say that if the main readership is the literary establishment (including literary prize juries, schools and universities), we are dealing with general literary fiction, and if the readership is the mass market, this is popular fiction. While popular fiction is often largely genre fiction, genre fiction is not always popular: some fantasy works have small audiences for example. Although I use the term genre fiction over popular fiction, Ken Gelder's analysis is helpful:

> Its logics and practices ... are primarily industrial and commercial; it is intimately tied to the category of entertainment ...; it mostly operates outside of official, educational apparatuses ...; it is closer in kind to 'craft' than to discourse and practices of the art world; and it deploys, to lesser or greater extents, a set of formal features (plot, convention, simplicity, event, exaggeration, pace and so on) that underwrite its identifications and structure the manner of its production as well as the means by which it is marketed, processed and evaluated. (Gelder 2004: 158)

This link between genre fiction and the mass market is clearly relevant in western contexts, but because the Iranian book market is largely politically and ideologically rather than economically driven, this way of defining literary products by their readership needs to be reconsidered. In the case of Iran, whilst economic considerations remain paramount when it comes to genre fiction/popular fiction, they are significantly less important when it comes to other literary products.

There are very few examples of science fiction in Persian today, although both speculative fiction – especially dystopian fiction – and fantasy are increasingly gaining traction. There are a few examples of texts in these genres in the twentieth century, especially from Abdol Hossein Sanat'izadeh Kermani. The Fantasy Academy is helping to promote this genre by holding awards and contests as well as publishing a monthly journal, *Shegeftzar*. This was preceded by the short-lived *Bo'd-e haftom* (2002–4), the first Science Fiction Club in Iran. One can think of books in these categories that have been well-received, such as *Don't Worry* (*Negaran nabash*) by Mahsa Moebali: an apocalyptic story in which a drug-addicted woman tries to secure her fix in the ruins of Tehran following a devastating earthquake. There is also the fantasy fiction *Khak-e adampush* (*The Human-Wearing Earth*) by Zoha Kazemi (2017), which sets a story full of both fantastic and realistic details 3000 years ago. Iranians outside of Iran – especially those writing in English – are expanding these genres with novels like *Cyclonopedia* by Reza Negarestani and *The Final Six* by Alexandra Monir, but sci-fi and fantasy still make up a very small proportion of the Iranian market, particularly when compared to the profusion of these genres in western countries. There are a lot of TV series that are linked to the genre of horror through their use of the occult, with stories of jinns and ghouls (Doostdar 2019), as well as some films (Bledstein 2019). These horror elements that are present on screen might make their appearance in books later. A reason for this relative lack of science fiction or time travel might be linked to the ideology of the Islamic Republic regime: neither nostalgia nor utopia are valid in an ideal ideological space.

Below, I want to look at the evolution of two popular genres – crime fiction (*dastan-e jenai*) and romance (*romans, dastan-e asheqaneh*) – in order to explain their interactions with the current literary field and to try to understand why one is booming but not the other. My argument is that despite some interest in the genre of crime fiction being expressed by both readers and publishers, internal constraints like censorship do not let the field expand, and crime fiction remains a marginal genre. On the contrary, and perhaps paradoxically, romances within the boundaries of Islam proliferate and are certainly not discouraged by the authorities; such romances are the most widely read and published popular fictions in Iran.

Crime Stories

Crime fiction comprises many sub-genres, including thriller, noir, mystery and spy novels. Whereas all literature, including classical Persian texts like the *Shahnameh*, have depicted death and criminal acts, crime fiction makes these things its primary focus: solving the mystery of the murder and understanding the psychology of the people involved. I detail some possible reasons why it is not a genre much practised in Iran below.

Kaveh Mirabbasi is a crucial figure who has translated crime fiction into Persian from English, French and Spanish. For several years, Mirabbasi had a column in the newspaper *Iran*, and is believed to have published one of the first 'native' crime novels in the country (Darab 2015). Mirabbasi has stated in the above interview that Sudabeh – a female character from the *Shahnameh* – has the qualities of a crime-fiction heroine, and his heroine, Sudabeh, is based on her (Darab 2015). He has written several volumes of a series published by Ofoq, *S like Sudabeh* (*Sin mesl-e Sudabeh*), which takes influence from canonical crime novels and roots them in classical Persian literature (Mirabbasi, phone interview with author, 8 October 2008). His predecessors include Parviz Ghazi Said, Amir Ashiri, Amir Mojahed, Mohammad Delju. Another important figure in crime fiction is Mehrdad Morad. Morad also makes some of his stories available online for free on his weblog and is active on social media platforms. In terms of publishers, Jahan-e Ketab has attempted to create a wider readership for crime fiction in Iran by publishing international works in the genre, mostly by popular French authors such as Charles Exbrayat and Georges Simenon.

In 2017, Qoqnoos – one of the oldest and largest independent publishing houses in Iran – began publishing a new series of crime fictions and thrillers (as well as some fantasy), through Hila publications, headed by Mohammad Hassan Shahsavari.[3] Since 2015, Qoqnoos and Hila has published, for

---

[3] Qoqnoos is one of the oldest independent publishers, and it is also a publishing house (*Bongah-e nashr*) with three other publishers working under its management: Nashr-e Qoqnoos, Nashr-e Hila, Nashr-e Afarinegan. Qoqnoos publishing house also has a distribu-

example, Laleh Zareh's *Young Skull* (*Jomjomeh-ye javan*) and *Without Coffin* (*Bitabut*), as well as *Pines are Upside Down* (*Kaj-ha varunehand*) by Saman Nuraei and *Crazy Mordad* (*Mordad-e divaneh*) by Mohammad Hasan Shahsavari. It is the first time that a series with such a significant number of titles has focused on genre fiction. This series started with a creative writing workshop at Book City (*Shahr-e Ketab*) by Shahsavari, who is keen to use genre writing. By developing the creative writing workshops, he also trained a number of writers in the genre, who would later publish with Hila. When I attended one of his workshops at Shahr-e Ketab in 2011, Shahsavari had not yet started to be interested in crime fiction but there were clear indications of his interest in exploring the issues of genre fiction and pushing his students to tackle genre conventions.

Although welcome, this Qoqnoos–Hila initiative is a very recent evolution, limited to a few titles. Another prestigious independent publisher, Cheshmeh, also started a book series of crime fiction but has published only two titles as of 2020. I argue that the genre has not been able to expand due to different factors, one of them being government control. Crime fiction is about the disruption of order. In an Islamic society where justice is of paramount importance, it is impossible for the government to acknowledge that crimes are sometimes left unpunished, or that the police force may fail to do its job to the extent that private detectives are needed. The Islamic Republic regime does not allow for the publication of alternative visions of justice, either. This is mitigated by the fact that a lot of TV series and films can be categorised as crime: they have a large viewership and support from the government. I explain below this apparent paradox, only mentioning here that the government blocks crime fiction from independent writers and publishers being published. Contrary to TV series, the government has not invested in promoting a certain type of crime fiction in literature because it is not impactful enough so its strategy is to censor the few that try to get a publishing permit. Some genres of crime fiction, like noir – which often focuses on the ills of a society and sometimes describes the underworld of prostitution and drug-trafficking– are banned because these things are not

tion centre (*Markaz-e pakhsh*). This centre works with many other publishers to assist in the distribution of their books (Mehr News 2016).

supposed to happen. Whilst it might be permissible to describe the ills of society if Islamic morality was to ultimately triumph, this cannot be the case in many sub-genres of crime fiction. In the noir genre, the story is about describing the ills of the society not about the crime as such. A restoration of order seems hardly possible in a genre that is all about the underworld. Salar Abdoh – an Iranian-American writer who has edited a collection of English-language noir stories set in the city of Tehran – describes the difficulty of publishing crime fiction in Iran thus:

> Imagine having to write in an alternate universe where there is to be no mention of sex, little genuine interiority of character, no delving into social issues, no politics, and nothing that could convey a society at some internal conflict with itself. (Abdoh 2014b: 18)

Another aspect of crime fiction which renders it incompatible with the social and political establishment of Iran is its strong focus on the individual. The genre's concern with the ascent of an individual, often against a big organisation like the government or the intelligence services, is problematic because painting such a picture of the individual versus the Islamic collective society is unacceptable in an authoritarian regime like Iran's. The pivotal figure of the private detective also does not exist in Iranian society, so such a character is not believable to Iranian readers. Censorship, prompted by the reluctance of the Islamic Republic to allow for the type of discourse on justice available in crime fiction, is accountable for the genre's failure to flourish in Iran.

There are, however, many instances of crime fiction in television series which portray some crimes and the eventual triumph of Islamic morality, because television attracts a much larger audience and is a better investment, for example the series *Michael* directed by Cyrus Moghaddam. Such programmes appear on the Iranian state TV IRIB and are sponsored by the government's Law Enforcement Force (*Niru-ye entezami*), the uniformed police, and its art institute, Naji Honar, founded in 2000. The particularity of these series is that they start with a disruption of the order and always end up with the state reinforcing it; they do not show the contradictions present within Iranian society, nor do they consider possible failures of the state. In these series, it is not up to an individual to restore justice, but to the state. These kinds of crime series on television have been permitted, supported and indeed flourished and found their audience. On the other hand, the government has not made the decision to fund similar narratives in novel form, because television is more popular than novel-reading and did not find it worth investing in books. It is thus only an apparent paradox that crime TV series flourish while crime novels are censored. TV series have a large viewership and the government has decided to invest in them. On the other hand, the government does not give publishing permits to crime fictions by independent writers and publishers because they do not convey the adequate message, contrary to the TV series and films that are approved.

Some Iranian writers who live in the west have published crime fictions in English and other European languages, but these remain exceptions. Salar Abdoh, mentioned above, who writes in English (Abdoh 2000, 2014a, 2014b), and Naïri Nahapétian, who writes in French (Nahapétian 2013, 2014, 2016, 2017a, 2017b), are two examples that come to mind, but the fact that their works have all been published since 2000 supports the view that the genre is only recently starting to become popular among Iranians, whether at home or abroad. In any case, these fictions are not circulated within Iran because of the gap between publishing inside and outside the country, a division I describe in the second part of the book.

The absence of substantial Iranian crime fiction is a counter-example to the globalisation of the genre studied by world literature scholars (Nilsson *et al.* 2017) and by scholars working on the 'glocal' implementations of the genre. As I argue throughout the book, since Iran is not integrated into the world literary market and has different internal mechanisms from the spaces studied by Nilsson *et al.*, it does not participate in this mechanism of globalisation. On the other hand, romances are extremely successful in the Iranian literary market, although they are very different from western ones.

Romances

Romances attract the interest of readers and account for a significant part of contemporary publications in Iran today. In the last two decades, one can estimate that they represent at least half of the country's literary production. A list of bestsellers published in 2018 by the Iranian state is a good reference, and it is corroborated by discussions with literary practitioners (ISNA 2018). This is particularly interesting and might be seen as paradoxical because the practices of censorship and self-censorship make talking about love difficult in Iran. Erotic romance novels are not published because the description of intimate relationships is not accepted, but there are many other topics on which to work in romances. In addition, there is a long tradition of love stories in Persian literature on which the romances of today build, with central characters such as Leila and Majnun, and Vis and Ramin (Naeej 2018). There is also the tradition of *Filmfarsi*, which has striking resonances with post-revolutionary romances. *Filmfarsi* encompasses popular films made before the revolution, which had similarities with Bollywood cinema. Because of its entertainment qualities, the genre has been dismissed, like romances, but recently critics have placed it in the Persian cultural tradition and shown its lineage with other forms (Partovi 2017). However, this scholarship has only made a real start in the last twenty years.

The increase in publications of romances – staple bestsellers in all western fields, but which have been absent from the Iranian literary field until recently – is a sign that readers' interests are becoming increasingly important in the expansion of the Iranian literary market, at least when censorship rules are not violated. Many contemporary bestsellers belong to the genre of romance. One of them, *The Morning After* (*Bamdad-e khomar*), which recounts the story of a girl who wants to marry below her class against the advice of her family, is particularly revealing of the topics which Najmabadi argues are most relevant to Iranian readers: class issues, individual choice versus family decision, passion versus reason (Najmabadi 2004). The novel's engagement with such subjects may help to explain its success. Sudabeh is an educated girl who falls in love with a man from a lower class than hers. To convince her of the inappropriateness of the marriage, her aunt Mahbubeh tells her own story of getting married to Rahim, a carpenter. Having to live in poverty, to work, to bear her horrible mother in law who lives with them and increasingly to tolerate the unfaithfulness of Rahim, Mahbubeh lives a life of suffering. Their son dies in an accident. Eventually, she leaves Rahim and returns to her family. Sudabeh seems to have absorbed the message, as she abandons her lover.

Romances in Iran are quite different from the western novels exemplified by Harlequin, but one can find similar patterns in both, particularly in terms of the focus on the love story and the development of the female character. There are several crucial differences, though, most strikingly regarding the endings of Iranian romances, which unlike their western counterparts are frequently unhappy ones. Another difference is that they often feature instances of gendered violence and domestic violence, whereas this is not at all a characteristic of western romances. Female characters are punished harshly for their transgressions, although the very fact that these transgressions are written about is a novelty in itself. Elham Naeej argues that there is a direct link between gendered violence in romance novels and gender stereotypes in society (Naeej 2018). The hierarchical gender ideologies represented in romances further entrap women in abusive relationships by valorising victimhood and submissiveness, demonstrating how mass-market literature re-constructs an image of the world, though filtered through generic rule. In a patriarchal and religious society like Iran, where marriage and family are of paramount importance, romance novels take a turn that is quite unexpected for western readers. Naeej demonstrates that more recent romances published since the 2010s tend to get away from the gender violence aspect and insist on the independence of the woman (Naeej 2020). Romances cater to a readership keen to read about love in a way that is deemed proper, Islamic and traditional by the censor. Romances which conform to the boundaries of Islam proliferate, and are certainly not discouraged by the authorities. One must wonder if this acceptance is due to the fact that such romances largely reproduce the patriarchal discourse on women by representing any rebellion on the part of the heroine as short-lived and ultimately tamed or not threatening the general order of society. In this sense, the fact that romances are not produced by governmental publishers is interesting in that it suggests that the control mechanisms are upheld by society itself and that self-censorship and patriarchal norms are internalised. The fact that the vast majority of writers of such romances are women reinforces the argument that patriarchal systems are not systems of oppression imposed solely by men; women have a large part in perpetuating them. Even with this caveat, it must be said that romances play a role in representing women as having agency, and encouraging their mostly female readers to consider their inner selves as important, especially the most recent publications.

There is a final portion of the Iranian literary field that is prominent and accounts for a significant amount of publications. These are the politico-religious genres which require some background explanation since they do not exist as such in western book markets.

Politico-religious Genres

It is essential to understand one characteristic of the literary field to put this genre's specificities into context. Because I devote the third chapter of this book to detailing the way the Iranian literary field works, here it is necessary only to give a broad account of the way the field has been divided according to politics after the Islamic Revolution. The Iranian literary field is polarised between two segments: independent (*khosusi*) and governmental (*dowlati*). There exist entirely separate circuits for writers, publishers and distributors according to which group such practitioners belong to, and these circuits maintain their own literary prizes and networks. The criteria for belonging are along political and ideological lines, with the major question being: Do you believe that the Islamic tenets of the regime are a priority when it comes to literary production or do you believe that literary production should be self-governing and autonomous from the state? Governed by an authoritarian regime, Iran's literary field is based on opposition or adhesion to the state ideology on culture and is thus markedly different to western market-oriented models for book industries. Publishers, as well as writers, literary juries and all literary persons, are distinguished along such political lines, and although there are nuances and blurring of these lines, as a rule, the two categories are quite fixed. Conversation between these two groups is rare, although not unheard of and certainly worthy of attention. One can see such conversations happening in spaces like Shahr-e Ketab, a non-profit institution mainly known as a chain of bookstores/cultural centres that have multiplied across Iran since 1995. The organisation has diversified a lot since the 1990s and now has many affiliated companies, including the publisher Hermes, which also does music publication and production. Shahr-e Ketab also organises book exhibitions and conferences, courses and workshops that are more open than the rigid university environment. In effect, they act as more or less neutral spaces where practitioners from both ends of the political spectrum can meet and argue on a relatively friendly basis. For example, in December 2017, I joined Professor Amir-Ali Nojoumian for his talk on postcolonialism in one of Shahr-e Ketab's Tehran bookstores on Bokhares Avenue. There were few men in the audience, which was mostly comprised of young women – one of whom told me that she was writing in two genres: Sacred Defence literature and Popular literature, by which she meant love stories. At first sight, these two genres are antagonistic and one might think that they belong to entirely different sets of writers. This woman was also a long-time member of the classes led by Professor Nojoumian, which dealt mainly with western literary theory. She was a good example of the bridging happening between those spaces, although the norm is the parallelism of the two circuits. Another exception of this bridging is the annual Tehran International Book Fair, the largest book fair in the Middle East, which is precisely about the intermingling of people, as demonstrated by Kaveh Ehsani in his chapter, where he argues: 'The Book Fair is Iran's version of a relatively autonomous public space' (2015: 219–20). The Book Fair is the only specific time during the year where divisions between the two fields abate, although the governmental field is over-represented, and some independent publishers are often banned from it. On the ground, many kinds of readers meet. Acknowledging this division between the governmental and the independent fields is crucial for understanding the existence of the politico-religious genre I now turn to.

In the sections above, I have focused on two genres which are limited, in different ways, by the specificities of the Iranian literary market and its history. Below, I want to focus on the circulation and reception of two genres that are supported by the government, and are thus on the opposite side of the literary divide: 'Sacred Defence' texts, which are about the 1980–8 Iran–Iraq War; and religious texts, which are about the important religious figures of Shia Islam. Both genres intertwine politics and religion, a combination that is at the foundation of the Islamic Republic regime in Iran. Although it could be argued that Sacred Defence texts belong to the genre of war literature and can be understood in these terms, it is my contention that where political motivations are one of many elements at play in western war literature, they are the driving force of Sacred Defence texts.

As in all authoritarian states, there is a specific kind of cultural production which is encouraged and supported by the state because it is aligned with its core dogmas. One cannot really speak of a mass market in such instances, since the field does not function as a market free from injections from the state, but the production and distribution of politico-religious texts nevertheless constitutes a vast industry in Iran. The aspect of genre is present in Sacred Defence texts in the sense that style, form and theme are similar, and they share a field of production, distribution and circulation. There is also a common readership – mainly schools, universities and governmental institutions – which receives these books freely, as do individuals who align with the state on the politico-religious primacy of the Islamic Republic. These texts comprise an important part of the production of books in post-revolutionary Iran and even though lots of them are formulaic and repetitive, they cannot be neglected in an analysis of contemporary Iranian literature. One thing to remember is that the large distribution of Sacred Defence texts has to be understood in the context of the state promoting its values. At first glance, the number of reprints and copies distributed of these kinds of work are much higher than those of independent books. However, this high circulation rate is mostly due to the government buying copies and circulating them to schools and institutions, as I have argued in my analysis of the Iran–Iraq War memoir, *Da* (Nanquette 2013b). The fact that the state, mostly through the Ministry of Culture and Islamic Guidance (also known as Ershad), buys numerous copies of books important to its ideology is well-known by literary practitioners although not documented as such for obvious reasons.

Sacred Defence Texts

Sacred Defence literature is linked to a vast field of discourse on the Iran–Iraq War – in Iran also called the Imposed War (*Jang-e tahmili*) – and represents a foundation of the Islamic Republic as it organises the political (defence of the nation) and the religious (defence of Islam and of the Islamic Revolution). While the revolution was a complex set of events, and has led to various narratives, the war is a foundational narrative of the Islamic Republic, the event that allows it to homogenise its discourse. Literature of Resistance (*adabiyyat-e paydari*) is an all-encompassing term for this narrative, which focused on describing the experiences of soldiers on the battlefield or the lives of citizens during the war. The scholar Hassan Mirabeidini explains that between 1980 and 1992 only, 1600 short stories and 46 novels on the war were published in Iran, authored by more than 258 writers (2007: 889). The publications have not abated since, despite the war being further away in time and an event that the young Iranian population has not lived through.

Thematically, the narratives follow the official story in which Iranians were engaged in a sacred defence of their territory against the invading Iraqi army. In such works, heroism, love of one's land and religion, as well as dedication to political leaders, self-sacrifice and martyrdom are defining values. This, more than anything else, distinguishes *adabiyyat-e paydari* from other war texts, which do not always connote alignment with the governmental discourse and in which writers express diverse opinions about the war, including strong condemnation. Sacred Defence literature is not entirely homogeneous, and it is increasingly less so; more varied discourses on the war are published now than at the beginning of the war, but the texts belonging to this genre do have a lot in common in terms of their production and circulation. In terms of form, they are often memoirs or life narratives, while thematically they insist on values like self-sacrifice and martyrdom, Islamic fraternity and purity. It is particularly interesting that Sacred Defence texts began to appear at the very beginning of the war. Kamran Rastegar observes that 'within months of the initial Iraqi invasion in September 1980, the revolutionary state had begun to develop key elements of what would become the sacred defense project' (2016: 67). There was almost no lapse between the commencement of the war and the production of such works.

During the war, the discourse was organised through several governmental institutions, key among them the Centre for Islamic Arts and Thought (*Howzeh-ye honari-ye sazeman-e tablighat-e eslami* – which translates literally to English as Artistic Centre of the Islamic Development Organisation), whose functioning is well studied by Fatemeh Shams (2015a). The texts of the Sacred Defence are published in the thousands, many by the governmental publisher Sureh Mehr. This publisher is an interesting example of a governmental publisher linked to the Centre for Islamic Arts and Thought that has its own censorship system. They do not need to go through the Ministry of Culture and Islamic Guidance before publication. They publish a massive amount of texts and are not slowed down by the censorship process. The fact that they are a parallel institution sometimes leads to the production of creative products and to disruptions of the system. Shams points to the publication of the music album *Toranj* by Mohsen Namjoo as an example of such a disruption (2015a). The centre itself has evolved from being a socialist place to a rightist pro-war institution. Unpublished texts and accounts of the war owned by families in various forms are even more numerous but they are not literary as such and are not accounted for in this book. There is also an expanding field of scholarship on the subject in English, with Narguess Farzad's work on Qeysar Aminpur (2007), and Asghar Seyed-Ghorab's work on revolutionary poetry (2012). Amir Moosavi has analysed in detail several key texts of the field of Sacred Defence literature, especially those by Ahmad Dehqan, which reveal cracks in the ideological discourse of the war (2015, 2016, 2017). Fatemeh Shams specifically studies the poetry that came out of the war, calling it 'Islamic Republican poetry.' She writes that

> Islamic Republican poetry indicates a literary phenomenon that bears a specific relation to the hierarchy of power and exhibits distinctive literary characteristics. Despite their ideologically charged content, many of these poems express popular sentiments that proved strongly resonant during troubled times. War represented a critical phase for Islamic Republican poets since they assumed control of the official literary scene and state-sponsored institutions and became the mainstream voice of poetry during the postrevolution era. (Shams 2016: 49)

According to Shams, Islamic Republican poetry is comprised of sub-genres like Ashurian poetry, which is dedicated to recalling the war as an event in line with the tradition of martyrdom in Shiism (2016: 21).

The body of scholarship on Sacred Defence literature, apart from the work of the above scholars, is scarce. There is scholarship on Sacred Defence texts in Persian, however a lot of it is published by governmental institutions and tends not only to reiterate the official discourse but to lack a critical approach.

Even more than thirty years after the war, Sacred Defence texts are still a space of contention for the Islamic Republic. I have written elsewhere about how one particular text – *Da*, the bestselling memoirs of a woman who fought during the war – constitutes an interesting case of negotiation. Although in one sense *Da* was the pure product of the Sacred Defence field, commissioned and published through its institutions, it also engaged with ideas about minorities and the importance of women to the war effort that were previously absent in most Sacred Defence texts (Nanquette 2013b). There is currently a realisation that new modes of engagement with the war are needed and that the narration of martyrdom in formulaic texts and films is no longer sufficient to interest the clear majority of the population who did not live through the war. Narges Bajoghli demonstrates through an engaging narration how governmental media producers are adapting their strategies to appeal to young audiences who are bored of the official narrative (2019). She describes how the media producers, who are often veterans, want to offer new strategies to counter the lack of engagement in the audience. Kaveh Ehsani similarly insists on the discontent that this unified narrative about the war creates. Today, 'instead of acting as a unifying experience that reinforces state hegemony, the legacy of the war is a widespread resentment that affects public culture and political attitudes' (Ehsani 2017: 1). Many want to reclaim the war and the diversity of experiences.

Literary Texts on Religious Figures

Outside of the Sacred Defence realm, there is also a vast field of religious texts that have literary aims and present themselves as literary. These are different from religious texts of exegesis, which include hagiography of the figures of Shiism; literature of the People of the House (*Ahl-e beyt*, namely the family of the Prophet Muhammad); texts for pilgrimage (*Ziyarat nameh*); and texts with prayers that make the tenets of Islam accessible – all of which constitute a large and crucial part of the Iranian publishing industry. The literary-religious texts do not represent a significant portion of the books published but they are important to take into account because, just like Sacred Defence texts, they are at the centre of the government's views of literature. These texts usually engage with the most important figures of Shiism and of the current regime, and the best place to look for them is in the textbooks of literature, since young adults and students are their primary readership. Reading these works is compulsory and educates students from a young age on the ideas of the Islamic Republic. In Chapter 5, I study children's literature in detail, but here I focus only on the general high school curriculum as being representative of the way the government views literary texts.

The curriculum for first-year high school students is the most heavily influenced by politico-religious texts. If we look at the 2016 Persian Literature textbook for first-year high school students in all fields of study, we find that about one third of the book contains religious stories, another third classical ethical stories from Nezami or Nasser Khosrow, and the rest contains foreign texts and texts about society. The politico-religious stories are comprised of a short story by Mohammad Eshtehardi, 'Summary of Lessons' (*'Kholaseh-ye danesh-ha'*) – a commentator on the Quran – from his book *Stories of Mystics* (*Dastan-ha-ye sahebdelan*); a poem about Imam Ali by Mousavi Garmaroodi entitled 'In the Shade of the Palm of Sanctity' (*'Dar sayeh sar-e nakhl-e velayat'*), from his book *Olive on the Bergamot Branch* (*Peyvand-e zeytun bar shakheh-ye toranj*); a story by the Sacred Defence filmmaker Morteza Avini entitled 'Chivalrous Warriors' (*'Darya delan-e saf shekan'*); 'Heroines of Iran' (*'Shir zanan-e Iran'*), a short story by Masoumeh Abad from her memories of the Iran–Iraq War, published in the book *I Am Alive* (*Man zendeh-am*); 'The Brave Men of Iran' (*'Deliran va Mardan-e Iran Zamin'*), a poem by Mahmoud Shahrokhi, poet of the Sacred Defence; and a poem about the Shia religious leader Musa Sadr entitled 'Dawn' (*'Sepideh dam'*) by the Syrian Nizar Tawfiq Qabbani. Curricula for the second and third years contain fewer religious texts and more contemporary Persian poetry. This is the time when students chose a major and have potentially less time to devote to the basics of the Islamic ideology.

Outside of the high school curriculum, there are also texts published by individual writers who engage literarily with religious figures. Some are for children and young adults, and this forms an important part of the government's efforts to publish them, as I show in Chapter 5 on children's literature. Others are for adults: one example is *Observed by the Moon* (*Zir-e negah-e mah*), published by Seyyed Mohammad Reza Darbandi, the current Director of International Relations at the Saadi Foundation, the institute for Persian language which I discuss in Chapter 3. It is the story of Fatemeh

Zahra, the daughter of the Prophet Muhammad, as told by her husband Ali, after her death. Ali recalls moments with her in an interesting intertwining of pseudo-erotic and religious tones. Ali insists that she was always the model of a perfect Islamic wife – proper, humble, never directly expressing her feelings but showing them through her devotion to her husband and children – but at the same time, he wishes she had been more open in expressing her love. The religious figures of Zahra and Ali are used here in a modern way to depict the love between husband and wife whilst also promoting the ideology of the Islamic Republic, especially in its definition of the ideal woman and her focus on her family.

Seyyed Mehdi Shojaei is another author who has written on the subject of Fatemeh Zahra and her husband. His books include *The Berthed Ship* (*Kashti-ye pahlu gerefteh*, Shojaei 1986). *Father, Love and Son* (*Pedar, eshq va pesar*) by the same author is about Imam Hussain (Shojaei 2013). He also has books on Imam Hassan Mojtaba, Imam Reza and Imam Mahdi. Shojaei is an interesting example of a writer who is popular, with high prints and good reception from readers, and is at the same time close to the governmental establishment: he has been a jury member at various governmental Fajr (Film and Theatre) festivals, and once belonged to the board of directors of the Centre for the Intellectual Development of Children and Young People (*Kanun-e parvaresh-e fekri-ye kudakan va nowjavanan*), an essential institution I discuss at length in Chapter 5. He is one of the most well-known governmental writers, and he is also respected by independent writers, which is not often the case. Most of Shojaei's works have been published by Neyestan – the publishing company he founded in 1987 – although two of his works have also been translated into English by Caroline Croskery for Candle & Fog, a publisher I examine in Chapter 7. Other texts in this line, respected by both independent and governmental writers, exist, but none are as well known or popular as those by Shojaei. There are fictions about the different Shia imams, about Imam Reza's sister Masoumeh, about the family of the Prophet Muhammad, and about Imam Mahdi. There are also fictions about Ali Khamenei, like *Fascinated and Triumphant* (*Maftun va Firuzeh*) by Said Tashakori, and at least one on Khomeini – *Three Meetings with an Unbelievable Man* (*Seh didar ba mardi keh as farasu-ye bavar-e ma miamad*) – by the well-known writer Nader Ebrahimi. But there are very few texts on

Khomeini, which is particularly surprising given the strong encouragement of governmental institutions in the form of a festival devoted to writing about Khomeini, which provides free creative writing workshops (Portal of Imam Khomeini 2017).

Conclusion

This chapter has given an overview of the contemporary Iranian literary field in terms of forms and genres. Perhaps surprisingly, romances are bestsellers, whilst genres like crime fiction are unable to flourish due to the nature of the authoritarian regime. Politico-religious texts form a crucial part of this literary field, and are heavily regulated and supported by the government, and the wide circulation and high sales volume of politico-religious texts is the direct result of the state distributing them to schools and institutions.

Giving an encompassing view of the literary texts published in Iran after the revolution according to forms and genres has allowed me to distinguish the Iranian literary field from western literary fields which the reader might be more familiar with. One distinctive point for western readers is to understand that in the authoritarian context of Iran, the independent sector that challenges the hegemony of the state is often calling for more market mechanisms and a freer market. This is a situation shared in other authoritarian contexts. However, this might be counter-intuitive for a western reader who sees the independent sector as asking for more reining in of the market.

In the following chapter, I continue to investigate the specificities of the Iranian literary field, paying attention to its digital forms. The internet has long been touted as a space of free expression, but what role has it played in the evolution of Iranian literature in the past four decades?

2

Digital Literature: The Importance of the Medium

Since 2011, the Iranian state has endeavoured to create an Iranian intranet, which would be tightly controlled and censored, and would replace connections to the global internet. Called the National Information Network (Shabakeh-ye melli-ye ettela'at), it is still a work in progress and the connection to the internet is still available. However, the access to blocked websites like Facebook requires the use of VPNs; there are moments of crisis, like in November 2019 when the state shut down most internet connections for several days; and its speed is also slower than the national intranet. This endeavour is similar to that of the Chinese state. It is interesting to see China and Iran moving in similar directions when it comes to internet connections and to this preference for national forms of intranet. In this chapter, I focus on the influence of the digital medium on post-revolutionary Persian literature. It is critical to understand how online platforms shape cultural products.

This chapter explains the forms literature takes in new media and analyses the importance of digital literature in the Iranian literary field. Following the first chapter that looked at genres, this one is about the medium, and interrogates its importance and influence. After literary blogs/weblogs – which in the early 2000s were crucial in redefining the field and introducing new forms of literature, especially short forms – Facebook and Telegram have been sites of literary innovation, particularly in genre fiction. Since the mid-2010s, Instagram has played an important role. This chapter therefore studies the impact of the digital medium on the evolutions of contemporary Iranian literature through case studies of literary blogs and literary Instagram, which stand at either end of the chronology of Persian digital literature. New media offer specific literary constraints in terms of length mostly, with possibilities to divert and to use multiple materials, including sound and images. They also theoretically allow for global distribution, although filtering has an impact on these digital forms of literary production. Finally, in the Iranian context which is restricted by a strict censorship, as I analyse in detail in Chapter 3, they are possibly a space of more open publishing. This is why it is important to question contemporary Iranian literature's links with new media, the forms they encourage, the effect they have on the whole system and on readers, and how literary practitioners have used them for creative purposes in the constrained Iranian environment.

Digital literature is not a distinct branch of Persian literature. However, because it does not encounter the same constraints as print literature, especially because censorship plays a lesser role, it has moved in different directions from print literature, and this has had an impact on the whole of the field. Literary blogs have been important sites of literary innovation since the 2000s, when digital literature started in Persian, and at the beginning of the 2020s Instagram is the most dynamic platform for such innovations. I concentrate on each of these to trace the evolution of contemporary Persian digital literature. I ask if digital literature is redefining Iranian literary discourse: does it democratise it and include writers who are not part of the literary establishment? What innovations in terms of form, topic, style does it introduce? How has it evolved between different platforms? What is the role of censorship in this process? I define the role digital literature plays in Iranian literary networks and ask whether its history evidences a literature that has global ambitions. This chapter examines digital literature by Iranian nationals, which includes material written by Iranians in Iran, as well as in languages spoken by Iranians in the diaspora, primarily English and French. It does not include blogs by Persian speakers from Afghanistan and Tajikistan or from Iran in languages other than Persian.

Iranian Literary Blogs in the Context of the Iranian Blogosphere

A blog, or weblog, is a personal site that has entries, 'posts', usually in reverse chronological order, characterised by its interactivity and dialogue with readers through comments on posts. In contrast to a website, a blog is easy to set up, usually free, and does not require much technical knowledge. I define a literary blog as a blog that engages with literature, for example by publishing texts, reviews of books, interviews with authors, or discussion about the literary world. Iranian blogs first emerged in 2001, when Hossein Derakhshan (known as Hoder), who is referred to as the father of the Persian blog, followed the first few bloggers who had published in Persian, to found his weblog in Persian and put together a guide to blogging for Persian speakers on the free site, *blogger.com*. Arash Falasiri and Nazanin Ghanavizi write of the rapidity with which interest in blogging expanded: 'Within a few months, the first free blog service, Persianblog.ir, appeared, initiated by three young engineers in Tehran. In less than a year, it had more than one hundred thousand blogs in Persian' (Falasiri and Ghanavizi 2015). The popularity of blogs exploded, in line with global trends: 'blogging reached a high popularity in 2004, the year that is also called "the year of blogs" throughout the world' (Falasiri and Ghanavizi 2015). Literary blogs had become a popular mode of writing within Iran by around 2002, the time the blog *Sleepwalker* (*Khabgard*), which I study below, was launched.

The Iranian blogosphere is numerically significant, although it is now a dated phenomenon. Persian has been reported as both the fourth (Alavi 2005: 1) and the tenth (by Technorati; see Sifry 2007) most-used language in the blogosphere. This difference emerges from different scales of measurement. Such rankings shift rapidly and often, and are to be taken with caution. Despite the exact ranking being contested, Persian is among the ten most used languages in this arena, which is surprising from a relatively small population – there are 110 million Persian speakers worldwide, including in Afghanistan and Tajikistan. Since these last two countries do not have good access to the internet, most Persian blogs come from Iran.

Many academics and journalists have portrayed Iranian bloggers as young people resisting the power of the state (Alavi 2005). More generally in Middle Eastern Studies, the dominant argument is that new media belong to the youth, resist the state, are inherently liberating and a cause to celebrate. The Iranian blogosphere has similarly been depicted as a space of resistance and a potential tool for the development of democracy. Although I agree with the idea that blogs can theoretically constitute an alternate public sphere, and more generally that social media facilitates communication between those oppressed by the state, such approaches do not capture the multi-dimensional character of the Iranian blogosphere. The Iranian blogosphere does not always speak to a straightforwardly oppositional politics. Babak Rahimi and David Faris' edited collection is a particularly important exploration of the ambiguities of new media in Iran: 'social media as a "many-to-many interactive" medium is a multilayered and permeable form of computer-mediated communication, and accordingly, its impact on offline domains of Iranian life or beyond is ambiguous and multidirectional' (Rahimi and Faris 2015). Other researchers have shown that many other discourses populate the Iranian blogosphere, including blogs by conservative, religious people, young or old, and have demonstrated how the Iranian state has been particularly successful at populating the blogosphere with its own interventions (Akhavan 2013; Falasiri and Ghanavizi 2015; Kelly and Etling 2008). This has been effective because 'unlike many other electronic devices, such as video players and satellite television networks, the Internet was generally received as of possible use to the state and was thus acceptable to Islamic Iran' (Falasiri and Ghanavizi 2015).

Furthermore, I am concerned that a discourse that insists only on the resisting power of the blogosphere shares traits with 'digital Orientalism' (Morozov 2011: 241–4). 'Cyberutopians', as Evgeny Morozov calls them, tend to forget that oppressive regimes benefit from using the internet just as much as supporters of democracy. They also often overlook the negative impact of the internet: 'as we are beginning to debate the impact of the Internet on how we think and learn – tolerating the possibility that it may actually impede rather than facilitate those processes – we rarely pose such questions in the authoritarian context' (Morozov 2011: 241). It is also worth noting that I am concerned with literary blogs only, although some of them have political resonance, and I show that these blogs in particular often reproduce the milieu of the offline world, probably more than blogs concerned with civil society issues.

Iranian Literary Blogs from a Comparative Perspective

A particularly relevant feature of the Iranian literary field that has a bearing on blogs is the existence of censorship, which I discuss at length in Chapter 3. *Momayezi* literally means verification, auditing or inspection in Persian. It is considered by those undergoing such verification to be an understatement.

Sansur comes from the French *censure* and perhaps describes the process more effectively (Atwood 2012: 38–41). Censorship has always been part of the Iranian literary field but the rules changed with the Islamic government, and the ideological and moral censorship of the Islamic Republic is unprecedented. Contrary to print books, the censorship of blogs is not carried out by the Ministry of Culture and Islamic Guidance but by the Prosecutor General of Iran and the Commission to Determine the Instances of Criminal Content (called the Committee Charged with Determining Offensive Content in the document below), which censor the internet with the help of the Cyber Police and the Supreme Council of Cyberspace.

Figure 2.1 represents the complexity of the relations between the different powers in charge of controlling the internet and implementing censorship. What is noticeable is that many of these institutions are very recent – 'four new bodies – the Supreme Council on Cyberspace, the Committee Charged with Determining Offensive Content, the Cyber Army, and the Cyber Police – have emerged since 2009' – and that some like the Cyber Police have emerged only in 2011.[1]

Some Iranian writers, who were published in print before the 2000s but resented censorship, took up blogs with enthusiasm, partly because initially this sphere was not well controlled, and even today, is not completely subject to censorship. Additionally, the emergence of blogs also saw new writers begin blogging about literature, thus indicating the appeal of the blog as a relatively uncensored site of literary production. Literary blogs are one of the most popular blogging genres in Iran. As of April 2015, 31,227 blogs were classified in 'Literature and poetry' on *Blogfa*, the main Persian weblog service, and 2,593 in 'Book', this category including many literary blogs. This statistical data is to be approached with caution. First, it is not entirely reliable, and second, many people in Iran view themselves as poets, and as such, might choose the category 'Literature and poetry' to classify their blogs, although most of the content is about life in general, interspersed with some of their own poetry. This statistic is only given to provide an idea of the categories people use to classify their

---

[1] For a detailed analysis of the evolving laws around internet censorship, including the different institutions and methods used, as well as interesting case studies, see Small Media's report (Robertson and Marchant 2014).

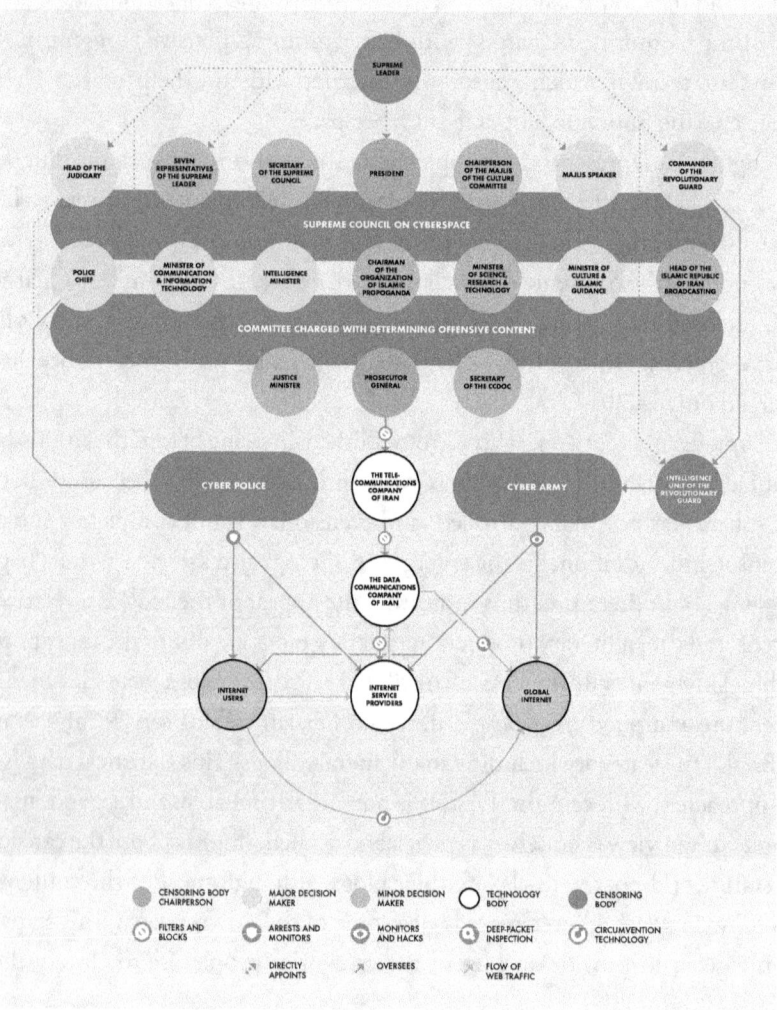

Figure 2.1 Internet censorship in Iran. Credit to Iran Media Program at the Annenberg School for Communication at the University of Pennsylvania and Hyperakt.

Supreme Leader
The most powerful decision maker in Iran, the Supreme Leader has broad, direct and indirect legislative and policy-setting powers over internet communications. The Supreme Leader appoints directors of key military, security and governmental posts, which also serve as members of bodies involved in shaping and implementing internet censorship in Iran.

Supreme Council on Cyberspace (SCC)
The top policy-making body for cyber activities in Iran, formed by the Supreme Leader in April 2012 to develop the state's domestic and international cyber policies in response to the "soft war" with the west.

Committee Charged With Determining Offensive Content (CCDOC)
The "filtering committee" is responsible for identifying web content to be filtered and blocked. The CCDOC creates lists of illegal websites and online content that violates public morals, contradicts Islam, threatens national security, criticizes public officials or organizations, or promotes cyber crimes or the use of circumvention tools. The SCC and the CCDOC share seven common members. This shows the lack of a coherent division of powers and responsibilities between officials in charge of making policies and those responsible for implementing censorship decisions.

Filtering List
The Prosecutor General's Office, as head of the filtering committee, issues the filtering list to the Telecommunications Company of Iran (TCI), the state-controlled company responsible for internet and communications services in Iran. The Data Communications Company of Iran (DCI), a subsidiary of TCI that manages Iran's public data network, implements some filtering orders and transmits the remaining list for filtering by ISPs.

Iranian Cyber Army (ICA)
The Iranian Cyber Army is an underground network of pro-government cyber activists, hackers and bloggers who monitor the internet and launch cyber attacks on opposition and anti-Islamic websites. It operates under the Intelligence Unit of the Revolutionary Guard.

Cyber Police (FATA)
A division within Iran's police department established in January 2011 to combat internet crimes and online social networks that spread anti-Islamic activities.

Telecommunications Company of Iran (TCI)
TCI manages Iran's ITC and telecommunications infrastructure, including mobile and internet communications, directly or through its subsidiaries. TCI is owned by the Iranian government and Etemad-e-Mobin Company, a private consortium with reported ties to the Revolutionary Guard.

Data Communications Company of Iran (DCI)
DCI, a subsidiary of TCI, maintains Iran's data network infrastructure, and is responsible for implementing filtering and blocking orders from the CCDOC. All Internet Service Providers (ISPs) are required to purchase bandwidth from the DCI.

Internet Service Providers (ISPs)
ISPs must comply with the CCDOC's filtering and blocking orders, and are also required to filter any materials that contradict Islam, the Constitution, insult the Supreme Leader or other religious figures, or any content that "undermines the independence of the country," disrupts national unity, stirs "pessimism and hopelessness in people against the legitimacy and efficacy of the Islamic government," or promotes "illegal groups and parties."

Content-control software
ISPs are required to install content-control software that automatically inspects, filters, blocks web content and monitors IP traffic and internet-user activities. These programs are configured to identify and filter websites, based on keywords that are customized by Iranian ISPs and network administrators.

Deep-packet Inspection (DPI)
Technology capable of monitoring and inspecting network traffic data in "real time" and determining whether content can pass through the network or be redirected, flagged, blocked, or reported to network administrators. China's ZTE Corp in 2010 sold TCI a DPI-based surveillance system capable of monitoring landline, mobile and internet communications. It is unclear how extensively the DPI system is being used in Iran, beyond interfering with anti-filtering tools.

Circumvention
Iranian authorities estimate that 20 to 30 percent of the country's internet users rely on circumvention tools to bypass state censorship, although such technologies are illegal. These tools vary in technological sophistication and in their capacities to allow users to browse the web undetected.

IRAN MEDIA PROGRAM
پژوهش رسانه در ایران

www.iranmediaresearch.org

blogs. For my analysis, I have considered as literary blogs those in which more than approximately 70 per cent of the content was about literature. By way of comparison, 'Humor' accounted for 4,047 blogs, 'Computer' for 8,060, and 'Education/research' for 5,987. 'Family' (private and public blogs about life in general) was the largest category with 45,479 blogs. It might be striking to note that, after general blogs, literary blogs are the most prolific, and that other categories come well after. This reminds us of the extent to which Iran is a literary nation, of people who see themselves as a nation of poets, and who hold their literary figures in high esteem, as the last chapter of this book details.

Before honing in on Persian literary blogs in detail, it is useful to offer a broader comparative perspective on the history and characteristics of blogs in other parts of the world, as some of their usage and characteristics are structural to the medium and not specific to Iran. If we assume that literary blogs follow the same tendencies as blogs in general, the history of blogging in English offers a useful comparison. Although blogs are less dominated by English today than when they first started, English is still the most commonly used language of the internet. At the beginning of this research, I had thought of making a comparison to the Sinophone blogosphere, because of the similarities in the literary fields. However, it seems censorship is less prevalent in the Chinese digital literary field, outside of political topics, than in Iran. Also, it appears that blogs have not played such a key role in Chinese internet literature. In an interview, Hockx gives this example: 'China's most famous blogger is Han Han, who is also a famous novelist, but his literary work never appears on his blog' (personal communication, 22 September 2015). Discussion forums seem to have been more important. In addition, the history is different, as Chinese blogs started with Sina around 2003; the decline came when microblogs like Weibo became popular (Abrahamsen 2015).[2] For blogs globally, 'In 1999 . . . there were 23 blogs on the internet. By the middle of 2006, there were 50 million blogs' (Chapman 2011). There has been a short delay in Persian blogs catching up with English ones because of the difficulty of adjusting to a non-Latin alphabet. Iranians within Iran did not have easy access to most platforms because these were in English. But when Hoder published a guide in Persian on how to blog, this started a trend and the history of Persian blogs has followed a similar path to English blogging since its emergence in 2001. What is interesting here is that Iran, which is largely isolated from worldwide trends politically, economically, and partly culturally, has followed a similar track to that of better-connected countries in the evolution of its blogosphere. The English blogosphere experienced a decline around 2005 (Chapman 2011). 'The conversation seems to have moved on from blogs to Twitter, Tumblr, Facebook and the rest. Blogs now feel very Web 1.0' (Sarvas 2014). The evolution of the Persian blogosphere derives from this English trend. As in other places, there has been a boom and then decline of Iranian blogs, in line with the emergence of other technologies.

It has been argued that women particularly benefited from and contributed to this boom in the blogosphere (Rahimi 2003). One important argument is that the anonymity of blogs allowed women to talk about their private lives and selves, which is not a given in a Persian society where outer (*zaher*) and inner (*baten*), visible and hidden, are fundamentally separated. Although there are no reliable statistics available about the gender of bloggers, who are often anonymous, it is clear from the popularity of some female bloggers that they are playing a role in opening up the online discourse. The activist and journalist Masih Alinejad, who has lived in the diaspora since

---

[2] Thanks to Michel Hockx for sharing his knowledge on this topic.

2009, used to have a blog but now publishes her stories on other platforms. Massoumeh Ebtekar, the first female member of the post-revolutionary cabinet in Iran, started a blog in Persian in 2006 and a year later in English (Ebtekar 2007–17). The well-known poet Fatemeh Ekhtesari, mentioned in more detail below, had a writing workshop online (Ekhtesari 2011–14). In all cases, at different ends of the political spectrum, these blogs appealed to several generations as well as an international/diasporic audience and demonstrated an attempt to move past gender bias in Iran in general and in the Iranian technological world in particular. The online role of women should not be overstated though, as Niki Akhavan reminds us, and should not be reduced to the argument that whereas women are oppressed in the public sphere, they are free online (2011: 63). In any case, I argue that the role of women is not as evident in literary blogs as in other blogs concerning general and social matters, including those on gender issues. One of the foundations of Iranian literature, the prevalence of men when it comes to literary situations of power, is still prevalent online. Indeed, although females are more active in the literary field today than ever before in Iranian history, and many bestselling authors are women, the book industry is still male-dominated, as women write only 20 per cent of published books in all categories, which includes the prolific field of religious writing (Small Media 2015a: 32).

In Iran, the boom in blogs after 2005 was curtailed, partly due to the state deciding to crack down on bloggers and arresting several prominent members of that community. With the contested presidential election of 2009, this decline accelerated. One main factor was that censorship was strengthened in all areas, including the blogosphere. In addition, a study of Iran's blogosphere finds 'a decline in overall blogging activity among our survey respondents, with nearly half reporting having stopped their activity, in large part because of time spent on social media' (Giacobino *et al.* 2014: 3). Indeed, it is maybe as much due to the restrictions of the medium and a tendency to use other platforms as to censorship that blogs have declined. The importance of social media is emphasised in many comments, and accounted for as an explanation for the decrease in the number of blogs (Khaledian 2015). There has been, during the 2000s and 2010s, a supplanting of blogs by other forms of internet literature: 'The growth of social media, and, in particular, social networking sites (SNSs) like Facebook, is also among the most important causes of the erosion of Blogestan' (Giacobino *et al.* 2014: 4). Quoting state-filtering practices, Arash Falasiri and Nazanin Ghanavizi also claim that 'the main reason for the apparent decline of blogging practices can be found in the effect of social networks as a new platform for self-expression and critical discourse' (Falasiri and Ghanavizi 2015) and go on to explain that 'the number of Iranians in the country joining Facebook increased dramatically after the 2009 incidents, in spite of the government's intermittent blocks of the site' (Falasiri and Ghanavizi 2015). Facebook has been blocked permanently since 2009. This is also evident in the fact that many creative writing workshops, which would be presented on blogs in the 2000s, can be found in the 2010s on Instagram and Facebook – for example one run on Facebook by the famous US-based Iranian writer Moniru Ravanipour. She runs a writing workshop online called the Story Writing Workshop for Gypsies (*Kargah-e dastan nevisi-ye koli-ha*), set up as a secret group on Facebook. It is only accessible by invitation. The workshop had a collection published as a book.

Another technological reason for the decline in blogs is the shift from the use of computers in the 2000s to smartphones and tablets in the 2010s. It is cumbersome to update a weblog from a smartphone, while smartphone users can easily log into and use social media applications, which all started to offer smartphone versions. Around 2011, 3G was introduced to Iran, so internet connections outside of home or the office became possible. In 2017, it was estimated that half of the Iranian population owned a smartphone (Azali 2017b). All these suggest that, while filtering has played an important role in the decline of blogs, other factors also influenced this decline, especially the fact that blogs are generation-oriented. Young Iranian people today primarily use other tools of expression, such as Instagram, Facebook, Viber, Twitter, Telegram and WhatsApp, accessed on smartphones. If blogs have not been replaced entirely, there is an intermedial exchange as they work in interaction with other tools. Blogs become personal archives of writings that have appeared in a multitude of other internet platforms (Giacobino *et al.* 2014: 32).

If there is a similar history between English and Persian blogs because of the characteristics of the medium, though, blogs in Persian have specificities due to the Iranian context that need to be analysed. There is a difference between print publishing and weblog publishing in Iran, due to two characteristics of online publishing: the novelty of the medium which allowed for more experimentation in style, form and content; and the particularities of censorship of the internet. Although censorship of the Iranian blogosphere by the Attorney-General of Iran is quite effective today, there are gaps present on the internet that are simply not permitted in print publishing. In addition, censorship took several years to become implemented effectively online; blog innovations bloomed during this period. Below, I analyse two influential literary blogs that assume different political perspectives, in order to give a sense of the kind of texts that are published in literary blogs.

Focus on Two Literary Blogs

Khabgard is a good representative of a certain type of literary blog, as it has been described as one of the best weblogs in different platforms, based on criteria such as the continuity of blogging; the use of a unique linguistic style; influence or authority; networking strength; and success in attracting audiences. It has also started trends, for example by creating a literary prize, although it only lasted a few years – the Bahram Sadeghi Prize. *Khabgard* has been described as an 'ultra-weblog':

> By this, I don't mean that it is superior (although it has the characteristics of a superior weblog). I mean that it is more than a weblog. It is a comprehensive website that encompasses different layers. From another point of view, it might be considered as an online magazine . . . but it is not really a magazine because it is overtly under the shadow of its blogger's personality. (Irani 2008)

Khabgard is run by Seyed Reza Shokrollahi, a journalist, writer and editor who used to work for well-known independent publishers like Cheshmeh and Ofoq, as well as for IRIB, the national radio and television broadcaster. This means that he had many connections and was familiar with the Iranian literary field when he began to blog. Shokrollahi started *Khabgard* in November 2002. It gradually evolved from a personal weblog to one that publishes short stories, reviews, articles and translations, written by himself as well as other writers, and became one of the most famous literary blogs in Iran. Shokrollahi's taste and attitude is pivotal in selecting and organising the website's articles and notes; indeed, the main page's subtitle is 'Critical View on Culture, Art and Literature'. *Khabgard* was not politically oriented in an obvious way until 2009, when Shokrollahi decided to publish political posts advocating reform during and after that year's presidential elections, and the blog was subsequently filtered.

As early as 2003, *Khabgard* published fortnightly reports about the book market and publications, which did not exist outside of mainstream media at the time. Contrary to the *Book of the Week* (*Ketab-e hafteh*) and *Book of the Month* (*Ketab-e mah*) published by Iran Book House, which mostly give summaries and details of books, these were reviews often with a particular viewpoint, not only aimed at describing a book. *Khabgard* also published the news and reports of the Book City (Shahr-e Ketab, now the biggest bookshop chain in Tehran) and supported the Book City's Short Story Award (Shokrollahi 2015). It also set up an online library with texts that had not been through censorship or the censored segments of works already in the market, with Persian short stories and translations. Shokrollahi's personal interest is in Persian proverbs and their link to folklore and history. He reproduces his posts about this topic from a column in the reformist newspaper *E'temad Daily*. Another well-known writer, Mohammad Hassan Shahsavari, has his blog *Back Window* (*Panjereh-ye poshti*) linked to *Khabgard*. *Khabgard* thus has supported and continues to support various literary enterprises both online and offline, and uses its influential internet presence to promote other projects.

What is striking in the blog's reviews of current books is how much they reproduce the conventions of offline literary discourse. We are dealing with a relatively small circle of established writers, more middle-aged than young, who navigate between independent publishers like Cheshmeh and literary prizes like the Golshiri. Is this also the case, however, within a more minor and personal literary blog that does not represent the milieu of reformist-oriented writers?

Abdol Jabbar Kakaei has a weblog called *Years to Today* (*Sal-ha-ye takonun*) (Kakaei 2007–present). It is an example of a personal blog that started later, in 2007, and is representative of an individual and complex take on literature, whereas *Khabgard* represents the viewpoint of the mildly reformist literary elite while being conservative in its use of language and philosophy of writing. Politically, Kakaei is a well-known conservative-oriented writer, but with a reputation outside of the conservative elements of society. He is also critical of some aspects of the Islamic Republic regime and has become disillusioned with it especially after the 2009 elections. This reminds us that conservative blogs contribute to the Iranian literary field since 'bloggers who are identified with hardline elements aren't necessarily agents executing orders' (Akhavan 2013: 39). Kakaei is a famous contemporary Iranian poet and songwriter who started to write after the Islamic Revolution. He is known as a 'poet of the revolution' (*Sha'er-e enqelab*), famous for his use of the forms of *ghazal* and *masnavi*. Among his texts, many are about the Iran–Iraq War, in which he participated, as well as about the religious ceremonies performed during the month of Moharram. He has published academic articles as well as collections of poems. Two of his books have been selected as Sacred Defence Book of the Year, a prize run by the Center for Islamic Arts and Thoughts (*Howzeh-ye honari-ye sazeman-e tablighat-e eslami*), funded by the state (*Ilam Today* 2006). Kakaei plays important roles in state-backed literary events. For instance, he was director of the 2014 edition of the Fajr International Poetry Festival – a governmental one. Kakaei is a supporter of the Islamic Republic regime, and has written poems expressing his admiration for Khomeini. However, at the same time, like many followers of the Supreme Leader, he has criticised the government and has become increasingly vocal about it after 2009. For example, he has a moving text about the attack on his son by Basijis (a volunteer militia linked to the Iranian Revolutionary Guards and the Supreme Leader) during the 2009 demonstrations, defending his son against the militia, who, according to Kakaei, betrayed what he and his friends had stood for during the revolution and the war (Kakaei 2009). Shams analyses this text as such:

> Parts of Kakai's letter to his son, which followed the latter's physical assault during one of the demonstrations of 2009, provides an example of how a leading official poet who had written numerous pieces in praise of war, Khomeini and the revolution quickly became disillusioned in the aftermath of the 2009 election. (Shams 2015b: 236)

Kakaei's blog is simple in its organisation. It features posts with his poems and songs, interviews, and sometimes reflections that criticise those in power in the literary milieus. In most cases, his poems have a political or religious undertone. *Sal-ha-ye takonun* started after the boom of blogs in Iran, in January 2007. Until 2008, Kakaei mostly used the blog for publishing his poems and interviews. However, from 2008 he started to share more, especially by writing introductions to his texts, reporting on some of his trips, for example to India, or recalling stories from his youth. Since 2012, he has also published posts on political issues, becoming vocal about his criticism of censorship. In one of his interviews with the newspaper *Shahrvand*, he talks in support of songwriters' freedom. He believes that decades after the Islamic Revolution, the negative side effects of censorship are detrimental to society. He affirms that this policy of the regime is against the Islamic Revolution, not in support of it. He also talks about self-censorship, and says that songwriters are censoring themselves in order to be able to sell their songs (Kakaei 2007). In a similar fashion, in a meeting for the Fajr International Poetry Festival, Kakaei emphasised the importance of the festival's organisation being in the hands of poets, rather than the state. He also expressed his regret for those whose books are banned by the state, and stated that he would do his best to help writers to get their books published. Kakaei thus presented the festival as a platform for inclusive and free speech (2007).

Interestingly, Kakaei's blog began after the popularity of Persian blogs had already peaked. One can see it as a way for a conservative writer to have an impact on the virtual literary milieu, as well as to steer the state's policies on culture, using his position of influence. Kakaei does not shy away from expressing dissent through his poems and songs, which speak on topics including censorship or the demonstrations of 2009. His blog supports Akhavan's argument that conservative voices are important in the Iranian blogosphere, including in the literary blogosphere, and that they are far from conveying a fixed propaganda discourse. If we focus only on reformist-oriented blogs like *Khabgard*, we are bound to perform another kind of 'digital orientalism', seeing only the utopian vision of blogs as a mode of resistance to a monolithic Islamic state. In reality, the Iranian literary blogosphere is multi-dimensional and includes a variety of voices. It is certainly possible to identify multiple forms of evolution and innovation that have taken place within the blogosphere. Below, I offer a more expansive exploration of the innovations brought forth by literary blogs.

What Evolution did Literary Blogs Bring About?

It is important to recognise that in terms of form, blogs have brought forth new literary genres, oriented towards concision, that are significantly changing the Iranian literary field. Being concise is important in blogging, which has thus stimulated forms like flash fiction. In particular, the genre known as very short story (*dastanak*) was encouraged by the nature of online interactions within blogs. One can see examples of such a form in group blogs for flash fiction like *Very Short Story: Group Weblog of Iranian Very Short Story* (*Dastanak: weblog-e goruhi-ye dastanak-nevisi-ha-ye Irani*) and it is worth noting that a *dastanak* blog won the best blog award in 2011 (Kamalinejad 2015). The genre is also present on other platforms that encourage even shorter literary forms than blogging. *Dastanak* builds on a long tradition of short literary forms in Persian literature, for example the *hekayat* (short story) in Sa'di's *Golestan* or Jami's *Baharestan,* and in poetry the *roba'i/do-beyti* (quatrain) forms, the most concise forms of Persian poetry.

As early as 1998, the newspaper *Hamshahri* published a collection of twenty-three stories from twenty-three writers in 100 words (Baharloo 1998). In 2011, a scholarly book tried to categorise these new short forms (Jazeini 2011). This trend towards concise stories accelerated with the arrival of blogs, and there have since been many festivals devoted to flash fiction, SMS fiction and other very short forms, called differently very short story (*dastan-e kutah-e kutah*), even very very short story (*dastan-e kutah-e kutah-e kutah*), and flash fiction (*dastan-e nagahani*) but *dastanak* is the most common term. This trend includes the governmental literature, which has been keen on promoting flash fiction on the Iran–Iraq War (as in the Internet Festival of Very Short Stories of the War – *Jashnvareh-ye interneti-ye dastan-e kutah-e kutah-e jang*). In this, Iranian literature follows a worldwide trend of increased recognition for the short form. The critic and translator Asadollah Amraei, for example, notes that the 2013 Nobel Prize in Literature was given to the short story writer Alice Munro, thus validating the genre as internationally prestigious. As a further example, novelist and literary critic Farahnaz Alizadeh has produced a collection of both Iranian and non-Iranian flash fictions (Alizadeh 2013b). Alizadeh states that she has collected flash fiction from blogs and festivals. One can therefore see a correlation between the development of flash fiction and the boom in blogs. In addition, many blogs have used the form of flash fiction and explicitly commented on its usefulness to the medium. As such, I believe the changes in Persian literary short forms were partly stimulated by blogs. Thus, we see that *dastanak* is a form that is built both on a long Persian literary tradition and develops from the encounter with modern media, with a good reception from readers and the literary establishment alike.

Similarly, the development of what has been termed the 'postmodern *ghazal*' has been encouraged by blog writing, although the genre was already in existence prior to the emergence of blogs. The genre can be defined as in keeping with the traditional form of the *ghazal* (a poetic form using a refrain and rhyming couplets, often dealing with love) but deconstructing its usual topic of love in some way. It is not new to have philosophical and social topics included in the form of the *ghazal* since modern poets like Simin Behbahani had already done that, but the darkness of the tone, the ironical stand and the extremisation of the societal topics make the postmodern *ghazal* stand out. One of the main composers of the postmodern *ghazal*, Seyed Mehdi Moussavi, states that not all poetry that breaks the form of *ghazal* is postmodern *ghazal*. For instance, the use of Finglish (transliteration of Persian words in English) words does not make a poem 'postmodern'. It is, for Moussavi, postmodern thought that renders poems 'postmodern' (Moghadam 2010). This might include: the use of deconstructed forms; textual self-awareness, evident in metafiction; or an engagement with epistemological and ontological crisis. Moussavi and fellow poet Fatemeh Ekhtesari developed the genre in their blogs, which were popular during the Green Movement that started in 2009. Ekhtesari was famous in literary circles and became more so after the Germany-based Iranian rapper Shahin Najafi sang a postmodern *ghazal* by her. Their weblogs were closed and blocked in 2009 in the post-election turbulence and are not accessible anymore. Moussavi and Ekhtesari left Iran a few years later as a result of heavy sentences on charges of blasphemy for the social criticism expressed in their poetry (International Campaign for Human Rights in Iran 2015). In an interview, Moussavi, who has been called 'the father of postmodern *ghazal*', says that there were poets who composed in such forms before him and his use of the genre on his blog, like Mohammad Said Mirzay and Hadi Khansari, although they might not have used the term 'postmodern' (Moghadam 2010). This is thus another example of a form that has not been developed through blog writing as such, but which blog writing has facilitated to the point that critics have identified a correlation between the two. It is also a form that has been important online but not so much in print.

In terms of topics, one can see that Iranian literary blogs, as in other blogospheres, have promoted popular genres that were not much part of the literary system. In Chapter 1, I analysed the scarcity of popular genre fiction in Iran, except for romances. Erotic fiction, which is impossible due to censorship in print, is more popular online and presents a new addition to the literary system, if not yet to the literary canon. Although there is a long tradition of erotic writing in Persian literature, to be found in poems of Sa'di and of fourteenth-century Obeid Zakani for example, the genre had not been favoured for a long time, if one excludes the early twentieth-century Iraj Mirza and his colloquial erotic poetry. 3kkk.wordpress.com was a popular pioneer blogging site dedicated to the production of erotic fiction and teaching about sexuality (Sekaf 2002–4). It stopped after the fortieth issue but its writers are still active on other social media platforms, and have introduced a wide vocabulary linked to eroticism into Persian. The stories vary in tone and are sometimes purely pornographic, while others tend towards literariness, but this topic has undoubtedly emerged in the Iranian literary field due to the existence of blogs, which have bypassed modes of both state-led and self-instigated censorship driven by social taboos in Iranian society. We find examples of erotic fiction on Instagram too, in the last section of this chapter.

It is also possible to identify interesting innovations on other levels, particularly in relation to language. Bloggers' style is described as 'blogspeak'. Blog writing is often less formal than traditional literary pieces and blogspeak is closer to middle-class language. In Persian, as in English, 'blogspeak' has an anti-elite flavour (Megerdoomian 2008). It often uses the spoken form of Persian (as opposed to the written one), as well as spoken vocabulary. It is less prone to using the classical rhetoric of Persian style, and more the everyday one.

There is one further aspect of Iranian blogs, however, which has not followed the pattern of other parts of the world and can be shown to be more conservative than in other contexts. Blogs have often been considered to encourage the formation of newly democratic online communities around the discussion and dissemination of literary knowledge. Scholars have argued that blogs, and the web in general, constitute a world-scale laboratory for democratic experiences by auto-organising citizens, opening up discussion to new audiences, helping with the organisation of transnational communities, and socialising knowledge. As such, it transforms the nature of democracy

(Cardon 2010). Aliasghar Seyedabadi, the founder of the weblog *Nevertheless* (*Hanuz*), explains how this works for collective blogs:

> The existence of several individuals in one sharing place leads to confrontations between different taste and ideas, which eventually leads to dialogue. Such dialogues are formed within the circle, but due to the nature of the medium, it opens up a path to a broader milieu . . . Group blogging cannot only be an exercise for us who are not used to dialogue, but also an exercise for accepting diversity and plurality and also respecting differences. (Seyedabadi 2004)

It is true that pages that are collective blogs like *Heavenly Circle* (*Halqeh-ye malakut*) play a role in creating a democratic platform for exchange. *Malakut* is the common domain for a collection of forty-one independent blogs, with a concentration on literature and the arts. How far, though, has this led to a democratisation of online communities?

In single-author blogs, the democratic process might emerge out of the potential for readers to comment on posts. Persian blogging could thus redraw the lines not only of language but, more importantly, of who can speak and define the language of literature. A connected feature is the blurring of the line between writer and reader. Writers like Leila Sadeghi have mentioned that they edit their texts based on the comments made on their blog posts (Mardani 2009). In a traditional literary culture where the writer has a high status, where there is a relationship of master/pupil between a famous writer and her readers, this complication of authorship is a sign of a possible redefinition of literary relations. One can think of Forough Farrokhzad, the famous poet, who looked for an established author to write a preface for her collections as a way of being introduced into the literary world. This convention and this hierarchy are not as present as during Forough's time but are still critical to print publications.[3] What happens to her status if the writer's text can be commented upon immediately after being posted online with the possibility for the writer to edit it? Such processes have also featured in some blogs in the

---

[3] In western literary fields, the importance of prefaces has decreased and a lot of the symbolic capital that was contained in the preface now appears in blurbs and cover endorsements.

diaspora, for example Reza Ghassemi's blog: 'Reza Ghassemi's initiative to establish an interactive relationship with his readers is of historical importance . . . In his online diary, readers could follow up on the daily progress of one of his latest novels' (Mina 2007: 203). However, these possibilities have hardly been seized upon by Iranian writers/bloggers, and Sadeghi and Ghassemi are exceptions rather than the norm in responding to readers' comments. Writers of popular romance fiction like Homa Pur Esfahani and Fereshteh Tat Shahdust are more open to readers' comments, and the process might work better with the form of popular novels because they are more attuned to their readers' expectations and aim for large numbers of readers.

In addition, literary blogs as a field reproduce much of the offline world. The example of the virulent 'vulgarity debate' started by Reza Shokrollahi, the editor of the literary blog *Khabgard*, who engaged with Hoder, is telling. Doostdar argues:

> that the vulgarity debate reflects a cultural and political clash between a *roshanfekr* (intellectual) class who consider themselves to hold a certain amount of authority in matters of language and culture and a larger group of people who see blogging as just the place to be free from any kind of linguistic or cultural authority. (Doostdar 2004: 5–6)

Doostdar convincingly shows that the debate reflected a tension between the *roshanfekran*, who have cultural capital, and the rebels against the traditional intellectual class, who might be endowed with other less-traditional forms of cultural capital. Blogs more often than not seem to reproduce the sociality that happens outside in the print world. Although *Khabgard* is managed by one person with writings from others and links to other blogs, and does not have the characteristics of a collective blog, it came to represent the viewpoint of elite writers with mostly reformist affinities on literature and society. As such, it is an elite blog, not designed for a large audience. It reproduces the structure of the Iranian literary field, namely the interdependency between the different agents. Indeed, one sees that writers for the blog are also judges of the Bahram Sadeghi Prize, for example.

It should be remembered that Iranian literature has often been accused of being elitist and working as a closed circle of establishment types, as the accusations above demonstrate. This is complicated, however, by the fact that there are governmental and independent circles within it, as I explain in Chapter 3. Although the point of going online is sometimes to leave the social spaces dominated by the state and gain relative autonomy, the politics of governmental versus independent are partly reproduced online. Interestingly, the 'vulgarity debate' sparked by Shokrollahi made him look as though he had sided with the government and wanted to censor the Persian blogosphere (Doostdar 2004: 27). Blogs are not, for Shokrollahi and his fellow writers, a way to popularise literature, but a channel through which to continue a conversation that was largely happening offline and was slowed down due to the closure of reformist newspapers and more restrictive censorship. Blogs, for Shokrollahi, may introduce a new medium but they do not revolutionise the people's relationship to literature. In particular, the authority of the writer remains unchallenged. In a sense, literary blogs have extended the length of a writer's networks and added an online authority to the offline one. As such, Iranian blogs did not contribute as much to democratising the literary discourse as they might have done in other literary spaces around the world. Doostdar insists that as

> spaces of expression, social interaction, and political activity, blogs are marked as much by exclusion as by inclusion . . . Empirical studies of blogs . . . cannot afford to lose sight of the reproduction of older forms of power and inequality, as well as the emergence of new one. (Doostdar 2010)

The example of literary blogs shows that inequality between men and women, and between those with cultural capital and those without, is sometimes transformed but mainly reproduced online.

It is also important to remember that there is a large digital divide within Iran (Abdollahyan *et al.* 2013), which means that certain segments of the population do not access the internet. Access to the internet, and especially to the creation of internet content, is dependent on demographic issues. The forms of literacy, including computer literacy, required for participating in the blogosphere exclude entire sections of the Iranian population based on age, gender, class and, particularly, education. There has been a lot of discussion on the use of circumvention tools (*filtershekan*), as tools that widened the access to the internet, and it is true that they are widely available (Small Media 2015b). A 2014 report by the Ministry of Youth and Sports found that 69.3 per cent of Iranian youth (between 15 and 29 years old) are users of circumvention technologies such as proxies or VPNs (ISNA 2015). This statistic only concerns the youth though, and older generations are using them much less.

There is a distinction between sites that are filtered (*filter shod*) or removed (*basteh shod*). Filtered sites can still be accessed within Iran with the help of *filtershekan*. These refer to any program or software that circumvents the filters that the government puts in place to block access to certain sites, including YouTube (Sreberny and Khiabany 2010: 82–4). However, they do require some computer literacy. Today, because platforms like Instagram are not filtered, they act as a more direct democratic platform for a population that has wide access to smartphones. Literary blogs have thus stimulated innovation in terms of form and genre: erotic fiction, the forms of the *dastanak* and of the postmodern *ghazal*, for example, were promoted thanks to blogs. The language of blogspeak also moved closer to everyday language. On the other hand, the authority of the author has not departed much from offline norms. Networks online more often than not reproduce offline networks, which are the sign of a closed literary milieu. This finding challenges existing discourses around the web as a site of democratic connectivity, as articulated in books that see the use of new media in the Middle East as liberating, and as an act of resistance (El Hamamsy and Soliman 2013: 8). The use of the internet in authoritarian regimes like Iran is not necessarily a force for change, or for good (Morozov 2011: 241). In the case of literary blogs, we do not see radical changes in terms of the literary establishment within Iran with the advent of blogs. However, we do see other significant changes, which are worth exploring further.

During the ten years of their intense activity, Persian literary blogs created new dynamics within the Iranian literary field. One such feature of this impact is the increased importance given to internet publishing. Much as in other literary fields worldwide, print publishing is generally seen as more prestigious and valued more than online publishing for a variety of reasons, one being that print publishing is usually selective, because it is expensive, whereas online publications can be self-published by the author. However, thanks to the internal selection processes that some literary blogs have adopted, internet publishing has gained some value since the 2000s. For example, the famous bestselling writer Mostafa Mastoor published the story 'Malakeh Elizabeth' on *Khabgard*, which was to be published later in a

2004 collection by the prestigious publisher Qoqnoos. The link between the weblog *Khabgard* and Book City, the bookshop chain that organises literary events and is a main cultural centre in Tehran, is another example of this closing gap in prestige. These examples show that the distance between print and online publishing is narrowing and that there are an increasing number of links between offline and online worlds, even though, as I mentioned earlier, the links often reproduce well-known networks and rarely include outsiders.

Some writers have also turned to online publishing exclusively for some of their novels. Mohammad Hassan Shahsavari, mentioned earlier, decided to publish his novel *Dear M.* on *Back Window*, a page that belongs to *Khabgard*. In an interview with the literary blog *Our Literature* (*Adabiyyat-e ma*), he says: 'Obviously, like any other writer I prefer my work to be published via the official channel, in print and by reliable publishers. But when you know that your novel will face censorship, then is there any solution but electronic publishing?' (Shahsavari 2013).

Publication via blogs has also provided the context for the development of sectors like digital distribution and on-demand publication, which are giving new breadth to Iranian literature within Iran and in the diaspora. In Iran, Fidibo is the largest digital library for books that have received publication permission. In France, Naakojaa is a large print and online library for books published within Iran and outside, which I talk more about in Chapter 6. In the UK, H&S Media is a firm that specialises in on-demand publication for Persian books that do not have publication permission. Its director notes the problems that Iranian audiences have in accessing these texts, however, explaining that 'because of international sanctions people in Iran cannot buy our e-books from Amazon or similar foreign-based sites' (Kamali Dehghan 2015). They have nevertheless found a solution by sidestepping the traditional model of economic exchange that renders the sale of books transparent. Instead, users in Iran donate a book's price to a charity and when they send its receipt, they are able to download the book. As a result, 'every month, at least 300 books are sold to readers in Iran using this method' (Kamali Dehghan 2015). There are also innovative platforms like Nogaam, also based in the UK, where books are crowd-funded by supporters, and then made available for free online (Small Media 2015a: 49). This transnational dynamic of circulation is politically significant in many senses: not only does it sidestep traditional publishing models but it also bridges the link between Iran and the diaspora.

Changes brought about by blogs to the Iranian literary field have been slowed down both by the impact of censorship and by decreased interest in the medium, as well as by the substitution of computers with smartphones, which are more oriented towards social media. Studies of the Iranian blogosphere demonstrate the effectiveness of censorship and the online arrival of government forces, in their effort to populate the web with its own discourse, after a brief period of freedom in the early 2000s (Giacobino *et al.* 2014: 4). But this should not make us forget that the limited reach and growth of blogs is also linked to the structure of the medium (Sreberny and Khiabany 2010: 43). It should also be remembered that slow internet access is a constant problem, which affects the development of the field. Although literary blogs brought about changes in the Iranian literary field, they did not revolutionise contemporary Iranian literature as expected, due to the restrictions of the medium as well as to factors specific to Iran: the effectiveness of censorship, dissent between independent and governmental literary fields, and the closeness of the literary milieu. The dissent between writers inside and outside the country is an additional factor. In Chapter 6, I detail how these transnational dynamics work.

For most of the 2010s, Facebook and Telegram, the most widely used messaging applications in Iran (Etehad 2017), have been the primary platforms for digital literature. From the mid-2010s, especially since 2018 when Telegram was shut down by the Iranian government, Instagram became the most used one. Many Iranian writers joined Instagram around 2014 during Hassan Rouhani's presidency. In the last section of this chapter, I focus on Instagram, which is closely linked to Facebook, which bought it in 2012.

Literary Instagram: Form and Evolution

Instagram is the most popular social media in Iran, with 20 million users in 2017, nearing around 3 per cent of its total members (Azali 2017a). It is not blocked, unlike Facebook and other social media. Within Iran, it is controlled by the Iranian cyber police. Because it is primarily a photo-sharing media with short written data capacity, it is interesting to study its role for the literary field. As such, it is a mode of promotion for texts published elsewhere, more than a new means of literary production. Most literary journals, for example, use Instagram as a platform to promote the texts they publish elsewhere. Only a few, like *Poeticas Magazine*, run by AmirHossein Khorshidfar, are Instagram-based literary journals.

As of June 2018, the most followed literary Instagram pages are those of the controversial writer and lyricist Yaghma Golrouee, with 577,000 followers, and Shahin Najafi, another controversial figure, singer, songwriter and writer in exile in Germany, with 465,000 followers in early 2018. Neither of them are traditional print authors and they are oppositional figures. They navigate between media and have an ostensibly controversial position. Instagram has mostly had an impact on the Iranian literary field by pushing popular fiction to the fore. It is also linked to a younger generation of writers, who are using the medium to publicise their work, whereas older writers do not do so. Some writers became instant bestsellers with their first published book thanks to careful Instagram background work, especially in the genre of serialised popular writing, *Pavaraqi* (literally page-turner), close to the romances discussed in Chapter 1. A writer of *Pavaraqi* posts serially and the genre is often romance, with some crime fiction. The term *Pavaraqi* was used to refer to the genre on Instagram by the writer Chista Yasrebi, who has more than 100,000 Instagram followers. While most people only hit the 'like' button, Yasrebi decided to use serial writing to increase readers' engagement with the text. Her Instagram fiction *The Postman* (*Postchi*) is a love story of a young girl, Chista, who falls in love with a mailman who afterwards become a soldier. They engage in a platonic love story, where Chista spends most of her time waiting for Ali to come back from different war missions, in Bosnia and Syria notably. In 2016, the book was published by the well-known publisher Ghatreh and the audio book by Novin. The book sold fourteen reprints in 2017, which is significant considering that the free PDF is easily accessible online and that the book has been read by followers on Instagram. In this, although on a much smaller scale because of the specificities of the Iranian book market, her work can compare to the famous Instagram poets of the English sphere, like Rupi Kaur, who has sold millions of copies of her printed book *Milk and Honey*, even though all the poems are available on her Instagram page.

Yasrebi is navigating between independent and governmental circles. She applies careful self-censorship to her texts, which can be described as aligned with most of the governmental discourse. The main characters in *The*

Postman are generally characters that the Islamic Republic approves of: they are honest, true to their love, and modest. There are some parts where the female character of Chista questions the surveillance of love by the regime and comments on censorship, for example:

> work, insomnia, writing, your work being rejected, and a giant called censor teaches you to get a scissor and cut your hair locks, cut your love, cut your emotions, cut all your humanistic feelings so that nothing remains for them to cut. Though you don't look like you anymore. Then you don't look like anything at all. (Yasrebi 2016)

However, such rare sentences are contained within a story that can reach a wide audience while keeping with the Islamic principles.

Another example of *Pavaraqi* is Roozbeh Moein and his *The Cold Coffee of Mr Writer* (*Qahveh-ye sard-e aqa-ye nevisandeh*), a fiction for young adults that mixes a love story and crime puzzles. It sold fifty-six reprints and 62,000 copies in the first year after its publication in 2017, a high number in the current Iranian book market, where most books sell around 1000 copies. The book became famous even before its publication thanks to Instagram, as Moein published excerpts from his story on his Instagram page with 62,000 followers, and built a readership by creating a sense of suspense. As a result, on the rainy day when his book was first published, a long queue waited to buy the book at the publishing house. The first print is said to have been sold in two hours (ILNA 2017). In this case, Instagram provided a platform for marketing.

In addition to serialised popular writing, as in literary blogs, some erotic content seems to be more permissible on Instagram than in print publication. Homa PourEsfahani's novel *It Wasn't Meant To Be* (*Qarar nabud*) was published without issue on Instagram, but she had to revise some of the erotic content and make alterations to receive the license to publish the print version. Whereas some words like 'kiss' are taboo in print publications, writers have published poems online that used taboo words without having issues. Parsa Hemmat has several erotic poems in his Instagram posts. For example, one of them reads:

با بوسه به آن ثانیه برگردانم/ آن ثانیه ای که ناگهان عریانم
این قدر نوازشم کنی می میرم/ کم مانده فرو بریزم از چشمانم!

With a kiss, take me back to that second/ That second when I'm suddenly nude

You're caressing me so much that I am dying/ About to collapse and flow through my eyes!

Some new forms can also be found only on Instagram, especially 'textgraphy' and 'she'rgraphy' (*she'r* means poetry), where Instagrammers select a few short sentences or a single verse and mix them with an image that matches. One can mention Mehdi Faraji, Fatemeh Ekhtesari mentioned earlier, Kazem Bahmani or Ahmadreza Ahmadi as important users of this form.

Most of these textgraphies and she'rgraphies are designed by illustrators, who mention the writers on their post. These are then shared among literary Instagrammers. As such, it is a new form that does not originate from writers themselves. It is an important distinction from literary blogs, which are text-based and coming from the writers. On Instagram, the text is not central, the image becomes so. We are thus faced with a hybrid genre, not purely literary.

Like literary blogs too, Instagram is more interactive and reader-oriented than traditional publishing. However, although some reply to readers' comments and engage with them, it does not seem to be the most common trend.

Figure 2.2 Fatemeh Ekhtesari's she'rgraphy on Instagram.

Some writers like Yaghma Golrooee even close the comments' button so that readers cannot comment on his posts. In general, one cannot see whether writers, even those who write popular fiction and are necessarily more reader-oriented, integrate readers' comments in their works. This was also the case with blogs. There exist a few exceptions, like the popular romance writer Homa PourEsfahani's whose published version of the novel *Bitter Chocolate* (*Shokolat-e talkh*), previously posted on Instagram, applies all her readers' comments, but they are rare. This is partly due to the medium, which asks for 'likes', not for long exchanges and discussion.

Instagram, contrary to blogs, has not had a major influence on forms and discourse in the literary field. Writers who post on Instagram usually post already published poems and Instagram is more often than not a means of promotion and communication, not of production of literary material. The most important area where it has had an influence on the whole of the Iranian literary field is in promoting popular fiction and content that could face censorship issues in print, especially erotic content.

Conclusion

The Iranian literary blogosphere has shown a complex history and evolution. It invites us to challenge some of the potentially Eurocentric assumptions that may remain engrained within new media discourses. Iranian literary blogs helped develop trends that would have taken longer or might not have happened otherwise. The influence of Instagram is more difficult to assess because it is more recent, having boomed around 2017. However, literary Instagram pursues trends that were also evident in literary blogs, especially the focus on popular genres.

In Chapter 9, I analyse how global contemporary Persian literature is becoming. The trends studied in this chapter form part of my argument as I return to the idea of the internet as a potential site for connecting readers of Iranian literature globally.

3

The Iranian Literary Field: An Overview

I went to the Tehran International Book Fair for the first time in 2009 and several times in the 2010s. The site was then in Mosallah, in the centre of the city, in the space of the huge mosque of Mosallah, still in construction. It was labyrinthine and not particularly appropriate as a book fair space but the atmosphere was cheerful and laid back. It has since moved to the south of the city. The crowd was dense in the outside spaces as well as inside. There were families as well as young people, happy to exchange in a fairly open space, in search of English textbooks. It was difficult to access some of the booths of the major independent publishers because of the long queues. I remember once the publisher Cheshmeh was so crowded I could not even get to see their books from afar. The governmental publisher Sureh Mehr also had a long queue on the year it published its bestseller 'Da'. The section of textbooks for high school and university exams, as well as English books, subsidised by the government in the form of governmental dollars (dollar-e dowlati) was always busy. On the other hand, not all but many sections devoted to the publishers from the Arab world, religious books and stands for the support to Palestine were deserted. It was a very direct expression of the polarisation of the literary field between independent and governmental sectors, about which I talk in this chapter.

This chapter first examines the polarisation of the independent and government sectors according to political orientation and explains the history of this division in the Iranian literary field. This polarisation is not specific to Iran and shares traits with literary spaces in authoritarian regimes elsewhere. There is a great deal of heteronomy of the field, being heavily governed by the Iranian state; however, the Iranian literary field is also increasingly being shaped by market forces. This first section describes how the polarisation works in concrete terms at the micro and macro levels, and the recent evolutions that have occurred. The next section considers the restrictions to the market, both those internal to Iran (from censorship to material constraints on paper supplies) and those external to Iran (sanctions, lack of copyright agreements).

A good categorisation of these constraints is provided by Gisèle Sapiro, who argues that they are:

> authoritarian regimes in which economic exchanges are strictly regulated and cultural products entirely controlled by an apparatus created for this purpose and/or by institutional centralization of the means of production and consecration. In these regimes, the State is an instrument of control put at the service of an ideological system – e.g. religious, fascist, communist – with a totalitarian ambition. (Sapiro 2003: 442)

Post-revolutionary Iran, as a religious ideological system, controls the means of production, distribution and reception, but only up to a certain point, as there is also a parallel or underground space. This also means that a whole literary field that questions some of the state's ideology on culture has gradually been created: the independent sector. As Sapiro describes:

> In all authoritarian regimes, cultural producers develop strategies in order to escape the political constraints ... Contrary to the attempts to unify the corporation and to increase professional homogeneity, the logic of the field opposes the dominant agents, who hold the monopoly of the means of formal consecration, and the dominated, who resist this system. (Sapiro 2003: 446)

In post-revolutionary Iran, the dominant agents are governmental, while the independent members of the field are the dominated. For Sapiro, 'three main strategies of thwarting can be identified: thwarting censorship in legal publications or in places like theatres by using a metaphorical code, allegory, or allusion; publishing abroad; illegal or clandestine publishing' (2003: 446). These are all practised in the Iranian context. It is important to understand the complexity of the process, that goes through evolutions and that includes self-censorship, as rules are largely internalised by the producers of texts who apply them. Both the governmental (*dowlati*) and the independent (*khosusi*) literature published in Iran are official (*rasmi*), since a work must be approved by the Ministry of Culture and Islamic Guidance in order to be published. The only exception is the 'parallel space', including underground or black-market literature (published without the permission of the Ministry of Culture and Islamic Guidance), and, to a certain extent, literature published online, for which censorship can be bypassed if one is tech savvy. I analysed the example of online literature as an exception in Chapter 2, and focus on the exception of underground literature in the section entitled 'The Underground Literary Space' in this chapter. In the final section, I analyse two institutions that represent how the field works on its margins: the Saadi Foundation, a recently founded cultural institution that focuses on Persian language, and the Union of Tehran Publishers and Booksellers. These are not literary associations as such, which have been difficult for me to access long-term, but they are institutions that help us to understand the struggle for cultural power, the overlapping of cultural institutions and the polarisation of the field that is occurring in Iran. I also touch on non-institutional places like circles (*dowreh*), cultural gatherings which act as counterpoints to express ideas in a less censored space.

History of the Division Between Governmental and Independent Sectors

One can trace the history of the polarisation of the literary field in Iran to the beginning of the Islamic Revolution and particularly to the cultural revolution, which started in universities in 1980 with a decree by Khomeini, and continued until 1983. At the time, the universities were seen as places where the western sciences predominated, as opposed to the religious seminaries of Qom, Mashad or Najaf in Iraq, where Shiite clerics did their training. Ali Rahnama and Farhad Nomani detail the sequence of events in the cultural revolution:

> On 26 April 1980, Khomeini explained his reasons for the cultural revolution: 'When we speak of reform of universities, what we mean is that our universities are at present in a state of dependence, they are imperialist

universities and those whom they educate and train are infatuated with the West'. (Khomeini and Algar 1981, quoted in Rahnama and Nomani 1990: 228)

This declaration clearly reflects one of the main slogans of the revolution, which was to break away from a dependence on western powers, especially the US and the UK, and to 'recapture the dignity of Iran as a Muslim country' (Siavoshi 1997: 512). The cultural revolution's aim was to Islamise universities, that is, to ensure that programmes and teachers were aligned with the new Islamic discourse so that they could teach it properly to a new generation of Muslim students. Kevan Harris emphasises the two methods through which this Islamisation was achieved, the first being to give preference to 'the devotees of the Islamic Revolution such as war veterans, martyr's families, and members of revolutionary organizations such as the literacy campaign and the construction crusade' (2017: 112); and the second being to investigate 'the moral and political record of each candidate' (2017: 393).

What effectively happened is that there was an institutionalisation of this division of society between 'the *maktabi* (followers of the school of Islam) and others as *ghayr-e maktabi* (not in line with the Islamic values presented by the leadership)' (Razavi 2009: 4). This was a crucial starting point for the polarisation mentioned above. From then on, one sees whole sectors defined according to the idea of being faithful to Islamic guidelines. In addition to universities, there was also an attempt to control the entire cultural field, although on a smaller scale. In 1980, the universities were thus closed and the content of some programmes and books rewritten, especially in the humanities, as they were considered to be westernised and promoting western science to the detriment of Islamic science. The Organization for Researching and Composing University Textbooks in the Humanities (*Sazman-e motale'e va tadvin-e kotob-e olum-e ensani-ye daneshgah-ha*), a publisher and organisation founded in 1985, now publishes books in the humanities that aim to centralise the discourse. Those who did not approve of this move were purged. Some estimate that 8,000 faculty members emigrated or were dismissed (Rucker 1991: 461). In 1983, universities re-opened. In addition to the new commitment to the Islamic Revolution, a major change from the pre-revolution was that university slots were allocated to the category of 'martyr', including martyr families, handicapped veterans and members of revolutionary organisations (Harris 2017: 112). In pragmatic terms, the cultural revolution was also initiated because of what was seen to be the failure of the Shah's regime to keep students under control (Razavi 2009: 4). Rahnama and Nomani have argued that the

> reopening of the universities, showed that the cultural revolution simply meant the exercise of control over the ideological purity and dedication of the students and professors. The educational process remained the same. The content of the majority of courses was not changed, nor was the method of teaching. (Rahnama and Nomani 1990: 229)

Sakurai agrees and says that 'the real purpose of closing the universities was to expel the militant students, especially the left-wingers who were defying the consolidation of clerical rule by Khomeini' (2004: 389). A similar process occurred in China, as Sobhe explains:

> Although Mao Tse-tung claimed that the universities must close because of their elitist tendencies, closing the universities and sending the educated to the rural places and communes would also eliminate the chairman's opponents who were among the intellectuals and scientists. (Sobhe 1982: 272)

Contrary to the Chinese Cultural Revolution, the cultural revolution in Iran was primarily focused on course planning and university policies; it did not entail vast movements of people from the city to the provinces (Hamdhaidari et al. 2008: 235), but it led to the exile of many of them.

Today, there is some level of consensus admitting the failures of the cultural revolution. I do not want to downplay its consequences, which have been real and massive. The cultural revolution has led to a purge of intellectuals and changed the cultural field in dramatic ways, in cinema, in literature, in public spaces, in education. It has had profound effects on core or symbolic elements of society, through the renaming of streets for example, but it was not the complete rewriting of culture that the Islamic Republic regime hoped it would be, and it happened on a smaller scale than the Chinese Cultural Revolution. It is also important to remember that it was a period of turmoil and that resources to implement the curriculum were lacking. Shervin Malekzadeh comments on this aspect in the context of primary schools: 'Even if the IRI had the wherewithal to produce a coherent curriculum of "Islamic" and ideological education, it hardly had the resources or means to implement such a program' (2016: 864). One particular aim that it did not achieve was the 'unity between theological schools and the universities' (Razavi 2009: 14). Qom stayed separated from modern universities. This division is complicated by the appearance of universities that are neither seminaries nor governmental, privately owned Islamic universities. Kalb argues about these: 'Financial independence, institutional autonomy from the state and elite support have carved out an autonomous space for this educational type that set it apart from the state system, the seminary or Azad University' (2017: 595).

The cultural revolution is also today criticised by those who had been its proponents and is seen to have alienated many, especially those with liberal tendencies who emphasise 'education and the use of logic and discourse rather than repression to create a strong intellectual atmosphere' (Siavoshi 1997: 514). For many critics from inside the establishment, Islam should not be imposed; people should embrace it because it is apparent to them that it is the best way to think and live. Therefore, an Islamic society should be able to withstand criticism. Similar to the taking of hostages in the American Embassy, the cultural revolution is an event that many of those involved in regretted years afterwards, most prominently the intellectuals who were at its forefront: 'almost two decades later, both Zibakalam and Soroush tried to distance themselves from the events during and after the cultural revolution' (Razavi 2009: 5). This is true of many on the reformist side, although not necessarily of hardliners. Although the cultural revolution was formally brought to an end in 1983, the Islamic Republic has still not ceased its programmes of Islamising science. This is often achieved through the financing of religious institutions and universities, such as Al-Mustafa University. In February 2018, President Hassan Rouhani explicitly condemned this movement of the Islamisation of science, claiming it was a huge waste of time, energy and money for something which was impossible to achieve. He also explicitly questioned the possibility of having Islamic physics or Islamic engineering (Hmeid 2018).

While in China, the Cultural Revolution was felt at all levels of society, the Iranian cultural revolution only affected some areas, such as universities, radio and television, and, of course, publishing. Despite the rather smaller scale implementation, it had a lasting impact on the general organisation of society, and especially on culture, dividing practitioners between governmental and independent organisations. In cultural production generally, censorship was slowly implemented to ensure all cultural products reflected the new Islamic values. Nevertheless, the effect on publishing took several years. In the following section, I analyse how this control of publications gradually took effect.

The Institution of Censorship

Censorship can be defined as the suppression or changing of ideas that can be deemed subversive for a society. According to Sapiro, 'In contrast with a market determined by a strict ideological control of the supply, economic liberalism has imposed the idea of a market governed by its own rules, those of free competition arbitrated by the consumers' (2003: 450). This is the model found in most western publishing industries. In Iran, there is strict control of publication, which is at the opposite end of the spectrum to economic liberalism. Control of publication did not begin under the Islamic Republic regime however.

> The establishment of institutions of censorship dates back to the nineteenth century . . . Other offices with different names but similar in nature have since been established despite the fact that all Constitutions (the first one was ratified in 1906) have in principle recognized the right to free speech and publishing. (Azadibougar and Haddadian-Moghaddam 2019: 161)

Under Mohammad Reza Shah, until the revolution, censorship was also important, pertaining to all political aspects. Many writers were banned and imprisoned for producing texts deemed too subversive. After the revolution, politics remains very much guarded; however, the eyes of the censor have also turned their focus to morality. This is because, as I explain below, the idea behind the new censorship regime is that literary works should fit within the Islamic definition and reflect the new Islamic society.

Policies on Book Publication

In this section, I look at the legal texts that define book publication and therefore censorship. Neither the term censorship (*sansur*) nor verification (*momayezi*) is mentioned in the legal texts that define the activities around cultural production. Azadibougar and Haddadian-Moghaddam argue that:

> in order to resolve the gap between the explicit statement of the Constitution and the contradictory practice of law, a Persian word, *momayezi* ('auditing, verification, examination'), is used to differentiate between present cultural policies, on the one hand, and censorship, on the other. This word denotes the readiness of a text for publication and presents the practice as a professional process, an editorial issue rather than censorship as a political process. Regardless of discursive practices that pretend otherwise, *momayezi* is essentially censorship. (Azadibougar and Haddadian-Moghaddam 2019: 161)

Article 24 of the Iranian Constitution, adopted at the end of 1979, states: 'Publications and the press are free to discuss issues unless such is deemed harmful to the principles of Islam or the rights of the public. The law shall determine the details of this exception' (Islamic Republic of Iran). In the years immediately after the revolution, there was a boom in printing and lots of pamphlets which had been censored under the Shah were printed. This only lasted for a few years. As Siavoshi describes:

> By the summer of 1982, repression had peaked, and the polity was sharply polarized. The result was a drastic decline in published materials, a crackdown on independent publishing houses, and the burning of hundreds of tons of pamphlets known collectively as 'White Books'. (Siavoshi 1997: 510)

From 1985, it became compulsory to obtain formal permission to print (*Parvaneh-ye nashr*) from the Ministry of Culture and Islamic Guidance (Lavasani 2013). In 1988, the Supreme Council of the Cultural Revolution introduced legislation leading to the creation of what is now called a pre-publication permit (*Mojavez-e pish az enteshar-e ketab*). According to the 1988 legislation, it was only children's books that had to be reviewed before publication; however, from this time on, all books had to receive a publication permit (Lavasani 2013). This is different from the permission to shoot that Iranian directors have to obtain before shooting a film: there is no permission to write a book to obtain. As such, the process of censorship is widely different in film and in literature, as a writer and a publisher invest a large amount of time in getting a book ready without knowing if it will be approved, whereas filmmakers get a permit before shooting. There are exceptions to that, and the writing of the script is done, as for books, without prior approval.

The Act of the Parliament approved in 1988 deems books not suitable for publication if they: negate religious principles; propagate moral corruption; incite society to revolt against the Islamic Republic of Iran, or are hostile to it; or propagate ideas and groups opposing the Islamic Republic of Iran. Other books are defined as illegal if they: defend imperial powers or the previous kingdom; incite feuds between tribal or religious communities; create hostility or disharmony among the people or the totality of the country; ridicule national pride or patriotic feelings, or generate a lack of self-esteem in relation to western or eastern cultures, civilisations or colonisation; or encourage attachment to any of the world powers or books that are against the independence of the country (Rajabzadeh 2002: 6). In practice, this 1988 legislation of the Supreme Council of the Cultural Revolution plays the most significant role in determining the rules for publishing books. This legislation was introduced relatively late – eight years after the establishment of the Islamic Republic regime. Until the re-election of President Khatami in 2001, the Supreme Council of the Cultural Revolution was the main actor in cultural politics (Devictor 2004: Chapter 1). The Supreme Council of the Cultural Revolution is not technically party to Iranian law, which has to be passed by the parliament and approved by the Council of Guardians (*Shora-ye negahban*). However, 'since its creation, the resolutions of this Council have the force of law, even if it is only in January 1987, on request of President Khamenei, that Ayatollah Khomeini, officially confers it the authority to formulate directive, rules and laws, independently from the Parliament' (Devictor 2004: 6). The Supreme Council of the Cultural Revolution is a revolutionary institution that is currently under the direct leadership of the Supreme Leader Ayatollah Khamenei. Its closest partner is the Ministry of Culture and Islamic Guidance. The members of the Ministry are always asked to join or head the sub-organs of the Council (Devictor 2004: 8).[1]

---

[1] For a thorough analysis of the way the Supreme Council of the Cultural Revolution works and a description of some of its sub-organs, see Chapter 1 in Devictor (2004). For a com-

When the reformist, Khatami, became president, there was a relaxation in the censorship regime, which was, nevertheless, not reflected in law. It happened mostly informally but led to an unprecedented boom in publications. Four hundred publishers were given the opportunity to publish their books without review before publication. A book such as *My Fate* (*Sahm-e man*) by Parinoush Saniee could be published at that time thanks to this relaxation, after having been banned several times in previous years (Nanquette 2016). I refer to this in Chapter 4 as 'the open door policy'. Publishers have stated that, at the time, they were told that they should only consult with the Ministry of Culture on issues that could be problematic (Lavasani 2013): this is when the publishers became their own censors, which was a move that many found problematic. When Ahmadinejad became president, the Ministry of Culture decided to re-examine all books and permissions and there was a huge backlog of books waiting for permission. There have not been major changes in this policy implementation strategy since.

As mentioned above, in 1988, the Supreme Council of the Cultural Revolution (*Shora-ye ali-ye enqelab-e farhangi*) and the Office for the Development of Books and Book Reading (*Daftar-e tose'eh-ye ketab va ketab-khani*), a sub-entity of the Ministry of Culture and Islamic Guidance, issued its first official text, entitled 'Objectives, policies and rules for the publication of books' (Supreme Council of the Cultural Revolution 1988). Its first article defines the goals of book publication:

> Promoting culture, fostering knowledge and strengthening the foundation and values of the revolution by securing the freedom of book publication, preserving the dignity of the pen, protecting the high status of science and thought, and protecting the freedom of thought in Islamic society. (Supreme Council of the Cultural Revolution 1988)

The text then defines general positive policies, insisting on the promotion of

---

plete description of the mechanisms of censorship in Iranian film, see Chapter 3 in Devictor (2004). She explains the details of the policies concerning the Islamisation of film and gives various examples of how directors deal with difficulties such as not being able to show affection, and Iranian women always wearing the hijab, even in private, including in bed.

knowledge through book publication, followed by several restrictive policies: 'Although the freedom of book publication reflects human and social freedom, it can be misused and damage public rights . . . The authorities should take the following points into account [to avoid this problem].'

What is particularly interesting is that some points in the 2010 legislation, which revises that of 1988, have been amended in significant ways or deleted altogether. For example, the points that prohibit books that 'Promote prostitution and moral corruption' and that 'Publicize one of the world powers and opposition, that is, against the independence of the country' have been deleted. The first deletion is explained in a note in the 2010 legislation stating that certain books are acceptable, 'if the negative aspects of the books are already explained in the introduction'. This includes books about moral corruption, framed as 'Use of sexual attraction and naked images of women or men under the title of an artwork or any other title', as well as 'Publishing pictures to promote prostitution, such as dance, drinking'. Some points were added in 2010, forbidding books that promote 'Zionism – and other types of racism', as well as 'Distorting important and historical events of Iran and Islam'. However, these are clarifications and specifications rather than significant changes. In addition, the positive point that books should be published as 'a rational and scholarly approach towards political, economic and cultural independence, especially in the light of the principle of "Neither Eastern, *Nor Western*"', has been deleted, showing that the importance of this non-aligned motto has decreased over the years. The 2010 legislation is a lot more detailed and longer. The relevant article stipulates the possibility of publishing certain types of books that could be considered problematic, as long as it benefits the community and they are written in a scholarly way: for example, atheism is possible; as is sexuality, for educational purposes and as long as there is no eroticism; and so are 'criticisms of the Islamic Republic in order to understand the issues and to reach an appropriate and constructive solution through reasoning and reforming without any defamation'. Anne Démy-Geroe gives a good explanation of what this might look like in cinema for the example of 'social issues films'. She says that

> Acceptable social issues films seem to show positive solutions or individualise the problems; problematic social issues films seem to criticise or imply criticism of government action or policy, show the country in a bad light

internationally (itself a trickily subjective judgement), or are seen to countermand Shi'ite Muslim ideology or values in some way. (Démy-Geroe 2020: 71)

There have also been many paragraphs added on the promotion of culture, thus insisting on the positive and not only the restrictive aspects of a text, for example, on the fact that the Ministry of Culture should 'support modern technologies in the publishing industry' or 'support the publication of the Persian translation of books published in other countries'. These are some of the details of the legislation currently in place, to which literary practitioners must refer when assessing their books and the likelihood that they will obtain a publishing permit.

The structure of the reviewing process is well defined, especially in the 2010 text. It mentions that the committee working on reviewing a book should do so within a month, with the possibility of a two-month extension. In effect, this time limit is rarely respected, as many writers and publishers know, and the time taken to have the work assessed can vary greatly. However, the process sometimes functions well. In a personal communication from Amir Hossein Khorshidfar, I learned that his long novel, *The Tehranis* (*Tehrani-ha*), was approved in only two weeks. He explained that he had submitted it just before the presidential elections that saw the re-election of the reformist President Rouhani in 2017 (Khorshidfar, personal communication, 20 December 2017).

The 2010 text of the legislation adds that the Ministry of Culture, in cooperation with other institutions, is responsible for preventing the printing and distribution of books that do not have an official permit and must send the publishers to the judicial authorities if needed. Thus, if books are published illegally, the Ministry of Culture should pursue the publishers, which in effect rarely occurs, as I show below in the section on underground books in relation to Mahmoud Dowlatabadi's pirated text. Finally, Article 5 of the 2010 text entirely concerns children's books, revealing the importance that the Islamic Republic regime places on the regulation of such publications, as I elaborate in Chapter 5, which is devoted to children's literature.

How Does Censorship Work?

Censorship happens both before the book goes to print, in order to obtain a publication permit, and after the book has been printed, to obtain a distribution permit. This is to make sure nothing has been changed in the book between the delivery of the publication permit and the printing of the book. This last step is usually quick, while the first step is long and complex. I am focusing on the publication permit here. Permanent publication permits have been delivered at some points in the last forty years and on a one-by-one basis at other points, in which each reprint needs to be reapproved. Blake Atwood gives interesting examples of some of the censorship issues and confirms that it is 'a truly subjective procedure, and the system as a whole is highly susceptible to current waves in the political ocean' (2012: 39). Many books are given permission at certain times, only to be banned by another censor, and vice versa. Several scholars have insisted on the relative variability of censorship at a given time. It is well known that censorship is not a monolithic institution: it varies according to who is Minister of Culture and Islamic Guidance and which censor is appointed to read your work. It is also dependent on the contacts one has (*parti-bazi*), as well as on bribery in some instances. This variability and unfairness are a concern for writers because the boundaries are constantly changing.

However, censorship is not only a negative imposition from the state. Scholars agree on the fact that 'a complex relationship exists between the state and authors and publishers' (Siavoshi 1997: 525). It is indeed important to 'present an alternative view of a more nuanced and complex relationship between the state and civil society'. Moreover, there is a 'variation of attitudes on the part of intellectuals encompassing disaffection, acquiescence, and accommodation toward the state (a society-related development). This evolution, in some post-revolutionary periods, has made possible the relative but inconsistent openness of the polity' (Siavoshi 1997: 525). It is not only the censors who shift the boundaries, but the writers and publishers who modify their attitudes towards censorship. It is also important to remember that several institutions can escape censorship entirely and have their own internal censorship process. This is the case with television, with the Centre for Islamic Arts and Thought and with the Centre for the Intellectual Development of Children and Young People (on which more can be found in Chapter 5 on children's literature), or with the governmental publisher Sureh Mehr, as discussed in Chapter 1. With reference to cinema, Devictor notes that these exceptions usually do not deflect the censorship process completely. However, there are sometimes conflicts, differences of opinion or a desire to be more autonomous, and these can block the system (Devictor 2004: 82). As we have seen in Chapter 1, this has sometimes been the case for books published by Sureh Mehr, especially those by Ahmad Dehqan.

In this chapter, I mostly discuss the censorship of books before production and discuss its process. However, it is important to note that the whole process of publishing, distributing and reading is censored in different ways at different stages. For example, some publishers are forbidden to attend book fairs. It was the case for several years in the 2010s that Cheshmeh could not participate to the Tehran Book Fair; in some years, some of their books were not allowed to be sold there. Also, independent literary prizes have been ordered to stop: the Hushang Golshiri Prize, a prestigious prize recognising contemporary writing, had to cease in 2014 after eleven years of existence. Mahmood Karimi-Hakak, a playwright, has described in detail how his texts and directing had been consistently censored and how he had to leave the country (Karimi-Hakak 2003).

Examples of Censorship

Since morality is crucial to the definition of Islamic society, it is usually not possible to describe any intimate relationship between a man and a woman, even if they are married and legally entitled to this relationship. As a result, writers use coded language to describe intimate life. The journalist Nazila Fathi describes some of this coded language:

> 'Two figures were moving under the sheet', is how Ms. Haj Seyed Javadi informs readers that two characters in 'Drunkard Morning' have a sexual relationship. The readers of Ms. Pirzad's 'We Get Used to It' learn that Arezou and Sohrab have kissed when Arezou asks Sohrab if he prefers the taste of the toothpaste to lipstick. 'All three', he says, meaning both and her lips, which are never directly mentioned. (Fathi 2005)

Ahmad Rajabzadeh undertook a thorough analysis of one year of censorship reports, for the year 1996, to determine how the process works, where the censorship is exercised and exactly on which points it focuses. Because his book is not readily accessible and has not been translated from Persian, I discuss it at length. This was during the Rafsanjani government, not a particularly open period, as I show in Chapter 4. In 1996, 1,528 book titles in literature were published: 73.9 per cent were Persian literature, 10.3 per cent were English and American literature, 4.7 per cent literature from other western countries, and 5.4 per cent literature from other countries. Literature was the most censored Dewey category, with 46 per cent of its titles not being accepted, followed by history at 25 per cent and philosophy at 24.5 per cent (Rajabzadeh 2002: 63). Books of comedy and satire, as well as books about war, were especially censored (Rajabzadeh 2002: 61), whereas poetry was the least censored, with most publications being reprints of classic poets (Rajabzadeh 2002: 199). Overall, 33 per cent of the books rejected or requiring revision were foreign fiction. Of these books, 73 per cent required revision and 27 per cent were rejected. Censors are thus more lenient with foreign works than they are with Persian books (Rajabzadeh 2002: 149). The least censored areas are the natural sciences, technology, children's books and the social sciences.

Rajabzadeh gives examples of the areas that are likely to be censored – when writing about women, for example: mentioning that women are deceived by men; spreading women's negativity about men; insulting traditional or chador-wearing women, Muslim women, sacred women and distinguished women in Islam and world history; insulting women in proverbs; insulting the relationship of women with their mothers-in-law; misogynist and unfair attitudes to women; depicting a relationship between a Muslim woman and a foreign man; writing biographies of corrupted women and corrupt neighbourhoods; or mentioning Iranian and women's lack of freedom (Rajabzadeh 2002: 75).

Rajabzadeh also goes into detail about sections or sentences that were to be removed. In the case of Forough Farrokhzad, several of her poems were censored due to their 'immorality' (mention of women, mention of a sacred figure, mention of cinema – seen as a symbol of westernisation). The following lines were censored:

'She creates natural children (بچه های طبیعی می سازد)'.
'His face is brighter that Imam Zaman (Mahdi)'s face
(صورتش از صورت امام زمان روشن تر)'.

'How good is cinema Fardin (چقدر سینما فردین خوب است)'. (Rajabzadeh 2002: 210)

Another interesting aspect of Rajabzadeh's study is that he analyses who does the censorship work. According to his investigations, there were almost 188 censorship officers in 1996. Some of them assessed one book and some of them around ninety books. Ninety per cent of the books were assessed by twenty-eight officers, which is a very small number. These twenty-eight censorship officers assessed books in all categories, from religion, literature and philosophy to the social sciences (Rajabzadeh 2002: 89). Thus, the censors are not specialists of one particular field. Some of them are also not very cultured, and Rajabzadeh points out that sometimes their Persian language skills are not particularly good (2002: 96).

Self-censorship

A feature of writing in post-revolutionary Iran is the importance of self-censorship. Its very existence testifies to the complexity of the censorship apparatus. Indeed, writers, publishers and translators have internalised the rules of what is morally and ideologically accepted and apply them. Writers, publishers and translators censor themselves to avoid conflict and social stigma both with their close ones and society in general, and with the government. As such, it is not only taboo subjects that are avoided. Self-censorship, which is not only restricted to the domain of literature, has a much more encompassing impact on writing in general. In the texts of Goli Taraqi for example, one can argue that she has chosen to retreat to a nostalgic writing about childhood to avoid having to deal with the description of contemporary society. When she chooses, rarely, post-revolutionary topics, she is careful in maintaining the appropriate level of criticism – for example in her short story 'The Encounter', where she writes about the maid Delbar, a new zealot for the Islamic regime (Taraqi 2013). Farzaneh Milani takes an interesting look at how self-censorship can be traced in the work of Simin Daneshvar. Although it applies mostly to the pre-revolutionary period, its mechanisms on the writing process are applicable to what happens after the revolution: only the norms have changed. Milani insists that Daneshvar was both an anti-establishment intellectual and also refused to submit to the demands of the avant-garde, so she would have been one of those less prone to applying self-censorship mechanisms. However, according to Milani:

> for many of Daneshvar's characters, censorship has corrupted and distorted many aspects of personal and interpersonal relations. Obviously such impairment of relations between the sexes in Daneshvar's fictive world cannot be attributed solely to censorship. But, however subtle and sophisticated her presentation of these all-too-often flawed relationships, the impact of repression shows through, both in her characters and in her treatment of them. (Milani 1985: 343)

In the post-revolutionary era, such avoidances similarly lead not only to certain topics, but also forms of writing and not writing. Self-censorship is deeply ingrained and comes from the assimilation of the Islamic norms.

What is the Ideal of Islamic Censorship?

In a society such as Iran during the early years of the revolution, the idea of censorship was not about banning certain texts or words, but about framing literary production to align it with the ideal of a new Islamic society. As such, censorship should not merely be seen as a negative force, as a push to condemn particular texts and ideas. Its idea was also to promote something new. One can see how this process works in different contexts. In countries that gained their independence from colonial powers in the twentieth century, one can also see similar patterns in the establishment of national literatures, sometimes through the local language, sometimes using the language of the former coloniser, with an important part devoted to censorship as a way to contain the literary. In the case of apartheid in South Africa, Peter McDonald has written a fascinating book that offers an analysis of censorship under this regime and argues that the entire endeavour was about defining literature. The appointed censors were established literary critics. They wrote sophisticated reports and became the guardians of literature, deciding what was literary and what was not. In this case, it was a theoretical endeavour, not a question of linguistic inappropriateness (McDonald 2009).

Similarly, in Iran, the new censorship model was established as a way to define what was literature or not. The new criterion was that it should be Islamic. This censorship model has evolved over the years and it is much more prohibitive today than it was forty years ago, when it was a prescriptive model for the literary realm. However, Rajabzadeh points out that in 1996 some works were still rejected because of their lack of literary merit – in the language of the censor – and he gives the example of *The Bold Halo of Sorrow* by Ameneh Ghazanfari, and *The Grey Nights* by Nasrin Sameni (2002: 119). However, according to Rajabzadeh and to the discourse in the literary field, most of the censorship work in later years is about deleting certain words and ideas. For example, every reference to alcoholic drinks or un-Islamic, immoral behaviour, as well as positive references to the west or criticism of contemporary Iran have to be deleted, whatever the context, even if they originate from a character in the story who is considered negative and could be thus seen to embody a criticism of these practices (Rajabzadeh 2002: 117–18).

It seems to be less frequent today to ask the writer to rewrite entire characters so that they appear more Islamic, although this was the case several decades ago. Goli Taraqi mentions that her character of Mr Alpha was deemed too westernised and had to be rewritten:

> Twenty years ago, I started a long novel, 'The Bizarre Comportment of Mr Alpha in Exile'. But in Iran I could not even publish the first chapter, since the censor wanted to know why I had sent this eminent professor of history to the capital of vice that is Paris. For sure, he would be corrupted! I assured him that Mr Alpha was a pious man who would resist all temptations, but the censor answered that I had to bring back Mr Alpha immediately. 'If he comes back, what about my novel about exile?' 'That is your business, Madam.' (quoted in Zanganeh 2007)

It is apparent that the censorship model has gradually changed and become prohibitive, which means that the state generally forbids what it deems non-compliant, but does not aim at orienting the entirety of cultural production in its direction. In 1996, the year analysed by Rajabzadeh, we are very much already at that point. This means that censors would mainly check for certain taboo words such as 'kiss', 'sex' and so on, and ask the writer to delete them and rewrite. Censors use search engines with a list of taboo words, sometimes without reading the entire text.

An important consequence of the prevalence of censorship is that the independent field has gained a badge of honour and specifically defines itself as opposed to the state. Even for some publishers who benefit from government money, it is important that they display their belonging to the independent field. This is again a characteristic of authoritarian states, as explained by Jarad Zimbler in the context of apartheid South Africa:

> However, as catastrophic as the effect of censorship may have been for individual authors and works, bannings came to be interpreted, paradoxically, as signs of election, as evidence that the publication or person in question had been deemed sufficiently political by the state. (Zimbler 2009: 609)

He adds: 'authors come to desire the state's displeasure' (Zimbler 2009: 610). In the context of music in post-Soviet nations, in this case Belarus, Yauheni Kryzhanouski argues:

> these strategies of bypassing make them appear as actors both engaged in difficult conditions (martyrs to the cause) and able to cleverly avoid sanctions (clever subjects who outsmart their dominators) . . . This symbolic capital can be mobilised in the internal rivalries of the artistic field. (Kryzhanouski 2017, 37)

It is an important element and I come back to this question of the symbolic capital of the independent field as being seen as opposed to the state when I analyse the Union of Tehran Publishers and Booksellers later in this chapter.

Other Internal and External Restrictions

While censorship is the greatest hindrance to the free production and circulation of books, it is not the only one. This section focuses on other restrictions faced by the Iranian literary field.

Paper Supplies versus Support of the Final Book Product

When the war against Iraq began in 1980, the government took control of the paper market by classifying paper as a strategic commodity, with the Ministry of Culture becoming responsible for the distribution of paper (*Donya-ye eqtesad* 2018). From then on, until 2007, this encouraged many people to establish publishing houses, because they would receive free paper from the government. The Union of Tehran Publishers and Booksellers and the Syndicate of Paper and Paperboard Manufacturers both protested against the policy, which was leading to a proliferation of publishers, many of whom were not professional and only published one book, while selling the rest of their paper quota on the market. In the late 2010s, around 80 per cent of the paper needed in Iran was imported (IRIB 2017). Because the country is highly dependent on the fluctuation of the US dollar, this leads to an unstable paper market. After the policy was evaluated by all professionals as not benefitting the sector, the paper subsidy was cut in 2007 and replaced by a subsidy on books to help boost the publishing market, shut down the black market in the paper sector and help reduce the price of paper. The Ministry of Commerce is now responsible for regulating the paper market (ISNA 2006). The book subsidy aids this market by purchasing books from publishers, helping domestic paper manufacturers, equipping libraries, and providing students with a 'book card,' with which they can buy books. This subsidy has been criticised as being biased towards the governmental publishers, who will often obtain more assistance than the independent sectors, but generally it seems to work better for the industry.

These changes have also brought Iran closer to western book markets by removing governmental support for the basic material, and working on the promotion of the final product. Many western countries have a strong cultural policy encouraging book production in some manner. In France, there is the Centre National du Livre (National Book Centre), linked to the Ministry of Culture, which supports many literary players in the industry, from publishers to writers and librarians, with a budget of 30 million euros a year. It gives grants to writers, translators, organisers of literary festivals, and promotes literature written in French all over the world. In countries with a language that has a small circulation, such as Norway, there are similar endeavours to promote literature: 'each year the Cultural Council is to buy 1,000 copies of every new title published by the publishers' associations and to distribute them free of charge to public libraries' (Fetveit 1987: 227). There is significant general support for the book market in Norway, including 'exemption from value added tax, fixed book prices, and special regulations for the direct sale of books' (Fetveit 1987: 228). Interestingly, Iran's policies thus aligned with several other places around the world at that time. Although its policies ressembled that of other countries, the Iranian book market is suffering from its lack of exchanges with the rest of the world.

Lack of Integration into the World Market

An additional issue related to the healthier production of books is that Iran is not a signatory to important international treaties on intellectual property, which means that foreign works are not protected by intellectual property laws. Copyright laws are in place around the world to ensure that authors receive the financial rewards from their work, but may also counter any distortion or adaptation of a work. They are important cultural policies designed to encourage cultural production. Iran is not a signatory to the Berne Convention, an agreement that governs copyright, first accepted in 1886, or to the Universal Copyright Convention, or the World Trade Organization copyright laws. However, in 2005, Iran joined the World Intellectual Property Organization as an observer member. Mahsa Salamati details the long process of discussing internally the legitimacy of international treaties in the context of Islamic law since the 1990s (Salamati 2019: Chapter 2). Iran also has a Law for the Protection of Authors, Composers and Artists Rights (1970), which protects works produced within Iran.

In Iran, anyone can reproduce foreign works or translate them without paying copyright to the foreign author. This has led to the book market in Iran being inundated with low-quality English textbooks or bad translations of foreign works. Retranslations are extremely common, especially for western bestsellers like *Harry Potter*, which count translations in dozens. Poupeh Missaghi argues that

> examples abound of practically unending retranslations of classical works. Here are just a few examples from an article by Marzieh Rasouli, published in the newspaper *Bahar* in 2013, with data from the National Library of Iran: *Animal Farm* by George Orwell: 34 translations; *The Little Prince* by Antoine Saint-Exupery: 28 translations; *Great Expectations* by Charles Dickens: 20 translations; *The Old Man and the Sea* by Ernest Hemingway: 20 translations; *Huckleberry Finn* by Mark Twain: 13 translations; *Crime and Punishment* by Fyodor Dostoyevsky: 12 translations; *Blindness* by José Saramago: 11 translations; *The Stranger* by Albert Camus: 10 translations; *Madame Bovary* by Gustave Flaubert: 9 translations. In contemporary literature, things are not that different. As we've seen in cases of Paul Auster,

J. K. Rowling, Herta Müller, Roberto Bolaño, Kazuo Ishiguro, Haruki Murakami, ad infinitum, several translations of an author's title might appear in the market almost simultaneously. (Missaghi 2015)

A study of publishers' views on copyright laws in Iran states that: '73 percent of publishers believe that Iran's copyright laws and lack of commitment to international systems has decreased the quality of translated books' (Sadat Hosseini and Matlabi 2013: 388). Azadibougar and Haddadian-Moghaddam rightly note that: 'the importance of copyright, or to be precise, the no-copyright ethics, has been influential in constructing the Persian tradition in its modern period in many ways' (2019: 157). This has also meant that the Iranian literary field has come to be seen as untrustworthy by the world market. Foreign publishers in international book fairs see Iranian publishers as thieves (Tangestani 2017).

There is a gradual movement towards adhering more closely to international rules, with some publishers, such as the well-known Ofoq, mentioned above, or Markaz, making an effort to buy copyright although they are not obliged to do so. Increasing numbers of people in the field realise that the current state of affairs contributes to the isolation of Iran from the world book market. Even on the domestic scene, '54 percent of publishers believe that the government and judicial bodies do not properly follow the violators of copyright law' (Sadat Hosseini and Matlabi 2013: 388). This is one of the reasons why the field lacks professionalism and why many publishers come and go quickly. In this context, sanctions are dramatically increasing the lack of integration of the Iranian book market.

External Restrictions to the Market

There have been economic sanctions against Iran by the US since the hostage crisis in 1979. In 2006, the sanctions increased, with a new resolution from the UN Security Council and the European Union, and again in 2012, all affecting the banking, trade and oil sectors. A lot of these sanctions touched the cultural field by restricting international trade and isolating Iran from the world market. For example, a European publisher who wanted to buy the copyright for an Iranian book could not do so because it was impossible to transfer money to Iran. There have always been ways around such problems, mostly through barter trade and exchange houses, but such exchanges could not occur on a large scale due to the difficulty of implementation and the risks involved. It is also an expensive process. In 2016, many EU sanctions were lifted after successful negotiations over the Iranian uranium enrichment programme, but those from the US were reinstated even more firmly in 2018. It is still impossible for the American company Amazon to directly sell products in Iran, although not impossible for Iranians to buy products from Amazon through middlemen or companies that act as intermediaries. However, this is only available to the tech-savvy and affluent, since the costs of products are greatly increased. Even if no commercial exchange is at stake, sanctions affect the cultural field. For example, Goodreads, an Amazon property, has been blocked in Iran since June 2019. Until then, Tehran was one of the top locations recorded by Goodreads users, along with cities like Jakarta, well above some major American and European cities. The sanctions have a deep effect on contemporary literary culture.

From Politics to the Market?

Despite these restrictions, one can see some openings with a slow integration of Iran into the world and the relative retreat of Islamic ideology to the margins of cultural production. There is a bit more logic of the market infusing the literary field. In other words, the field is increasingly less heteronomous with respect to the state. I would like to give two examples of this: the increase in publications of romance literature, which I examined in Chapter 1, as well as the rate of translations from English, which I discuss in Chapter 4: about 30 per cent of literary texts are translations, mainly from English, not from the language of the Sacred text, Arabic, despite the reticence of the state towards what it calls the west's 'cultural imperialism'. In Iran, translations are some of the most important literary products.

English-speaking countries do not publish many translations – the US is well known for translations only accounting for 3 per cent of all publications – but many European countries do, including France, which prides itself on what it calls 'French cultural exception', a politics based on supporting French cultural products against others. These translations are often supported by the state. In Iran, it is not necessarily the state that funds translation. Translations of religious texts from classical Arabic are usually published by governmental publishers, but this is not the case for most translations of prose from European languages, or from Asian languages such as Japanese, which is popular, and consequently, they are published by independent publishers because they sell well. Although most readers will go to Persian texts for poetry, they will often go to western texts for prose and overlook Iranian prose writers, as I explain in Chapter 9. This is to the point that it is the translators who have their names on the book cover and people often choose books according to the translator, not the author. The prestige of works in translation and of translators in Iran is unheard of in western countries, where scholars such as Lawrence Venuti have studied the 'invisibility of the translator' (Venuti 1995), an invisibility that does not apply to the Iranian context (Saeedi 2019). Most writers and intellectuals are also translators, and translation is a respected intellectual field, unlike western countries, where it has minor status, partly due to historical reasons and the link between the development of modern thought and translation. Interestingly, however, it is not a well-organised profession. There is no powerful syndicate for translations or programmes devoted to developing translation. Translation studies as an academic field is also a recent development, starting with journals such as *Translator* (*Motarjem*). Thus, although it is a field endowed with much prestige, it is not very organised and this prestige primarily works at the individual level. There has not been an increase in the number of translations throughout the years but the steady and high numbers are significant.

This importance of the translation of foreign works, which has remained constant throughout the years of the Islamic Republic, as well as the increase in romance novels, are signs that the Iranian literary field has integrated some logic of the market into its state-driven policies and is not completely isolated from worldwide tendencies. Although a very authoritarian context still exists, where heteronomy to the state is prevalent, the field has gained a little more autonomy from the state since the foundation of the Islamic republic.

This is evidenced by the recent arrival of a new portmanteau term in the political landscape: *khosulati*, which is composed of *khosusi* (independent) and *dowlati* (governmental). It is mostly used in politics to refer to the privatisation of governmental institutions but it has also had some relevance in the cultural field since the 2000s. 'One of the greatest "achievements" of the reformist-dominated Parliament (2000–2004) was indeed to speed up the process of privatization' (Khiabany 2007: 486). The media and communication sector has been particularly affected by these changes and the arrival of a new space between independent and governmental. The appearance of this term describes well the complexity of the relations between capital and the state, which keeps its political hands on large media institutions but has needed to diversify its programmes and appeal. Most recently, even the institution of censorship, traditionally in the hands of the state, has been partly privatised, to the dismay of literary actors. In 2019, for example, the state gave a contract to a private company to censor 13 million pages in a few months, possibly due to a backlog in the books waiting for analysis at the censor's office. The company would likely use a software to be able to censor a huge number of pages in a short amount of time (Shokrollahi 2019). This might just be a one-off to clear the backlog, but if this is repeated, it will drastically change the institution of censorship and its dynamics. The term *khosulati* has also been used to describe some sectors of the educational field, as 'neither dowlati nor khosusi' (Kalb 2017). Some cultural institutions have characteristics of both and have been described as a composite in recent years. Book City (Shahr-e Ketab), the bookshops that function as literary institutions that I talked about earlier, can be considered as *khosulati*: they are independent but belong to the municipality and their owners have very strong links to the political elite. Mostly, *khosulati* publishers are based in Qom and are religious publishers which have been privatised.

In the following section, I analyse the parallel underground space, which is the unofficial sector of the Iranian literary field that is most autonomous from the state. Iran has both a black and a grey book market that play some part in its system. Books circulate online in PDF format, they are shared between families and friends, and excerpts are reprinted without reference. Mahsa Salamati has closely studied Iranian shadow economies of cinema and shown how the informal components are at the centre of the market not at the margins or underground (2016). Shahnaz Salami argues similarly that the

> metaphor of the underground to designate the realities of the informal circulation of cultural goods should not lead us to think that what is at stake is a marginal section of the economy of the communication of the

country. On the contrary, informal networks occupy a central position. (Salami 2014: 21)

The important point to take from these analyses is also that the formal and informal are porous in the Iranian context. Amin Moghadam mentions this in the context of border crossings and trade with Iran's neighbouring countries: 'The arbitrary opposition between formal and informal economies is contradicted by these forms of individual autonomisation based on *savoir-faire*, competencies and daily negotiations developed in spaces that, while foreign, remain close in spirit' (Moghadam and Weber 2016a: 179).

The informality of Iran's book circulation has not yet been studied, and it certainly occurs on a smaller scale compared to cinema, but it is important to remember that publishers work within this system and are aware that they are competing as well as working with grey and black book markets. Salami has estimated the consumption of underground cultural goods at 9 per cent per week for illegal books, versus 39 per cent per week for legal books. Also, 44 per cent of books are obtained on the parallel market, 25 per cent on the black market and 78 per cent through friends and family (Salami 2014: 12). This is why the number of copies printed is only an indication about the actual reception of texts, that circulate more than is the case in western book markets. While the number of copies sold is not high, it is important to remember that a lot more readers read one copy than the number of copies bought. According to discussions with literary practitioners, I estimate this is at least double, maybe triple; so for 1000 copies bought, there are maybe between 2000 and 3000 readers.

The Underground Literary Space

Another way in which this informality is playing out is of course in the underground literary space. While Chapter 2 discussed some of the non-official literature online, here I discuss only print publications. There are different ways to refer to the black market and its diversity of practices in Iran: underground (*zirzamini*); offset (*ofset*); smuggled (*qachaq*); xeroxed (*ziraks*); or white cover (*jeld-e sefid*) because of the colour and neutrality of their covers. Underground books do not have an ISBN and are not referenced by the National Library of Iran or the Iran Book House. Since it is an illegal trade, it has been difficult to research this aspect of publishing in Iran. Although it is not a secret, people do not readily talk about it, for obvious reasons of security. I do not have figures nor definitive data on the percentage of books published on the black market, but my fieldworks in Tehran have led me to the conclusion that first publications of literary texts are not a prominent section of the market. This ran against my expectations. Knowing about the vast black market in film, and considering the restrictions imposed on the literary field, I expected underground publications to be more numerous and more central to how the field works. However, they are not culturally valued and thus most writers would avoid them if possible. In addition to a lack of prestige, it also means that most of the time, writers will not only be unpaid but must also pay for publication, which is not financially sustainable. Here it is important to remind the reader that I am not discussing the books published as originals which are actually translations, a very common practice, nor the photocopied books of varying quality that inundate the streets. An important sector of this black and grey market – which I do not discuss here but which is important to bear in mind – involves the re-publication of previously published texts, such as classic books that still do not have permission for publication, including *The Blind Owl* by Sadegh Hedayat, or lesser quality publications of texts that have previously been published by traditional publishers, either in Persian or translations, and are reprinted and distributed by street vendors or in the metro. Some publishers make minor changes to the text and print it as their own, which crosses the line between copyright infringement and plagiarism. These lower quality counterfeit reprints are produced in significant numbers and disrupt the market, as they divert important sales revenues from traditional publishers and booksellers. I am only concerned about first prints of original texts. Nevertheless, the economy of underground publication is not a secret, nor is it well hidden. It is well known that several Tehran publishers around Revolution Square (*Meydan-e enqelab*) print and distribute underground publications, as I described in my introduction. The area, which is in close proximity to the University of Tehran, boasts dozens of publishers and bookshops. It is also packed with street vendors who sell banned books in broad daylight. They set up their books on a blanket on the pavement along Enghelab and adjacent streets. The Enghelab area is thus the place to go if one wants to look into underground and black-market businesses.

In the following, I discuss the different categories of underground publications of first literary publications.

Books Which Have Been Awaiting a Publication Permit for a Long Time

Amir Ahmadi Arian is one example of a writer who waited three years for a publishing permit then decided to print his book, *The Disappearance of Danyal* (*Ghiyab-e Danyal*), underground. He is a well-known writer and journalist who left Iran for Australia and then went to the US in 2009. In an interview, he mentioned that he did not expect his book to be stuck at the Ministry of Culture and Islamic Guidance for several years (Khosravi 2016). According to him, apart from a sex scene, the book had no other issue. He expected the censors to ask him to rewrite the scene and move on, but instead the book stayed with the censors for several years. So, he decided to print it himself, first in 100 copies, then when the copies were sold in a couple of weeks, another 100 copies. After that, deciding that the book had had a proper print life, he put the book online for free download. Ahmadi Arian points to the fact that for him, underground publication was not a radical gesture. He had to do it to reach readers, but he did not do it as a rebellious act. He also said he was reluctant to put his book online because so many people download thousands of books that they never read and he wanted his book to circulate and be read (Khosravi 2016). The other choice he had would have been to publish with an Iranian publisher abroad, but he argued that they usually have very little impact on readers within Iran (Khosravi 2016). I come back to this argument on the relationship between literary Iran and the diaspora in the second part of this book.

Books That Will Never Receive Publishing Permits Under the Current Circumstances

These include the memoirs of the former Empress Farah Pahlavi, who is *persona non grata* in Iran, but also translations of western classics that are deemed improper and immoral, for example, *Lolita* by Vladimir Nabokov, which was recently translated by Akram Pedram Nia, published in Afghanistan by the publisher Zaryab and smuggled into Iran (Qiasi 2014). It can be found in bookshops in Enghelab.

Books That Are Circulated Illegally Without the Consent of the Writer

One prominent example in this category is Mahmoud Dowlatabadi, the famous novelist, whose novel, *The Disappearance of the Colonel*, to be published by Cheshmeh, has been waiting for a permission to print since 2009. The book has become a symbol of the different views on censorship and literature, and it is seen as political. In the meantime, his novel has been published with his approval in different European languages, first in German as *Der Kolonel*, then in English as *The Colonel*. He has also toured throughout Europe and done some readings of the Persian version (Amiri 2014); however, he does not want his book to be published underground or online in Persian and is still waiting for permission. This has not stopped counterfeit copies being published. Dowlatabadi has urged readers not to read these versions, which he says are not the original text. The book has been published in Afghanistan and distributed underground in Iran. It was also rumoured that the German publisher Gardoon had published it, but its publisher, Abbas Maroufi, stated that this was false and that the Gardoon logo on the cover was fake. Dowlatabadi is very critical of the Ministry of Culture and Islamic Guidance, which, according to him, allowed the book to be published and distributed in these ways (Amiri 2014). The Ministry of Culture and Islamic Guidance has been able to collect 4,700 copies of the illegal novel but it is unknown how many copies had already been sold (Amiri 2014). *The Colonel* is an example of a book that is deemed subversive by the Ministry of Culture and Islamic Guidance, but for which the writer wants a publication permission and is not ready to move underground. Dowlatabadi is one of the most well-known contemporary writers and can afford to be seen as fighting the authorities.

Books Which Have Received Publishing Permits Then Were Banned

Many books go through the process of being permitted then banned. A book by the intellectual, Abdolhossein Zarrinkub, *Two Centuries of Silence* (*Do qarn sokut*), is the account of the 'silence' that followed the conquest of Persia by the Muslim Arabs and is very critical of that period. The book resonates with a discourse shared by many in Iran about the decline of the country after the Islamic conquest. It was hugely popular and many people relate to its discourse, as demonstrated by Reza Zia-Ebrahimi, who analyses the 'memory-narrative of Iran's past that emphasizes the nation's continued cultural survival in the face of invasions by hostile hoards' (2016: 840). *Two Centuries of Silence* was published years before the revolution and banned just afterwards. Since then, it has been published underground several times. It has also circulated online in PDF format. It received a permit to print decades later and has been published by Nashr-e sokhan since (Dehbashi 2012: 196). It is an example of books that go through different lives.

Several conclusions can be drawn from these examples: first, as we have seen above, the censorship of certain books occurs in an environment of uncertainty. There is no certitude about the publication of a book or about whether its publication will ever be allowed. Second, the Ershad and security forces allow certain activities to occur, although they are supposedly forbidden. Is this because they do not want to invest time and effort in controlling literary phenomena which are deemed minor, or is it to leave a certain amount of freedom to readers and literary practitioners? Third, the permission to print sometimes becomes a political statement on the part of Ershad; it is endowed with high symbolic significance. For example, it is well known that Sadegh Hedayat's *The Blind Owl* has not been given permission to be printed but that it circulates online and is readily available in the streets around Enghelab. Ershad allows this to occur but insists that they will not give permission for it to be printed. Thus, we return to the idea of the censors defining this classical book as unworthy, while most critics and readers both nationally and internationally recognise it as a masterpiece.

In the final section of this chapter, I focus on two cultural institutions, the Saadi Foundation and the Union of Tehran Publishers and Booksellers, to put these reflections into perspective with concrete examples of institutions influencing the literary field.[2] One critical issue relating to many sectors in Iran, including in the cultural sector, is that there are many parallel organisations whose work overlaps and who sometimes contradict each other.

---

[2] This chapter benefited from an interview in Tehran with Mohammad Reza Darbandi, the director of international affairs of the Saadi Foundation, on 14 March 2017. I am grateful for his time and insights. I have also met informally with a past president of the Union of Tehran Publishers and Booksellers.

I encountered such overlap many times when studying the Saadi Foundation. This foundation is focused on language, not literature, so it is slightly outside of the main focus of this book; however, the Saadi Foundation was more readily accessible than other institutions such as the the Academy for Persian Language and Literature (*Farhangestan-e zaban va adab-e Farsi*). The Saadi Foundation's members were more responsive, perhaps because it is a new governmental institution that is keen to publicise its activities, with this accessibility determining my decision to work on it. Such fieldwork decisions are not insignificant when working on a country such as Iran, where fieldwork is difficult. In the future, I aim to do more work on literary associations and institutions to complement these reflections.

The Saadi Foundation

How Do Endowed Foundations (Bonyads) Work?

The Saadi Foundation is one of the many endowed foundations, or *bonyads*, that are essential to the Islamic Republic regime. Devictor describes the *bonyads* as such:

> They constitute a vital element of the Iranian institutional system, even if they are still particularly opaque and difficult to access, including for the majority of those Iranians in charge ... Traditionally, they are managed by clerics and have non-profitable aims, for the general interest ... They do not seem to all be regulated by the same status and some institutions called *bonyâd* ('foundation') can fall within the jurisdiction of private law and some others of public law ... Their funding traditionally falls within the jurisdiction of gifts and religious taxes. (Devictor 2004: 68, Chapter 2)

Niki Akhavan provides a further explanation of their mechanisms, making a comparison with socialist systems:

> Although most are under the supervision of the Leader (the highest political and religious position in the country), the bonyads have institutional autonomy. At the same time they receive direct and indirect financial support from the state and enjoy tax exemptions and subsidized access to foreign currency and loans, among other benefits. They are neither subject

to state oversight (as might be the case in a centralized socialist system where the state directly controls more resources and doles out social services and payments to the needy and such) nor accountable to market forces or shareholders (as might be the case in a largely decentralized system with private ownership subject to some state regulation). (Akhavan 2016: 185)

In the current context of Iran's isolation from the world, the foundations act as 'effective agents and vehicles of Iranian soft power and regional influence' (Bullock Jenkins 2016: 156). Moreover, as Bullock Jenkins adds, 'the parastatal nature of the *bonyads* allows them to alternately associate with or dissociate from aspects of the Iranian state's policy of the day for expedience with particular soft power effect' (2016: 159).

Kevan Harris mentions competition between institutions as an important element shaping the politics of the new Islamic Republic regime: 'parallel institutions in the Islamic Republic permitted state officials to placate and channel contradictory pressures from different segments of the population as well as competing elements of the new political elite' (Harris 2017: 92). The Saadi Foundation, a recent cultural endeavour, belongs to this landscape:

A range of foundations have been active in book and magazine publications, art festivals, and exhibits, as well as the establishment of museums and other cultural spaces . . . cultural and media outlets were among the properties confiscated and turned over to the foundations. In 1980, for example, all the country's movie theaters were handed over to the Foundation for the Oppressed. (Akhavan 2016: 187–8)

Functioning of the Saadi Foundation

The Saadi Foundation was established in 2010 to promote and support Persian language and literature outside Iran and to support educational, research, cultural and media activities at the international level, as stated on its website. It aims to be the equivalent of the French Alliance Française, the Chinese Confucius Institute or the German Goethe Institute. It is mostly focused on language teaching, but also organises cultural events. Its primary achievements have been to collaborate with universities and institutes around the world to establish language programmes. The Saadi Foundation is currently headed by Gholam-Ali Haddad Adel, an important figure in the

Islamic Republic regime. Haddad Adel is an advisor to the Supreme Leader Ali Khamenei, with whom he has family ties, and he has been very active in cultural organisations in the past decades. He is the current president of the Iranian Academy of Persian Language and Literature, among many other influential positions. The Saadi Foundation is a non-governmental institute, but it receives most of its funding from the government. With the addition of some private funding, it can be called a semi-governmental institution. As Haddad Adel mentioned in an interview: 'We have had a little financial support from some banks such as Pasargad Bank and Shahr Bank in Iran. We are looking forward to financial support from Iranians inside and outside Iran who care about their culture and language' (Baqer Sakhaei 2016). The budget might evolve significantly year on year, but for 2016, it was 7 billion tomans, approximately 1 million American dollars (Soleimani 2016), which is relatively small.

The Saadi Foundation's goal, as stated in its constitution, is:

> to strengthen and develop Persian language and literature outside Iran and to create concentration, coherence in activities related to this field, and to make optimal use of existing capacities of the country. The bonyad aims to undertake strategic management and implementation of educational, research, cultural and media activities toward development of Persian language and literature abroad, in coordination with Islamic Culture and Relations Organisation. (Saadi Foundation 2010)

The Saadi Foundation has published dozens of textbooks for students of various levels, mostly published by Fatemi. They also publish an educational journal called *Fanus* through the Persian Language Centre in Belgrade.[3] Its audience is adult intermediate and advanced Persian language students in all countries. The journal's managing director for a few years was Mohsen Soleimani, the Iranian Ambassador to Serbia and representative of the Saadi Foundation around the world. They have published a couple of bilingual

---

[3] Iran was the guest of honour at the 2016 International Belgrade Book Fair. Iran has rarely been a featured guest in international book fairs in the last four decades and it is interesting to see the links with Eastern Europe, especially Belgrade. A whole network of Iranian film-makers and illustrators in Serbia are also maintaining these links.

books, in English and Persian, including *The Water Urn* (*Khomreh*) and *Iranology* (*Iran shenasi*) by Houshang Moradi Kermani. The first book was published in collaboration with the independent publisher, Candle & Fog. Although the Saadi Foundation's focus is on the Persian language, it has a more widespread ambition that extends to the literary. In an interview, Darbandi told me that they consider literary activities to be in their orbit, although not currently a priority (14 March 2017). It is also possible that their ambitions to have an impact on the literary field are curtailed by other institutions which are older and have more cultural capital.

The Saadi Foundation collaborates with Iranian universities and research centres. It has signed memoranda of understanding with Payam-e Noor University, the Academy of Persian Language and Literature, Allameh Tabatabai University and Islamic Azad University. There are also collaborations with Al-Mustafa University, which is a school of theology. Their main work is to send instructors abroad, write and publish textbooks, and organise Persian courses in Tehran. This exchange programme is called Courses to Increase Knowledge (*Dowreh-ha-ye danesh afzaei*) and in 2019 it had around 200 students from different countries, who come to Iran for language courses during the summer. Some of their work is directed at non-Persian speakers, some of it at the second or third generation of Iranians abroad who might not know Persian or those who only speak it and want to become proficient in reading and writing.

Power Struggle with Other Institutions

The overlap issue is crucial to an understanding of some of the problems in the cultural sector, especially with the Saadi Foundation. As Kevan Harris argues, 'parallel institutionalism became a defining characteristic of the Islamic Republic' (2017: 81). He works on socio-political organisations but his argument is also applicable to the cultural field: 'Instead of merging various welfare organizations into a single social-policy apparatus, the state repeatedly proliferated new organizations to compete with old ones and new activities for existing organizations' (Harris 2017: 82).

As mentioned above, the Saadi Foundation is attempting to centralise the work of several other institutions. For many years, there were four main institutions that were working on developing and promoting Persian language programmes throughout the world: the Ministry of Foreign Affairs; the Ministry of Science, Research and Technology; the Ministry of Culture and Islamic Guidance; and the Organization of Islamic Culture and Relations. In 2010, Haddad Adel suggested to the Supreme Council of the Cultural Revolution that it merge these four organisations so as to optimise their work and avoid overlaps (Darbandi, personal communication, 14 March 2017). Since then, the Saadi Foundation has been responsible for this task, with the ministers of each ministry mentioned above sitting on the board of directors and having a say on its programmes. Other members of the board include the Minister of Education, the Head of the Academy of Persian Language and Literature, the Secretary of the Supreme Council of the Cultural Revolution, the Head of Al-Mostafa International University, the Head of the Islamic Republic of Iran Broadcasting, as well as five experts in the field of Persian language and literature selected by the Head of the Academy of Persian Language and Literature, confirmed by the board and approved by the Supreme Council of the Cultural Revolution.

Article 13 of the Saadi Foundation constitution states: 'In countries where the Organization of Islamic Culture and Relations has cultural representatives, the Foundation would not establish a separate representative centre' (2010). The teachers sent to the countries concerned remain under the supervision of the political representative of the Islamic Republic of Iran through its embassies. This means that in the countries where there has been a long tradition of teaching Persian, the Saadi Foundation is not active. It is to be noted that the Saadi Foundation was only founded in 2010 and although it is attempting to have an impact on teaching Persian language across the world, it is in competition with older institutions and universities. In European countries especially, there have been institutions of Persian language and literature for centuries. Some might be happy to collaborate with the Saadi Foundation, which gives away books and provides teaching for free as part of its soft power strategy, but some are reluctant to engage with a foundation that is directly financed by the Iranian government.

In France, for example, which has several long-standing institutions of Persian language and literature, the University of Strasbourg had a visiting professor from Iran between 2005 and 2017 and does not collaborate with the Saadi Foundation. In France, the role of the Saadi Foundation seems to be restricted to Persian language classes through the cultural centre of the embassy, which caters only to a certain category of audience. In the UK, at the School of Oriental and African Studies in London, there are exchanges with the Ferdowsi University of Mashhad but not with the Saadi Foundation. In Australia, which only has one university teaching Persian, the Australian National University in Canberra has started collaboration with the Saadi Foundation. Its level of collaboration with the Saadi Foundation is somewhat low: they receive guidance on teaching, and in some years, they have teachers sent to them; however, the textbooks used are not those of the Saadi Foundation but those of the Council for the Dissemination of Persian Language (*Shora-ye gostaresh-e zaban-e Farsi*).

This is an interesting example of the negotiations occurring between different institutions that are struggling for power. The Council for the Dissemination of Persian Language was under the Ministry of Culture and Islamic Guidance until the Saadi Foundation was established (Statute 6). Since then, the *Shora-ye gostaresh*'s tasks and duties have been determined by the Saadi Foundation. Their staff outside Iran work under the supervision of Iranian Embassies (Article 16 of SF statute), collaborating with the embassy to organise events such as the Persian Language and Literature Olympiad.

The Iranian Society for the Promotion of Persian Language and Literature (*Anjoman-e tarvij-e zaban va adab-e Farsi-ye Iran*), as suggested by its name, does work that can be seen as overlapping, since it also focuses on developing and teaching Persian and sending teachers abroad to teach the language. Starting in 1971, its activities ceased between 1979 and 1982. It is currently headed by Mehdi Mohaghegh, who is also a member of the Saadi Foundation's board of trustees.

The Saadi Foundation is a good example of the struggle for cultural power occurring in the cultural field in Iran. It is struggling to establish its place among institutions that have been doing similar work for a long time. Without the power of Haddad Adel, this would never have been possible. Even with it, there is a reticence by older institutions to come under its leadership and abrogate some of their powers. Although its place in the literary field is quite peripheral due to its focus on language, I have chosen to include the Saadi Foundation in this analysis because other governmental literary institutions function in a similar way to it. As such, it is a good representative of other literary institutions: they receive public funds, their mission overlaps with other institutions, and they work with a mission in mind without much consideration for the market or readers.

The Union of Tehran Publishers and Booksellers

I would now like to focus on an independent institution that is crucial in the Iranian literary field: the Union of Tehran Publishers and Booksellers (*Etehadiyeh-ye nasheran va ketabforushan-e Tehran*). Since 75 per cent of the nation's book production occurs in Tehran, this union is the most important in the country. A governmental union, the Union for Cooperative Publishers of Iran (*Etehadiyeh-ye sherkat-ha-ye ta'avoni-ye nasheran-e Iran*), has also existed since 2001 but its power is restricted to governmental publishers, its history is shorter and its range is smaller. It is more and more active though in organising the national section of the Tehran International Book Fair and representing governmental publishers at international bookfairs. The fact that two unions exist for publishers exacerbates the tensions between the independent and the governmental fields.

History and Functioning of the Union

The Union of Tehran Publishers and Booksellers was officially established in 1958 under the Act of Union in order to support the rights of publishers and booksellers, develop relationships between Union members, provide better services for customers, and facilitate the relationship between the Union and the government, the private sector and other relevant unions. There are other unions in Iran that are active in specific areas of publishing, such as the Union for Textbooks and the Union for Children's Books. The Union of Tehran Publishers and Booksellers aims to facilitate communication between these different unions. All people active in the publishing industry and/or booksellers may request Union membership. Many publishers are also booksellers, so both categories often overlap. The board of directors has seven members who have weekly meetings. The board is elected every four years, with the directors selected from Union members. There are different committees in the Union, such as the Technical Committee, the International Committee, the Committee for Complaints and the Committee for e-Publishing. The Union also publishes a journal that is a reference for people working in the field.

The first managing director was Nasrolah Sabuhi, the publisher for Markazi bookstore and the son of a well-known cleric, Abdolah Vaez Tehrani. After the Islamic Revolution, Ali Mohammadi, who was close to Ayatollah Khomeini, became the temporary managing director for three years, which was the only time that the Union was under the direct influence of the government. In 1982, the seventh president, Ali Mohammadi Ardahali, of Mohammadi publications, was elected. For several years, Said Hassan Kiayan, also director of the publishing house Cheshmeh, was the director. The director in 2020 is Houman Hassanpour, who also heads Aryaban publications. According to their website, the Union comprised 1,200 members in 2016.

What is its Place in the Field?

A crucial issue in analysing the place of the Union in the field concerns its link to the government. One way to assess this is by looking at funding; another is to examine which parties the Union best represents: governmental or independent publishers? As a Union, it should not receive funds from the government. In a 2014 interview, the managing director mentioned that it relies on membership fees and donations for funding (Khosravi Yeganeh 2014). He also mentioned that it makes some profit from organising workshops, for example during the Tehran and Frankfurt Book Fairs. The relationship between the Union and the government is complex. More often than not, the Union acts as an intermediary between independent publishers and the government and lobbies for modification to the law so that it better supports publishers. However, like all cultural institutions with an official status, it has to work with the government if it wants to make things happen. In 2013, the Rouhani government wanted to leave the responsibility of 'censorship of information before publication' to publishers, not to the Ministry of Culture and Islamic Guidance. The Union protested against the suggestion because they believed that publishers would have to invest a lot of money and time in publishing books that would later be censored and not receive permission for distribution (Lavasani 2013).

All the heads of the Union have been independent publishers, except for three years immediately after the revolution. This in itself reflects the general line of the Union, which, it should be repeated, elects its own head. There were instances when the Union had to fight against the government, for example in the early years after the revolution, when the government wanted to establish publishers without the necessary credentials or experience, so it would be able to publish its books. The Union then refused to grant recognition of these publishers as such and thus acted as a barrier to unlawful acts in this regard (Tasnim 2018). The election of a governmental publisher at its head would be seen as encroaching on its aims, one of which is negotiating with and not being controlled by the government. This brings me back to the argument about the symbolic capital of independent actors, as opposed to the governmental ones, who have the political and, up to a point, financial capital. This independence from the government as a form of capital is a trait of many authoritarian regimes. Narges Bajoghli has a similar argument in her book on media producers, where the distinction between 'not ours' (*gheyr-e khodis*) and 'ours' (*khodis*) is a crucial demarcating line:

> Regime cultural producers face a conundrum that results from the structural conditions of wielding power in a revolutionary government: they use their political power unapologetically, yet they lack social and cultural capital. This capital, especially in the art world, is often held by *gheyr-e khodis* who have easier access to international markets and the Iranian diaspora. Internally, *gheyr-e khodi* artists and intellectuals hold pride of place, and because they have been heavily censored and policed inside Iran, they end up retaliating socially against the regime supporters whom they blame for the censorship. (Bajoghli 2019: 8)

This dynamic is crucial to the understanding of the literary field today.

I have focused on two organisations in this chapter to demonstrate the overlapping of institutions in the Islamic Republic and the dynamics of cultural prestige and capital of the independent field. Of course, there are other relevant examples of institutional functioning. For example, the legacy of the Iranian Writers' Association (*Kanun-e nevisandegan-e Iran*) is still important among literary practitioners, although it has been forced into exile in Paris since 1982. Founded in 1962, the Iranian Writers' Association was an intellectual institution acting 'both as a safeguard against doom and a professional guild with a defined responsibility to protect and preserve the rights and interests of the Iranian writer' (Karimi-Hakkak 1985: 197). It was decidedly secular, and although there were different trends, mostly on the left of the political spectrum. It was one of the first examples of the divide between writers and the government. Under the Shah, the association was unsuccessful in fighting censorship and was paused for a few years until 1977. It is then that it organised the famous ten nights of poetry at the Goethe Institute in Tehran, which marked a turning point before the revolution:

> the Ten Nights is beyond question the most significant group event in Iranian intellectual history and must be considered an early milestone in the Iranian Revolution. It not only provided an occasion for young literate Iranians to see and hear in person and for the first time those writers and poets who had for years remained wrapped in a reverential halo of intellectual opposition to a repressive regime, but what is more it dispelled much of the popular fear of assembly and peaceful demonstration of that opposition. (Karimi-Hakkak 1985: 211)

While the Association's activities blossomed in the first years of the revolution, it clearly went against the grain of the new Islamic government and had to go underground from 1981, then into exile in France in 1982. It is still active there, but has mostly lost its connections with Iran. However, its legacy is remembered in the independent field and its opposition to the government was critical in building a certain spirit of resistance among writers (Sepanlou 2002).

Another important consideration about literary institutions is that there are many informal circles, or literary salons, around literary figures in Iran, which do not function as institutions, but play an important role in the functioning of the literary field, the *dowrehs*. In her analysis of Afghan literary practices in Iran, Olwszeksa defines a *dowreh* as 'an informal circle of intimates . . . who meet periodically and rotate the venue among the homes of members . . . *Dowrehs* may have a literary focus, and poetry and short fiction may be read and discussed at them' (Olszewska 2015: 134). Some prominents writers like Mahmoud Dowlatabadi hold their *dowreh* in their home. Some are organised around reading a text like the *Shahnameh*, while others are more about sharing work and exchanging on specific points around cultural issues. In a country where institutions are polarised and political, these gatherings act as counterpoints. They are places where expression is less censored, less self-censored and where the formality of interactions is downplayed.

Conclusion

The governmental literary field is endowed with most of the political capital and benefits from support from the state: for example, getting a good stand at the Tehran Book Fair or sending books by post for free and thus saving on distribution fees. However, the independent field has attained a higher level of prestige and symbolic capital. To a certain extent, both the independent field and the underground market continue to fight for independence from the government and, in doing so, also make a political statement. Sapiro describes this process in the following terms:

> the struggle against the political control of the cultural production has contributed to the foundation of the principle on which the relative autonomy of the literary field rests, even though, as we have seen, in authoritarian regimes, the defence of autonomy is associated with a political struggle to which it is subordinated. (2003: 449)

This chapter has traced the history of the divide between the two fields, explained at length the processes of censorship, analysed the obstacles to a larger circulation of Persian literature and delved into the grey and black markets. My position is that addressing this issue is critical to understanding the complexity of the field as a whole. It is important to understand censorship mechanisms, the different layers of censorship and how the field has responded to it. In the authoritarian context of Iran, it is also important to note that literary practitioners who challenge the hegemony of the state have started in the past decades to call for more market mechanisms and a freer market, as is the case in other authoritarian contexts. In this sense, the independent book market in Iran, which often challenges the state, is at the opposite end of what we call the independent sector in western book markets, that often calls for more influence of the state and less of the free market.

After this overview of the functioning of the field, in the following chapter I use data from the Iran Book House to visualise the production and distribution of literary texts within Iran since the 1979 revolution.

4

Book Production within Iran: A Look at the Numbers

In December 2017, I met with Esmaeil Afghahi, the co-author of The Statistics of Books in Iran: Statistical Data of Book Publishing in Iran from 1979 to 2016 *(Tabriznia and Afghahi 2017). PhD student Elham Naeej had met with him a few months before when I asked her if she could go to the Iran Book House for me and get their CD cataloguing publications. She told me that they had stopped publishing the CD, but that Esmaeil was willing to help with data. Thanks to her, I exchanged with Esmaeil, who kindly sent the Excel spreadsheets I am discussing in this chapter and who was happy to be named in this book . In 2017, I met with him in central Tehran and we talked about his co-authored book, about my research and about his prospects. This anecdote is an example of the difficulty of accessing resources in Iran. Whereas libraries are fairly easily accessible, the access to the Excel sheets was dependent upon chance and upon a kind student who helped me to find the right person, himself willing to help a researcher. Such reliance on chance encounters and fieldwork, although at the basis of my work on contemporary Persian literature and of this book, is not applicable to all Iranian topics or periods, and is dependent upon the possibility of travel to Iran. This is the positive side of chance encounters and there are negative anecdotes which I am omitting, as well as many instances of encounters that did not happen. It is crucial to remember these constraints when reading this book and in general research that relies on fieldwork in Iran.*

In this chapter, I use the data of the Iran Book House to analyse the production of books within Iran after the 1979 revolution and its ties to politics. This is an example of how the methods of digital humanities and book history can be used to help us to understand a literature that has not often been its object of study. While several projects in these fields have been successful with classical Persian literature, contemporary literature has mostly been left out of it, partly because of the difficulty of accessing reliable data since the 1979 revolution.

I do a quantitative study of book production to give precise figures to phenomena that are often only sketched. Contrary to western markets, where sales are easily traceable, there are no reliable statistics on sales in Iran and no centralised database available on books. In addition, the government is an important buyer of certain categories of books, which disrupts the sales number. It is not documented but it is well known by literary practitioners that the Ministry of Culture and Islamic Guidance buys numerous copies of books important to its ideology. The most reliable data we have on the Iranian market is thus the publication of books, before the sales. The study juxtaposes this data to the discourse of literary practitioners I have been exposed to when doing fieldwork in the literary field in Iran between 2006 and 2017. As such, it confirms some ideas, for example the ebb and flow of publications according to politics, and contradicts others, such as that governmental publishers publish higher quantities of texts than independent ones. I use the Iran Book House (*Khaneh-ye ketab*) data as my primary source for understanding the production of books within Iran. One must bear in mind that because it is a governmental institute, it does not take into consideration books that are produced outside of the official networks and that do not get an ISBN, that is, all books published underground in black and grey book markets. However, as I explained in Chapter 3, underground original publications are scarce. On the other hand, the circulation of pirated books is high, but I am concerned with the production of books here, not their circulation. As I mentioned in the previous chapter, there is a higher circulation of each copy of a book than the number of copies sold or printed. I use three sets of data all related to the Iran Book House and compare them to determine how the production of literature works in post-revolutionary Iran.

Method and Resources

In many western countries, the most reliable data on the production of books over a certain period would come from national libraries. In Iran, although the National Library is also a valid resource, the most reliable data on contemporary books are provided by the Iran Book House, which is a governmental institute, officially established in 1993 (Masoudi 1998). Why is this so? Before getting a permission for distribution, each publisher must hand out two copies of the book, one to the Iran Book House and one to the Ministry of Culture and Islamic Guidance. The Iran Book House is the institute that receives all the books that have been published, checks them and logs them. It also copies a few pages and archives them. The Iran Book House is thus the primary source for understanding the production of books within Iran. While the National Library is mainly for book professionals and researchers, the Iran Book House aims to inform a wider audience. It thus also publishes journals, for example journals that list books published weekly and monthly in each discipline – *Book of the Month* (*Ketab-e mah*) and *Book of the Week* (*Ketab-e hafteh*) – in addition to their daily updated website, and runs cultural events including Iran's Book of the Year Awards, the Parvin E'tesami Literary Prize and the Jalal Al-e Ahmad Literary Prize. The Iran Book House has also been the ISBN representative in Iran since 1994. A distinctive ISBN is assigned to each edition and variation (except reprints) of a book. The Iran Book House gives ISBNs to publishers depending on their activity: for example, to a big publisher, it might give a package of a hundred ISBNs. In this way, publishers do not have to be in touch with the Iran Book House for each book they publish.

In this chapter, I use three key resources. The first one is a report that the Iran Book House published in 2016 on statistics of book publishing in all categories between 1980 and 2016, on the occasion of the publishing of one million books since the revolution (Gholami Jaliseh 2016/1394). They updated the report and published it in English in 2017 (Tabriznia and Afghahi 2017). I refer to both the English and the Persian versions since they have some variations. The second resource is data that I have obtained directly from the Iran Book House for literary books. In the first chapter, I outlined what I consider literature, with a broad definition that does not distinguish between high and low literary texts, and that overlaps mostly with the Dewey category. This data is in the form of Excel sheets, containing all information on books in the category of literature only, for the same period. The third resource is the report *Writer's Block: The Story of Censorship in Iran* produced by the independent research lab, Small Media (Marchant 2015), a UK-based institute that defines itself as an 'action lab, providing digital research, training and advocacy solutions to support the work of civil society actors that provides assistance to at-risk communities globally'. A lot of its work is on Iran and is about empowering marginalised communities there and supporting civil society initiatives. Small Media have also worked on the database of the Iran Book House but because they do not have direct access to Iran, their method was to scrape the data from the Iran Book House website. Their report, like the Iran Book House one, is also focused on books in all categories, not only literature. I thus have two resources that have data on the entirety of book production and one that is only on literary book production. I contend that the production in literature does not differ enough from the whole of the production for this difference in the resources to be an issue when comparing them. However, this needs to be remembered when analysing their particularities.

I compare these three resources, concentrating on links between book production and the politics of the government at the time; the decline of the number of books published over the years since 1979; the decreasing number of translations in comparison to original texts; the increased centralisation of book production in Tehran; and the relative minority of governmental publishers compared to independent publishers.

Digital Humanities, Book History and Contemporary Persian Literature

Before I get into the analysis of book production, I want to stop to reflect on the construction of the data, and on the place of this kind of analysis in Iranian studies.

The Small Media report, produced in the UK, is accessible online, but the published report *Statistics of Book Publications in Iran* is not accessible outside of Iran and not easy to find within Iran (Tabriznia and Afghahi 2017). However, it is possible to get the report in the Iran Book House or at the yearly Tehran Book Fair, where the Iran Book House has a stand. The co-author of *Statistics of Book Publications in Iran*, Esmaeil Afghahi, helped me get access to the data in the form of Excel sheets from the Iran Book House.[1]

---

[1] I would like to thank my PhD student, Elham Naeej, for her help, in making this connection.

It contains between ten and thirteen variables depending on the years: title of the book, writer, publisher, translator, sub-category, original versus translation, Dewey classification, number of pages, number of reprints, number of copies printed, price, province of publisher, details about publisher. In the digital humanities, it is important to not 'deny the critical and interpretive activities that construct that data and digital record and make them available for analysis' (Bode 2018: 20). In this case, one can see some variables are not included every year. There is also the issue of selecting 'literature' as a category in a large database, with a potential for error, although the Iran Book House followed the Dewey classification, which is standard. As for the construction of the large database itself, I am not aware of the processes in place, nor the criteria for selecting books under certain categories. It is also important to remember that we are dealing with contemporary resources and data, that are constantly evolving. It is not an archive, fixed in library bookshelves. This evolution should be remembered, especially when we are studying the most recent years.

A part of my argument in this chapter is that because the three resources largely overlap and confirm each other, the minor inconsistencies between them are negligible. It is particularly important to note that Small Media and the two resources from the Iran Book House come from opposite political sides, since the Iran Book House is a governmental institution while Small Media is an institution based outside of Iran which is clearly opposed to some of the foundational tenets of the Islamic Republic regime: they publish reports on censorship, on the LGBTQ community, and on minorities in Iran for example. The fact that their readings of the data overlap nonetheless is testimony to its validity, as well as to the relative accuracy of the construction of the data.

Studying within a framework of digital humanities, defined here for my purpose as the use of computational methods for humanities disciplines, is relatively recent in Iranian studies. Persian digital humanities focuses on educational and research resources to make available texts of Persian literature, usually classical texts, including manuscripts or visual texts. An important part of this work relates to collecting and digitising. This is the case of the Roshan Initiative in Persian Digital Humanities at the University of Maryland, as well as other initiatives around the world, including major libraries like the American Library of Congress. There are also publications using text mining, comparing for example lines of classical poems. Concerning contemporary Iran, most resources are within Iran, such as the University of Tehran's *Hamshahri* collection, which collects the data of the newspaper *Hamshahri*. As far as contemporary Persian literature goes, the only project that I know of, based in the US, is 'Persian translated' by Alireza Taheri Araghi, who started collecting titles of Persian books published and translated into English. Just like the rest of the digital humanities, which started with the archiving of texts, digitisation programmes and creation of textual corpora for large-scale analysis, digital Persian literature has primarily achieved results in these areas. This chapter combines it with book history and uses a method that has thus far not been practised much in the field of contemporary Persian literature to offer new perspectives and contribute to reflections on Persian digital humanities and book history both within Iran and abroad. It shows that using them tells us different stories from the ones told by traditional literary methods. They give us access to information that is critical if we want to understand the Iranian literary field, that would not be available without them.

Literary Production and its Ties to Governments

Literary practitioners in Iran almost always mention the years of Khatami's presidency (1997–2005) as a golden age for publishing, and criticise the periods preceding and following it. How does this compare with the data on the topic? Figure 4.1 shows the evolution of the total market volume – that is, the total number of books published (book titles from Figures 4.2 and 4.3 by number of copies from Figure 4.4) – according to both Small Media and the Iran Book House. There are a few discrepancies, especially at the end of the period, but the general trend is the same: it shows a sharp decline from 2005 to 2006 – as much as 51 per cent, according to Small Media.[2]

The Iran Book House report states that literary production increases and decreases according to governments (Tabriznia and Afghahi 2017: 18). According to the report, in the early years of the Islamic Republic and

---

[2] I have used the graphs in both reports but uniformised their presentation to make the comparison between them easier.

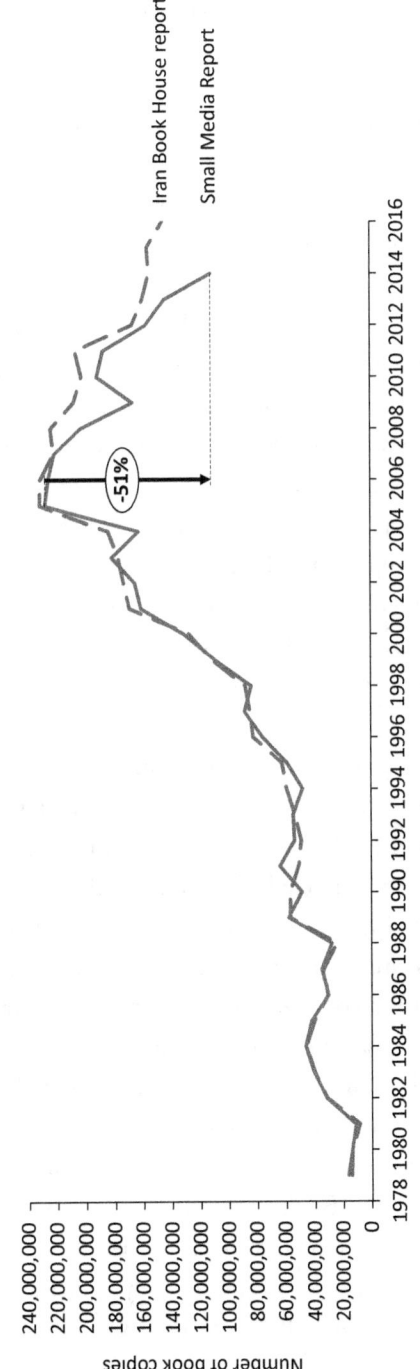

Figure 4.1 Market volume, from data extracted from the Iran Book House report and the Small Media report.

during the war with Iraq and Ali Khamenei's presidency (1981–9), book production was low. It did not increase much during the reconstruction period under the presidency of Hashemi Rafsanjani (1989–97). It reached a peak during President Khatami's government (1997–2005), while during President Ahmadinejad's presidency (2005–13) there was a decrease. Data for Rouhani's presidencies (2013–today) shows a small increase but is too small to be interpretable (Tabriznia and Afghahi 2017: 18). This evolution is also what Small Media reports in its analysis (Marchant 2015: 9).

Below are the two curves that the Iran Book House report and Small Media report have for book production over the years. Figure 4.2 from Small Media shows the number of books published since 1979. One can see that the Khamenei presidency, which also coincided with the war against Iraq, was a period of stagnation for book production. Rafsanjani's presidency, a conservative presidency, saw an increase. It can be noted that the liberal Khatami was his Minister of Culture and Islamic Guidance for a time, but Rafsanjani also had two other conservative ministers during his presidency. Ahmad Masjed-Jamei, a reformist, had the position for the last years of Khatami's presidencies. It is only with Khatami's presidencies that production boomed. The reformist period had 'a policy known as "open doors", when the books received a permanent publishing license, some large publishers were allowed to be responsible for their own books and some permanent publishing licenses were issued to certain publishers' (Tabriznia and Afghahi 2017: 19). There was a decrease with Ahmadinejad's first term, which banned altogether some writers, without allowing them to even go through the process of submitting their books to the Ministry (Marchant 2015: 17), and then another decrease at the beginning of his second term in 2009, which saw massive upheavals in the country and which had an important impact on literary life. Actors in the sector mention 'making up books' (*ketabsazi*, literally, building books) as a factor to take into consideration when counting books during Ahmadinejad's presidencies (Marchant 2015: 42; Shahneh Tabar, interview, 27 May 2014). This would allow the Iran Book House to count as books some texts which would usually not be included, such as academic theses or collections of academic articles. Such books would scarcely make a contribution to the book market, but the strategy has been used so as to save face and counter those who said book publication decreased dramatically during Ahmadinejad

(Marchant 2015: 17). Figure 4.3 shows similar data from the Iran Book House report, which includes a couple more years of data from Rouhani's presidency up to 2014, with a small increase in publications since. There are also small positive events in this period like the re-licensing of the independent publisher Cheshmeh in 2014.

One can see that the curves from the two reports are very similar, apart from a few discrepancies in the last years, maybe due to errors in data extraction. The fact that they are identical, although they have different agendas in producing the figures due to their different political belongings, is a sign that the data is solid.

Number of Books Published versus Number of Copies per Book

Literary practitioners in Iran say that the number of copies per book published is now at an extremely low number, but that this was not always the case. What do the numbers tell us? The two graphs of Figures 4.2 and 4.3 show the numbers of books published. An important aspect to remember is that the number of copies is a different matter altogether. There has indeed been a huge decline in number of copies published per book over the last decades. Whereas it used to be an average of 8,000 copies in the early years of the Islamic Republic, a standard number in the late 2010s is around 1,500 copies per book title. Figure 4.4 gives the average number of copies per book and confirms this drastic decline that literary practitioners mention (Tabriznia and Afghahi 2017: 34).

The fact that the price for books has increased drastically, in a shrinking economic space, might be a reason for this decline, although this does not explain everything. For example, between 2011 and 2014, the price of a book doubled in a period of four years (Gholami Jaliseh 2016/1394: 14). It is difficult to assess book price increase independently, because in Iran inflation has been high in the last forty years, for all consumer goods and services. The Central Bank of Iran notes there was a rise in products of 100 per cent during the same period. The rise of e-books, the ever-presence of pirated books, and the absence of copyright laws are other factors explaining this decrease, as I discussed at length in Chapter 3.

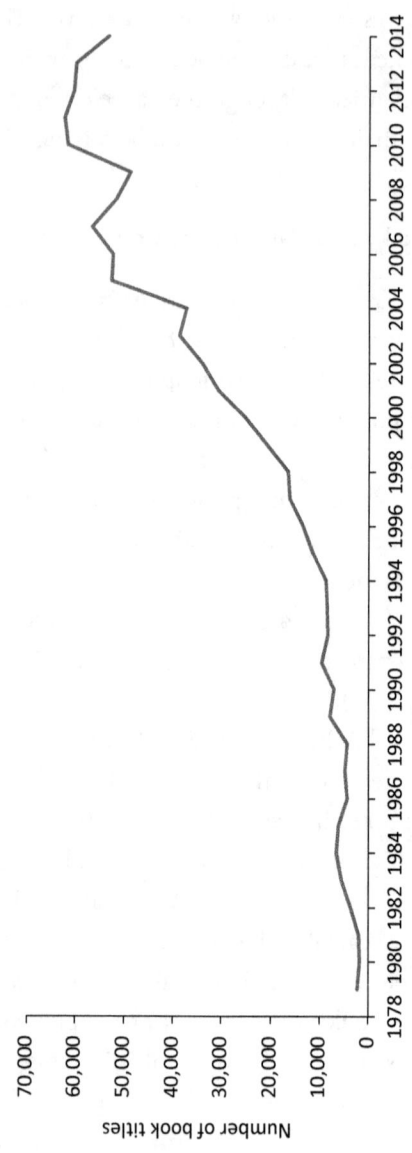

Figure 4.2 Number of book titles produced per year according to Small Media, from data extracted from the Small Media report.

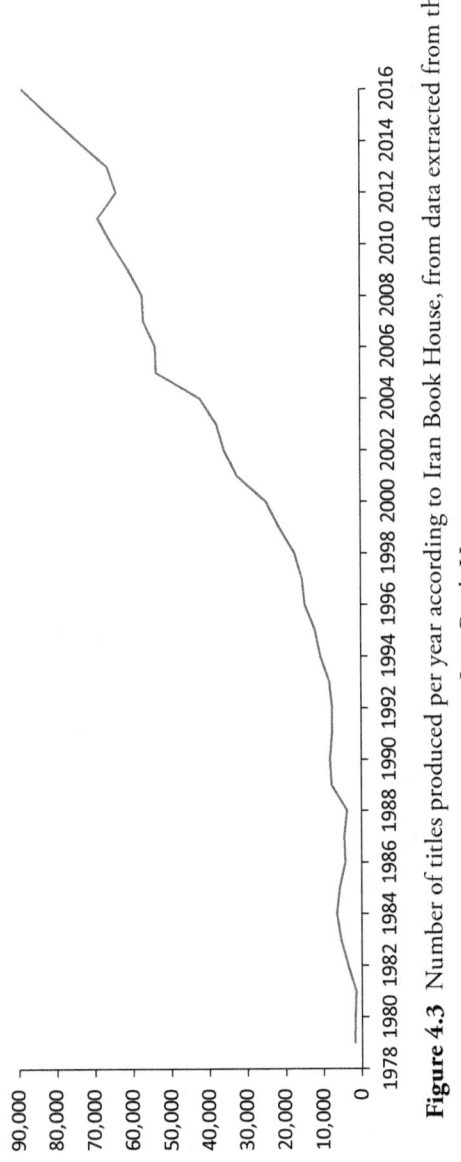

Figure 4.3 Number of titles produced per year according to Iran Book House, from data extracted from the Iran Book House report.

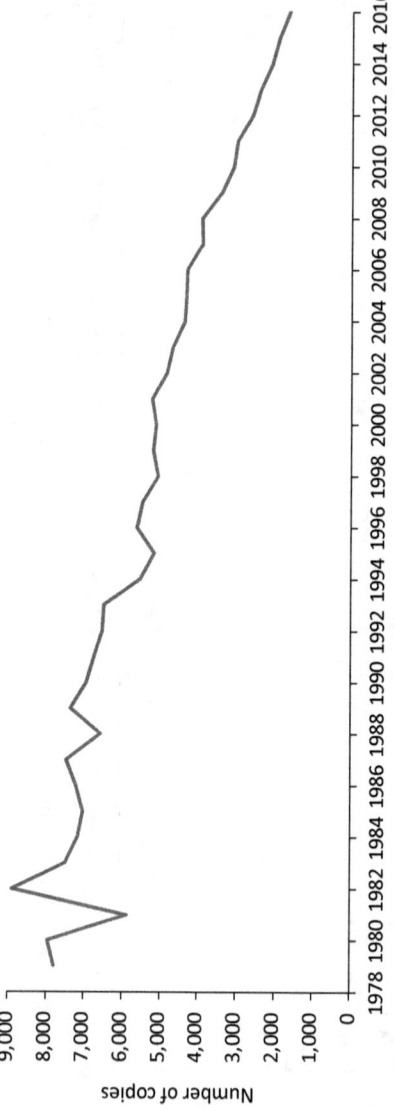

Figure 4.4 Average number of copies produced per book title per year, from data extracted from the Iran Book House report.

Categories of Books Published

Opinions vary on which categories of books are most published among literary practitioners, although many mention that religion is very high, a lot higher than literature. The Iran Book House discusses religion coming first with 17 per cent of publications, then children's and young adult literature, as well as applied sciences, each at 14 per cent, and literature 13 per cent (Tabriznia and Afghahi 2017: 21). Literature is thus relatively important compared with and almost on a par to the most published categories.

Gender of Literary Practitioners

I have not done a comparison of the gender of writers from the Excel sheets I have, since this would require assigning a gender to hundreds of thousands of names. Small Media's report on how the categories of books compare to the gender of writers seems to be a general appreciation, as they do not seem to have organised their data according to gender either. Small Media's report says:

> Women are most prolific in the sphere of literature; it is in this field that they comprise the greatest proportion of active authors. The proportion of women that have published works in the fields of technology and natural sciences is fairly similar to that of men . . . The least women-friendly genre is religion. Women face numerous obstacles in climbing the ranks of the clergy, and make up just a small contingent of the seminaries in Qom and Mashhad. As a result, male writers are responsible for much of Iran's religious output. (Marchant 2015: 29).

This can be compared to a general discourse that women are active as literary writers, as argued by journalists like Nazila Fathi: 'Over the past decade, Iran's best-selling fiction lists have become dominated by women, an unprecedented development abetted by recent upheavals in Iranian society' (Fathi 2005). She adds that women publish as much as men in today's Iran, 'but the women's books are outselling the men's by far'. Although Fathi does not confirm this with data, this is the perception in the field, maybe because women suddenly becoming active in the field makes them hyper-visible. The Iranian Students News Agency, a governmental institution, reports that, in the bestselling books over a fourteen-year period, the top three are by women. In the forty-seven books ranked, twenty are by women and twenty-seven by men ISNA (2006b). Farzaneh Milani confirmed this in her study: 'The number of women novelists now is 370 – thirteen times as many as ten years earlier and about equal to the number of men novelists' (Milani quoted in Fathi 2005).

Whereas women writers thus seem to be important in terms of numbers and reputation, this is not the case for other literary practitioners like publishers. The Iran Book House's revised report in English does not have statistics about the gender of writers, but it has them for the publishers: 'The female directors have published 13 percent of the books' (Tabriznia and Afghahi 2017: 85). This is indeed a very small number. Shahla Lahiji was the first woman to open a publishing house after the revolution; she started Entesharat-e roshangaran in 1983. The Cultural Institute for Women Publishers (*Anjoman-e farhangi-ye zanan-e nasher*) started in 1997, then disappeared, and re-opened in 2005. The environment for women publishers is volatile.

Translation versus Original

The issue of translated texts versus texts in Persian is a fraught one, as it relates to issues of dependency on foreign markets and foreign languages, and on the quality of local production compared to the foreign one. Therefore, it is crucial to get the numbers right. I discussed the issue of translated fiction texts versus texts from contemporary Iranian writers in the previous chapter, but here I am concerned with the numbers. There is no doubt that Iran publishes many translations. But so do a lot of non-English-speaking western countries. Gisèle Sapiro explains that in the late 1990s, the percentage of translated texts is '15–18% in France and Germany, 25% in Italy and Spain, 40% in Greece' (Sapiro 2015: 6). In literature, France publishes as much as 35 per cent of translations, and 'English is far and away the most translated language: it represents two thirds of the books translated into French' (Sapiro 2015: 6).

I have shown elsewhere, based on the UNESCO database *Index Translationum*, that English is the most translated language in Iran, with

> 7981 translations between 1979 and 2011, significantly more than French and Arabic, which account for only around 700 translations each. Despite

the official rhetoric of the Islamic government against its American counterpart and against imperialism, including cultural imperialism (*tahajom-e farhangi*), Iranian market trends are in accordance with American and English-speaking cultural dominance across the globe, as most of the translations into Persian of foreign-language texts are from English. In the same 30-year period, however, there have been only 350 translations from Persian in the US. (Nanquette 2017b: 3–4)

Because of the dominance of the book market in English, it is now a global phenomenon that all literatures translate a lot of English books. The fact that Iran, which is isolated somewhat from the global book market, follows similar trends, is noticeable in itself. That is, its isolation is not to the point where it would only publish local literature.

What is maybe more important is to look at the evolution of the field of translation. Have there been significant changes in the proportion of translations versus originals? Figure 4.5, from the Iran Book House report, shows an increase in the number of publications of original books compared to translations over the years (Tabriznia and Afghahi 2017: 26). Whereas in 1994, around one third were translations versus two thirds originals, in 2015, there were around 19 per cent of translations versus 81 per cent of originals. The production of books in Persian has increased four times more rapidly than that of translations in a thirty-year period. Is it due to policies that aimed to minimise cultural imperialism? Is it a consequence of the 'building up of books' (*ketabsazi*) of the two Ahmadinejad governments (2005–13) and the fact that most of the books with which *ketabsazi* is concerned, such as academic theses, except for those in language studies, are in Persian? The Iran Book House report warns against the possibility that this data might be difficult to analyse as originals include 'all the compilations, collections, poetry and etc' (Tabriznia and Afghahi 2017: 27).

I compare the graph of Figure 4.5 to the data for the category of literature I have gathered from the Iran Book House, bearing in mind that the comparison does not look at the same data, since the Iran Book House's report is for the whole of book publications, not literature only. This is to understand trends. In my data for literature, I take three years as indicative waypoints. In 1982, there were 276 translations versus 490 originals, so translation made

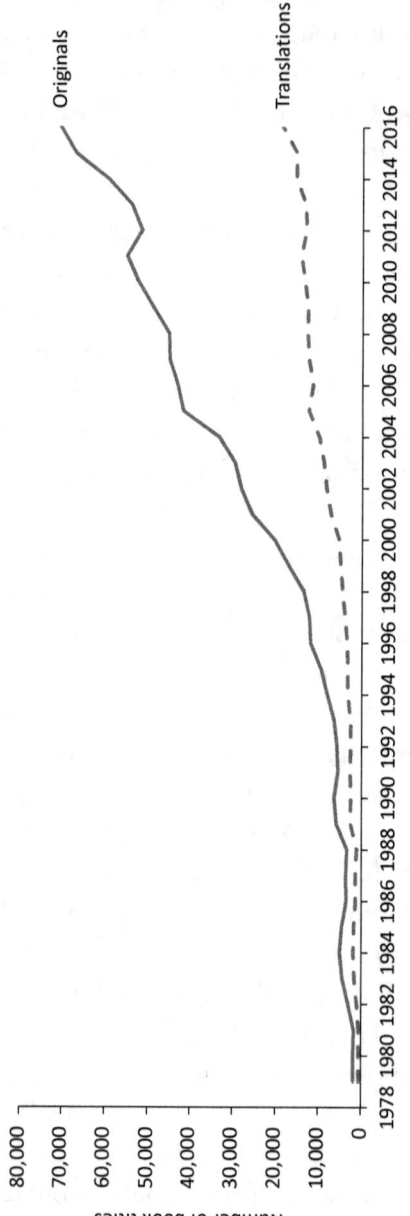

Figure 4.5 Number of book titles produced per year per type, from data extracted from the Iran Book House report.

up 37 per cent. In 2002, there were 5,556 originals versus 1,741 translations, so 24 per cent was translation. In 2012, there were 10,116 originals and 3,129 translations, close to 31 per cent of publications. This confirms the data for the whole of publications: there are more originals than translations in recent years than there were forty years ago. However, the numbers fluctuate. There is a general decrease of translations over the period, but in some years translations pick up. This contradicts parts of the discourse among local literary practitioners, who insist that translations are an increasing part of the market. This discrepancy is partly due to the fact that the literary practitioners I speak with are mostly in the field of literature, and not in applied sciences or religion. Indeed, the Persian version of the Iran Book House report on the books published in the year 2014 confirms the high percentage of translations in certain areas. The biggest area for translations is children and young adult's literature: 45 per cent of its publications come from translation; then come applied sciences at 30 per cent, then comes literature at 29 per cent. Other fields like religious or academic books are primarily originals (Gholami Jaliseh 2016/1394: 152). Chapter 5 is entirely devoted to the analysis of children's literature, as it represents a specific subfield with its own, quite successful, dynamics.

This data seems contradictory to the discourse in the field about the increase of the role of translations in literature. Indeed, when I browse bookshops in Tehran, I am always struck by the fact that foreign fiction seems more numerous than Persian. I elaborate on this in Chapter 1 as well as in the last chapter of the book. The perception in the field is that translations of fiction account for a good part of the sales. Critics often comment on the fact that Iranian readers do not read contemporary Iranian fiction. However, publications of original Iranian poetry might compensate for this, since they have increased over the last forty years. A study by Ali Khazaei Farid and Nasrin Ashrafi seems to confirm this hypothesis. It focuses on the category of '*dastan*' (story), and shows that the number of translations is more important than the number of originals (60% against 40%). However, there was a decrease of translations over the years from 65% in 2001 to 55% in 2010. The authors mention the policies of *bumi sazi* (indigenisation) of the Ahmadinejad governments (Khazaei Farid and Ashrafi 2013: 12) to explain this decrease of translation. This confirms that there has been a decrease of translations over the years, even in the field of literature, which is the field traditionally with a lot of translations. While the discourse in the field is about the dominance of translation, since most of my interviewees were referring to stories, not to other genres, and certainly not to poetry, which are less dependent on translations, this explains the discrepancy between the numbers and the discourse.

Centralisation of the Production

Iran's publishing industry is very centralised. Although I lived in Esfahan for a few months as a student and have spent extended time in Shiraz, I have myself mostly spent time in Tehran when working on the literary field. This is because most of the literary events and all the main publishers are in the capital. I have chosen to analyse the centralisation of the books' production on a given year to give an idea of the number of books published per year. The Iran Book House reports that although Tehran has always been the central point of publication, it has become increasingly so. The graph in Figure 4.6 confirms this argument (produced from data of Tabriznia and Afghahi 2017: 28). 'The publication of books in Tehran increases compared to all the other cities and this gap has widened in the recent years' (Tabriznia and Afghahi 2017: 29). This is in line with what I have noticed on the ground, where few literary activities happen even in major provincial cities like Esfahan or Shiraz. This is not particular to Iran though. The French literary field is also extremely centralised with most literary activities and prestigious centres in Paris.

The curve in black shows the production in Tehran and the dotted line indicates that in the provinces. Without the productions from Qom and Mashad, which are religious centres and thus account for a lot of religious texts, the production in provincial cities would be insignificant.

I compare this to the data for the year 2012, presented in Table 4.1. For a total of 13,245 books published, 9,957 were published in Tehran: that is 75 per cent. Although my data only contains books categorised as literature, the cities coming just after Tehran are cities where religious books are dominant, Qom and Mashad. The category of literature is large enough to include literary texts with religious elements but it excludes the vast production of

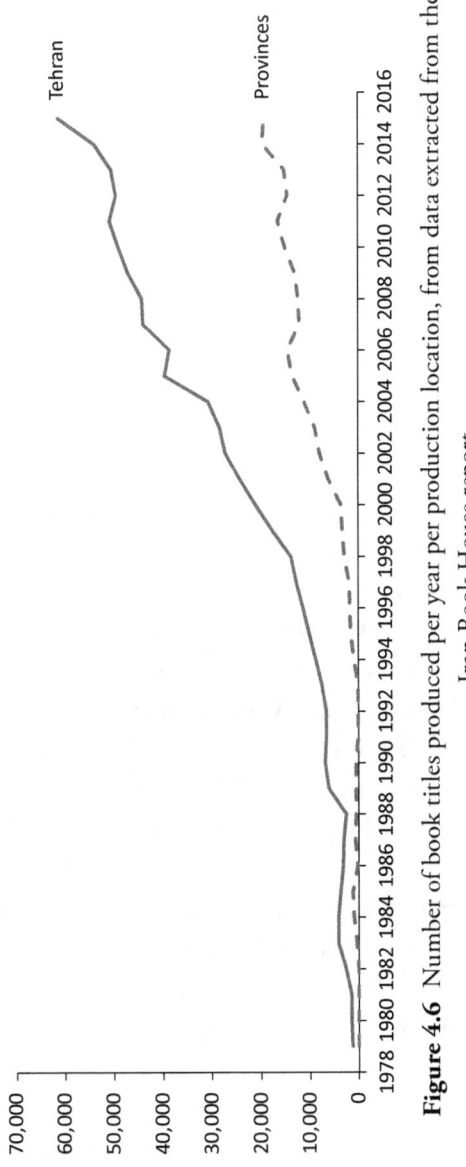

Figure 4.6 Number of book titles produced per year per production location, from data extracted from the Iran Book House report.

Table 4.1 Number of books published per city for the year 2012, from data extracted from the Iran Book House report.

Tehran	9,957
Qom	991
Mashhad	518
Tabriz	197
Esfahan	164
Rasht	144
Shiraz	138
Karaj	125
Qazvin	80
Kashan	56
Kerman	49
Sari	47
Semnan	45
Sanandaj	43
Zanjan	41

Quranic exegesis, biographies of Islamic figures or Islamic commentaries. Therefore, it might look different with the whole of books' production. The next major cities, Tabriz, Esfahan, Rasht, Shiraz and Karaj (a suburb of Tehran), publish less than 200 books per year. I have not included the cities publishing fewer than forty books per year.

Small Media, which considers all categories of books, says that 76 per cent of titles printed since the revolution have been produced in Tehran (Marchant 2015: 43), thus its number is very similar to mine, although it looks at the whole of the production during the period, while I look at one year only.

Why is centralisation important to consider? Small Media rightfully notes that the 'massive centralisation of production wouldn't be such a big deal if Iran had an effective distribution network to carry regionally-published books to the rest of the country, but the necessary infrastructure is concentrated almost exclusively in the capital' (Marchant 2015: 44). The centralisation of the production is indeed a concern since it is not compensated by good distribution networks. De facto, the provinces of Iran get scant access to new publications.

Are the Publishers Independent or Governmental?

Small Media notes that the most prolific publishers, maybe contrary to expectations, are not religious and governmental publishers, but publishers working in the academic field, although these are not mutually exclusive. The field of book exams preparation (*ketab-e konkur*) is huge. The entry examination to university (the *konkur*) is crucial to the higher education system and represents a whole industry in itself, with specialist publishers like Mobtakeran and Gaj competing for the market. The data I have includes the category of literature only, so does not take into account such books and academic textbooks, but one of the five most prolific publishers that Small Media underlines, Mobtakeran, is also in the top ten in literary publishing, according to the Excel sheets from the Iran Book House, so it overlaps with my data. Mobtakeran was established in 1986 and its stated aim is to increase scientific awareness. It is also heavily involved in educational activities pre- and post-university, holding a mathematics Olympiad and scientific workshops.

Of course, Figure 4.7 needs to be compared to the total number of books published. The Iran Book House reports that from 1979 to 2016, governmental publishers published only 12 per cent of books (Tabriznia and Afghahi 2017: 81). They show that most books are produced by independent publishers. Today, independent publishers publish seven times more books than governmental publishers (Tabriznia and Afghahi 2017: 78).

It is important to remember that even what I call independent publishers are not entirely independent from the government. I have explained at length in the introduction my use of the terms governmental versus independent, and what this entails. During some periods, most publishers received paper supplies from the government, which was an important financial contribution. It is also common for independent publishers to receive direct funding from the government occasionally; however, this issue is difficult to investigate, as an independent publisher, which builds its credentials on its independence from the government, would not want such assistance to be known about. Therefore, it is important not to draw a strict line between the two categories: all publishers in Iran, except the underground ones, have to stay in line with the government exigencies.

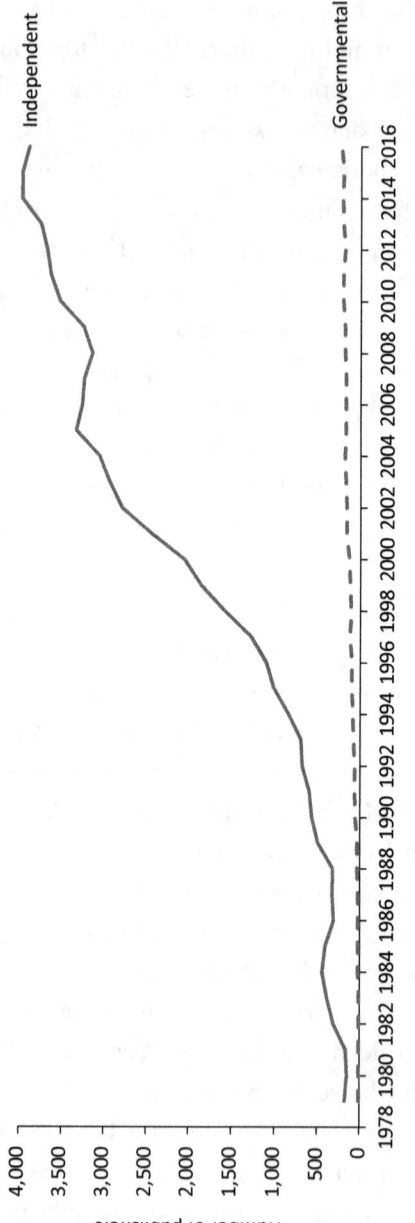

Figure 4.7 Number of publishers per type, from data extracted from the Iran Book House report.

These data clearly show that independent publishers are in a very large majority compared to governmental publishers in terms of numbers of books published, since they published 88 per cent of the total volume of books over the period 1979–2016. It is true that some governmental publishers are enormous in size thanks to the support they get, like Sureh Mehr, the publishing press of the Centre for Islamic Arts and Thought, but most of the production, in terms of numbers, is done by independents. The Iran Book House reports that 'even though the state-run publishers benefit from state budgets and generally do not rely on the income of their book sales, overall they cover 12 percent of the book market' (Tabriznia and Afghahi 2017: 83). This contradicts a recurrent discourse among scholars and literary practitioners working on contemporary Iranian literature. The data proves, to the contrary, that although governmental publishers do not really struggle because they do not need to abide by the law of the market since they are injected with money from the government, governmental publishers are a minority: most of Iran's book production comes from independent publishers. The independent publishers, on the other hand, often lack political support. This is not the case for all of them, as some are aligned with the ideas of the Islamic Republic, but the major literary independent publishers are usually not supported politically.

Underground Publications and Self-publishing

One could argue that underground publications come to disrupt this analysis and that not taking them into account in this chapter does not give a complete view of the field. It is true that underground publications are there, sometimes quite visible, especially in the publishing area around the University of Tehran in the centre of the capital, and this is why I have analysed them in qualitative terms in the previous chapter. However, as I argued in Chapter 3, my fieldwork has led me to the conclusion that it is actually quite a small proportion of original publications. Here I am not referring to the reprints, pirated and poor-quality copies of previously published books: this forms a huge market, where books circulate for a lower price than in bookshops. I am only concerned with new publications, since the circulation of pirated books is a question of circulation, not of production. As mentioned in the previous chapter, underground publication is not prestigious, and it is expensive since writers have to pay for publication themselves. Mohamad

Zendehru, a member of the Union of Tehran Publishers and Booksellers, states that self-publishing (*Khod-nasheri* or *Nasher-moalef*) can be divided into three types (Zendehru 2014):

- A writer gets a publishing permit from the Ministry of Culture and Islamic Guidance and publishes the book without having a publisher involved. There is no publisher's name for this type of books. Such books are often published by organisations and institutions that do not specialise in publishing.
- Writers pay fully or partly the expenses to a publisher.
- Online publication, which does not require permission from the Ministry of Culture and Islamic Guidance but follows the rules of the censorship of the internet. I have detailed this aspect of publications in Chapter 2.

While I expected more books to be published underground given the restrictions in publication, it is a marginal segment. There are important numbers of self-publishing houses, but they do not publish large quantities of books and often come and go rapidly. Their very number contributes to the issues faced by publishers who criticise the field's lack of professionalism. The Persian version of the Iran Book House report states that in the ten years between 1993 and 2014, 3,584 self-publishers have published one book each, while only ten have published more than fifty books (Gholami Jaliseh 2016/1394: 102).

Conclusion

Where is book production going? The data I have for literary publishing only goes until 2015–16, encompassing the first two to three years of Rouhani's first presidential term. This is too early to give definitive answers, but there seems to be a slight increase in publications. It was also a period where you could notice small positive changes like the re-licensing of the independent publisher Cheshmeh. Small Media and the Iran Book House have drastically different numbers of total publications for the latest years, which is interesting since they showed similar patterns in the earlier periods. However, what I have noticed during several fieldwork trips since 2013 is that publications have not increased as much as anticipated despite the reformist presidency of Rouhani. This might be due to the fact that *ketabsazi* has gone down but expectations of a boom in the cultural field after Rouhani were certainly not met. In general, only the Khatami years were overly positive for literary production.

This chapter is an example of the possibility to use methods and ideas from digital humanities in the analysis of contemporary Persian literature. Studying different resources, all devoted to book production, has produced verifiable and cross-checkable answers. These resources, all coming from the Iran Book House, have been selected and treated in different ways, and by two different institutions that have different aims and agendas in publicising them. The fact that they come from one source could be seen as an issue, but as I argued above, it is a relatively reliable source in the current Iranian context. The fact that the results nonetheless overlap, apart from the very last years, which are possibly subject to inaccurate recordings in the database, makes me confident in their validity in helping us to understand several elements in the field: the link between books' production and who is in government; the decline of the number of books published over the years since 1979; the decreasing amount of translations versus original texts; the increased centralisation of book production in Tehran; and the relative minority of governmental publishers compared to independent publishers. The conclusions in this chapter show that having a broad view of the field and using a variety of sources is key to understand it in all its complexities.

5

Iranian Children's Literature: A Success Story Nationally and Globally

At the Tehran International Book Fair, one of the biggest sections is devoted to children's books. It is a space that makes for a stark contrast from the austere booths of the Islamic publishers. It is filled with activities for kids, balloons, and families wandering joyfully. It was always a pleasure to wander in this section when I visited the Book Fair.

At the Book Garden (Bagh-e ketab), an enormous bookshop and learning centre which opened in 2017, the section of children's literature is also the most impressive and reflects the professionalisation as well as the worldly perspective of the field. Like in any big western bookshop with a children's section, there are statues of children's favourite characters and a whole array of consumer items linked to their stories: mugs, bags, and toys.[1]

These exemplify the important differences existing between the fields of adult and children's literature in Iran. They function separately, have different institutions and a different history. Children's literature has been more successful internationally than Iranian adult fiction and it is also a field that is more professionalised than the one for adults. In this chapter, I analyse children's literature to understand phenomena that have been occurring in

---

[1] The place belongs to Tehran Municipality and was constructed during Mohammad Baqer Qalibaf's term as mayor. It is interesting to note that the whole area, which also comprises the National Library and the Museum of Sacred Defence, is rather welcoming, with greenery and fountains, and does not compare with other austere Islamic buildings. Thanks to Omid Azadibougar for pointing this out as well as for his helpful feedback on this chapter.

Figure 5.1 The Book Garden in Tehran, Children's literature section, author's picture.

the larger field. The chapter analyses the history of Iranian children's literature in the past decades, zooms in on the important institutions supporting it, and theorises both its importance to the Islamic republic and its reception nationally and globally, explaining its relative success. This chapter forms a bridge between the two parts of the book, the first one being on the literary production within Iran and the second one on circulation outside of the country. The chapter touches upon these two elements as children's literature is a genre that has been produced with visibility nationally and that has travelled internationally more than other genres, which is why I devote some space to its study. It is a case study for a success story for contemporary Iranian literature.

In post-revolutionary authoritarian Iran, children's literature has been invested in by the Islamic Republic regime because of its usefulness. Authoritarian regimes control culture as much as they do politics and they start with the child because she is the new citizen who needs to be taught the new values. The Soviet Union invested similarly in teaching the Soviet child its values, as testified in the Cotsen Children's Library archive of Princeton University Library. This strategic development of the child however is by no means specific to authoritarian regimes. Jacqueline Rose, in her study of the classic Peter Pan entitled 'The Impossibility of Children's Fiction', argues that the writer is addressing an ideal child and rarely has real readers in mind. For her, the child in children's literature is always an adult fantasy (Rose 1984). What we see is a heightened degree of fantasy in authoritarian regimes' children's literature.

Brief History of Children's Books

The definition of what constitutes children's literature can be contentious. I use the definition from *The Encyclopedia Iranica*: 'Children's literature is a genre employing themes, language, and illustrations geared to the developmental levels of children, introduced in Persia in the 13th/19th century' (Ayman 2011). In her thesis, Nafisa Abdelsadek considers classical tales like *Kalilah va Dimnah* or *The Shahnameh* as part of the network of children's literature. It is true that these texts have been read to and by children for hundreds of years, but in this chapter, I am concerned with children's literature as a distinct field, produced and distributed for children only. Children's literature as a genre specifically directed to children is relatively recent in Iran, as in many countries. Although there existed moralistic tales and poems for entertaining children, children's literature only came as a specific genre in western countries around the eighteenth century with writers like John Newbery and Jean-Jacques Rousseau. In Iran, in the nineteenth century, Mirza Mahmud Khan Meftah-al-Molk's *Disciplining Children* (*Ta'dib al-atfal*) is seen as the first Persian book for children. It is 'a collection of twenty-one stories translated from Arabic translations of French originals' (Ayman 2011). 'Meftāh-al-Molk noted that, in his translation, he had avoided rhymes, Arabic phrases, and didactic verses, in order to render the text more accessible to children. The black-and-white illustrations were by contemporary Persian artists' (Ayman 2011). In the first half of the twentieth century, an increase in children's books went along with attempts to modernise the education system. Increasingly, translations of European children's stories were published, magazines for children were produced and well-known writers began to write children's stories. This was part of a worldwide movement, 'connected with post-Second World War reconstruction and revival of economies, as well as developments in society such as improvement in healthcare, education, and employment opportunities' (Abdelsadek 2011: 152).

In 1958, Mehdi Azar Yazdi published *Good Stories for Good Children* (*Qesseh-ha-ye khub baraye bache-ha-ye khub*), a collection of classical Persian stories like *Kalila va Dimnah* and *Golestan*, simplified for children, which has been a bestseller since. I remember still seeing these books in every bookshop in Tehran fifty years later and having read some of them to practise my Persian. Azar Yazdi won a UNESCO award in 1966 for his work, as well as the Imperial Award for Book of the Year in 1967. Today, the Iranian national day for children and young adult literature bears his name.

Iranian Institutions Devoted to Children's Literature and Culture

The 1950s and especially the 1960s were crucial for the development of institutions that helped built a professional children's literature field. It is noteworthy that such institutions have been critical in Iran to develop what was long seen as a field unworthy of research and efforts. Today, largely thanks to them, it is one of the most dynamic sections of the literary field, in many ways more professional than adult literature, as I detail later. The history of the development of children's books is entangled with that of institutes devoted to children's education. The fact that these institutes have persisted for decades, throughout the twentieth and twenty-first centuries, alerts us to the continuities in the field of children's literature. The revolution was a major turning point, at which most of the staff of these institutes changed, but Abdelsadek shows convincingly that there are also many things that did not change and that some of the changes were superficial. For example, the Institute for Translation and Publication of Books (*Bongah-e tarjomeh va nashr-e ketab*), directed by Ehsan Yarshater, made 'a systematic effort to provide reading materials for children from kindergarten through adolescence' (Ayman 2011). These were mostly translations from classic western works, with a lot of young adult fiction. When analysing its work, she argues:

> a considerable number of the Bongah's publications were reprinted after 1979, indicating that despite the mergers and new names, much of the early work of the organization was still found to be acceptable and continued to

be published and read even after the changes brought about by the Islamic Revolution. (Abdelsadek 2011: 157)

In 1962, a group of educators founded the Children's Book Council, or CBC (*Shora-ye ketab-e kudak*), which became a crucial institution for the development of Iranian children's literature, on which I write more below. In 1965, in an effort to develop literacy and culture throughout the country, the Empress Farah supported the creation of the important Centre for the Intellectual Development of Children and Young People (*Kanun-e parvaresh-e fekri-ye kudakan va nowjavanan*), shortened as the *Kanun*. This has been influential since, not only in children's literature but also, as I show in Chapter 9, in music, film and visual arts, as well as in creating public libraries – including in the provinces, often neglected in Iran which is very centralised. The *Kanun* also owns the largest network of English institutes in Iran, the Iran Language Institute. It has a significant function because it makes accessible English children's literature, cartoons, satellite channels, and so on. As mentioned above, the *Kanun* produced films and its key role in building Iranian cinema after the revolution is well recognised in Iranian cinema scholarship. It also acted as a meeting place for many cultural practitioners and helped forge connections. In particular the *Kanun* produced a lot of the films that have children at their centre that formed part of what has been called the Iranian New Wave. Child characters are in a way easier to use since they do not have to abide by the strict modesty laws surrounding men and women's behaviour. Scholars like Hamid Reza Sadr discuss child characters in Iranian films in the first two decades after the revolution, like Bahram Beyzai's *Bashu, Little Stranger* (1986), or Abbas Kiarostami's *Where is the Friend's House* (1987). In addition to the support of the *Kanun*, the topic of children and their filming were less subject to censorship (Sadr 2002). This is also the case with the publication of children's literature by the *Kanun*. Although it is critical to understand the role of censorship in the production of children's literature and cinema using children, it is also important to remember that indirectness or what scholars like Michelle Langford call allegory, is a critical component of Iranian cultural production. Langford shows that Iranian cinema uses allegorical techniques not only to avoid censorship, but as a way of crafting stories (Langford 2019).

In terms of book publishing for children, the *Kanun* emphasised original work, many based on folktales. As a result of these institutes' efforts, children's literature started to carve itself a place in the Iranian literary field: 'Toward the end of the decade children's literature was introduced into the curriculum of Persian teachers' colleges' (Ayman 2011). The *Kanun* is relatively independent as it is not directly linked to the Ministry of Culture and Islamic Guidance and thus its production follows specific regulations, which are more flexible. Most importantly, the *Kanun* has its own censorship system. Like the publisher Sureh Mehr discussed in Chapter 1, it does not have to go through the Ministry of Culture and Islamic Guidance for approval. This gives it enormous autonomy. The *Kanun* and the Children's Book Council (CBC),

> while complementing each other, focus on different areas involved in the production of children's literature; the CBC deals with fixing criteria, selecting works and compiling book lists, training critics, international liaison, and awards, whereas the Kanun is involved with the publication and distribution of books. (Abdelsadek 2011: 153)

With the Islamic Revolution, children's literature took a different turn. Children's literature was seen as a way for the new Islamic government to implement the 'Neither Western nor Eastern' motto and to give new meanings to the idea of the child. The CBC and the *Kanun* continued their activities nonetheless, with different management. In the early years of the revolution and until the end of the 1980s, many of the books published by the *Kanun* were on the themes promoted by the Islamic Republic regime. 'Of 332 children's books published by the Kānūn between 1358 Š./1979 and 1368 Š./1989 at least eighty were on themes related to religion, the revolution, and support of the war with Iraq' (Ayman 2011). This tendency subsided in subsequent years, and one could see books on more diverse topics. Writers like Houshang Moradi Kermani, who writes about rural life and about poor families, based on his own experience, have been very successful after the revolution. His writing fits well with the ideas of the revolution, promoting the lives of the downtrodden (*mostaz'afin*). It also depicts Iranian traditional life, far away from the concerns of big cities. Interestingly, he is also one of the writers who is well translated into European languages and tours the world to meet Iranian communities.

There have been some endeavours to create forums like the *Kanun* that would be entirely independent and not under the umbrella of the government, but most have not succeeded. Mehdi Hojvai recalls the foundation of the journal *Domain of Children Literature* (*Qalamrow-ye adabiyyat-e kudakan*), founded by independent writers, which stopped after six issues. He also recalls how some members of the group, including Amir Hossein Fardi, Hossein Fatahi, Sousan Taghdis and himself started a weekly meeting in the library of *Park-e shahr* and requested the Ministry of Culture and Islamic Guidance to grant them a forum permit, but were denied it (Hojvani 2001: 34–6).

An institution like the Children's Book Council has been central to the development of children's literature as a field. A non-governmental organisation founded by Touran Mirhadi, until the revolution, it was headed by Leyli Imen. As stated on its website, it 'joined the International Board on Books for Young People in 1964 and represents the Iranian National Section'. After Imen, Noushafarin Ansari became the head and has been in this role since. The key achievement of the Children's Book Council has been *The Encyclopaedia for Young People*. An Institute for Research on the History of Children's Literature in Iran (*Daftar-e ta'lif-e farhangnameh-ye kudakan va nowjavanan*) was established under the supervision of the Children's Book Council board of directors, with Touran Mirhadi as the manager of the encyclopaedia. The first encyclopaedia volume was published after thirteen years in 1992. It had published sixteen volumes in 2018, with a total of twenty-five anticipated. The encyclopaedia is written for an audience consisting of children and teenagers aged from ten to sixteen. The reasons for creating a new encyclopaedia and not translating the international encyclopaedias for children and young adults is linked to the fact that the members of the Institute thought that western encyclopaedias had biases, especially when narrating ancient history. Western encyclopaedias mostly point to Greece as the origin of most human thinking and inventions, whereas Iranian scholars have different views (Daralshafaei 2013: 153). The members also had a different version of the history of Islam to tell. The encyclopaedia, managed by Mirhadi until her death in 2016, came out of progressive educational methods that Mirhadi implemented in a school setting – especially in the Farhad school – inspired by educational methods like Montessori's, where the child, not the teacher, is at the centre of the education system. This translated into the encyclopaedia's writing by the fact that groups of children and teenagers are always part of the writing project. They are consulted on entries to the encyclopaedia and experts take their guidance into consideration. As such, the child reader is at the centre of this work (Bani-Etemad and Mir-Tahmasb 2018).

Concerning the relationship of institutes of children's literature to the government, Abdelsadek argues: 'The number of non-governmental institutes working in the field of children's literature in Iran is increasing, and this is one of the major differences between the pre-revolution and the post-revolution period, especially the post-Khatami period' (Abdelsadek 2011: 160). There is, for example, the Association of Writers for Children and Youth (*Anjoman-e nevisandegan-e kudakan va nowjavanan*), a non-governmental organisation and independent association. It was established in 1999 by a founding board of nine writers of children's and young adult literature.

The increase in the production of children's books is up to the point where these have been the most published books, after religious books, since the revolution.

> The greatest increase has been in the number of titles of children's books. During the eight years before the revolution, a total of 1,541 children's books were published. By 1992, the annual number of children's book titles published, including translations, averaged 1,500 titles, and the total number of copies printed surpassed all other categories, averaging about 15 million. (Siavoshi 1997: 520)

This is confirmed in the data from the Iran Book House I analysed in the previous chapter. Whereas religious books account for 17 per cent of the total production, children's books come close with 14 per cent (Gholami Jaliseh 2016/1394: 25).

Why is Children's Literature an Important Field for the Islamic Republic Regime?

The fact that there is less potential to be censored in children's books partly accounts for the popularity of the field. Children's books can relatively easily avoid topics dealing with morality or politics and can present stories that have clear messages for the young reader. One can see a parallel in films produced in the early years after the revolution, when many of the well-known filmmakers preferred child actors.

> Their prevalence [children's prominence in movies] was driven by film organizations making child-centered films, such as the Center for the Intellectual Development of Children and Young Adults (CIDCYA), which spanned the second Pahlavi and the Islamic Republic periods, and by the new regime's gender segregation and censorship politics, which encouraged directors to use children as substitutes for females. (Naficy 2012: 209)

The *Kanun* was crucial in driving such films with children to the fore, as it was in driving children's book publication.

However, I want to insist on the fact that the Islamic Republic's focus on children's literature is not only a factor shaped by negative forces like censorship. It is also a positive endeavour – in the sense that it is not only a reaction – to redefine the human as Islamic. As discussed in Chapter 3, censorship has to be seen in its prescriptive aspects, not only as a prohibitive force. The revolution was also cultural and was aimed at creating a new Islamic being. Children's books are a way to create this Islamic being more easily than to redefine university students as Islamic, who are already adults with ideas and opinions. I have also shown in Chapter 3 how the cultural revolution that was aimed at Islamising universities was largely a failure, in that although many professors left and were replaced, the content of the education was not dramatically revised. Children's books are not only produced in mass because it is easier and less risky to do, but also because they represent a field in which the Islamic Republic regime has to be heavily invested if it wants to take its revolution to the core of the human.

An article published by the Institute for the Compilation and Publication of Imam Khomeini's Works (*Moasseseh-ye tanzim va nashr-e asar-e Imam Khomeini*) underlines this endeavour and insists on the fact that their goals were to get rid of the values of the aristocratic and consumerist (*masraf zadeh*) system of the Shah, to be replaced with stories about the values of the revolution like war, martyrdom and the fight against colonialism (Parviz 2018). It insists that it is important to write without metaphor nor 'secret' (*ramzi*) and that children's literature should show the true and realist aspects of Iranian society, including through stories on rural life, which represent a simple life favoured by the Islamic Republic regime. As a conservative institution, it is critical of some of the work of the Children's Book Council or the *Kanun*, which it sees as excessively promoting western ways of writing children's books, which do not integrate much religion.

It is crucial to note that the number of translated texts in children's books has decreased dramatically over the decades, compared to original works. An important endeavour after the revolution was precisely to be less dependent on western powers and create original Iranian stories. In less ideological terms, there was a desire to 'find ways of publishing more science books based on the fauna and flora of Iran, as well as to improve the quality and the accuracy of translations' (Abdelsadek 2011: 164). This has largely succeeded, as we can see from the evolution of the percentage of original works versus translation. In 1968, it was 17 per cent; in 1975, 27 per cent; in 1988, 50 per cent (Hojvani 2001: 25). These numbers overlap with those discussed in the previous chapter.

Children's literature is important to any political system that trains children to respect certain values, but it is more urgent and critical for ideological regimes. It becomes a means through which to shape the future, by shaping the thinking of its future men and women. In Iran, governmental institutes have heavily invested in the field since the revolution. But so have non-governmental institutes, as we have seen with the example of *The Encyclopaedia for Young People*, which is an endeavour that presents a different view of human history from that developed by western knowledge, although it does not strictly follow the expectations of the state either. In a film about Touran Mirhadi's life, it appears clearly that the *Encyclopaedia* aims to give a better understanding of Iran to Iranian children and that it is reliant on knowledge produced by the west only up to a certain extent. As such, it appears as a national scholarly endeavour, insisting on the unity of the Iranian nation. The very existence of a film on Mirhadi, by the famous director Rakhshan Bani-Etemad, shows the importance of the figures of children's literature and its development in the cultural context of Iran (Bani-Etemad and Mir-Tahmasb 2018). It is also a clear example of the links between the field of cinema and the field of children's literature through the portrayal of this female figure.

Despite its involvement in building a new Islamic child, there are limits to what the Islamic Republic regime can control and do. One of the reasons for that is the overlapping of institutions and the multiplicity of decision-making centres, as I have shown in Chapter 3. Another factor is the arrival of new technologies, especially the arrival of satellite TV in the 1990s and internet in the 2000s. Despite satellite TV being banned since 1994, it is widely used by large segments of the population. TV programmes, which are widely viewed by children, convey different messages from children's books. In the first decades after the revolution for example, Japanese cartoons were the primary cartoons children watched because they were easier to access due to the sanctions, more in line with the ideology of the Islamic Republic regime than western cartoons, and children generally enjoyed them more than the low-quality puppet animations made nationally. After that, satellite TV changed the viewership, and the programmes became a lot more diverse. Western cartoons have been favourites for decades. It is difficult for the state to control satellite TV. It has thus proven impossible for the political system to monopolise the field of children's culture, although it is a field where it had a lot of impact. This is partly because when market trends diversify, like with the advent of new technologies, it becomes impossible to monitor the variety of products available. Once the market makes its entrance into a state-dominated field, the state will often lose some of its power as it cannot control the diversity of the expectations of audience.

National and International Recognition Linked to Professionalisation of the Field and Quality of Illustrations

Unlike adult books which – as is evident throughout this book – have been slow to gain international recognition, Iranian children's books have been globally recognised for several decades. There are three main reasons for this global success: the field has been supported by powerful institutions nationally; from early on, the field was professionalised; and quality illustrations have played an important part in their success. Another factor contributing to this success is that the children's books circulating globally are not heavily politically oriented. The international market is often different from the internal one, as we see with Iranian cinema and as I analyse in the last chapter. It is not entirely the same products circulating globally and nationally.

Having discussed the institutions above, I would like to analyse the field's professionalisation and the role of illustrations as crucial to the development of the field of children's literature. Whereas Iranian adult literature only started to use literary agents quite recently, after around 2005, children's literature is a field that has seen the potential for using agents earlier; it also became more professional several decades earlier. This is partly due to the work done at the institutional level. Once support institutions like the *Kanun* were in place, it was easier for other industry professionals to develop around the field, including literary agents, who play a crucial part in the global circulation of literary texts. It is through agents that rights are sold in international children's literature book fairs, rights for the text as well as derived products, which are important in children's literature (paraphernalia with characters from the book for example). Book fairs are, in western countries, the primary place for exchanging literary texts and their rights. Kia Literary agency, headed by Lili Hayeri Yazdi, an example of an agency specialised in children's books, started its activities in 2002. Before starting her own agency, she had worked for the *Kanun* as a cultural adviser and rights manager, promoting the books of the *Kanun* in the book fairs (Hayeri Yazdi, phone interview with author, 5 April 2018), showing again the link with the institutions discussed earlier. Very early on, despite the fact that Iran was not a signatory of the Berne Convention, the *Kanun* had been buying rights for foreign children's books, establishing itself as a fair player in the children's book market. Iranian children's book publishers today benefit from several decades of this fair play. Foreign publishers see them as fair players, in opposition to some adult publishers, and there is a trust that has been built over decades. As the illustrator and animator Noureddin Zarrinkelk, who was involved in the beginnings of the *Kanun*, comments: 'One of the reasons why Kanun was well recognised, on an international scale, was the mature, balanced, and gentle relationship it had with other countries' (Daryaee and Beigpour 2016: 5).

Finally, the good quality of the illustrations accompanying the text has been crucial to the international success of Iranian children's books. Worldwide, 'the inclusion of illustrations in books for children became a more common feature as the cost of printing fell in the twentieth century, and became a convention that indicated that the work was intended for children' (Abdelsadek 2011: 234). Illustrations are so important to Iranian children's books that often foreign publishers only buy the illustrations, preferring to add their own text, according to Hayeri Yazdi (phone interview with author, 2018). This overreliance on the visual aspects of children's literature is important to understand some of its global success. As I demonstrate in Chapter 9, Iranian visual arts are increasingly recognised internationally and benefit from private and governmental support. The illustrations of children's books add to the success of Iranian cinema and visual arts, which I expand on in the last chapter. One can link this success to the illustration component of children's literature, which is similarly well supported. In 1989, there was the first exhibition of illustrations for children and young adults' books at the Contemporary Art Museum in Tehran, an institution I discuss in Chapter 9. It was a prestigious event, sponsored by the Ministry of Culture and Islamic Guidance, named 'Children's Book Illustrators in Iran' (Abdelsadek 2011: 240). It was followed in 1991 by the First Asian Biennial of the Works of Illustrators of Children's Books in Tehran. In 1993, this Biennial became an international one. Another important exhibition in this area is the Cartoon Biennial of Tehran, also held in the Tehran Museum of Contemporary Arts from 1993. The entanglement of children's literature with visual arts, seen here in the link with the Tehran Museum of Contemporary Arts, partly explains its international success. As I explain in more detail in Chapter 9, there is a movement from literature to visual arts, and the importance of illustration for children's literature is a crucial example of it.

Before the revolution, in 1974, famous illustrator Farshid Mesghali received the international Hans Christian Andersen Medal for his lasting contribution to children's illustration. He has been living in the USA since the 1980s. Iranian illustrators have continually received recognition at children's book fairs: for example, Mohammad-Ali Bani-Asadi who won the New Horizon Award of the 2012 Bologna Children's Book Fair and in 2015 the Hans Christian Andersen award. 'Between 1360 Š./1981 and 1368 Š./1989 ten children's books published by the Kānūn won awards for their illustrations in international competitions' (Ayman 2011). As a comparison, writers of children's books have often been nominated for international awards but did not win the prizes: 'Among these individuals, some of our authors have been nominated for the Hans Christian Andersen Award: Hooshang Moradi Kermani in 1992, Mohammad Reza Yousefi in 2000 and most recently M. H. Mohammadi the candidate for 2006' (Ghaeni 2006, 18). Farhad Hassanzadeh has been nominated for the international Astrid Lingren Award 2017 and for the Hans Christian Andersen Award 2018.

The Iranian Illustrators Society (*Anjoman-e tasvirgaran-e Iran*) is an institution supporting Iranian illustrators. It is a mostly independent group of critics, writers and illustrators working in the field, that influence the profession by introducing the best books each year – sometimes these include foreign books – and organising a prize, the Flying Turtle Award (*Lakposht-e parandeh*), which is crucial in the field of illustration. Flying Turtle compiles a list of selected books each season by evaluating published books and at the end of the year gives Golden and Silver Flying Turtles to the best books of the year. All foreign books contained in this catalogue enjoy a 'Translation & Publication Grant Program' given by the Ministry of Culture and Islamic Guidance. Like most literary institutions, even some of the independent ones, it benefits from subsidies from the government. It is interesting to note that there is a combination of independent and governmental links: they organise the Flying Turtle Award in coordination with Book City as well as with the Children's Literature Studies Periodical, which are independent organisations.

There is another institution that is specifically supporting illustrators, through its support to book fairs, which is the Iran Cultural Fairs (*Moasseseh-ye namayeshgah-ha-ye farhangi*), which belongs to the Ministry of Culture and Islamic Guidance. It was established in 1992 to organise cultural events, especially the Tehran International Book Fair, as well as fairs at home and abroad, in order to promote books and reading. It is a purely governmental institution, so many illustrators would prefer not to work with it and choose instead to get help from the Iranian Illustrators Society or the *Kanun*. As in adult fiction, there is rivalry between governmental and independent publishers for influence. My analysis has shown that the institutions most relevant and with most prestige in the field of children's literature are the independent ones. Although being mostly independently funded, they sometimes receive support from the government, in the form of loans, free paper and so on.

Illustrations of good quality, that appeal to foreign publishers, have largely contributed to the international success of Iranian children's literature. It is also the case that the field became professionalised earlier than adult literature, with important and powerful institutions supporting it and helping to develop a whole industry, including new literary persons, literary agents, who almost do not exist outside of children's literature. The field of children's literature is a success story that shows what happens when a field gets support. Increasingly, the industry around it develops itself and if there is good enough quality, receives international recognition. This is precisely what has been lacking in adult literature, which has been struggling on its own. The support to the independent field is negligible; only the governmental literary field gets appropriate support, but the products are too specific and too ideologically oriented to be of interest to a large literary market. Even if they circulate in a Muslim, mainly Shia, context, their outreach is limited to that sphere. In this sense, children's literature is quite similar to post-revolutionary Iranian cinema and, up to a point, visual arts, which has benefited from various support and which has been recognised internationally for a long time, as I show in the final chapter of this book.

Conclusion

This chapter has traced the history of contemporary children's literature in Iran, especially by discussing the institutions promoting it in the post-revolutionary period. They are noteworthy because of their long history and survival after the revolution. Although they adapted to the new Islamic context, it is important to note that they have been built on a solid tradition of children's literature. These institutions are in large part an explanation for the circulation and success of Iranian children's literature nationally and worldwide. Their history has helped to make the field professional for several decades, something which is still in progress in adult fiction. Another important aspect to explain the healthy functioning of children's literature is the quality of the illustrations, which play an important role in their circulation, and sometimes even the main one. One can thus see the entanglement of children's literature with visual arts, a field I discuss in the final chapter where I compare literature to other media.

This chapter concludes the first part of the book, where I have discussed the production and circulation of Iranian literature within Iran. In the second part, I move to these topics outside of the Iranian borders and analyse the literary relations between the Iranian diaspora and Iran as well as the circulation of Iranian literature in languages other than Persian for non-Iranian readers.

PART 2
THE LITERARY FIELD IN THE DIASPORA

6

Iran and the Diaspora: Irreconcilable Divisions?

In an interview with the renowned filmmaker, Dariush Mehrjui, Shiva Rahbaran discusses the relations between Iran and the diaspora:

> Shiva Rahbaran: 'In the eyes of many Iranians in exile, you are an ally of the regime.'
> Dariush Mehrjui: 'Yes, I know. You in exile believe that anyone who lives in Iran is a traitor.' (Rahbaran and Mohajer 2016: 97)

I would argue that the reverse is also true: Iranian writers within Iran believe those who have left are traitors. This is an exaggeration and provocation, and is valid for literary practitioners mostly, and I explore all the nuances to these points in this chapter, but the overall framework is that of a division between the two entities of Iranian literature: within Iran and in the diaspora. This division is especially the case if Iranian writers use a language other than Persian. The idea that Iranians should be faithful to their native language is prevalent, and the use of an adopted tongue is often frowned upon, even if many Iranians celebrate the success of writers from Iran who get recognised in western countries.

When I started working on the literary production of the Iranian diaspora, at first in France, I expected to work on the multiple exchanges and collaborations between Iranians across the world. It is only slowly that the evidence of my findings led me to the conclusion that, although the discourse of collaboration is there among certain Iranians, the reality is different and what is striking is rather the scarcity of the diaspora–Iran exchanges when it comes to literature. It is important to reiterate that this is not so much the case in other arts, music, cinema, visual arts, which are benefitting from more international connexions. In the literary field, there are many people who work hard to make such connections become a reality but this is still a work in progress.

This chapter argues that the Iranian diaspora is a case of a diaspora spread widely, that is relatively well-connected otherwise, but not when it comes to global literary exchanges. It reflects on the division that exists between literary practitioners who leave Iran and those who stay. Diaspora writers deal with a crisis of legitimacy within Iran. Mistrust between Iranians from within and the diaspora is still prevalent, due to historical and political grudges. The fact that books by Iranians published abroad are banned in Iran or cannot be easily bought increases these tensions. The divide is visible in the gap between the market within and outside Iran, while cooperation only occurs on a small scale. I study some examples of attempts to overcome the division of the diaspora as well as the blockages to cooperation, such as the initiatives of the publishers Naakojaa and Candle & Fog, and literary blogs in the diaspora based on interviews and case studies with literary practitioners from the US, the UK, Iran, France and Australia. I show how the gap between Iran and its diaspora translates when applied to cultural production. Like some scholars of the Chinese diaspora, such as Shu-mei Shih in her essay 'Against Diaspora' (2010) or Rey Chow's 'Against the Lures of the Diaspora' (1993), I disagree with the idea that diasporic formations necessarily have to be cohesive and coherent to have a positive impact on their members. Many scholars working on Iran whom I expand on in the chapter have discussed the lack of cohesiveness of the Iranian diaspora and warn us against the idea of fetishising diasporic formations. To me, this lack of coherence can be a positive factor that shows Iranians' deep commitment to their new place of living, self-reflective understanding of their positioning within the society and reluctance to frame themselves as an 'Other', whatever this means. The chapter does not offer close readings of texts published by diaspora writers, like the memoir *Reading Lolita in Tehran* by Azar Nafisi or the graphic novel *Persepolis* by Marjane Satrapi, as they have been extensively studied. It gives an overview of the literary Iranian diaspora and discusses its relations to the literary field within Iran. The two need to be seen as separate entities as their dynamics are distinct. There is thus a literary field in Iran and a diasporic Iranian literary field.

The Iranian Diaspora: What Does it Look Like?

In this section, I give an overview of the Iranian diaspora itself and its cohesiveness. I discuss questions of identity briefly, because identity has been at the core of the last few decades' research on Iranians in the diaspora, before focusing on its literary aspects. Using the term Iranian diaspora means that there is a community of reference. I show in the first section that this community is contested and certainly not unified but has valence nevertheless. Amy Malek rightfully describes the evolution of the use of the term: 'while originally considered as *exiles*, Iranians became more frequently described as part of a *diaspora*, reflecting the growth of Iranian communities and institutions, and shifts in their self-identifications in the intervening years' (Malek 2015: 26).

Overview of the Iranian Diaspora

As explained in the introduction, I loosely use Cohen's reflections on the notion of diaspora. Iranians in the diaspora can be divided according to their education, host country, class, date of arrival, political affiliation and religion. The response of the host society to the Iranian community is also crucial to the form it takes and its evolution. In Chapters 6, 7 and 8, I reflect on how the different receptions of Iranian writers in France, the US and Australia are linked to the expectations of the readers of these host countries. Shahram Khosravi confirms: 'Responses differ due to a range of reasons, e.g. historical relations between Iran and the host country, the degree of shared social and cultural interests, the size of the Iranian migrant group and the status of Iranians in the host country' (2017). My analysis applies to the literary field but is at points valid for larger segments of society.

Numbers on the Iranian diaspora are contentious but one can use the figure of 3 million as a good approximation (Hakimzadeh and Dixon 2006). The post-revolutionary period has witnessed multiple waves of migration. The first wave, from 1979 to the end of the Iran–Iraq war in 1988, primarily formed what Cohen terms a victim diaspora (1997). These were people who fled the nascent Islamic Republic regime, which was in the process of establishing itself, as well as the war with Iraq. The second wave, between 1988 and 2009, formed more of a cultural diaspora, combined with a labour diaspora, as economic conditions became more difficult in Iran. The third and most recent wave involved cultural political migrants, but also economic migrants, and started after the political repression following the 2009 Iranian presidential election. Thus, it can be said that today the Iranian diaspora consists of a combination of several different Iranian groups who left their country for social, cultural, economic and political reasons.

It is important to note that these waves concern long-term and long-distance movements. However, there have always been many movements between Iran's neighbouring countries, which do not count as diasporic, but nonetheless add to these reflections. Amin Moghadam argues: 'Foreign travel came to combine tourism with more-or-less occasional import-export activities, based partly on ties of family or friendship and partly on an understanding of territorially-based opportunities for trade e.g. in free zones or border areas' (Moghadam and Weber 2016b). This is especially the case for populations such as the Kurds and Azeris, who frequently interact across borders. There have been important studies on the history of the Iranian migration and on Iranian communities' integration in western countries after the revolution. The Iranian-American community, which is particularly numerous and vibrant, has been the object of many studies, so in this section I focus on some less examined European countries. There are also important Iranian communities outside of western countries – in the Middle East, especially in the United Arab Emirates and Turkey, in Japan and Malaysia, which have been scarcely studied, apart from the works of Fariba Adelkhah on Japan (Adelkhah 2016) and Amin Moghaddam on the UAE, Armenia and Iraq (Moghadam 2015; Moghadam and Weber 2016b). Adelkhah reflects on the idea of the Iranian migration as journey, *safar*, and inscribes it in the *longue durée* of historical migrations of Iranians (2016).

Histories of Iranian migrations and the identity of hyphenated Iranians have been well studied, so here I only want to assess briefly the results of these findings forty years after the revolution, determinant to understand the literary links between Iran and its diaspora. The case of Iranians in Sweden is representative of a general discourse on the Iranian diaspora as a whole:

> There is a general belief that Iranians in Sweden are easily 'integratable' into the host society. This public imagination is partly accurate since the

social and economic context Iranians come from is not very different from the Swedish one. Iranian migrants in Sweden come mostly from the urban middle class and are well educated. They prefer living in cities and show preference for spatial integration. (Khosravi 2017: 75)

It is also the case in the UK, where a survey showed that 56.7 per cent of respondents held a postgraduate degree and nearly 36 per cent an undergraduate degree (Sreberny and Gholami 2016: 8). This is also a characteristic of the Iranian community in France. According to Nassehy-Behnam, '78.5 percent of Iranian immigrants in France have at least a university degree. Despite this impressive figure, close to half (46 percent) of Iranians in France are unemployed and many highly qualified Iranians are unable to find suitable jobs' (Nassehy-Behnam 2000). Iranians in France are no exception when it comes to this characteristic associated with migration from developing countries to western countries, whereby many well-qualified people hold positions for which they are overqualified or are not able to find work at all. Despite these numbers, the main discourse among members of the Iranian community in France and elsewhere is to insist on how well they are adapting to the new country and how much they contribute to it. In the US, organisations like the National Iranian American Council (NIAC) and Public Affairs Alliance of Iranian Americans (PAAIA) reinforce this discourse about Iranians as 'good migrants'. This discourse was present, for example, in debates over the US Visa Waiver Program that was announced by the US State Department in January 2016.[1] Nadereh Chamlou of the NIAC, a non-profit organisation with the stated mission of 'advancing the interests of the Iranian American community', said: 'We feel we are being singled out. Iraq and Syria are warzones and I cannot comment on Sudan. Everywhere we have gone as Iranians, we have been exemplary citizens'

---

[1] The US State Department announced in 2016 a change to its Visa Waiver Program, which allowed visitors from thirty-seven countries to enter the United States without a visa. From January 2016, those who had travelled to Iran, Iraq, Sudan or Syria on or after 1 March 2011, were not able to enter the United States without a visa. They had to apply for a visa through the regular process. This change came under the Visa Waiver Program Improvement and Terrorist Travel Prevention Act 2015. It applied to bi-nationals of those countries during 2016. In 2017, rules around visas tightened again.

(Smith 2016). This 'fitting with the image' stance largely comes from the fact that diasporic Iranians see themselves as secular. The insistence on Iranian migrants as secular is reinforced by diasporic Iranians themselves in order to counter the criticism against Muslims that is current in western countries. Iranians want to disassociate themselves from extremist Muslims. There is often a strong anti-Islamic discourse by Iranians in the diaspora, and an insistence on the glory of the Persian past before Islam. In Sweden, Khosravi says:

> This hegemonic anti-Islam discourse among Iranians in Sweden contributes to the segmentation of the diaspora. The anti-Muslim sentiments among Iranians have deepened the gap between diasporic stances, as well as the references to the homeland where Islam plays a significant role in society and culture. (Khosravi 2017: 75)

This phenomenon has also been well studied by Reza Gholami, who showed how Iranians in the UK distinguish themselves as not being Islamic as a form of diasporic consciousness (2015). In the spreading of this discourse, it is important to note the role played by the institutions that Khosravi calls 'diaspora brokers' (Khosravi 2017: 76). These institutions are essential in creating a certain image of Iranians for themselves, that they aim to share to the world and to host countries.

This image might be contradictory with what the host countries see as characteristics of the Iranian diaspora, the religious identity being an important part of it. Compared to a country like France where secularism is deeply ingrained, in the UK, Iranian Muslims are quite visible and some practice Islam in an ostensible way with the help of institutes that specifically cater to this religiosity. This is not contradictory with what Gholami has argued; it is more a case of cultivating different forms of diasporic consciousness. One religious institute is Kanoon-e Towhid in London, which is directly linked to the Union of Islamic Students Association and to the embassy of the Islamic Republic in the UK, although it has been reformist-oriented at some moments (Van den Bos 2012). In France, which has mainly attracted secular people, some Iranians have become interested in Sufi brotherhoods (Nassehy-Behnam 2000). In Sydney, there is also a Nimatullahi Sufi Center. In the context of post-revolutionary youths within Iran, Roxanne Varzi has studied the appearance of 'Sufi cool', mixing New Age and Islamic elements (Varzi 2006: 10). As Varzi argues, their practice of spirituality is different from religious practice. There is a similarity with the Sufi brotherhoods developing in western countries, to which many people who describe themselves as 'secular' belong.

An important characteristic of the Iranian migration after the revolution is actually its religious belonging. It is a different religiosity from that imposed by the Islamic Republic regime, as the example of British Kanoon-e Towhid shows, or it is a religiosity coming from religions other than Islam, or ways to practise Islam that are not welcome in the Islamic Republic, such as Sufism. Many members of Iranian religious minorities left Iran after the establishment of the Islamic Republic regime. In certain countries, such as Australia, there existed programmes specifically for Baha'i migration, and Baha'is effectively compose an important segment of the Iranian population in Australia to this day. In the US, certain neighbourhoods are well known for welcoming Iranian Jews, like Beverly Hills in Los Angeles. Effectively, Iranians' religiosity thus appears to be more present in their everyday life than what is stipulated by the upholders of the pro-secular discourse. Religiosity embodies far more complex and nuanced forms, in its differentiation both from the traditional Islamic practices and from the religion of the Islamic government.

The question of the identity of Iranians has been prevalent in the field of literary studies, hence my going into some details about it above. There are several scholars working primarily on Iranian-American writers, such as Persis Karim (Karim 2006, 2015; Karim and Khorrami 1999; Karim and Rahimieh 2008; Rahimieh and Karim 2008), Jasmine Darznik (2008), Amy Motlagh (2008), Sanaz Fotouhi (2015) and Leila Samadi Rendy (2017). In Australia, there are studies on Iranians as a migrant community, but not much in literary terms, apart from Fotouhi (2017) and my own work (Nanquette and Alizadeh 2017). In Europe, one can mention my work on Iranian-French writers (Nanquette 2013a), the work of Nima Mina and Christian Palm on Iranian-German writers (Mina 2019; Palm 2017), and Vanzan on Iranian writers in Italy (Vanzan 2009). In Chapters 7 and 8, I detail some of the arguments put forth by these scholars in the contexts of the US, France and Australia.

A characteristic of these studies is that they focus on one national context only. As such, they miss the possibility that some of the phenomena encountered in these Iranian texts might be transnational. Amy Malek, in her anthropological work, confirms that there are very few studies of the connections between diasporic locations and on the transnational aspect of the Iranian diaspora (Malek 2019b). Such studies are more prominent in the field of Iranian cinema, for example in the work of Mahsa Salamati (2019), who studies the circulation of cinema transnationally, but there is a need for analysis of literary exchanges among the Iranian diaspora as a whole. In this section, this is what I am to do. I keep the focus on western countries because of my personal involvement with them: in the past ten years, I have lived in France, the UK, the US and Australia. I have thus been engaged with the Iranian diasporic communities in these locations, whereas I do not have personal experience of them in other places. Crucial work on Iranian writers in other locations such as Malaysia or the UAE remains to be done.

The Connectedness of the Diaspora: Links to Iran and Other Diasporic Locations

In the digital era, when Iranians around the globe interact on a regular basis with their family and friends both within Iran and in other diasporic locations, the discourse about the Iranian diaspora's lack of coherence might come as a surprise. It seems to contradict the assumption that being connected online transforms into strong community ties. One sees this strengthening of ties thanks to online communication in other diaspora, such as the Haitian one (Parham 2004). This discourse is nonetheless common among scholars in the field. A report on Iranians in Germany published in 2015 suggests: 'This fragmentation of the Iranian diaspora impedes the formation of a collective identity and obstructs the ability of Iranians in exile to organise and act as one' (Heinrich Böll Foundation and Transparency for Iran 2015: 7). Many

> qualitative ethnographic studies (predominantly concerning the first generation of emigrants and refugees), . . . have concluded that there is a marked reluctance among emigrant Iranians to engage with compatriots or participate in institutionalised activities (Sanadjian 1995, 2000; Ansari

1988; Kamalkhani 1988; Khalili 1998; Mobasher 2012). (Heinrich Böll Foundation and Transparency for Iran 2015: 16)

Sonja Moghaddari reinforces this point: 'research in social sciences has spoken of a "fragmentation" within the Iranian "community", or talked about "communities" in plural' (2015: 106). Many studies argue that the stigmatisation directed towards Iranians reinforces the lack of engagement with other Iranians: 'when a community is collectively engaged with concealing or downplaying their identity, they are also less likely to draw further attention by establishing ethnic or culture-based organizations and institutions in their host society' (Sadeghi 2015: 127).

Despite a strong desire to maintain an Iranian identity – however it is defined – there is a high level of assimilation in host countries (Mahdi 1998: 94). This observation for the US appropriately applies to the case of Iranians in other countries and explains why the links between the Iranian diasporic communities are not always strong. The links that are created tend to be to the homeland and to the host country, not to other diasporic communities. In France, as I elaborate in the next chapter, this can partly be explained because of the diverse political affiliations and activities of Iranian members of the diaspora, which hindered people from communicating on other matters. Consequently, there has not been a strong sense of community built over the forty years of post-revolution migration. As Nader Vahabi suggests:

> Generally, Iranians living in France constitute a population presenting a considerable diversity, so much so that one can say there is no 'Iranian community' but culturally and politically very diversified Iranian groups. The attachment to France is less that of a new community of belonging than the expression of values where the individual is prioritized over the group. (Vahabi 2015: 38–9)

Political affiliation, more than class or religion, seems to be a dividing force, with Iranians divided between leftist parties, such as the Communist Party (*Tudeh*), the *Fadaiyan-e khalq*, and the *Mujahedin-e khalq* (both left-leaning political organisations), and the monarchists, who support the Shah's son, Reza Pahlavi, exiled in the United States. In a study of the Iranian diaspora in Belgium, Vahabi uses the term 'diaspora by default', which is a good term to describe the Iranian diaspora in general. He emphasises that the diaspora is politicised but not community-oriented (Vahabi 2011). Amin Moghadam also coincidentally uses the term 'by default' to discuss Iranians who circulate in the countries on the borders of Iran, Armenia and Iraq (Moghadam and Weber 2016a).

One can see that although second- and third-generation Iranians still feel a connection to their homeland, they mostly decouple their origin and their 'homeness'. This leads to the fact that although they might perform Iranian rituals like celebrations of Persian traditions, speak Persian at home and engage in other performances of Iranianness, they do not feel a strong connection to Iranians outside of Iran located in other countries. This could be seen not as a lack of cohesiveness but as a sign of Iranians' commitment to their new home and I would agree with Shu-Mei Shih on the necessity of ceasing to consider diasporic formations as inherently positive: 'To decouple homeness and origin is to recognize the imperative to live as a political subject within a particular geopolitical place in a specific time with deep local commitments' (Shih 2010: 46).

There are some exceptions to this lack of connection to other members of the community. For example, Khosravi uses the example of the creation of the Tirgan Festival in Stockholm, which is directly inspired from the one in Toronto. He argues that Tirgan, a biennial summer festival of Iranian arts and culture, is mostly a creation of the Iranian diaspora, as this is celebrated inside Iran only on a small scale in provincial areas. In this sense, Iranians in Sweden link not back to the motherland but to another diasporic location (Khosravi 2017). One might see more such recreations happening as years go by, but these do not appear to be representative of the Iranian diaspora. An additional explanation is that, although there were Iranians living abroad and forming associations before 1979, with the role of intellectuals and writers being crucial in diasporic locations during major events like the Persian Constitutional Revolution in 1905–11, it is only after the Islamic Revolution that one sees a mass of people migrating and establishing themselves outside of Iran. This means it is only a forty-year-old diaspora, which is recent and still finding its ways to navigate the attachment to the motherland among political divisions. In March 2019, for the occasion of the fortieth anniversary of the revolution, the first ever conference on the

Iranian diaspora happened at San Francisco State University, entitled 'Forty Years & More'. The inaugural Center for Iranian Diaspora Studies at the same university, directed by Persis Karim, opened only in 2017, building important scholarship on the history of Iranian-Americans. After several decades, the conference constituted the first instance when we could see the emergence of a field in such a clear way, although there have been many reflections on the Iranian diaspora throughout the last four decades, including through community associations like Iranian Alliances Across Border (Bajoghli and Kharrazi 2015).

There are recent evolutions though that might contradict this discourse and analysis. Sreberny and Gholami note that attitudes are changing:

> it can be suggested that views and attitudes around issues of community in the Iranian diasporic context are changing. That is, an increasing number of people believe that not only does a community exist but they also feel some sort of a connection to it. (Sreberny and Gholami 2016: 9)

Scholars like Amy Malek also show that there is increasingly a sense of the diaspora as unified and as sharing in the same memories. She uses the example of pre-revolution family photographs to prove her point:

> diasporic remediation of audio-visual family archives of 'back home, back then' made available online in a time of increasingly simple digitization and online sharing is creating and circulating Iranian diasporic sites of memory and a collective (post)memory connecting dispersed populations in affective, imaginative, and symbolic ways. (Malek 2019a: 17)

Such new studies will be critical in understanding the ways in which the Iranian diaspora connects. Iranian and Persian film festivals across the world, as well as festivities around Persian New Year (*Nowruz*), which is the major Iranian celebration (Malek 2011), work as a way of temporarily getting together, even though there is a dispersion of the community at the end of the events.

Among some segments of the Iranian diaspora, this sense of belonging to a diaspora is even more present. The Baha'is are an example of this, as they tend not to maintain ties with Iran since they cannot travel there (they are considered apostates and discriminated against), but as members of a religion that insists on its universality, they forge strong ties with other Iranian Baha'is around the world (McAuliffe 2008a).

Niki Akhavan demonstrated in her book *Electronic Iran* that there are some instances when the gap between Iran and the diaspora is bridged. She gives the example of the debates around the naming of the Persian Gulf, as opposed to the Arabian Gulf, that some media had started using in the early years of the internet. It was the first internet mobilisation, started by the diaspora, which was followed up by the Iranian state (Akhavan 2013: 31). As such, it gave the impression that the two were reconciled, when it came to nationalism. However, she sees this mobilisation as an exception rather than a rule, when national pride is at stake, and argues that the rise of the internet did not help much in closing the gap:

> Outside the country, the embrace of the new medium within the Diaspora brought the promise of reconnecting with a lost homeland, but it often also provided evidence of the depth of the chasm between an imagined Iran and the real Iran. (Akhavan 2013: 107)

Akhavan argues that there is a mistrust towards the diaspora when saying: 'Physical location remains an issue in determination of loyalty' (2013: 73). During my fieldwork in Iran, many of the literary practitioners I talked to discussed the disconnection between Iranian writers who have left their homeland of Iran through the metaphor of the tree cut from its roots. They argued that if Iranian writers lose the connection to their people and their language, with a Persian language that evolves rapidly, they cannot produce quality works. A scholar like Mirabeidini, who has written the most comprehensive books on contemporary Iranian literature, does not include the writers from the diaspora in his catalogues. This attachment to the motherland and the mother tongue as the marker of Iranianness is a contemporary position. Indeed, Iranians in medieval times have largely contributed to sciences by writing treatises in Arabic, while continuing to write poetry in Persian. The two were not exclusive. In contemporary times however, writing in both English and Persian does not seem to be an accepted norm and Iranians within imply there is a choice to make. For the Islamic Republic regime, 'Any calls for an open society or the end of state censorship on the part of the Iranian dissidents have been construed as collaboration in the secular plot against religion, and, therefore, prima facie cases of treason' (Sprachman 2017: 180). While for a large number of Iranians within Iran, the view is more nuanced, all diasporic Iranians can potentially be seen as traitors by the state, and as participants to what the Islamic Republic calls the soft war waged by western powers.

Precedents to the Division

While the current gap between Iran and its diaspora is often commented upon by scholars of Iran, it is important to remember that there have been other times when Iranian culture was largely decentralised. The most important moment is before and during the Constitutional Revolution, when many intellectuals and writers who would become the leaders of the movement, lived outside of Iran. Their first reflections on Iran's encounter with modernity started in places such as Turkey, India, England or Germany. It is also the case that many politicians were in exile at the time. Christophe Balaÿ reminds us that it is in the literary magazines and journals published outside of Iran, like *Hablo al-matin* in Calcutta, *Akhtar* in Istanbul or *Kaveh* in Berlin, that the first essays of literary criticism appear and that Iranian thinkers develop their reflections on modernity. It is also through these magazines that they simplified Persian writing (Dabashi 2012). Mirza Agha Khan Kermani, Malkam Khan, Dehkhoda and Jamalzadeh did so (Balaÿ 2017: 472). Another example is Jamalzadeh's short story 'Persian is Sugar' ('Farsi shekar ast'), which is widely considered to be the first modern short story in the history of Persian literature, and appeared in the magazine *Kaveh* published in Berlin, before being published in Iran in the collection *Once Upon a Time* (*Yeki bud, yeki nabud*) (Balaÿ 2017: 158). In these paragraphs, I use the terms modern and modernity to follow the scholars who have worked on this literary period and categorised works along these lines. The pairing of the words modernity versus tradition is frought in the study of Iranian history and I do not go into these debates, but I encourage the idea of going beyond them and using frameworks like that proposed by Houchang Chehabi who speaks of cosmopolitan versus local instead (Chehabi 2018).

After the Constitutional Revolution, one can think of Sadegh Hedayat's *The Blind Owl*, published in Bombay in 1936 and described as the first modern Persian novel. Hedayat also spent a large amount of his life in Paris, where he eventually committed suicide. After the Constitutional Revolution, there was generally less of a disconnect between Iran and its diaspora until the 1979 revolution. There are important movements, especially of students studying abroad and contributing to the thinking leading to the revolution (Matin-Asgari 1991), but it is on a small scale and restricted to specific segments of the population, mostly the upper middle-class.

With the Islamic Revolution and the war against Iran, one sees a mass migration of Iranians, including many thinkers and writers, primarily to western countries. It is the first time in history that such an important proportion of the Iranian population lives abroad. Although at first, they come mainly from the economic, political and intellectual elite, as well as religious minorities who find the new Islamic Republic intolerant, they gradually include people from all walks of life.

It is also important to historicise this decentralisation to an even earlier period. If we reflect upon the decentralisation of Persian culture in the context of the Persianate world, we can better understand the difference of the new diasporic cultural production. From the fifteenth century until the end of the nineteenth century, Persian was a *lingua franca* in a vast space ranging from Turkey across Central Asia to India. It had a transregional influence. However, Kevin Schwartz argues that the genre of the *tazkireh* (biographical anthology), which had crossed borders relatively freely until then, starts to become localised and restricted to the capital of Qajar Iran in the nineteenth century (Schwartz 2018). As the Qajars constructed Iran as a nation state, the influence of Persian as a language and a culture across the region diminished. Schwartz is only interested in one genre, the *tazkireh*, and Persian did continue to have an impact through other forms, especially in newspapers as I mentioned above, but the process of centralisation around Tehran and of linking literature and culture to the state had begun. After the Qajars, the scope of the Persian language starts to shrink and Persian texts and practices become less interlinked. This process continues throughout the twentieth century and, after the revolution, we can see that the focus on the language is replaced by an insistence on Iran as an imagined community, which is what I study in this book – a space of belonging and an identity beyond the language. Literatures from Iranians across the world thus produce small clusters of Iran outside its borders, either in Persian or in the local languages, English, French, German and other languages.

The lack of interaction between Iranians from within Iran and in the diaspora is largely restricted to the literary field, which is also the most elitist of all cultural fields. In the case of music, for example, one can see exchanges happening on a large scale and with a lot more interaction than is the case with literary texts. Nahid Siamdoust argues:

> The relations between Iranians inside and outside of the country, and their mutual impact on one another, have been instrumental to creative endeavors in this field. As late as two decades into the Islamic Republic, Iranians inside Iran were for the most part still listening to expatriate productions streaming in from Los Angeles, and the flow of music was largely unidirectional. By about 2005, the flow had nearly entirely reversed, as music made in Iran had achieved such sophistication that not only were expatriates listening to music by the likes of Benyamin – who now, in fact, like others such as Ehsan Khajeh Amiri, even goes on annual concert tours to Europe, Canada, and the United States – but expatriate artists were also collaborating on various levels with artists in Iran. (Siamdoust 2017: 138)

After this general discussion on the Iranian diaspora, I want to assess how these analyses apply to the literary field. Of course, it is more difficult to exchange printed books than it is to exchange information online. Electronic books only partly remedy this. As I show in the case of the publisher Naakojaa, one critical aspect for bridging the gap between Iran and the diaspora is to have real-life exchanges, in addition to virtual exchanges. Publishers in the diaspora are numerous and they have published a substantial amount of texts in the forty years since the revolution, both from writers within Iran who could not get their books published inside the country or did not want to, and from diaspora writers. Studying them in detail is critical to understanding the relationships between the literary fields in Iran and in the diaspora, as we cannot speak of a unified field. The diaspora publishers are the main actors trying to overcome the lack of connectedness described earlier, and below I study some of their challenges. One should remember that heavy sanctions and restrictions on cultural exchanges between Iran and the locations where Iranians live in the diaspora make it particularly difficult to bridge this gap, as I detailed in Chapter 3. Books by Iranians published abroad are banned in Iran or cannot be easily bought for example. Books by writers living in Iran need to be translated into European languages, but because of sanctions, financial exchanges between publishers in Iran and abroad are forbidden. The very fact that publishers in the diaspora try to overcome these challenges and successfully publish and exchange is to be celebrated.

Attempts to Overcome Divisions Between Iran and the Diaspora in the Literary Field

Naakojaa

Naakojaa, based in Paris and founded in the early 2010s, is the largest Iranian publisher outside of Iran. I compare it first to another Paris-based publisher and bookstore, Khavaran, to show how Iranian publishers abroad have evolved. Khavaran was established in 1983 in Vincennes, a suburb close to the centre of Paris. It was managed by Bahman Amini, who worked as a writer for an Iranian magazine before he moved to France in 1981. Amini did not receive help from French institutions and relied solely on his Iranian network to promote his books. Khavaran primarily published prison memoirs and books that were banned in Iran. In addition to books in Persian, Khavaran published a few French books in collaboration with a French publisher and commissioned some works. Khavaran was also a meeting place for Iranian intellectuals in the 1980s, especially for leftist intellectuals who composed the majority of readers; Amini himself was politically active and had been a political prisoner in the 1970s in Iran. Thus, Khavaran provided a platform that connected literary texts and political engagement. In the 2000s, Khavaran moved to a different location in Paris and scaled down its activities. The bookstore discontinued its Persian specialty, and the Persian books were stored in the back of the store, invisible to most customers. Ultimately, Khavaran closed down permanently in 2015 due to financial loss and lack of clientele. This was also the case for Ketab Corp, owned by Bijan Khalili, a Persian bookstore in Los Angeles, which closed down its bookstore in 2015 after thirty-five years of activity, to move to a much cheaper, entirely virtual platform.

Diaspora bookstores like Khavaran that functioned as cultural centres have increasingly been replaced by others. Naakojaa is one example. A major characteristic that differentiates the new Iranian bookstores from the old ones is a less marked political engagement and party affiliation as well as the potential to attract a larger spectrum of Iranian and non-Iranian readers. This evolution reflects not only an evolving book economy, less focused on print, but also changes in the Iranian population structure in western countries, as the older generation is replaced by younger intellectuals.

The cultural, political and social support networks linking France and Iran are generally weak, and the Iranian community in France is fragmented, as I discussed earlier. However, perhaps paradoxically, the post-2009 generation of Iranians in France, of which Naakojaa is representative, is more connected to Iran. The first generation of migrants, because of their strong political activities and the inflexibility of the Islamic Republic regime, could not return. This is not the case for many younger intellectuals, who can travel back and forth. This is not to say that the post-2009 generation is not politically active, but it is generally not affiliated to one party and has a subtle understanding of the political struggle thanks to its active interaction with the complex Iranian system.

Naakojaa is a publishing house founded by Tinouche Nazmjou in 2012. It also runs a bookstore based in Paris, the Librarie Utopiran. After the second term of President Mahmoud Ahmadinejad, when censorship in Iran grew stronger, Nazmjou – a translator of theatre and theatre director, who had extensive publishing experience – decided to start his own publishing house in Paris, where he had lived in his teenage years (Shahid 2017). He focused on digital distribution as a way of reaching Iranians globally. Contrary to most publishers in Iran, Naakojaa respects the Universal Copyright Convention. It offers a contract and copyright protection to writers, which provides an appealing option for writers in Iran. Naakojaa receives around a hundred manuscripts per month from Iranians around the world and publishes three or four works each month (Nazmjou, personal communication with the author, 2016). Naakojaa's goals are to publish quality texts from lesser-known writers based in Iran and abroad or on subjects that are less commonly treated, and to promote reading throughout Iran and France. E-publishing makes a difference in Iran, insofar as it replaces the many poor-quality scans that circulate illegally. Furthermore, considering that Iranians are scattered around the world, it makes sense to create electronic publications that are easily accessible. In a personal communication with me in 2015, Nazmjou also insisted that the texts must have an appeal for western audiences too.

Naakojaa offers a website with articles, notes, discussions, videos and the collected works of most of its authors, and it thus acts as a cultural platform (Nanquette 2017a). It also presents books published by other publishers in Iran, offering a broad view of the Iranian literary scene. Naakojaa further uses social media to promote its publications. In addition, Naakojaa's bookstore, Utopiran, carries printed Persian books and books in French about Iran and organises cultural events linked to Iran. Other activities of Utopiran include readings of texts and presentations by authors, and biweekly book club discussions in Persian and in French. Naakojaa aims to be a place of literary dialogue, as reiterated by its director: 'Naakojaa is not just a bookstore; it's a place for reviewing books and, more importantly, it's a place for dialogue and exchanging ideas and comments about world literature and its impact on life and our society' (Mehtari 2012).

Like the newer generation of diasporic Iranians, Naakojaa is not as visibly attached to a political party as earlier generations of publishers and bookstore owners in Europe. Naakojaa can be described as a committed publisher with an explicit policy of publishing books that have been censored or banned in Iran, those that authors think will probably be banned, and those that have been published and then banned by the government. Such books are catalogued under a category called Travel to the Other Side (*Safar be digar su*). For example, Naakojaa has published the poems and short stories of the Iranian writer, translator and journalist Sepideh Jadiri, whose poems are banned in Iran and who founded the first Iranian Women Poets award *Khorshid*. She lived in Italy for some time as a guest writer of PEN International, and her poems have been translated into English, Dutch, Swedish, Kurdish, Turkish and French. She also translated *Blue is the Warmest Colour*, a graphic novel about female homosexuality that has been banned in Iran (Nanquette 2017a).

Naakojaa's sales model is broadly based and usually offers several purchasing options, including directly from Naakojaa or from other providers such as Google, Lulu (a US-based independent print-on-demand and self-publishing bookstore) and Amazon in most European countries. Naakojaa's revenue comes only from the sale of books, as it does not receive financial help from French institutions, although this might change in the future if it produces French translations, as institutions such as the Centre National du Livre are devoted to supporting such translations. As Nazmjou points out, the e-publication of books is what allowed Naakojaa to reach the readership based in Iran, but because of its limited spending power, the sales from e-books were low. Nevertheless, this is still the main source of revenue.

Naakojaa's relative success compared to other publishers in the diaspora is partly due to the fact that it includes Iranians from around the world and maintains ties to Iran, as well as its focus on the digital. With this shift, local practices and diasporic spaces such as the Khavaran bookstore – where intellectuals met regularly and organised literary meetings for members of the community – have now been replaced with a diasporic space that is partly virtual. In addition to its role as an electronic space for promoting dialogue and networking among Iranian intellectuals in diaspora, Naakojaa also functions as a local physical space and a bookstore that hosts readings. Indeed, the effectiveness of digital spaces when not linked to local spaces should not be overstated. Important studies about the Iranian digital space, whether the website Iranian.com (Alexanian 2008) or weblogs (Akhavan 2013), insist on caution when speaking of an Iranian digital space 'as a kind of virtual community' (Alexanian 2008: 129). It is important to remember that articulations of identity online have 'consequences in the offline world' (Alexanian 2008: 133). The virtual and the local are linked, and the virtual does not replace the local but is closely intertwined with it (Nanquette 2017a). Naakojaa is a good example of the articulation of physical space and the virtual space that reaches readers both in the diaspora and in Iran. Although Nazmjou himself has not travelled to Iran since 2009 due to its strong stance against censorship, he is still the series director of an important collection of plays with the Tehran-based publisher Ney. He also regularly organises programmes of exchanges between French and Iranian playwrights, and is allowed to do so by the government (Mehr News 2019).

As such, this shows us that the disconnect between the diaspora and Iran is not irreversible, but that bridging it requires careful consideration. At the same time, the virtual space needs to be complemented by a local, physical space. Naakojaa appears as one of the new publishers that navigate these mechanisms, like Nogaam and H&S Media in the UK, and that distinguish themselves from the older publishers of the diaspora like Forough in Cologne; Ibex in Maryland; Khavaran in Paris; in Sweden; and Gardoon in Berlin.

However, the very fact that Naakojaa is situated outside of Iran and has a clear political line against censorship, makes it prone to criticism by literary producers in Iran. Many of my interlocutors in Tehran told me that they would never work with it because it is too risky or just because it works outside of Iran. Many also did not know about it. Naakojaa is part of Uncensored Tehran Book Fair, an event recurring every year since 2015, started by Small Media at the same time as the Tehran Book Fair. Several publishers in the diaspora join forces to put together a small book fair, selling books and sometimes organising readings in several cities across Europe and, since 2019, in North America. In this event, where publishers are united through their opposition to the censorship of the Iranian Republic regime, we see a symbol of the division between Iran and the cultural diaspora. Not that Iranian literary practitioners within Iran are confortable with censorship, but it is, as I demonstrated in Chapter 3, a space they have to navigate to continue their work.

In the next section, I want to look at a publisher with a different model – that is based both in Iran and in the diaspora – to assess its success in bridging the gap between Iran and the diaspora.

Candle & Fog

The publisher Candle & Fog was registered in 2001 in Iran and in 2003 in the UK (Afshin Shahneh Tabar, interview with the author, 27 May 2014). It is a small publishing house, having only published around seventy books since then, mainly in English, primarily literature, along with a few academic books. The founder and manager of Candle & Fog, Afshin ShahnehTabar, explained that the idea of registering Candle & Fog in the UK came from the lack of international interest in Persian literature, particularly fiction and novels. The decision was also made as a result of Iran not being a signatory to the Berne Convention. As such, Candle & Fog's central aim is to present Iranian books, translated into English and other languages, mainly French and German, at international book fairs: it insists on being part of the global community of publishers and on selling rights at these fairs. It also uses platforms such as Amazon for sales, whereas a publisher based only in Iran could not do so because of international sanctions. Candle & Fog is not the first Iran-based press which publishes translations in European languages; however, it is innovative in being the first to include bestsellers and popular literary texts, and in having a heterogeneous catalogue without many of the ideological books that typical Iran-based publishers exporting abroad have. It also has a policy that is markedly different from purely state-funded institutions. Many government institutions and projects have insisted on translation into European languages; however, these are often books about Islam or books that are closely aligned with state ideology. For example, the government literary agent POL (*pol* means bridge in Persian) supports the translations of books about the Shia form of Islam and about Iranian traditions, as well as children books, which are less polemical (Jafari Aghdam 2012–). Candle & Fog takes a different approach. Publishing bestsellers alongside canonical texts is not a traditional editorial policy in Iran, where books are very much segmented by genres and along an ideological spectrum as I discussed in Chapter 1. Candle & Fog's list of publications is heterogeneous, including highbrow texts such as Nima Youshij's poems (Talebi and Rasouli) and a biography of the Prophet Muhammad (Beygi), as well as lowbrow texts such as *Silk and Roses*, a story of an Italian family with some erotic content (Mahshid). Their bestselling books in English, *Robin Hood of the Desert* by Masoud Behnoud and *The Water Urn* by Houshang Moradi Kermani, each sold more than 3,000 copies (Behnoud 2011; Moradi Kermani 2014) (Shahneh Tabar, interview, 27 May 2014).

Below, I take a close look at one of their publications to unpack how the book travelled through this publisher, its translator and to readers: *Kimya Khatun*, by Saideh Ghods, a novel which is about the life of Kimya, the stepdaughter of the classical Persian poet Rumi (Ghods and Phillips 2012). Rumi is close to the heart of most Iranians and his life story and his encounter with Shams are known by everyone. In the novel, Kimya is married to Rumi's Sufism teacher and friend, Shams, forty years her elder, and ultimately dies at his hands. In Persian, the book has sold more than 80,000 copies, and been reprinted twenty-five times so it is considered a bestseller. It received the 2005 E'tesami Literary Prize and was nominated for other awards. *Kimya Khatun*'s reception was polarising: it was criticised by Rumi scholars for historical errors, as well as vilified because of what was seen as a feminist discourse. It deals with an erudite topic in a sentimental form. The book cover of the English version reinforces this sentimental trajectory, with a drawing of a broken heart and in its centre a miniature painting of a woman. *Kimya Khatun* was translated into English by Sara Phillips, who was commissioned by Candle & Fog with the help of the literary agency Gazelle (Phillips, interview with author, July 2014). It is one of the first contemporary Iranian bestsellers to have been translated into English. Despite this, it has not attracted much attention among English speakers. If we put aside possible issues with the translation itself, Candle & Fog has limited marketing means and mainly sold it on Amazon. It was not able to secure reviews in European newspapers. It sold 1,500 copies, which is relatively low for European standards of publication but standard in the Iranian context (Shahneh Tabar, interview with author, 27 May 2014). This book is an example of the many constraints an Iranian publisher has to deal with. Candle & Fog was able to go around international sanctions and market it through a major e-commerce website but it works with a small pool of translators and it has rare connections to the major literary centres, so is not able to organise much publicity.

Politically, Candle & Fog navigates the troubled waters governed by the Islamic Republic regime. Afshin Shahneh Tabar emphasises the lack of support from the Ministry of Culture and Islamic Guidance to independent publishers, and has been critical of its non-alignment with global trends and conventions. Although it is not a governmental publisher, Candle & Fog is Iran-based and works with government institutions, such as the Saadi Foundation discussed in Chapter 3, which promotes the Persian language globally. One of the Saadi Foundation's books, a reissue of *The Water Urn* (*Khomreh*) by Moradi Kermani, a children's classic from 1989, was a co-publication with Candle & Fog (IBNA 2015).[2] Candle & Fog's funding is not clear, and although it does have some independent characteristics, such as publishing a wide variety of texts, it also has some characteristics of governmental publishers. For example, it cancelled its programme for the 2015

---

[2] *Khomreh* is a popular children's story in Iran, first published by Sahab publisher in Iran in 1989. In 1992, it was translated into German and then into four other languages. Nine movies have been made on the basis of this story.

Frankfurt Book Fair due to the Iranian Minister of Culture's decision to boycott the fair in response to Salman Rushdie's presence. In terms of scale, Candle & Fog cannot be compared to Naakojaa, because it is not as prolific and does not have the same scope. While it is more flexible than a purely Iranian-based publisher, thanks to its UK headquarters, it is still constrained by the laws of Iran. It is more accountable for its politics than Naakojaa because it has to work on a daily basis with institutions within Iran. It is also constrained by a lack of international exchange, which makes it difficult to be transnational on a broad scale.

In the previous two sections, I looked at publishers who aim to make Iran and the diaspora converse. One could argue that they are constrained by their status as institutions and their necessity to make a profit. Outside of publishers, what do the literary exchanges between Iran and the diaspora look like?

Diasporic Literary Blogs

In Chapter 2, I examined Iranian literary blogs and analysed how some of them connected categories of people that might not connect offline. It is often argued that the internet connects people beyond national borders and I would like to assess whether Iranian literary blogs in the diaspora have indeed increased transnational exchanges. The internet has typically been associated with a connective potential to reinforce 'imagined communities' between diasporic and resident national communities (Anderson 1992: 12). However, the Iranian blogosphere challenges these somewhat utopian assumptions. Despite the hopes raised by the internet, the enduring dissent between the diaspora and Iranians from within proves difficult to appease. The literary networks are distinct and we cannot find an integrated literary space online. They do interact and exchange by commenting on each other's blogs or Facebook posts but there is a strong 'diaspora effect' (Giacobino *et al.* 2014). One blogger summarised it as such:

> You are not the same person that you were before you left Iran and the audience notices this. You are like a product which has changed its flavour [sic] and thus needs to market itself again and recreate its audience. (Giacobino *et al.* 2014: 27)

A striking point when considering Iranian literary blogs in the diaspora is that most of the interesting conversations happen in the Persian language; not much happens in European languages, except maybe in German. Sudabeh Mohafez has a website about her life and work, as well as a literary blog that innovates by using small texts of ten lines, along the genre of the short story (*dastanak*) analysed in Chapter 2 (Mohafez 2007–13, no date). In Germany also, Yadollah Kouchaki Dehshali (no date) publishes some of his texts online, and Ali Schirasi (2004–15) had a website with poems interspersed among political texts. No Iranian writer based in France has written a literary blog in French to my knowledge. The most well-known French-Iranian writer online, Reza Ghassemi, writes in Persian. His blog, *Davat, Literary Journal* has now been banned within Iran for more than ten years. When bloggers in the diaspora try to reach audiences within Iran, the effectiveness of the censorship inside Iran shatters their efforts. There are options to break the filters, and although many use them, this is nonetheless a serious impediment to many others who are not tech-savvy and just surf the web. Transnational literary circulation seems to occur more on social media than on older forms like blogs. On Instagram, and before on Telegram, as I showed in Chapter 2, one can find more interactions between the diaspora and Iran, with writers based in the diaspora exchanging ideas with readers inside Iran. Poets like Fatemeh Ekhtesari and Mehdi Moussavi still have their followers within Iran while living outside it.

Conclusion

Naakojaa is an example of a publisher that tries to bridge the gap between Iran and the diaspora and which has succeeded up to a point, but not as much as hoped when it opened. Candle & Fog works on a small scale only. Literary blogs in the diaspora do not reach Iranian readers within Iran. The best medium to bridge the gap is social media; however, it is not particularly tailored to the literary format. It does not lead to the creation of literary content as such, although it helps to spread it, as I discussed in Chapter 2 with Instagram. Although the Iranian diaspora is well-connected in general, it has not led to literary transnational exchanges on a large scale. Distrust between the diaspora and Iran, as well as heavy sanctions and restrictions on cultural exchange are the main reasons. In this chapter, I have not analysed in detail the impact of the sanctions and difficulties for exchange, since I have discussed them at length in Chapter 3. They are however crucial to understanding the dynamics between Iran and the diaspora, although factors less linked to current political dysfunctions are also part of the picture.

7

Translation and Reception in the US and France

I met with the writer Shahriar Mandanipour in Cambridge, Massachusetts, for the first time in 2011 and a few times after that until 2013. The last time I saw him was in Sydney in 2016. We discussed his latest novel, Censoring an Iranian Love Story, *talked about his writings published in Iran and about contemporary Persian literature. After each meeting, he increasingly reminded me of the figure of Gholam Hossein Sa'edi, who died in 1985, a famous playwright and writer who struggled during his exile in Paris. Mandanipour can be considered successful by many standards: his two novels translated into English have sold well, he is reviewed in prestigious newspapers like* The New York Times, *and he continues to write. However, he is someone that literary practitioners within Iran inevitably point to when they want to argue that as soon as a writer leaves the country, his relation to the Persian language and therefore his writing declines. During my fieldwork, literary practitioners often pointed out Mandanipour, widely considered as a sophisticated writer with stories like* Violet Orient (Sharq-e banafsheh) *when he lived in Iran, but criticised him for his later novels written for an English audience, especially* Censoring an Iranian Love Story, *discussed in Chapter 9. I do not necessarily agree with this argument that the loss of connection to the land leads to a loss of connection to the language: sometimes, the practice of a new language opens doors one could not see before. It is however true that the Persian language evolves rapidly, more so in the last century than it did for a thousand year. In this sense, a writer who does not speak the language every day and does not hear the evolution will use a language which can be outdated. What is reflected in this story about Mandanipour is the division between Iranian literary practitioners within Iran and those in the diaspora. We are back to the irreconcilable divisions of the previous chapter.*

There is no exhaustive database grouping information about Iranian publishers, writers and their texts in the diaspora, so the next two chapters use a mix of quantitative and qualitative data to analyse translations and reception from modern Persian literature into European languages. In France and the US, many highbrow texts and poetry in Persian are translated, with little attention paid to a wider market or to bestsellers. Australia exhibits some particularities due to a different history of migration (the Iranian migration is less upper and middle class than in Europe and North America). Australia is a literary field where Iranian literature has been more influenced by the demands of the Australian reader, and especially the thirst for refugee stories, where they areprevalent, while rare in Europe and America. In this chapter, I focus on literary production in the US and in France, making a comparison between the two spaces. Numerically and symbolically, an important part of Iranian literature abroad is written and published in these two countries, hence my focus on them. In the following chapter, I focus on Australia.

Translation of Modern Persian Literature in the US

In this section, I analyse the practice of translation from modern Persian literature into English in the United States over thirty years, defining where the translation field intersects with the academic, political and literary fields in the case of Persian texts. I stop at the beginning of the 2010s because there are changes in translation patterns after that date. My analysis relies on a Bourdieusian perspective in its study of a list of 100 literary texts of modern Persian literature, starting with Mohammad-Ali Jamalzadeh's *Once Upon a Time* (1921), translated and published between 1979 and 2011 in English. The chapter describes the production milieu of modern Persian translations in the American market and analyses them in quantitative terms. I focus on the American literary field because this is where most of the Persian translations into English are produced: according to the data I have compiled, 88 per cent of English translations of modern Persian literature are published by American publishers, compared to only 10 per cent by British and 2 per cent by Canadian publishers.

The *Index Translationum*, an international bibliography published by UNESCO, indicates that the most translated authors from Persian, into all languages, are classical poets (Omar Khayyam, Jalal al-Din Rumi) and religious authors (Baha Allah, Abd al-Baha and Morteza Motahari) (UNESCO 2012a). In the US, Rumi is a poetry bestseller (Tompkins 2002). Azadibougar and Patton interrogate this fact: 'This case is even more curious given that literary circulation usually favours prose forms rather than poetry' (Azadibougar and Patton 2015: 174). The *Index Translationum* database is to be taken with caution as it relies on the data provided by each country and is not always consistent on what is defined as a book. However, if one considers that it shows trends more than accurate statistics, it is an important tool in understanding the global economy of translations. Among these most translated writers, no contemporary Persian author can be found in the top ten, not even Sadegh Hedayat, the father of the modern Persian novel (UNESCO 2012a). These trends are hardly surprising considering that Iran is known for its poetry, which possesses the highest cultural capital, as discussed in Chapter 9, and, to a lesser extent, for its religious and philosophical thought. However, the invisibility of modern Iranian authors requires analysis, since the translations of modern and contemporary texts reveal ideological trends to a greater extent than those of classical texts.

Lawrence Venuti's political approach to translation is particularly suitable for the case of translations from Persian in the US, although my analysis is a counter-argument to his theory about the invisibility of the translator.[1] In his study of the translations of modern Japanese literature into English in the 1950s and 1960s, he argues that these translations establish a canon for a foreign literature (Venuti 1998). Western readers come to think that these texts are typical of the country and therefore represent it (Venuti 1998). The translation becomes about the culture from which it emerges; translation has an 'enormous power in constructing representations of foreign cultures' (Venuti 1998: 67). As for translators, choosing one text to translate is to exclude another and thus to privilege one aspect of the country over another

---

[1] For an example of responses to Venuti, see Pym (1996).

(Venuti 1998: 67). Similar to the Japanese case, contemporary readers often view translated modern Persian literature as a metaphor for modern Iran, as evidenced in comments on Amazon or Goodreads, as I expand on in Chapter 9. It is thus important to concentrate on modern Persian texts in this study – hence the decision to start from 1979, with the Islamic Revolution, because the event is a turning point in cultural relations between the United States and Iran. I decided to end the study in the early 2010s, as I saw new trends appearing then, with the translation of bestsellers such as Parinoush Saniee's *The Book of Fate*, which is studied in Chapter 9.

I have compiled a list of the literary texts of modern Persian literature, starting with Mohammad-Ali Jamalzadeh's *Once Upon a Time* (1921), translated and published between 1979 and 2011 in English, which amounts to 100 texts. I started building the list based on Alireza Anushiravani's unpublished 'Annotated Bibliography of Persian Literature in English Translation from 17th Century to the Present', and completed it by searching the *Index Translationum*, the catalogue of the Library of Congress, the database of the online bookseller Amazon, and by asking several literary translators in the US if they knew of texts that were not included in my list.[2] While it may not be exhaustive, my list contains far more titles than *Index Translationum* thus making it more than merely representative. I added all the details on the books published: author, title, translator, date of publication in English, date of publication in Persian, place of English publication, name of publisher in English, and genre; as well as details on the translator: occupation and ethnic origin; and details on the publisher: type and location. I have not included the translations into English published in Iran, as they scarcely circulate internationally; they are usually not sold in the US and are thus not accessible to the general American reader. In terms of genre, I have included fiction (novels and collections of short stories), essays, drama and poetry, but I have excluded children's or young adult books, as well as anthologies that were not specific to Iran, such as works encompassing writings by Middle Eastern writers, as my purpose was to focus specifically on the Iran–US cultural relationship. I have also excluded translations of short stories published

---

[2] I have asked several Persian to English translators working in the field in the US to check its accuracy and I thank them for their diligence.

in journals and reviews, because they do not reach a general audience and because they were too difficult to gather. I used pivot tables to analyse the data compiled in this list.

In this section, I start by exploring the American market for translation, specifically translations from Persian, and describe the production milieu of modern Persian translations. I then analyse in quantitative terms modern Persian translations (ethnic origin of translators, primary activity of translators, proportion of publishers by activity, location of publishers by region, number of texts translated per author, translated genres). The American literary market is notorious for its small number of translations as a proportion of all books published, amounting to only 3 per cent.[3] For literary texts specifically, a study by the National Endowment for the Arts found that out of a total of 12,828 works of fiction and poetry published in the US in 1999, only 297 were translations, 'that is, only a little over 2% of all fiction and poetry published, and far less than 1% of all books published' (Allen 2007: 25). This small percentage can above all be explained by the fact that because English is the language of the hypercentre, translation flows are from English into other languages, while translations into English from other languages are few. Johan Heilbron argues that there is an 'inverse relationship between the centrality of a language in the international translation system and the proportion of translations in national book production' (Heilbron 1999: 439). This is entirely confirmed in the Iranian case: although English as a global language could play a mediatory role between Persian and other languages, it does not do so, as I demonstrate below.

Another explanation that takes us away from translation and relates to culture is linked to the economic domination of English-speaking countries in the world system. Investing in cultural dominance requires capital, which has been available primarily to the US, and to a lesser extent to the UK (but not Australia or New Zealand, for example). We can thus argue that

---

[3] The *Three Percent* website, a site devoted to translation, is unfortunately not accurate in its count of translations. In 2011, for example, they list one translation, whereas my bibliography has three. Moreover, my bibliography only includes modern Persian texts, and the addition of translations of classical texts will necessarily raise the numbers. Their database is thus not usable as such for the Persian case.

being members of the world's dominant culture, American readers are not interested in reading productions from the outside. As a comparison, in a semi-central language such as French, the percentage of translations is much higher, as I showed in Chapter 4. In peripheral literary cultures, translations are produced in significant volume. In Iran, as I have explained, translations represent a high percentage of publications and enjoy considerable commercial success. Furthermore, in literary translations, the percentage is higher.

I would like now to assess the claim expressed by literary practitioners working in and with Persian whom I interviewed, that Persian literature is rarely translated. In terms of the percentage of translated texts compared to the national production, Iran does not appear to be under-represented in the American literary sphere in comparison with other minor languages. Let us compare it with another minor language from the Middle East, Turkish. In Iran, 0.08 per cent of all Persian texts published make it to the American market in translation, while 0.05 per cent of Turkish texts make it to translation in the US.[4] Iranian literature is thus not particularly underprivileged, at least in terms of books published, but it has a low circulation, which gives a different meaning to the comparison with Turkish texts. Turkish texts are indeed more visible on the American market, partly thanks to the bestselling Turkish writer, Orhan Pamuk, winner of the Nobel Prize in Literature. There is no Iranian equivalent to Pamuk, who is invited to talk at many events and is widely marketed. The American market is large and the US is still the country that produces most Persian translations, followed by Germany and Russia (UNESCO 2012b). Thus, although it produces few translations from the Persian, the US publishes the most significant portion of translations from Persian in the world, since its publishing industry is the largest. These two points challenge the discourse that Persian is not well represented. This claim needs to be complemented and qualified by an analysis of the

---

[4] I have taken 1996 as a basis as it lies in the middle of the time period considered. I compared the total number of publications per year based on the UNESCO statistics to the number of publications from the language translated in the US over the thirty-year period. Although the production of publications evolved differently in different countries over the thirty-year period, this allows us to see a trend in the percentage of publications from each language (UNESCO).

production milieu that implements these translations, focusing on institutions, translators and publishers. An analysis of this milieu shows that it relies on individual initiatives, and that it is largely scholarly and ethnically Iranian. These characteristics are important to explain the low level of circulation of contemporary Persian texts in the US.

As patronage helps to decide how much to translate, as well as which texts are to be translated, it is important to look at the role of institutions in the promotion and financing of translations (Lefevere 1992). The Iranian government sponsors translations of religious texts and of texts that spread the Islamic revolutionary message. The Islamic Culture and Relations Organisation (*Sazman-e farhang va ertebatat-e eslami*) sees this as one of its tasks. The organisation is a broad entity that coordinates the exchange of cultural activities between Iran and the rest of the world. Translation is mentioned at the very end of its list of preoccupations in its charter and is focused on spreading the Islamic revolutionary ideology: 'Writing and translation of books and periodicals with a view to introducing the Islamic-Iranian tenets, teachings, culture, and civilisation as well as facilitating cultural exchange with other countries'.[5] Apart from religious texts, there is little governmental support from Iran that either encourages the publication of Persian literary texts abroad or promotes Persian culture in its non-religious forms. The Saadi Foundation, as explained in Chapter 3, has only published a couple of books aimed at international readers. Therefore, the entire task of translation relies on the individual initiative of, for the most part, Iranian-Americans. An exception to this was the Association of Iranian American Writers (AIAW), co-directed for many years by Persis Karim, with founder and past co-director Manijeh Nasrabadi. The association closed in 2013.

In contrast, the French case shows how crucial such patronage is in the promotion of a literature abroad: not only is French language and literature

---

[5] See the tab 'Functions' on the Islamic Culture and Relations Organization website, http://en.icro.ir/index.aspx?siteid=257&pageid=9642 (last accessed 31 January 2014. This insistence on revolutionary propaganda is evidenced from the fact that 'Sacred Defence' texts narrating the war with Iraq are sponsored and their translation is promoted by several government institutions, as discussed in Chapter 1. A few texts have thus found their way into the American market: for example, texts by Ahmad Dehqan translated by Paul Sprachman.

put forward, but translations are also financially encouraged and publications sponsored, drawing on significant human and financial means (Sapiro 2010: 433). These absences in the Iranian case account for the literary withdrawal of Persian, which is difficult to export and translate. As a result, the field of translation of Persian is restricted to a small milieu which is not affected by this general withdrawal and can make things happen, albeit on a small scale: Iranian-American scholars.

If we analyse the characteristics of the translators, we see that 76 per cent of translations were done by at least one translator of Iranian origin (see Figure 7.1). One example of a prolific translator is Mohammad Ghanooparvar, Professor of Middle Eastern Languages and Cultures at the University of Texas. He moved to the US before 1979 and graduated from the University of Texas. Between 1982 and 2008, he translated four books on his own and two with other translators.

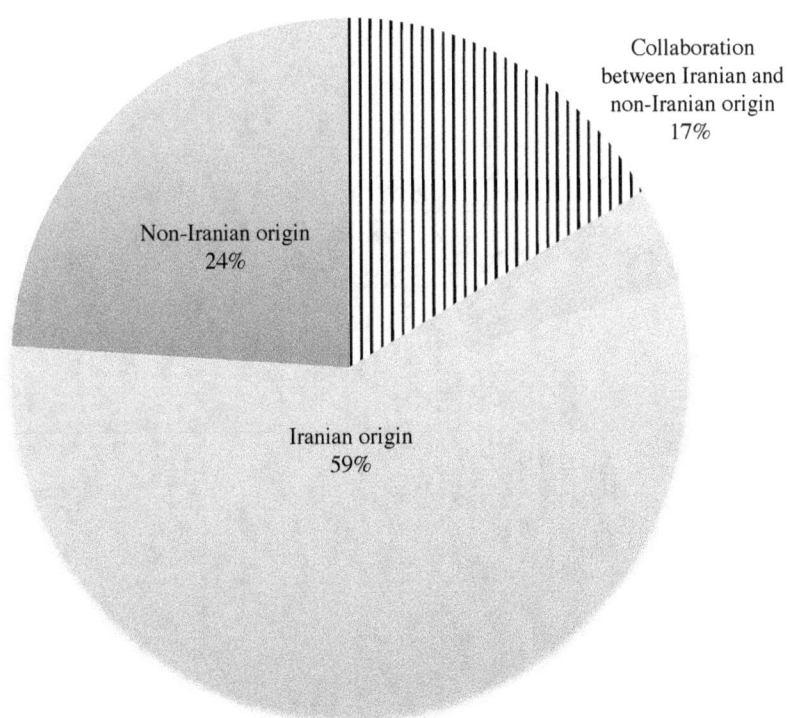

Figure 7.1 Ethnic origin of translators.

Moreover, 61 per cent of translations were done by a translator whose primary career is in academia (see Figure 7.2). This phenomenon can be explained in economic terms, since few literary translators from minor languages like Persian can afford to live solely on the proceeds of their translations. Translation is thus mainly a secondary activity. In addition, scholars can use their credentials as academics for the profit of their translations and do not need to build other credentials to be trusted by publishers. Finally, they can rely on an already constituted professional network linked to the university. As evidenced by interviews with translators from Persian, economic gain is not a priority for them as they either are not paid for their translations or receive relatively small amounts. Their remuneration is often only in the form of receiving copies of the book. As they have other primary ways to earn a living, mainly in academia, their interest in translations is

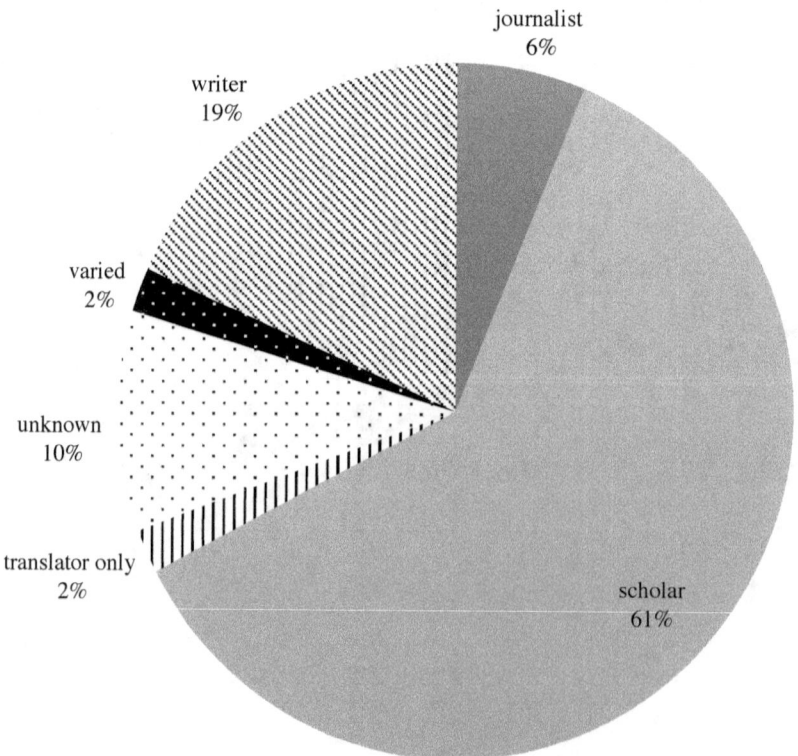

Figure 7.2 Primary activity of translators.

not economic. The Persian translation field is thus primarily linked to the academic field. It brings little economic capital but can bring some cultural capital, although translations do not always count as such in the review of tenure-track positions in the US.

Despite the importance of scholars in the field of translation, it is interesting to note that university presses do not play an essential role in publishing modern Persian translations. Scholar-translators, thanks to their institutional affiliations and the networks they benefit from within a particular university, could have privileged access to university presses, but usually opt for small and independent ones. I have divided publishers into three categories of activity: trade, university, and small and independent presses (see Figure 7.3). This latter category is broad and encompasses all small and independent for-profit and not-for-profit publishers, often specialised in one field.

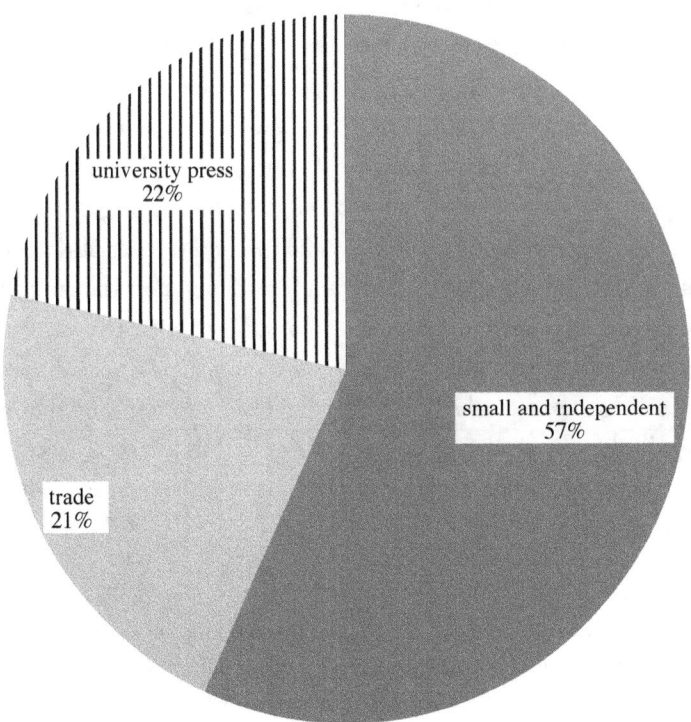

Figure 7.3 Proportion of publishers by activity.

Indeed, while university presses represent 40 per cent of the publication of translations in the US, they only represent 22 per cent in the Persian case (UNESCO 2012c). Of this 22 per cent, some universities play a vital role: for example, the University of Texas Press, partly thanks to the numerous translations by Mohammad Ghanoonparvar and because of the activities of the Department of Middle Eastern Studies. When analysing location (see Figure 7.4), the University of Texas Press accounts for the important number of publications coming from publishers located in the south of the US. Contrary to expectations, publishers are not located overwhelmingly where the Iranian community is to be found, on the West Coast. Indeed, publishers in the west represent only 20 per cent, whereas 56 per cent of Iranian-Americans are located in California alone (Hakimzadeh and Dixon 2006).

Figure 7.4 reminds us of the importance of the East Coast as the traditional area of publishing dominance, as well as showing exceptions such as the University of Texas Press, whose prominence can be explained by the fact that its Department of Middle Eastern Studies is very active.

The reliance on individual initiatives and networks demonstrated in this analysis of the production milieu supports the fact that personal connections are essential in the choice of texts. Lewis Coser noted the importance of informal networks in the analysis of American publishers (Coser 1982). Several sociologists have since studied the decision-making processes in cultural production (Franssen and Kuipers 2013), and the Persian case confirms the findings in this area. Usually, translations depend on the contacts of the publisher with certain translators and their affinity with a particular author. Interviews I conducted with translators and publishers revealed that translators are usually the ones who decide what will be translated, and they generally seek a publisher for an already completed work. Publishers rarely commission works, contrary to what occurs with more central languages.[6] Usually, they

---

[6] There are some exceptions, for example *Afsaneh: Short Stories by Iranian Women* (Basmenji 2005), which was commissioned by Saqi for a series of volumes by women from the Middle East, with other volumes by Bangladeshi and Pakistani women (Kaveh Basmenji, telephone interview with author, 20 April 2012). The trend in publishers commissioning translations seems to have increased in recent years. Sara Khalili, for example, was commissioned to translate Goli Taraqi's *The Pomegranate Lady and Her Sons* by W. W. Norton and Parinoush

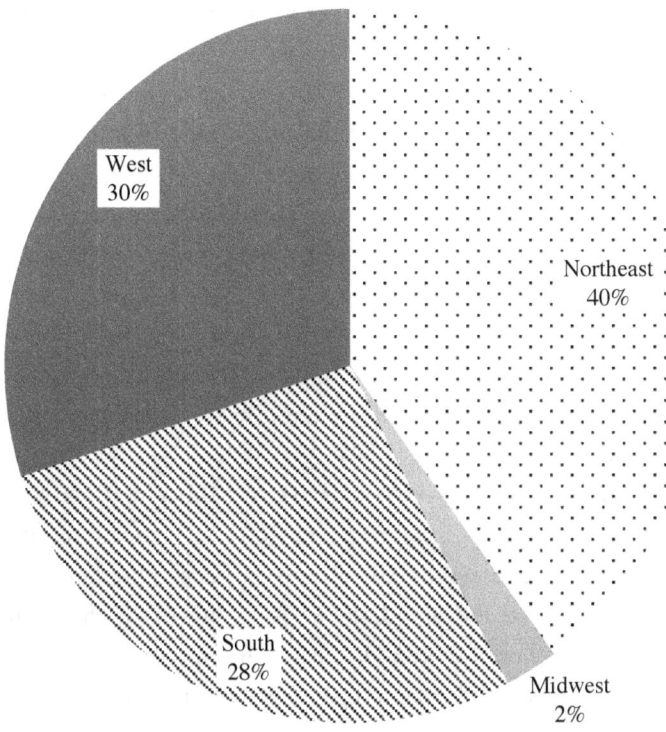

Figure 7.4 Location of publishers by region.

receive offers from individual translators and have no translation strategies as such. The role of the translator is thus essential, as most Iranian writers do not have literary agents who could promote their books in the US or look for an American publisher. This statement, however, should not overshadow the fact that the agency of translators is limited by the rare acceptance of their work by publishers: many translations are simply not published. Translators take the risk and invest their time without a guarantee on their work, and translation should certainly not be romanticised (Bokobza 2004). An exception in this regard, as I discuss in Chapter 9, is Shahriar Mandanipour, who has both an agent and a translator. Yet, it is not the publisher Knopf that commissioned the translation; it is the agent who found the publisher after

Saniee's *The Book of Fate* by Little, Brown, both published in 2013 (Sara Khalili, personal communication, 5 February 2014).

the translation had been partly completed (Sara Khalili, telephone interview with author, 20 April 2012).

As we have seen so far, the production milieu of translations from modern Persian literature is small, largely ethnically Iranian, and linked to the academic field. Do these characteristics have a bearing on the choice of texts translated? Probably, if we consider that these translations represent a stable landscape, very much like the long-term thinking and research privileged in academia, and contrary to the perpetual novelty demanded of the trade publishing sector. Indeed, an analysis of the choice of translations shows that they do not significantly evolve in terms of genre or content over the thirty-year period and that they are not directly linked to political events, except perhaps for the writings of Jalal Al-e Ahmad.

Can we note trends and evolutions over the thirty-year period? Between 1979 and 2011 – apart from 1992 and 2001 when no translations were recorded – from one to eight texts of modern Persian literature were translated in each year. Over the period, there has not been a significant increase or decrease in the number of translations. In addition, the distribution of genres over the period does not change: no genre is more translated than any other in any period.

For the authors who have been translated at least three times, as shown in Figure 7.5, translations are spread over time, with just one exception: Al-e Ahmad, who had six of the seven translations of his works published between 1982 and 1988. This can be explained by his importance as an ideologue of the Iranian revolution. In the years closely following the event, there was a desire to explain the revolution to Americans by translating its thinkers, and this is one of the reasons why he was translated more than other writers. In her thesis on Persian-English literary translation flows, Bahareh Gharehgozlou studies the evolution of translations between Persian and English. She does not focus on the US as I have done here, but on the English language, across three historical periods: 1925–41, 1942–79 and 1980–2015. Her analysis convincingly shows that the first period (1925–41, which I have not studied in this chapter) was dominated by translations of classical works, and that modern and contemporary texts started to be published only around the 1960s, but reached their highest number after the revolution (Gharehgozlou 2018: 99).

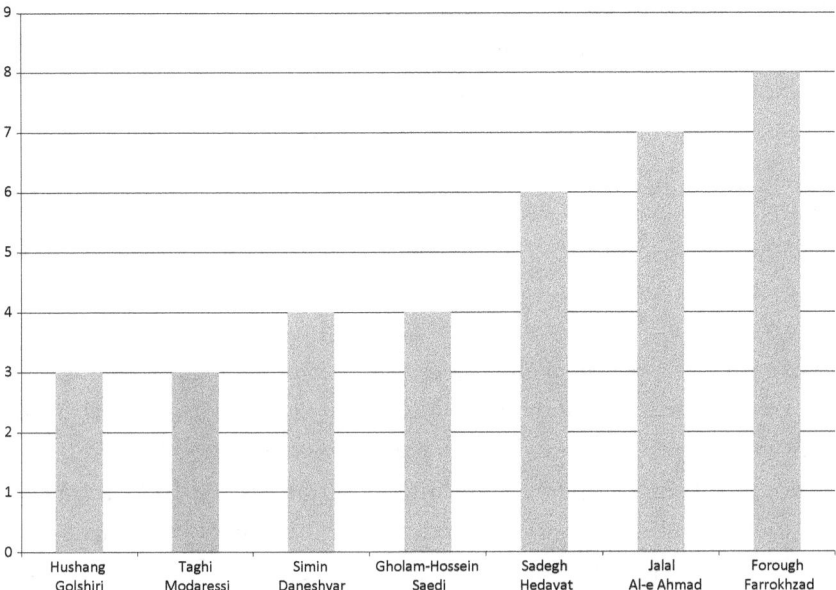

Figure 7.5 Number of texts translated per author.

Several texts by the same author have also been translated multiple times, such as Daneshvar's *Savushun*, Al-e Ahmad's *Westruckness* (also translated as *Westoxication*, *Occidentosis* and *Plagued by the West*), and Farrokhzad's collections of poetry. Farrokhzad is the most translated author, with eight books published in English. In addition, some authors, many having lived outside of Iran for a long time, have had more than one book translated: this is the case for Bozorg Alavi, Sadeq Chubak, Esmail Khoi, Mohammad-Ali Jamalzadeh, Majid Naficy, Shahrnush Parsipur, Moniru Ravanipur, Ja'far Modarres-Sadeqi and Goli Taraqi. In addition, Habib Ahmadzadeh and Mahmud Dowlatabadi, who have only lived in Iran, have had more than one book translated.

Apart from the exception of Al-e Ahmad, the analysis of the data shows that the translation of texts does not in fact follow political events, as there is an average delay of twenty years between publication in Iran and translation in the US. This is not unique to the field of Persian translation, and can be found in the translation from other languages as well. It takes time for books to circulate, to be picked up and to be translated and published, unless they are bestsellers and chosen as priorities by publishers. There is no evidence to show that the pattern of the delay has changed over the years. There is neither an increase nor a decrease in this delay of translations despite the recent American focus on Iranian politics. Thus, Iranian texts do not make it into the American market because of a greater need to understand contemporary Iranian culture in broad terms. Except for Al-e Ahmad, translations are done independently of current political events, although no text is devoid of political considerations. In this case, identity politics and the insistence on the definition of what constitutes Iranian identity (religious/secular; Middle Eastern/Indo-European) is often an element behind translators' choices.

Below, I complement this quantitative analysis of the data with an analysis of the content of the texts. The choice of texts clearly reveals elitist criteria (hence the absence of popular literature until the early 2010s), and avoids classical orientalist tendencies. In general, the texts chosen for translation are intellectual, and the translations retain visible traces of 'Iranianness'. The texts are not easy reads nor popular. For example, there is still no translation into English of romance bestsellers, such as Fattaneh Haj Seyyed Javadi's *The Morning After* (*Bamdad-e khomar*).[7] The first time a popular text was published was in 2013, *The Book of Fate* by Parinoush Saniee, translated by Sara Khalili, the translator of Mandanipour.

One can note an extension of this intellectual characteristic in the way the texts are translated. Whereas Venuti argues that the major strategy in translation in Anglo-American culture is the domestication of texts according to the horizon of expectation of the reader, the case of modern Persian literature is a counter example. Indeed, one encounters elements such as footnotes within the text, which interrupt the flow of the reading and highlight the text's foreign origins. In the collection of short stories translated by Kaveh Basmenji for example, in the first short story by Simin Daneshvar, one finds footnotes on words such as *korsi* (a table with heating underneath), on a month of the Persian year, or on the meaning of a Persian word (Basmenji 2005). Many

---

[7] Caroline Croskery has translated the book in its entirety and has registered copyright but has not been successful in reaching an agreement on the publication with the author, so the book has not yet been published (Croskery, telephone interview with author, 14 March 2012). The novel was translated into German in 2007 as *Der Morgen der Trunkenheit*.

texts display strong elements of Iranianness that need to be explained. This leads to what Venuti calls the 'foreignization' of the text, which he opposes to 'domestication'. This method of translating can also be considered as a phenomenon of identity politics: insisting on Iranian elements as a way of affirming an identity threatened both by the politics of the Iranian government and by emigration. Indeed, Iranians who reside abroad constantly have to redefine their Iranianness along religious, cultural and political lines. For example, defining oneself as a practising Muslim in a secular western country and at the same time fighting the religious establishment in Iran requires a difficult balance.

At this stage, a brief comparison with translations from Arabic is in order to understand the choices made by translators of Persian, which are quite different from their Arabic counterparts. According to Said Faiq, translations from Arabic suffer from highly political uses and bear the traces of orientalism (Faiq 2004). To a large extent, this is not the case with translations from modern Persian literature, although there are some exceptions with respect to highly political use. The texts chosen for translation and the way in which they are translated generally do not show traces of orientalism or have clear political goals. Translators tend to choose canonised texts. This may be why their choices are classic. For example, one cannot find the Iranian equivalent of translations of Hanan al-Shaykh, which respond to the need of the American reader to know about Muslim women, their sexuality in particular, often written in an exuberant and provocative way. The orientalism linked to Iran is not to be found in translations but in memoirs published directly in English by Iranian-Americans, which are largely orientalist in their use of the female Middle Eastern figure and have a clear didactic purpose to educate the American reader about Iran (Keshavarz 2007). Although most texts of modern Persian literature available in English can be seen as didactic, those written in Persian and translated were not written with an international audience in mind, and thus there is little space for them to be didactic about Iran. The translation and its paratexts (for example the foreword, translator's preface, notes and cover) cannot transform them entirely into cultural documents that they were not intended to be at the beginning. This difference with translations from Arabic might also be directly linked to the smaller volume of texts translated from Persian. Unlike texts written directly in English, like

Reading Lolita in Tehran, which are tailored to the interests of an Anglophone audience, translations from Persian do not fulfil the same purpose. I argue that translated texts are chosen according to their canonicity, following a canon defined by Iranian-American scholars, whereas texts directly in English focus the attention of the reader more explicitly on the content and on explaining Iran to outsiders.

In terms of genre and form, translators translate poetry, short stories and novels in an almost equal proportion, as Figure 7.6 shows, with a small proportion of poetry and short stories being collected in anthologies (20 per cent). Can we say that translators' choices are linked to a genre, or do they choose what is canonised and collectively thought to be best, whatever the genre? Because the division between translated fiction and poetry approximately corresponds to overall production in Iran, I believe it is not the genre that is the primary criterion for choosing a text for translation. However, the

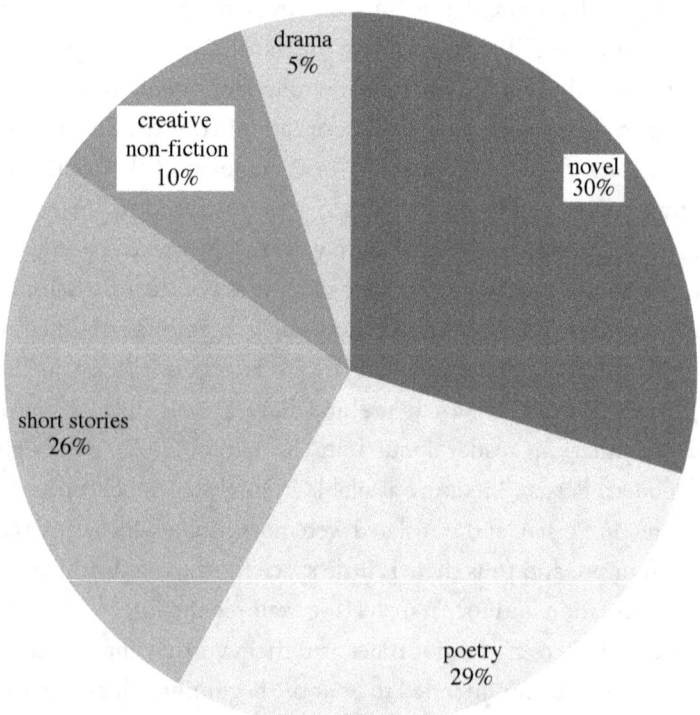

Figure 7.6 Translated genres.

equal division between poetry and fiction does not correspond to the expectations of American readers, who do not read much poetry.[8] An explanation for this trend is that translations use the positive image of classical Persian poetry, tapping into the interest in Rumi's poems as a poetry bestseller and redirecting this interest to modern Iranian poetry. It also reflects the Iranian canon, which is heavily reliant on poetry.

Nevertheless, the choices of particular texts for translation do not entirely correspond to the Iranian canon from within Iran. Some texts, such as Mahmoud Dowlatabadi's *Kelidar*, have not been translated, and the poetry of Ahmad Shamlou and Simin Behbahani only partially so. Some authors are over-represented when compared to the Iranian canon, especially Al-e Ahmad, both for his fiction and essays, as well as authors who belong to the Iranian-American community, such as Taqi Modaressi. Moreover, the texts by Modaressi – who writes in Persian and rewrites his own works in English – are on the border between translation and creation: it is difficult to 'speak of an original and a translation: *The Pilgrim's Rules of Etiquette* is not so much a translation of his Persian *Adab-e ziarat* as a separate work emerging from the same creative process' (Beard 1998). This over-representation of authors belonging to the Iranian-American community can be interpreted as a desire by the same community to build a counter-canon to the Iranian academic one from within the motherland, which does not sufficiently acknowledge the products of its exiles. It is also a reflection of the personal connections mentioned above, as it points to the inscription of Iranian-American writers within a network.

One final characteristic that should be mentioned in relation to the choice of texts is that American translators tend to privilege diversity. Contrary to what occurs in the field of translations into French, where the main French translator of modern Persian texts, Christophe Balaÿ, is devoted to translating the entire oeuvres of Zoya Pirzad and Fariba Vafi, and has a contract with the publisher Zulma for this endeavour (Balaÿ, interview with author,

---

[8] A 2004 report on American literacy in the US shows that the most popular types of literature are novels and short stories, read by 45 per cent, or 93 million adults, while 12 per cent, or 25 million people read poetry, and just 4 per cent, or seven million people reported having read a play (Bradshaw and Nichols 2004).

25 May 2011), there is no systematic endeavour to translate the whole oeuvre of any Iranian author in the US.[9] In the US, the scholarly Iranian-American community is devoted to representing a tentatively comprehensive corpus of canonised modern literature, with an Iranian-American twist.

Although the reception of modern Persian literature is more widespread in the academic milieu, with special issues in academic journals for example, the circulation is too small to be relevant to the American literary market. Yet even in the academic milieu, modern Persian literature is not well known. It has not become mainstream in academic reading and circulates mainly among Persian specialists. For example, the last edition of the American reference work on world literature published in 2018, the *Norton Anthology of World Literature*, does not contain any modern Persian texts: modern Persian literature does not yet belong to world literary history, although classical Persian literature often does.

Although Persian is not underprivileged compared to other minor literatures in terms of the quantity of translated books, it is largely invisible on the American literary market. A lack of concern for economic issues and commercial viability might be an explanation. According to my discussions with literary practitioners, economic capital is not a priority for translators of modern Persian texts. As translators earn a living through other careers, especially in academia, their interest in translation is not economic. Thus, in addition to the creative pleasure they bring to the translator, translations emerge mainly out of a sense of necessity in the translator and because they bring them additional cultural capital. Additionally, translators are hesitant to 'domesticate' the text, in Venuti's terms. It is worth remembering the trajectory of Pamuk's translations from Turkish into English: he only became known internationally after the translation of his sixth novel, *My Name is Red*. His previous translators were heavily criticised and Pamuk had three different translators before finding his 'definitive' one (Türkkan 2012: 160–1).

---

[9] Pirzad's books have an interesting trajectory in European languages. Her first novel was first published in German in 2006 as *I Turn Off the Lights*, then in French in 2011 and finally in English as *Things We Left Unsaid* in 2012. Many modern Persian texts are currently translated into German first, not into English. Mahmoud Dowlatabadi's *The Colonel* is another example.

This section has also revealed the role of the Iranian diaspora in shaping what can be considered the canon of modern Persian literature in the US, which is slightly different from the Iranian canon in Iran. The translations from Persian say more about the Iranian-American community, which represents the majority of literary practitioners devoted to it, than they do about Iran–US relations. They speak about the desires and expectations of the Iranian-American community regarding the place of Persian culture in the US and represent what they want the American reader to know, as well as what they consider the best of modern Persian literature. They partly desire the recognition of modern Persian literature, and not only classical poetry, as a significant contribution to world literature. The counter-example of a book translated from Persian which has sold relatively well, *Censoring an Iranian Love Story*, which I study in Chapter 9, consciously addressed the American reader during the translation process, and further demonstrates the gap between the Iranian literary producer and the American reader.

Despite the discrepancy between the production of translations of modern Persian literature and the horizon of expectations of the American reader, there is space for innovation. Against Venuti's argument, the ethics seem to me to lie in adopting a less elitist position and using more domestication strategies, so that American readers can relate to Persian texts. It is not yet time for foreignisation. In his introduction to a special issue on translation in the Middle East, Samah Selim's arguments follow a similar line to mine:

> Venuti's important argument (1998) for an ethics of translation that recognizes and preserves the specificity and singularity of the other takes on curious twists when applied to non-European languages like Arabic or Urdu, which are fully imbricated by the power relations that have structured imperial modernity. In the context of Orientalism and the history of violence, both discursive and real, that it has made possible, the line between foreignization and alienation, or 'radical strangeness' (Jacquemond 1992,149), seems dangerously fine. (Selim 2009: 10)

This is what I have argued in this chapter for Persian, which is inscribed in a similar context of power relations, even if I have shown there is less orientalism to be found within the body of translations from Persian than from Arabic. By adapting more to the expectations of the American reader without compromising on literary quality, as the example of Mandanipour's text shows, there might be great potential for modern Persian literature.

In the next section, I look at the production of Iranian texts in France and make a comparison to the environment in the US. I am interested in a slightly different topic, not the translations from Persian into French, but the texts written by French-Iranian writers, as alternative ways to reflect on the literary relations between the two countries.

Iranian Texts in France

Although the size of the Iranian population in France is relatively small compared to other European countries, Iranians in France have played a major role in the cultural, political and intellectual landscape of the Iranian diaspora. France has been a crucial place for the production of Iranian texts outside Iran since the 1979 Iranian revolution, written predominantly by secular intellectual writers. During the first thirty years after the revolution, literary texts by Iranians in France were dominated by works in Persian narrating the anxieties of exile. After around 2009, literary production in both the French and Persian languages increased, and a new generation of Iranian intellectuals gradually transformed and diversified the production of their texts and changed its distribution through their work for literary institutions such as bookstores and publishing houses – as the case of Naakojaa analysed in the previous chapter shows. Like the US in the space of translations from the Persian, we thus see a change around the early 2010s in the type of books produced. As I discussed with the example of the publisher Naakojaa, the new literary generation of Iranians in France has, perhaps paradoxically, more connection to Iran than the post-revolutionary migrants of the first generation, whose strong political engagement meant that they could not return home and lost many of their connections to Iran.

Below, I briefly sketch the history of Iranian migration to France and describe its demographic profile and its diasporic characteristics. The social and political characteristics of the Iranian diaspora have an influence on the way Iranian culture, and particularly literature, circulates in France. It provides clues to understanding texts, especially when put into the broader context of Iranian migration. Indeed, why do Iranian-French texts differ so much from texts by Iranian-Americans, which have been vastly studied in recent scholarship? I make frequent comparisons between the Iranian literary field in France and the United States and explain the differences between the two. I discuss literary connections to Iran and to the other diasporic literary communities maintained by Iranian writers in France.

The history of Iranian migration to France can partly be explained by the important role France played in the Iranian imaginary in the nineteenth and twentieth centuries. France's involvement in Iran was largely based on cultural cooperation, with French being the most widely spoken foreign language in Iran until World War II, when it began to be replaced by English. French was the language spoken by the elite, as well as the language through which Iran came to learn about Europe, especially its literature, with French works and translations introducing Iranians to new genres such as the novel (Balaÿ 1998) and unrhymed poetry (Ahmed 2012; Hadidi and Carnoy 1994). The Iranian education system comprised many French Catholic missions and their schools: before the revolution, in Tehran alone one could find the Lazarist schools of St Louis and Jeanne d'Arc, the Franco-Persane school, the Alliance Française, the Lycée Razi, and the Alliance Israélite schools (Nateq 1994). The Iranian system was largely modelled on the French one, especially in the institutions that formed the elite, such as the Dar al-Fonun, which was inspired by the Ecole Polytechnique (Nateq 1994). After Mohammad Ali Shah's coup against the constitutional government in 1908, some intellectuals and politicians opposed to his regime fled to Paris, including the prominent man of letters Mohammad Qazvini (Nassehy-Behnam 2000). Many members of the Qajar dynasty, which ruled Iran from 1785 to 1925, including Ahmad Shah, also settled in Paris after forced exile. In the first half of the twentieth century, Iranian elites sent their children to France to pursue their studies, and it is from this time on that one can trace the formation of an Iranian community in France. As Reza Arasteh notes, 'In 1918 there was a total of 500 Iranians studying in Europe, of whom 200 were in France, 34 in England, 9 in Germany and the rest in Switzerland and other countries' (1962: 444). By mid-century, more Iranians were choosing to migrate to Germany and the United States instead: in 1958–9 there were 4,000 Iranian students in Germany and 3,700 in the United States, with only 800 in France and 600 in England (Arasteh 1962: 448).

One can distinguish several periods in the history of Iranian migration to France: the Qajar period, including the Iranian Constitutional Revolution; the Pahlavi period; and the post-revolutionary period. During the Qajar and Pahlavi periods, Iranians primarily moved to gain an education in France, and sometimes they decided to stay. Students formed the main population of Iranians in France until the 1970s, like in other countries of Iranian migration. Some of them were part of the Confederation of Iranian Students, opposed to the Shah (Matin-Asgari 1991), which was strongly represented in France, Germany and the United States. Iran's modernisation process after World War I and the lack of political freedom during the Shah's rule shaped the political activities of Iranian dissidents during this period. Before the revolution, 'what was published outside Iran was mainly in the form of opposition literature consisting of political tracts and pamphlets' (Sepehri 1988: 6). Unlike the pre-revolutionary period, however, the post-revolutionary Iranians who migrated to France were more diverse and included refugees and activists with different political affiliations, some of whom stayed in France temporarily before they moved on to other countries.

In 2006, the number of Iranians in France was estimated to be between 24,000 and 26,000 (Vahabi 2015: 38).[10] This is much lower than the estimated population in Germany, which numbers around 160,000 in the same year. However, the significance of the Iranian diaspora in France is not captured in these numbers, primarily because France has traditionally hosted a higher proportion of intellectuals and prominent political figures including, for example, the first Iranian president, Abolhassan Bani Sadr; Massoud and Maryam Rajavi, the leaders of the Mujahedin-e khalq (an Islamo-Marxist political organisation), and Farah Pahlavi, the former Iranian empress.

In the following section, I trace the evolution of literary production by Iranians in France with an emphasis on the dramatic changes since the arrival of the third wave of post-revolutionary migrants in 2009. Different periods in the history of Franco-Iranian relations have been studied – for example,

---

[10] Nader Vahabi uses figures from INSEE (National Institute of Statistics and Economic Studies) and OFPRA (French Office for the Protection of Refugees and Stateless People).

during 1807–8 (Amini 1995) and between 1907 and 1938 (Habibi 2004) – and there is also a comprehensive study of their 400 years of dialogue (Hellot-Bellier 2007). There are also some accounts of the general image of Persia and Iran found in western literature (Ansari 2005). Moreover, the reception of Persian literature in France from 1600 to 1982 has been thoroughly studied (Hadidi and Carnoy 1994). An edited collection has analysed Franco-Iranian relations across a variety of disciplines, including literature (Delfani 2009). In my book, I analysed the Iranian cultural production in France since the 1979 revolution (Nanquette 2013a). Recently, a monograph has studied selected Franco-Persian texts (Daneshvar 2018). Continuing these researches, I integrate below the most recent developments.

There is a need to look at the broader cultural landscape of Iranians in France to better understand the literary texts being produced there. There are dozens of Iranian associations in France scattered across the country. Some of them are professional (such as associations of dentists or lawyers), and others are devoted to promoting Persian culture and language through language classes (Idjadi 2012). They work as cultural institutions devoted to maintaining and perpetuating Iranian culture, and they primarily serve Iranians. They often function as community centres, although occasionally events cater to a wider audience and are purposefully intended to attract the French and demonstrate the richness of Persian culture. These include Aftab and the Pouya Cultural Centre, as well as the Cultural Centre of the Islamic Republic, which represents the Islamic Republic regime's cultural viewpoint. However, unlike in the United Kingdom, there is no Iranian school and no religious or faith-based groups. One reason for this is that France has traditionally attracted secular people.

In terms of cultural production, there are several Persian journals and newspapers published by Iranians in France. One should, however, be cautious when counting such texts, as some publishers do not observe the requirement for an ISBN or ISSN, and this makes the publication untraceable. In addition, Persian publications are not consistently listed in western bibliographical databases because of the Persian alphabet. It is more likely that works that have both a Persian and a European-language title will be found there. Between 1979 and 1989, the Centre for Iranian Documentation and Research recorded more than forty Persian or Iranian periodicals published in France, ranging from political to cultural to general interest (Centre for Iranian Documentation and Research 1989). These formed the basis of a healthy Iranian newspaper production on French soil. However, most of these publications were short-lived, printing just a few issues before closing down, mainly due to the lack of sufficient resources or low readership. There were fewer journals and magazines published in the 2000s than previously. One of the longest on the market was *Arash: A Persian Monthly of Culture and Social Affairs*, which started in 1991 and closed down in 2014. The cultural and political journals of the first three decades after the revolution have not been replaced by other print journals. However, there are new initiatives, such as Naakojaa, which has a strong online presence and which is analysed in detail in Chapter 6.

For the first three decades after the Iranian revolution, orientalism and occidentalism were essential intertextual references in Iranian texts published in France as the basis for their images of the Other (Nanquette 2013a). While some texts overcome these references and complicate the image by resisting such discourses, they are exceptions. As I have suggested elsewhere, in contemporary French and Persian texts 'literature happens only when images are deliberately complicated' when the simple opposition between Self and Other fails (Nanquette 2013a: 10). Since the arrival of the post-2009 generation, there has been a change in the nature of Iranian literature production in France. Although it took a few years before the new wave of Iranian immigrants began producing more substantial work – due to their adaptation to the country and to the typical time lag when it comes to migrant cultural production – around 2010–11 there was a noticeable increase in Iranian literary production in France. For example, between 2012 and 2019, a series edited by Ata Ayati at L'Harmattan, called *Iran in Transition* (*L'Iran en transition*), published more than sixty literary and scholarly books on Iranian topics. The texts that were published also became more diverse and are thus less easily categorised. Overall, the first decades of literary production by Iranians in France were represented by books such as Esmaeil Fassih's *Sorraya in a Coma* (1985), describing the war with Iraq, the beginning of exile, and the difficulties of migration. More recently, new literary texts in which the agony of exile has been replaced by an acceptance of one's diasporic identity, especially among those who write in French, has appeared. There is also the emergence of entirely new genres such as crime novels in the field. However, for those who continue to write in Persian, exile remains the main topic. Unlike the Iranian-American texts (where Iranian autobiographies and memoirs swept the market), the themes and the genre of the autobiography do not occupy a central place in France. This is true for both the first wave of Iranians who came to France after the revolution and the more recent arrivals.

In 2009, the arrival of the third wave of Iranian migrants to France led to a dramatic change in cultural production. In the 2010s, some new genres have appeared that make the categories presented in my 2013 book more difficult to sustain. It appears that the field of Franco-Iranian writing is becoming more diverse and that the authors are moving beyond the few clearly defined topics and genres. For example, in recent years in France, Naïri Nahapétian has published several crime novels (2009, 2012, 2015, 2016) that delve into the problems of Iranian society and engage with political and social issues such as drug trafficking. These novels often focus on large cities, particularly Tehran and Esfahan. This is unusual because of what I have described in the first chapter as a scarcity of the crime novel genre in Iran. Even in the United States – where the genre is so popular that it might be expected that Iranian writers would use it more than in France – it is only a very recent addition to the field of Persian literature, along with noir novels and short stories, such as those by Salar Abdoh (2000, 2014a, 2014b). In France, collections of short stories have also begun to appear, such as *Flashes of Life, Persian Stories* (*Éclats de vie, histoires persanes*) (Mousavi 2013), which provides nostalgic glimpses of the life of an Iranian woman in French exile. Apart from Ali Erfan, who has always used the genre of short stories, such collections are usually favoured by Iranians writing in Persian only, and it is rare to read them in French (or in any other European languages, for that matter). Indeed, writers of Iranian origin who write in French have preferred genres that are more accessible to a French readership, such as novels. There has thus been a radical reshaping of the Franco-Iranian literary field in recent years, as evident not only in literary texts but also in cultural institutions, as I analysed in Chapter 6 with the opening of the bookstore Naakojaa.

This shift in the cultural production of Iranians is not specific to France. Sanaz Fotouhi discusses English-language texts by Iranians and argues that there was a clear shift with the onset of a third wave, which coincided with major historical event: the aftermath of the 2009 presidential elections in Iran and the global awareness about Iran's human rights problems against political prisoners through social media, as well as Iran's raised presence in international news headlines due to nuclear talks. (Fotouhi 2016: 112)

I have also seen a shift in the translations of Persian texts into English in the US in the first section of this chapter, with more diverse texts being published, integrating bestsellers.

Conclusion

The analysis of translations of Persian texts into English in the US and of texts by French-Iranian writers in France have shown the complexity of the literary relations between the US and Iran and between France and Iran. The changes that happened in the early 2010s, with more varied texts coming to the fore, are signs that these relations are increasingly complex and multi-layered and that the modes of writing and translating that happened after the revolution have been challenged by new paradigms.

8

Iranian Writers in Australia

When I moved to Australia in 2013 and started to get in touch with Iranian writers and the Iranian community, what was striking to me was the prevalence of the discourse on refugees, talked about in both positive and negative terms. There was just no way to avoid the topic, which is often at the centre of Australian politics. Increasingly, throughout the 2010s, it also became the case that migrants and refugees became a hot topic of European politics, but in Australia, it was already reflected in the literature at the time. Stories of migration and of seeking asylum by Iranians compose an important part of Iranian-Australian texts, whereas they had not been part of my literary encounters when I discussed with Iranian-American and Iranian-French writers.

In this chapter, I compare Iranian writers in Australia to the other Iranian diasporic locations discussed previously, mostly the US and France in Chapter 7, revealing the similarities and differences in the literary production between the various locations. It will become apparent that Iranian writers in Australia – perhaps because of, rather than despite, the short history of migration – have adapted to their Australian readers quickly by using English and modes of writing preferred by Australian readers.

The Iranian community in Australia is rapidly expanding. Who are the Iranian writers in Australia? What is the history of their migration? What kind of work do they publish and with which publishers? What kind of reception do the texts receive? Which literary and/or community institutions support them? What relationship do they have with Iran and other diasporic communities around the world? I first sketch the history of Iranian migration to Australia, describing its demographics and the characteristics of the Australian diaspora, also focusing on the cultural connections to Iran and to the other diasporic literary communities maintained by Iranian writers in Australia. I then focus on literary production and reception, with an emphasis on texts written in Persian, but also discussing the significant number of texts written in English. Finally, I examine the literary institutions that facilitate this production.

The Iranian Community in Australia

While the longer history of migration of Iranians to North America and Europe has led to the numerous and important studies discussed earlier on different aspects of these communities, the relatively recent history of migration to Australia may explain the lack of a comprehensive study of Iranians in this context. As the numbers become more significant, however, one can expect to see more studies emerging. Currently, there are only a few works that examine the Iranian community in Australia, some focusing on religious identity and issues of belonging (McAuliffe 2007, 2008a, 2008b), on adaptation as migrants coming from a Muslim country (Tenty and Housten 2013), on youth (Adibi 1998), on Iranian women's sexuality (Khoei *et al.* 2008) or the integration of the Iranian community into Australian society (Gholamshahi 2009). The only studies on cultural production are by Mammad Aidani, who focuses on refugee narratives (2010, 2014), and Sanaz Fotouhi, who studies cultural events, including literary production (2017). Inspired by these works, this chapter examines the literary production of Iranians in Australia, further expanding our view of the diversity of the contributions of Iranians in the diaspora.

History of Iranian Migration to Australia

One can distinguish several periods in the history of Iranian migration to Australia. Before the 1979 revolution and the subsequent mass migration, Iranians in Australia were primarily involved in the oil industry (Department of Social Services 2014). The Shah's visit in 1974 brought Australia to the attention of Iranians, but it was only after the revolution and the war with Iraq in 1980 that increasing numbers of Iranians began to migrate to the country. Even so, in the first decades after the revolution, the primary destinations were North America and Europe. During the first decade after the revolution, Iranian minority groups, such as the Baha'is, arrived in Australia. In 1981, a humanitarian programme was set up to help Baha'is fleeing religious persecution: 'By the end of the decade, around 2500 people had arrived under this and other refugee programs' (Department of Social Services 2014). In the late 1990s, many professionals came to Australia, but still in small numbers compared to the level of migration to other countries in North America and western Europe.

It was only in the late 2000s that the numbers of Iranian migrants to Australia boomed, and this was due to several factors: 'The major jump in late 2010 reflects a combination of conditions in Iran, changes in Australia and changes en route' (Farsight 2015: 3). In the early 2010s, the significant level of migration includes asylum seekers, following the political unrest of 2009, who arrive either by boat or – if they have already been recognised as refugees by agencies such as the UNHCR – by plane, along with skilled workers arriving on working visas: 'Figures on skilled migration show the perhaps surprising statistic that people from Iran were the 9th biggest nationality arriving under the points-tested skilled migration stream in financial year 2011–2012, with 2,390 arrivals' (Farsight 2015: 1). Of course, those coming by boat might also be skilled workers, but they are not permitted to apply as such through standard asylum-seeking procedures and if they take the latter route must endure an arduous process. The Australian Department of Immigration stated that in 2014 Iranians were the first nationality arriving by boat as refugees and, according to the Australian law of the time, being detained: 'As at 30 April 2014, there were 4,258 people held in immigration detention facilities. Of these 4,258 people, around 27% were from Iran, 16% were from Vietnam, 12% were from Sri Lanka, 11% were Stateless and 5% were from Afghanistan' (Department of Immigration and Citizenship 2014). There have been various contested policies since 2013 about the way Australia deals with asylum seekers arriving by boat, leading to criticism from the UNHCR and human rights organisations, especially regarding its offshore processing and the opening of detention centres in Papua New Guinea. The number of boat arrivals has decreased dramatically since then. An important part of the cultural production of Iranians in Australia deals with these harsh policies, as I show below.

Demographics and Nature of the Community

The Australian Bureau of Statistics' 2011 Census recorded more than 34,000 Iran-born people in Australia, an increase of 52.8 per cent from the 2006 Census. This is equivalent to only half of the Lebanon-born community and one tenth of the China-born community, according to the Australian Government's Department of Social Services. Half of the Iranians are based in New South Wales; they are generally younger than other migrants born overseas; and a significant proportion are Baha'is, Armenians or Assyrians. This characteristic is shared with other Iranian diasporas around the world, which are composed of many religious minorities: Baha'is, Jews, Assyrians, Armenians and converts to Christianity. Figure 8.1 reflects the significant numbers of non-Muslims among Iranians in Australia (Census Explorer 2011), in contrast to the Iranian society in Iran, which defines itself as primarily Shia. Tenty and Housten have different numbers but confirm the importance of non-Muslims among Iranian migrants:

> Religious affiliation of Iranian migrants varies considerably in comparison to other Muslim-dominated diasporas. For instance, approximately 99 percent of Turkish migrants in Australia adhere to Islam (although many are not orthodox Sunni); in contrast, the statistics suggest that only 32.5 percent of Iranians in Australia are Muslim, the remainder recorded as 27.1 percent 'other religions' with around one-fifth (20.8 percent) recorded as Christian. In addition, a large portion of Iranian migrants in Australia are of the Baha'i faith . . . The 2006 ABS census states that there are 17,000 people adhering to that faith in Australia, 45 percent born in Iran. (Tenty and Housten 2013: 636)

Religious minorities continue to face difficulties in Iran and this is why they are over-represented among migrants. It is thus erroneous to think of the Iranian population in Australia as entirely Muslim, as a significant proportion clearly is not, and this is the case in other diasporic locations, such as the UK and the US, as I demonstrated in Chapter 6. Figure 8.1 uses the data from Census Explorer 2011. Nationally, 2.2 per cent of people identified with Islam.

The median income of Iranians in Australia is significantly lower than

Islam	46.6% – 16,089
Baha'i	22% – 7,602
No religion	17.8% – 6,140
Not stated	6.1% – 2,096
Western Catholic	1.2% – 406

Figure 8.1 Religious affiliation of Iranians in Australia.
Source: Census Explorer 2011.

the Australian average, with a higher unemployment rate, although Iranians are generally more educated than the Australian population (Department of Social Services 2014): '58.9 percent of Iranian-born migrants aged fifteen or older had some form of qualification . . . The education attainment of Iranian migrants is even higher than that of Australia's general population at 52.5 percent' (Tenty and Housten 2013: 640). The places they choose to live in are varied. In Sydney, as is apparent in Map 8.1, Iranians live on the North Shore around Hornsby, St Ives and Chatswood, relatively affluent suburbs, as well as in the more middle-class and working-class western suburbs of Blacktown, Parramatta and Auburn. The New South Wales suburb with the highest number of Persian (excluding Dari) speakers is Castle Hill (Census Explorer 2011).[1] In her study of the Iranian community in Sydney, Soheyla Gholamshahi found that even some lower-class Iranians tended to settle in the affluent suburbs of northern Sydney so as to be close to Iranian community networks, highly valuing their support despite the very high cost of living (2009: 260–1).

The Iranian diaspora in Australia generally has a lower socioeconomic status than other Iranian communities around the world. As Gholamshahi confirms: 'A significantly low proportion of the Iranian community in Australia is from the upper classes compared to those in the US, Canada, England, France or Germany . . . but the variety of ethnic minority groups represented is comparable' (2009: 271). In addition, because their migration

---

[1] Non-Persian Iranians, with Azeri, Arab or Kurdish backgrounds, for example, are usually educated in Persian in Iran, so here I equate Iranians to Persian speakers (Dari speakers are included in a different category).

Map 8.1 In cross-hatching, the number of people who speak Persian (excluding Dari) at home in the Sydney area. Source: Adapted from Census Explorer 2011.

is relatively recent, the support networks are weak: 'Similar to other "newly-arrived, small and emerging communities", the Iranian community lacks legal, political, social and cultural representation, which disadvantages it (Gholamshahi 2009: 272).'

In Australia, there is a strong divide between Iranians who arrived as refugees and those who did not. As I have discussed elsewhere, in interviews with Iranian migrants in Australia, Mammad Aidani – a scholar and writer based at the University of Melbourne – found that most considered the term 'refugee' derogatory and called themselves migrant, traveller or *koli* (gypsy) in Persian (Nanquette 2014b). As such, Iranians who arrived as skilled workers tend to disassociate themselves from newcomers who have arrived by boat. This taboo of being a refugee also needs to be understood in the context of the Iranian community in Australia, where, as Fotouhi points out, using the term 'refugee' 'adds another layer of otherness' (2017: 22). There is an inescapable degree of homogenisation and objectification once people's stories are subsumed under the category of 'refugee'. This makes it only more crucial for Iranian-Australians to write about the way asylum seekers are dealt with in Australia, as individuals tend to disappear among a general portrayal of victims fleeing persecution.

Relationship with the Homeland and Diasporic Networks

Like in France, Iranians in Australia tend not to congregate in cohesive communities. This is only reinforced by the fact that Iranian migration to Australia is relatively recent. As I have discussed in Chapter 6, there is a high level of assimilation among Iranians to host societies. This is also the case for Iranians in Australia, although it is worth noting that there is more reliance on community services among lower-class Iranians than among middle- or upper-class Iranians, who are more integrated and tend to make use of services only at the beginning of the settlement process (Gholamshahi 2009).

With regards to the links to Iranians within Iran, as I have explained at length in Chapter 6, writers abroad are often disconnected from readers in Iran, even more so if they write in a language other than Persian, and this is certainly the case in Australia. The digital era is only partly bridging this gap in cultural exchange, and usually this bridging does not work if there is no physical exchange to reinforce the digital engagement. The cultural, political and social support networks linking Australia and Iran are generally weak and the Iranian community in Australia is fragmented. There are some community associations and organisations that are Iranian-specific, but Iranians in the diaspora have generally tended to avoid the creation of closed communities like those seen in other diasporas. Iranians in interviews often mention this aspect themselves and make a comparison with the Chinese, who rely heavily on community networks (Tenty and Housten 2013: 634). While this also occurs among certain Iranians, it is less common. The relatively weak networks are partly due to the significant numbers of political migrants, who, if they come from groups with entirely divergent opinions, such as the People's Mujahedin or supporters of the Shah, will find it impossible to meet for tea and discuss matters concerning Iran. Australian government programmes that support cultural exchange, for example, point to this recurrent problem as hindering integration due to 'mistrust between groups within their own community' (TAFE NSW Outreach 2007). There are other explanations that are linked to specific elements concerning Iranian migration. Firstly, it is much more recent than the history of other migrants in Australia and, secondly, it may simply reflect the structure of Iranian society itself, which might be reproduced after migration. Although an attachment to Persian culture creates a sense of common belonging, reports show that 'Iranians in Australia do not make up a single homogeneous and cohesive community, but rather a number of communities in Australia' (Adibi 1998: 127).

Iranian Texts in Australia

In the following section, I trace these characteristics of recent migration and lower socioeconomic status of migrants in the literary writings of Iranians in Australia.

What is the Literary Production Like?

Due to differences in the history of Iranian migration to Australia compared to other parts of the world, as well as to different readers' expectations, the Iranian-Australian literary field is substantially different from the other Iranian diasporic spaces in the US and Europe. There are common areas – for example, shared themes of exile or trauma – but also many differences, especially in the genres and themes used, with many works by Iranian-Australian writers focusing on the refugee experience. This is the most striking characteristic of Iranian-Australian literature and clearly distinguishes it from other Iranian literatures around the world: in Australia, Iranian asylum seekers and refugees have been telling their stories. This phenomenon does not exist in Europe or North America, although there are also Iranian refugees there. There are a few exceptions, for example, a book edited by Nushin Arbabzadah, concerning Iranian refugees in Britain, but even this does not engage with the experience of seeking asylum in Britain as such (Arbabzadah 2007).

This focus can be explained by a growing trend in Australian literature in general, which reflects an interest in refugee stories, leading publishers to look for them and publish them. Australia's awareness of the subject of refugees and asylum seekers has risen in recent years, and this has led people in the literary world, as well as journalists and human rights lawyers, to become interested in these stories, using them as political tools to promote the rights of asylum seekers. As such, the Iranian production is to some extent a consumption-led practice as many books about the refugee journey by authors of other nationalities – such as Vietnamese – have done well, both among critics and financially: for example, Anh Do's *The Happiest Refugee* or Nam Le's *The Boat*. Elsewhere, I described these works as '*testimonio*' (Nanquette 2014b), referring to accounts given by refugees to Australian writers or journalists who narrate their stories. Another reason for the proliferation of refugee narratives is that the Australian asylum-seeking process is harsher than that in Europe and has become increasingly so in recent years: this has only pushed more people to narrate their refugee experience.[2] There is the added factor of refugee narratives being part of the memoir boom; Graham Huggan argues:

> What is clear is that 'refugee literature' can easily be turned into another marketable form of cultural voyeurism, capitalizing on the endangered, the impoverished, and the needy, and manipulating the vicarious experience of suffering as a means towards establishing a false solidarity with the oppressed. As with other kinds of multicultural writing, there is exoticist mystification at work here. (Huggan 2007: 130–1)

There is clearly a realisation of this exoticist and reductionist danger by Iranian writers who have been refugees and some reject the idea of being categorised under this term. I use the term with caution but since this is such a different category to Iranian writings in the rest of the world, it seems important to use it and to reflect on its characteristics as many writers embrace it and make the most of the Australian readership's interest in refugee stories.

In this chapter, as in previous chapters, I use the term 'Iranian' to describe texts published by writers of Iranian origin for whom Iran remains

---

[2] Since 1992, unauthorised migrants arriving by boat in Australia have been held in detention until their asylum claims are processed. Since 1994, the time spent in detention has had no legal limit. At a later date, detention centres were also set up offshore in schemes such as the Pacific Solution 1 and 2. This included excising some of Australia's offshore territories such that people arriving there did not have an automatic right to seek asylum in Australia, as well as the transfer of people arriving by boat to detention and processing centres in other Pacific Island nations.

an important frame of reference, despite many also holding Australian nationality and/or preferring to be described as Australian. The works by Iranian writers published in Australia are divided according to language. The themes of the works in both English and Persian vary widely, ranging from the depiction of the revolution and its trauma, to the narration of migration and the associated nostalgia for home, to stories totally unrelated to Iran, like Ali Alizadeh's rewriting of the story of Joan of Arc (2017).

Like the Franco-Iranian writers studied in Chapter 7, first-generation Iranians in Australia tend to write nostalgically about Iran, narrating the difficulties of exile or the process of exile itself, and also speaking about loss. A representative example is Mammad Aidani, who left Iran after the destruction of his home city, Khorramshahr, during the Iran–Iraq War. He went into exile as an adult, first to Italy and then to Australia. He has written scholarly articles, collections of poems, one novel and several plays. In the foreword to his novel, he quotes from a letter he sent from Brisbane to his family in Iran in 1983, when the country was still at war with Iraq. At the time, he had just started to write *A Picture Out of Frame*:

> The war is still going on. I'm also worried about my solitude, and lack of sleep, my deep isolation in this city and my mental restlessness and not knowing the language. I feel that I am suddenly buried within my memories. (Aidani 1997: ix)

Zardosht Afshari has written academic studies on his plays (Afshari Behbahanizadeh and Zahedi 2013).

As I show below, it is possible to discern an evolution in the field over time, with more diverse stories appearing, just as in Franco-Iranian literary production and in the translations from Persian into English in the US. However, it is still a young field, younger than diasporic Iranian literature in Europe or North America.

Texts in English

REFUGEE STORIES AND PLAYS

The main characteristic of the texts written in English is their focus on refugee stories, in the genres of plays, short stories, novels or poems. Examples include the anthology of refugee writing, *Another Country*, originally published by

Sydney PEN in 2004 and republished in 2007 (Scott and Keneally 2007). While there are poems, and even collections of stories by child refugees, interestingly, plays are a quite common genre in Australia, especially in relation to narrating refugee experiences, with long traditions of verbatim theatre for example. This is less the case for Persian literature in general, whether in Iran or in other diasporic places. The process of performance, especially when narrating a refugee experience, seems to be an essential characteristic promoting its relevance in the contemporary Australian context (Wake 2010). Indeed, verbatim theatre especially is a prominent genre in Australia.

Included in the *Another Country* anthology is *Refugitive* by Shahin Shafaei, who arrived in Australia as a refugee and is a playwright. *Refugitive* is a one-man play: a conversation between a man on a hunger strike and his hungry stomach. They converse about his escape from Iran by boat, his detention and the reasons for his hunger strike. The play is a humorous and satirical response to the debate surrounding a hunger strike that occurred in 2000 at the Curtin Immigration Detention Centre (Nanquette 2014b). *Refugitive* premiered in Sydney in January 2003; it was also performed at the Sydney Writers Festival and then toured throughout the country, with a total of 300 performances. It is an example of a work by an Iranian writer directed mainly at a general Australian audience, which was well distributed and well received. Today, as well as being a playwright, Shafaei, who started to draw on his theatre background while still in detention, also organises theatre workshops for refugees of all nationalities. Another play in this vein is *Manus* by Nazanin Sahamizadeh, which uses verbatim theatre, relaying interviews with asylum seekers on Manus Island, including with the well-known writer and journalist Behrouz Boochani. It toured in Iran first in 2017, and then in Australia.

Another Iranian refugee who is a strong voice for refugees and who has written numerous non-fictional accounts and critical essays about the treatment of people seeking asylum in Australia is Behrouz Boochani. He is a Kurdish-Iranian journalist and human rights activist, who was held on Manus Island for six years as part of the Pacific Solution. He has written many pieces in major Australian newspapers such as *The Guardian (Australia)* and *The Age* and his writings have also been translated into English in literary magazines such as *Mascara* and *Overland* (Boochani 2015). In 2017, he released a movie shot clandestinely in the detention centre of Manus Island and in 2018 he published the book *No Friend but the Mountains* on his time there (Boochani 2018; Kamali Sarvestani and Boochani 2017), which has been widely discussed in Australia and globally. He was granted refugee status in New Zealand in 2020 and he is not technically an Iranian-Australian writer, but he engages with Australian topics and publishes in Australian journals. He has been recognised as making a significant contribution to Australian literature with the awarding of the Victorian Prize for Literature and the Victorian Premier's Prize for Nonfiction in 2019 for his book *No Friend but the Mountains*, translated by Omid Tofighian (Boochani 2018). In 2019, the *Australian Book Review* offered, for the first time, the *ABR* Behrouz Boochani Fellowship, worth a total of $10,000, demonstrating his leadership on the topic. Although he was the most vocal of Iranian writers on the issues of Australian asylum-seeking policies, he also does not want to be categorised as a refugee only and he is conscious about the way refugee stories can be simplified and lead to one narrative: that of the pitiable refugee looking from freedom (Boochani 2018).

Refugee narratives are very much divided along national lines. When I started this research, I expected to see interconnections between writers of Persian language in Australia, mostly Afghans and Iranians, who belong to nationalities with a high number of asylum seekers coming to Australia. Although it is important not to generalise, the national belonging is often reproduced during the journey, and later on either in detention centres or in Australia, and this translates in the texts produced. In the Iranian cultural centres or in the associations of Iranian students at universities, Afghans rarely mingle. The reasons are complex, and I will not go into them, but one of them is the construction of the Afghan as an Other in Iran (Bjerre Christensen 2016).

Memoirs

Works in English by Iranian-Australian writers also take the form of memoirs, following a worldwide trend of memoirs by writers of Iranian origin – I have mentioned earlier the scholarship published on the genre in the US. In Australia, there have been important studies on the use of this genre by writers from Iraq, Afghanistan and Iran (Whitlock 2007). Many of these works can be categorised as new orientalist narratives (Nanquette 2013a), insofar as they, intentionally or not, reproduce western stereotypes about Iran and systematically oppose Iran to the new country of liberty, Australia.

Zarah Ghahramani's memoir, the first to be published in Australia, offers a case in point (Ghahramani and Hillman 2008). She describes having been kidnapped in the streets of Tehran and imprisoned in Evin, Tehran's political prison, for one month, because she had participated in student protests. She was then barred from attending university and placed under surveillance. In Iran, months after her imprisonment, she met the Australian journalist Robert Hillman, to whom she narrated her story. He offered to help her to obtain a visa for Australia, which she refused for a long time. However, on the insistence of her parents, who were increasingly worried, she finally decided to migrate. The book is what Farzaneh Milani describes as a 'hostage narrative' (2011: 228) as well as a memoir of her childhood in a loving middle-class family and the events leading up to her arrest (Nanquette 2014b). Milani distinguishes between 'prison memoirs', which often testify to women's courage, and 'hostage narratives', which portray them as powerless victims (Milani 2011: 228). The book was written with the help of an Australian writer, which is not insignificant, and directed towards a western audience. Interestingly, despite the Australian component, the book has been well received by international audiences, perhaps thanks to its American publisher Farrar, Straus and Giroux. As Nima Naghibi notes, prison memoirs, as well as captivity memoirs, which sometimes overlap, are a favourite genre among western readers. In her discussion of Ghahramani's work, Naghibi demonstrates that the narrator deliberately constructs her identity, with a focus on being westernised and as belonging to a minority in Iran (her mother is Zoroastrian), thereby differentiating herself from the Muslim majority, of which a western reader might be wary (Naghibi 2016: chapter 2). Naghibi also argues that Ghahramani's work shares traits with Harlequin romantic fiction, which portrays women as highly sexualised captives of masculine power (2016: chapter 2). Pointing out the inequality in the economy of exchange between writer and reader in such memoirs, Naghibi argues that the reader offers their compassion in exchange for 'the spectacle and consumption of the abject suffering body' (2016: chapter 2).

Similar to Iranian-American memoirs, Zarah Ghahramani's memoir is a widely circulated work. It was reviewed by *The Guardian* and *The New York Times*, and widely discussed in Australian newspapers. More often than not, the reviews of the book focus on Iranian politics rather than the text as a literary object, which can be explained by its drawing on the genre of prison memoir. In several reviews, it is compared to another Iranian captivity narrative, *Prisoner of Tehran*, written by the Canadian Marina Nemat (2008). It is interesting that one of the few texts that has crossed the Australian border and appealed to an international audience is a memoir by an Iranian woman that is based on the model of those that have been so successful in North America in the first decade of the twenty-first century, starting with *Reading Lolita in Tehran* by Azar Nafisi and continuing with Marina Nemat. Reviewers' comments on Amazon of Ghahramani's book are usually by North Americans and the fact that it was published in Australia has not hindered its reception as a prison memoir in Canada and the US.[3]

Another Iranian-Australian memoir is by the writer of Jewish origin Kooshyar Karimi, who narrates his childhood in a poor, marginalised Jewish family (2012). He recounts how his Jewish mother had married a Muslim and pretended she had converted to Islam while still teaching her children about the Jewish faith. Karimi describes how he eventually fled Iran with his family, after having been tortured and forced to cooperate with Iranian intelligence (which was spying on Iranian Jews), allegedly because, as a doctor, he had performed abortions. He also wrote a book about the abortions he performed in Iran, focusing on one woman's story in a typically orientalist saviour-like narration (Karimi 2015).

In 2017, Shokoofeh Azar published a fictionalised memoir in the magical realist style titled *The Enlightenment of the Greengage Tree*, which has been well-received by Australian literary critics and shortlisted for literary prizes. She also writes children's stories and short stories. Her book was published in Persian in 2019 and circulates underground in Iran and through her Australian publisher Wild Dingo in the Iranian diaspora. Less widely distrib-

---

[3] As of July 2020, there were twenty-four reviews on Amazon.com, ranking the book 4.3 out of 5 stars. http://www.amazon.com/My-Life-Traitor-Iranian-ebook/product-reviews/B0046A9M9A/ref=cm_cr_pr_btm_link_1?ie=UTF8&showViewpoints=0&sortBy=bySubmissionDateDescending.

uted memoirs are those by Saeed Fassaie (2015), Banafsheh Serov (2008), Ali Alizadeh (2010) and Mehran Rafiei (2017). Alizadeh's book is not a memoir as such but a fictionalised story of the turbulent twentieth-century history of Iran (2010). It is innovative in its form, including fictionalised passages as well as poetry. One of Alizadeh's personal characteristics is that he identifies as an Australian writer, not as an Iranian, although he prefers to say that he has 'no home' (Alizadeh 2010: 1). Alizadeh believes that the Australian obsession with multiculturalism has led him to increasingly be identified as an ethnic writer, although he only writes in English and has written on many topics not related to Iran.

Finally, a new genre of humorous memoir has also appeared, with the book *Good Muslim Boy* by Osamah Sami (2015), which received the 2016 Multicultural Prize at the NSW Premier's Literary Awards. Born in Iran to Iraqi parents, with a cleric father, Sami describes his teenage years in Iran and Australia, where he moved with his parents at the age of thirteen, sharing his funny stories about love, family relationships and death.

Poems

Ali Alizadeh is the most prolific Australian writer of Iranian origin writing in English. His poems engage with issues of violence, immigration and injustice in Australian society and around the world (Alizadeh 2002, 2006, 2011). Mammad Aidani has also written collections of poems (Aidani 1993, 1995). Other poets include Roshanak Amrein, who has published several collections of poems in English using a German-based Iranian publisher (Amrein 2010, 2012); Tara Mokhtari, who has published one collection of poems and relocated to New York (2013); and Mohsen Soltany Zand, who wrote poems about his detention in Australian centres, many of which were published in the Australian literary magazine *Southerly*, and has since published a collection of poems (2010), among other writings. In 2017, a special issue of *Southerly* focused on texts by writers of Persian origin and on the relationships between Australia and the Persianate world (Nanquette and Alizadeh 2017). It included stories, poems, nonfiction as well as essays and offered diverse texts by Iranian-Australian writers.

As mentioned above, in the Australian-Iranian context, the number of texts written in English is greater than those published in Persian. These texts also largely match the expectations of Australian readers by using the genre of the memoir and telling stories about the process of seeking asylum in Australia. Works written in Persian not only have greater difficulty gaining circulation because of the language barrier, but also because of a lack of institutional support.

Texts in Persian

One should be cautious when attempting to determine the exact number of texts published in Persian, as some publishers do not observe the legal requirement for deposit. In addition, as mentioned in the case of France, Persian publications are not consistently listed in Australian bibliographical databases because of the Persian alphabet. Having said this, the Iranian-Australian texts written in Persian that I have traced include all genres. Among them are poetry collections, such as those by the well-known Iranian-Australian poet, Granaz Moussavi, based in Melbourne. Moussavi has published five collections of poems, three in Iran, one in Australia and one in Afghanistan, and is also a film director, known for her 2010 movie *My Tehran for Sale*, the first feature co-production between Iran and Australia. Her poems have been translated into many languages, including English (Nanquette 2014a).

Other poets include Pirayeh Yaghmaee, the daughter of a famous Iranian poet, Habib Yaghmaee. She is the author of children's books and a member of Sydney PEN, and has also published poems in literary journals, often in Iran, but has not yet published her own collection. Zahra Taheri, a scholar at the Australian National University in Canberra, also writes poetry in Persian, and published a couple of collections in US publications in the 1990s (Taheri 1990, 1997). Nasrin Mahoutchi-Hosaini writes in both English and Persian. She has had several short stories published in Australian journals, including *TEXT* and *Southerly*. As mentioned above, many plays have been written by Iranians. Apart from those in English focusing on refugee experiences, plays have also been written in Persian, and sometimes translated into English, for example those by Mammad Aidani (Afshari Behbahanizadeh and Zahedi 2013).

These writers are the most well-known Persian writers in Australia. However, there are many others who publish occasional texts on different platforms. Cultural centres occasionally publish collections in Persian, with a limited audience. The Aknoon Cultural Centre, for example, has published works that include an anthology of short stories and poetry, edited by Djamileh Vambakhsh. This particular publication, *Periodical of Poetry and Stories from Aknoon* (*Gahnameh-ye she'r va dastan-e Aknoon*), was the product of a year of weekly meetings at which writers gathered to discuss their work. The writers who participated then self-published the anthology and distributed it within the community. The anthology is composed of stories, reflections and poems by writers who have achieved various degrees of success, including some who had already published in Iran or abroad – for example, Ali Jafari and Elaheh Manafi Dastyari – and many others who were publishing for the first time.

There are also journals and newpapers published by Iranians in Australia. None of them are entirely literary, tending to be more community journals, but because Iranians are attached to their literary heritage, there are often interviews with writers, articles on literature or publications of poetry and stories. There have been at least seven journals published in Persian since the 1980s: *Payam-e hamyar*, *Peyk-e hamyar*, *Oziran*, *Funak*, *Bamdad*, *Arash* and *Danestani-ha*. *Payam-e hamyar* ran between 1986 and 1997. It included stories about Sydney, essays on poets such as Parvin E'tesami, or on classical poets, the presentation of people from the community, letters, reviews of exhibitions in Australia, advertising ranging from migration agents to patisseries, short stories, articles on the role of women in Iranian society, and reports on the Persian books available in the Sydney Persian Library. Some Iranian-Australian writers also published work in the journal, for example, Fahimeh Shojaiyan, Abbasali Ghasemi and Ali Jafari. In 1997, the Hamyar Centre invited the poet Sayeh to Sydney and the event was reviewed in the journal. Some parts of the journal were also in English; for example, short pieces giving advice to Iranian High School Certificate students. This journal ran to sixty-one issues.

The first Persian journal in Australia was *Arash*, founded in 1984, while the most recent is *Oziran*, a bilingual Persian-English journal. *Oziran* started in 2006 and shares stories about Iranian-Australians. *Danestani-ha* has articles in both English and Persian about world events, reporting the news to Iranians who cannot read English. *Peyk-e hamyar*, *Funak* and *Bamdad* are journals that provide information to the community, with advertisements and practical advice about daily matters. There are also some journals published in English, such as *The Persian Herald* (since 1997).

Reception and Readership

The reception base of the Persian texts and journals is small, as they only circulate within the Persian-speaking community, primarily among Iranians. Sometimes a work or an issue of a journal is taken to Iran by one of the members of the centres, but in general they do not circulate internationally. Why is this the case?

In addition to the usual problems of a peripheral literature such as Persian discussed throughout this book, writers in general in Australia encounter the tyranny of a small market. The variety of cultural products is not huge simply because the market is not big enough, while competition with the UK and the US markets is also detrimental to Australian publishers. Like with the other literary markets, the same restrictions to circulation apply: writers in Australia rarely return to Iran, especially if they have been granted a visa as a refugee; the western embargo also applies to cultural products and is effective – in part because of the difficulty in organising financial transactions; and thirdly, there are problems of censorship within Iran. As a result, the Iranian-Australian and the Iranian literary spaces run in parallel and rarely meet. There are exceptions, such as the works of Granaz Moussavi, who moves back and forth between Iran and Australia. However, unlike her previous works, one of her latest collections of poems, *Red Memories* (2011), could not be published in Iran and she had to self-publish in Australia. Her very latest collection was published in Afghanistan. Clearly, this artisanal distribution process means reception is scarce.

In Australia, there are no Persian publishers, contrary to the many Iranian publishers existing in Europe and North America. As such, Persian writers cannot rely on local networks, and must find their way through more complicated channels. As mentioned in Chapter 6, transnational Iranian cultural networks have proven to work well mostly if they are reinforced by occasional physical exchanges at the local level.

Literary Institutions for Iranians in Australia

In the final section of this chapter, I discuss the few literary institutions Iranian writers rely on in Australia. Literary texts are produced and distributed within a network of agents and institutions, and it is partly because of their lack in Australia that the Iranian literary field remains small and the work is not widely circulated.

Overview of Iranian Cultural Institutions in Australia

Although there is an important Persian library in Sydney, there is no Iranian writers' association or Persian bookshop, or a specialist publisher of Persian texts. However, there are a few cultural networks throughout the country on which Iranian writers can count. The most common associations are local community networks in places where the Iranian population is relatively numerous. In Sydney, there are two major cultural centres. One of these is the Aknoon Cultural Centre, Kanoon-e Aknoon, mentioned above, founded in 2007 and located in Hornsby. This centre organises weekly meetings where authors can read their stories and poems and discuss them. In addition, once a month, the meeting is devoted to the discussion of a book that everyone has read. In 2015, I attended one of their reading sessions with about thirty participants, some of whom were published writers, although none were widely published and most were trying their hands at writing. As Fotouhi notes, 'Aknoon is also the umbrella organization for a number of ongoing activities, including [the] Ayla Drama Group, writing workshops, and reading groups' (2017: 10). Ayla was founded in 2010 by Mehran Mortezaei. Eleven shows have been produced so far, with around 400–500 attendees each time (Fotouhi 2017: 30–1).

There is also the Iranian Cultural Association in Sydney (*Anjoman-e farhang va honar*), located in Chatswood. It organises monthly meetings, which include readings of participants' stories and poems, readings of traditional Persian poetry, the performance of Persian music, and talks on Iranian cultural matters. Fotouhi describes the poetry nights:

> These poetry nights, where people get together to read poetry of the masters, as well as their own, are one of the longest running of the community's activities in Sydney . . . They attract anywhere between 50 to 150 or more people each session, depending on the time of the year. (Fotouhi 2017: 11)

She insists on the importance of these poetry nights for maintaining the sense of Iranian identity (Fotouhi 2017: 12).

Universities also have Iranian associations which organise cultural events, such as screening Iranian films, monthly book clubs with readings of books from the Iranian and international canon, and celebrating special events such as Persian New Year (*Nowruz*). Finally, there are also creative-writing workshops in Persian. For example, Djamileh Vambakhsh, mentioned above for her editing of an Aknoon anthology, ran a creative-writing class for Persian speakers at Hornsby TAFE, initially just for women, and noted that: 'This allows women to tell their stories as fiction, as if it happened to someone else . . . You never tell your stories to anyone because you don't know who you can trust' (Levett 2007). Other creative-writing workshops include one organised by the poet Pirayeh Yaghmaee and the writer Nasrin Mahoutchi.

One can find similar associations in other Australian cities – in Canberra, Adelaide, Perth, Brisbane and Melbourne. Fotouhi confirmed the small scale of these community activities: 'Although these groups do run activities, they are mostly publicized through word of mouth; almost all of their websites seem to be lacking in interactivity and up to date information' (Fotouhi 2017: 10).

The Example of the Persian Library in Sydney

In the last section, I focus on the Persian Library in Sydney, which is arguably one of the longest running and most active cultural institutions on which Iranian literary practitioners in Australia can rely.

There are some small Persian libraries around Sydney and elsewhere, situated in community centres such as Hornsby, but the only major one in the country, the Persian Library (*Ketabkhaneh-ye Iranian-e Sydney*), is located in Parramatta, a western suburb of Sydney.[4] The library collection began with the books collected by the Iranian Welfare Association (*Sazman-e hamyari-ye Iranian*), founded in 1986 with the help of the Australian Department of Immigration. The library in its current form opened in 2005. Starting

---

[4] This section is based on two interviews with Sirous Razaghipoor, the current treasurer of the Persian Library, who is on the board of directors and one of its founding and most active members. I interviewed him in 2015, and my research assistant Setayesh Nooraninejad interviewed him again in 2016. I am grateful to both of them for helping me understand the history and work of the library. The library closed in 2020 during the COVID pandemic.

with 1,200 books, it now has approximately 17,000, primarily in Persian and including children's books. The collection is built on donations from Iranians, mainly from Iran but also from Australia and the US. It also has a small section of books about Iran in English. The library runs on a volunteer basis. It has been recognised as a charity organisation by the Australian Government. It has received very little financial support from the Parramatta Council and functions on the basis of membership fees and small sales of duplicate books, among other small sources of revenue. The library currently has 1,250 members, although not all of them are active.

The Persian Library is not politically oriented, holding books on different religions and political parties. This has contributed to its success in reaching many Iranians. It is one of the biggest Persian libraries serving the diaspora worldwide, despite the relatively small number of Iranians in Australia. As a comparison, Paris, with its small but influential and long-established Persian community of intellectuals and writers, does not have this kind of independent library, although there is a library in the cultural centre run by the Islamic Republic of Iran.

The Persian Library in Sydney organises cultural events in Persian, such as exhibitions or commemorations of important Iranian cultural figures, as well as events such as Nowruz and cultural workshops for children. The library has also invited writers such as Shams Langeroodi, Mohamad Mohamad Ali and, in 2016, Shahryar Mandanipour, through the Aknoon Cultural Centre, with which it has close links. It is the most significant Iranian cultural institution in the country, and while its resources are limited, it succeeds in attracting a wide and varied audience, arguably the widest of any Iranian cultural institution in Australia. It does not produce many texts or organise many events, but it functions as a cultural base, allowing Iranians to connect, and is, as such, an important place for other more production-focused institutions such as publishers.

Conclusion

Iranian literary production in Australia is varied due to the individual experiences of the writers, but several common traits are identifiable: the predominance of works that recount the refugee experience, the significant number of works written in English, versus the relative scarcity of texts published in Persian. The greater use of English reflects the experience of Iranians in Australia. They have arrived in Australia relatively recently compared to the longer history of migration to North America and Europe, and they cannot rely on similar cultural networks. Moreover, there are no Persian publishers based in Australia, which means Persian texts must travel transnationally to be published, either in Iran or in other parts of the diaspora. The predominance of texts in English also reveals how much the Iranian literary community has adapted to the expectations of its Australian audience, using its language, English, and its preferred genres, such as memoirs and stories about seeking asylum. Iranian writers in Australia, perhaps because of the brief history of migration rather than despite it, have quickly adapted to the demands of their Australian readers.

In Chapters 6, 7 and 8, I have studied the literary production of Iranians in the US, France and Australia as well as their relations with their host countries and the motherland. My findings have been that literary relations with Iran and in between countries are scarce but relations within national spaces are multi-layered and evolving in interesting new directions, especially since the 2010s. In Chapter 9, I think more conceptually about contemporary Iranian literature in its global dimensions and in its relations to other arts in the Persian cultural system. I reflect on possible directions for Iranian literature when it is considered as world literature.

9

Post-Revolutionary Iranian Literature in the World and in the Persian Cultural System

In this concluding chapter, I bring together the reflections from the first part of the book on the place of post-revolutionary Iranian literature in contemporary Iran, and those from the second part of the book on its circulation outside of the Iranian borders. I discuss the position that post-revolutionary Iranian literature has in these two spaces and reflect on how this has evolved in the past forty years. The chapter starts by analysing two books that have had an important circulation outside of Iran. Like the case study of children's literature in Chapter 5, they show in negative what happens in the rest of the field. As I discussed in Chapters 6 to 8, contemporary Iranian literature is not very visible outside of the Iranian borders, apart from a few exceptions like these two books. I then make a comparison between literature and other arts to find what is specific to literature in the place and circulation of Persian art products. I compare literature with Iranian cinema, which has given Iranian culture a specific global presence, with specially produced art house films for festivals and an important body of scholarship focusing on its various aspects. I also compare literature to Iranian visual arts, which, more recently, have been prominent on the international art scene. I show that the success of Iranian films is linked partly to cultural film policies which do not yet exist in the literary field and which are only starting to appear in visual arts. Iranian literature, apart from children's literature, lacks such support. Finally, I argue that Iranian literature is slowly being replaced in the Persian cultural system both within Iran and abroad, by visual media. This is a major shift in the history of Persian culture which has been dominated by the literary for centuries.

Is Iranian Literature Global and Does it Matter?

In the following section, I analyse two books by Iranian authors that have had some global circulation outside of Iran. One is a popular romance novel that had a wide circulation in Iran and has circulated in western languages, *The Book of Fate* (*Sahm-e man*) by Parinoush Saniee. The other is *Censoring an Iranian Love Story* by Shahriar Mandanipour, which has been published in English without the Persian original being ever published. Both can be described as books that sold well, if not as bestsellers like some of the Iranian-American memoirs such as *Reading Lolita in Tehran*. Since the 2000s, women of Iranian origin have written many autobiographies directly in English and published them in English-speaking countries. There is diversity among diasporic memoirs, but many are tailored to the interests of an Anglophone audience and play a role as cultural documents. They describe life in Iran both before the Islamic Revolution and during its turbulent days, as well as the war with Iraq and the process of adapting to a new western country. Apart from these memoirs, contemporary Iranian texts that are selling well in English-speaking countries are exceptions to the general lack of circulation of contemporary Iranian literature, which is why it is important to analyse *The Book of Fate* and *Censoring an Iranian Love Story* to see their differences and what has worked, as in a negative.

Censoring an Iranian Love Story

Censoring an Iranian Love Story, by Shahriar Mandanipour, written in Persian, but never published in that language, was translated into English by Sara Khalili, and published by Knopf in 2009. It tells the story of Dara and Sara, two characters invented by the writer Shahriar, who fall in love and exchange letters in coded form in their favourite books at the library. The story is intertwined with the story of Shahriar, who navigates a relationship with censorship and especially with one censor, Mr Petrovich. The writer crosses out the lines that he thinks might be censored, so the reader gets to read different possibilities of narratives and an insight into which sort of love story is possible to write in Iran after the Islamic Revolution. Mandanipour was well known and recognised as a sophisticated writer before leaving Iran in 2006 for a writing fellowship in the US. He has not been back to Iran since.

He is very vocal on issues of censorship and this book is the narrative embodiment of his ideas on the topic. The novel had the support of a major and prestigious commercial publisher for its promotion. As a result, *Censoring an Iranian Love Story* is one of the only modern texts written in Persian, not in a European language, published in the last forty years, which has been reviewed in two major American literary magazines, *The New York Review of Books* and *The New Yorker*. Boochani's recent book also shares this characteristic. Both reviews are positive overall and do not fall into the routine tendency of social criticism of Iran instead of literary criticism. Their reservations concern formal elements and narrative features, and there is a good balance between their literary points and their comments on social conditions in Iran.

In terms of sales, based on interviews with publishers and translators in the diaspora, it can be estimated that usually between 500 and 2,000 copies of translated modern Iranian texts are sold by small and independent publishing houses in the US market. For university presses, the sales are around 1,000 copies (Nanquette 2017b). *Censoring an Iranian Love Story* is one of the only books that sold well which had a resonance outside the realm of intellectual circles. It sold around 16,000 copies in the two years between 2009 and 2011.[1] Whereas some texts by Shahrnush Parsipour, for example, have been well circulated outside of Iran in terms of numbers, they are mostly directed at a cultured readership or at students in Middle Eastern studies, whereas Mandanipour's text targeted a broader readership and this is reflected in its being reviewed in major American newspapers.

As for its reception by general readers, Mandanipour often receives letters from readers and has had some positive feedback in readings organised across the US, but this reception is difficult to quantify (Mandanipour, interview with author, 6 December 2011). A good way to assess its actual reception is to look for online reviews. Table 9.1 compares the reviews of *Censoring an Iranian Love Story* with those of the bestseller memoir in English, *Reading Lolita in Tehran*, and the book I analyse below, *The Book of Fate*, on several

---

[1] In December 2011, two years after its publication, Knopf had sold a total of 13,000 copies in both hardcover and paperback in the US. For the UK sales of the book, as of December 2011, Little, Brown has sold approximately 3,000 copies. Thanks to Sara Khalili for providing me with this information.

Table 9.1 Reviews of *Censoring an Iranian Love Story*, *Reading Lolita in Tehran* and *The Book of Fate* online, as of August 2019.

	amazon.com		goodreads.com		
	reviews	stars	reviews	ratings	stars
Censoring an Iranian Love Story	18	4.1/5	314	1,657	3.65/5
Reading Lolita in Tehran	666	4.1/5	7,262	108,787	3.6/5
The Book of Fate	57	4.4/5	529	6,420	4.22/5

websites as of August 2019. Although written originally in different languages – English and Persian – these three books by Iranian writers are representative of different categories in terms of sales, *Reading Lolita in Tehran* being the top bestseller. The websites I look at are not exclusively American: for example, Goodreads is especially transnational. However, amazon.com is dominated by American reviewers, as reviewers of other nationalities tend to write on their national websites. These reviews thus give an indication of the American and transnational reception.

Censoring an Iranian Love Story thus appears as the first translated contemporary Persian text that has received a relatively good reception in the American market largely and among critics in particular, but it has nonetheless had a small circulation compared to memoirs in English by Iranian-Americans, such as *Reading Lolita in Tehran*.

What explains the relative success of this Iranian novel? First, the text has been helped by the prestige of the publisher Knopf and the networks that a big trade publisher draws upon when it comes to interviews, literary events and reviews. Second, as the author and translator worked together during the writing and translating process, they had a vision of what should be achieved by this book and how to address a western audience (Sara Khalili, telephone interview with author, 20 April 2012). I argue that *Censoring an Iranian Love Story* was written for an English-speaking, or more broadly, a western audience, and part of its success is due to this attention paid to the audience. The fact that the text has not been published in Persian and does not have a fixed status in Persian because it is unpublished, reinforces this characteristic. Its writing process, in which the author took into account the translator's point of view when writing the later sections of the novel, is particularly enlightening.

Moreover, the writer lived in the US at the time of the publication and promotion and thus has a direct relationship to his readership. In an interview with the author, Christopher Lydon does not even ask the question of the targeted audience, but stated that Mandanipour wrote the novel for an English-speaking audience, to which the author answers: 'I dare not to say that this book is just for western readers. Maybe it's a sort of testimony about our culture, our writers' (Lydon 2009). Mandanipour is reluctant to say that he did not think about Iranians when writing it, as no writer would like to consciously so restrict his audience, and to forego the possibility of addressing his Iranian fellow citizens, but he also says in the interview that the novel is an explanation to American writers of what censorship really means: when you have to wait five years to get a permit to publish; when your book becomes a sort of poison because it constantly reminds you of all the years wasted (Lydon 2009). Moreover, the explanations of Iranian history or certain words clearly address English-speaking readers.

Apart from Mandanipour's novel, there have been no other reviews of translated modern Persian novels, either in *The New York Review of Books* or in *The New Yorker*, in three decades. Of course, there are other media for book reviews apart from traditional newspaper supplements, such as online magazines, blogs, as well as minor publications that have reviewed modern Persian literature. Simin Daneshvar's canonical *Savushun* has been well reviewed in such publications for example. There are several reviews of Persian texts, like by Parsipur mentioned above, in *Kirkus*, an American book review magazine. However, such journals are aimed at a specialised audience and do not reach the general public, while in mainstream media and television, modern Iranian literature is entirely invisible. Promoting books on radio and television is an important aspect of the marketing process:

> Interviews and features seem to work better than reviews . . . 'as one gets a sense of who the person is and what they're doing.' So here we see what Booth terms 'the memoir complex' at work, the audience's interest in the story of the author, and their conflation of it with the actual fiction they will be reading (Büchler and Guthrie 2011: 51).[2]

---

[2] The space here is the UK but the analysis is relevant to the US and some other western book markets.

This was partly at work with Mandanipour because he is personally invested in issues around censorship and there was a desire from the American audience to hear from him and his direct experience of it and of life in Iran.

The Book of Fate

The Book of Fate, translated by the same translator as Mandanipour's, Khalili, was published in 2013, translated from a text published in Iran in 2002 that had enormous success (Saniee 2013). Written by a woman, it describes the life of a strong fictional woman, a religious but unconventional character. Not only has it been successful in Iran in terms of sales, but it has also become a cultural phenomenon within Iranian society. Although not endowed with the cultural prestige of literary prizes because it is a popular novel, but not entirely a romance, it has been talked about in Iranian literary forums, and become part of a discourse on the state of Iranian society. It is also one of the Iranian bestsellers that has had the widest international circulation and success globally. Why is this book, narrating the life journey of a woman married to a communist activist, significant? What does its circulation tell us about the movement of ideas and characters and about the book market globally? Here I focus on translations into English, which are the most significant in a cultural world where English is the hyper-central language (Heilbron 1999), but *The Book of Fate* has been translated into many other European and non-European languages – like Japanese.

The Book of Fate is a novel set in twentieth-century Iran and narrates over fifty years the life of Massoumeh, a girl from a poor and religious family who is married to a communist after her family forbids her to marry her sweetheart. The man is a stranger and the family do not know he is a political activist. The narration follows her struggles to get an education and a career and to look after her children by herself, when her husband Hamid proves his disinterest in family life, as well as the sacrifices made along the way. As with many books, there have been issues with the publication of *The Book of Fate* in Iran. It was initially denied permission to be published, then a first edition was released taking advantage of reformist president Mohammad Khatami's ruling, which stated that each publisher could print a few books without seeking the permission of the Ministry of Culture and Islamic Guidance (Daghighi 2005). By 2005, the book had been reprinted fourteen times, but its permission to print was revoked under the presidency of Mahmoud Ahmadinejad (Mardomak 2010). It received permission again to be printed after the Nobel Peace Prize-winning lawyer Shirin Ebadi defended its case legally. By 2019, it had been printed in thirty-six editions in Iran. However, despite its huge success among readers, it did not win any literary prizes and it has received mixed reviews from critics, many of whom dismissed it as 'popular'. However, others supported it from the start, most notably in the leading cultural magazine *Bukhara* (Shahrestani 2004: 384).

Parinoush Saniee is a sociologist and psychologist based in Iran. She insists in interviews that her novel is a documentary about a certain type of woman who has not had the opportunities available to the younger generation. She thought she would have difficulty publishing an academic book on the subject and decided to write a novel (Daghighi 2005). She also states that her novel shows the consequences of the status of women in Iran better than she could with numbers and reports. A major topic of discussion about this book within Iran has centred on the feminist message. Even though the discussion about Iranian women is an important aspect, and political in itself, discussing it also serves to overshadow the other important aspect of the book: its otherwise political message and its portrayal of political groups opposing the Islamic Republic regime. *The Book of Fate* offers a nuanced message about Iranian women. In particular, its ending, where Massoumeh continues to sacrifice herself and refuses to marry her childhood sweetheart because it would displease her children, can be seen as attenuating the discourse of empowerment present in the rest of the narration.

The book's global circulation is linked to several factors. First, this bestseller by an Iranian woman writer builds on the familiarity constructed among the western readership on Iran by diasporic memoirs, which have introduced western readers to the Islamic Revolution. Second, it rejects the stereotypes depicted by diasporic memoirs and benefits from introducing a new discourse. It portrays a different Iranian woman and engages in a global discourse on feminism, offering an alternative Islamic version of feminism as described by Ziba Mir-Hosseini: 'A movement to sever patriarchy from Islamic ideals and sacred texts and to give voice to an ethical and egalitarian vision of Islam can and does empower Muslim women from all walks of life to make dignified choices' (2006: 645). We see Islamic feminism at work in this book, as Masoumeh argues against the most conservative proponents of the Islamic Republic regime, and defends her position and will to be independent, as that of a true believer. It offers a nuanced portrayal of Iran and shares a complex vision of Iranian women. It portrays women who are religious but unconventional characters, and who do not hesitate to question the Islamic Republic's mandates. The circulation of this bestseller demonstrates how a different point of view on feminism, one based on the values of Islamic feminism and insisting on the idea that Islam is compatible with feminism, has the agency to interpolate – to use Bill Ashcroft's term – dominant systems of publication and circulation as well as the potential to transform western expectations of Muslim women. The Iranian woman's voice has to situate herself vis-à-vis the dominant discourse of feminism, and she 'must insert that text into the western-dominated systems of publishing, distribution and readership' (Ashcroft 2001: 48–9). The book's distributed agency comes from a combination of writer, agent, translator and publisher that disrupts the genre of writing by and about a Muslim woman.

The Book of Fate benefitted from significant support for its circulation in English, especially thanks to its literary agent, Laura Susijn, and it enjoyed success among international readers. It was first translated into Italian and won the Boccaccio prize for best international book in 2010. After receiving this prize, the book attracted the interest of the English publisher Little, Brown, who commissioned Sara Khalili for the translation. Later on, Little, Brown secured funding for the translation and obtained the Sharjah International Book Fair Translation Grant Fund. Its copyright was then sold to a Canadian press, House of Anansi, for sale on the North American market. Along with the numbers of reviews noted in the table above, *The Book of Fate* appeared on the list of *World Literature Today's* '75 Notable Translations 2013', along with Ismail Kadare, Marguerite Duras and Amos Oz.

Within Iran, *The Book of Fate* has been valued for its take on Iranian society and politics, including the status and role of women (Etemadi and Dehbashi 2004–5: 270), but not exclusively. On the other hand, it has received a feminist reading primarily from English-speaking audiences, both general readers and critics, because this is a discourse to which such readers can relate more easily. An interview with the English translator Sara Khalili confirmed the importance of this feminist reading for the western context

(Khalili, interview with the author, 22 July 2014). Khalili said she was interested in this book and accepted the offer to translate for three reasons: she was interested in the story of Massoumeh as a woman and her role in society; she was interested in the story of personal growth of a woman building a life and a career for herself; she also liked the retrospective view of what working-class society experienced during the revolution. Khalili has translated many books from the Persian for large and small presses, and chooses carefully the texts she wants to work on and promote. Her choice of this text was deliberate and her insistence on its feminist aspects reinforces the trajectory of the book along this line. She played an important role in helping build the agency of *The Book of Fate* in its global circulation.

The two books translated by Sara Khalili discussed above are some of the only books that have sold well and targeted a non-academic readership from Iranian literature, written in Persian, in the English-speaking markets. Why are these exceptions?

Should Iranian Literature Really Be More Global?

Throughout this book, I have studied the structural issues with Iranian literature being disconnected from global flows of exchanges, from sanctions to censorship and other constraints at the national and international level. But why should Iranian literature be global? Why does it matter? World literature debates are sometimes about which national literature gets a slice of the international attention. This is not my concern here and I do not think Iranian literature should necessarily be more visible globally for the sake of being visible. What is concerning is that its seclusion means that it restricts its possibilities and that it does not develop as richly as possible. The seclusion of Iranian literature means that there is no long-term back and forth between Iran and the world. It is difficult for Iranian writers to inscribe themselves in the world. As a result of this isolation, it is very rare to see writers concerned with addressing a global audience. It is also the case that many writers write 'local' (*bumi*) texts, that have difficulties attracting a western audience. It does not mean that texts with very local elements cannot be attractive to international readers though. However, the inscription in the world is an important aspect for stories to travel.

As I detailed in Chapter 3, and contrary to the independent sector in cinema which I discuss below, the independent sector in literature is small and has not been able to flourish. It also lacks professional organisation and the government is not interested in supporting it to become more professional, apart from the exception of children's literature. For example, literary translators do not have representation, only the International Federation of Translators exists, which is for technical translators. Most of the initiatives are governmental, like the Centre for the Organisation of the Translation and Publication of Islamic Studies and Humanities Abroad (*Markaz-e samandehi-ye tarjomeh va nashr-e ma'aref-e eslami va olum-e ensani dar kharej az keshvar*) founded in 2007, which is a governmental initiative and only translates texts that are in line with the Islamic Republic's mandates. In a country which is divided between governmental and independent, this means that independent literature not only is not supported but also is constrained and slowed down.

There are a number of agencies that aid publications, both governmental agencies and charitable foundations (*owqaf*). However, all of them support scholarly texts, and do not support the creation of contemporary literature. There is, for example, the Research Centre for Written Heritage (*Markaz-e pazhuheshi-ye miras-e maktub*), which publishes mostly philosophical, religious and scientific texts, not literary ones (Afshar 2009: 480–3).

Another example of this lack of support towards professionalisation of the field is the quasi absence of literary agents in the Iranian literary field, except again, for children's literature. In other literary markets, scholars note that:

> these agents have a central role in the shape and modes of international literary exchanges. They can push up the bidding and the negotiation on various grounds, such as the actual cash deposit, the level of royalties, the territories in which the target publisher will be allowed to distribute the translation, and even the duration of the contract ... In short, literary agents take an active part in the reconfiguration and fragmentation of translation territories. (Buzelin 2005: 209)

Iran is not alone in this lack of literary agents and it is important to remember it is a relatively new phenomenon in western countries. It is also the case in other non-western book markets, like in India, that literary agents are new players in the field (Gonsalves 2016). As I have shown in Chapter 5, it is only in the field of children's literature that literary agents have been active in promoting Persian books. In fiction for adults, the job does not really exist. There was the Gazelle agency for some time, which worked with independent publishers for fourteen years and bought rights at book fairs, but it stopped its activities. In 2019, there were only a few literary agencies not specialising in children's books still active, all on the governmental side: the government literary agency POL, which supports the translations of books for children as well as about Shia Islam and Iranian traditions as well as some novels (Jafari Aghdam 2012 onwards); the Nowruz Literary Agency from the Alhoda International Publishing Group; and the agency Tamass, created in 2014, which work along similar lines. Their main audiences are in the Islamic world, and they do not appeal to many foreign publishers outside of Islamic countries.

Because of this general lack of professionalisation of the literay field, no equivalent to cinema's festival circuit exists in literature. Felicia Chan has studied the role of festivals in promoting national cinemas, and the case applies to Iran (Chan 2011). Film festivals give prestige and value to Iranian films before returning them back to the nation (Salamati 2019: 18–28). In anglophone literature, literary festivals and prizes are essential in the creation of cultural value (English 2005). Since contemporary Iranian fiction is not recognised internationally in such book fairs, festivals and through prizes, it also lacks prestige within the country. There is for example no equivalent in Persian to the International Prize for Arabic Fiction, commonly known as 'the Arabic Booker', created in 2007.

Privately, there has been a recognition from professionals in the field that the status quo does not benefit the Iranian publishing industry and several important publishers are making an effort to play by the rules of the international game, although they are not obliged to do so legally within Iran, and to develop associations and literary initiatives. However, this is still tentative, and the trust with foreign publishers will take time to be constructed. As long as this is a case-by-case basis, it is unlikely that the field as a whole will benefit from it. Again, it is important to reiterate that this analysis should not obstruct the fact that they are initiatives that work, and individuals are working hard on overcoming the above-mentioned constraints. It was invigorating for me to talk with publishing staff at the publisher Ofoq to discuss their views on translation and copyrights and how Iranian publishers should play along globally. My point is that these are exceptions and until they become the rule, the field will not move dramatically towards more openness.

These structural issues are particularly striking when we compare literature with other Iranian arts. In cinema, support from the state has been critical to help develop it, while in literature, the independent sector has been crushed by harsh policies. The Islamic Republic regime invested in the media with a wider audience, cinema, and in children's literature, which had potentially high impacts on the formation of a new Islamic society.

The Global Circulation of Iranian Cinema

As Azadibougar argues, 'Comparing the status of the Persian novel with Iranian cinema, both nationally and internationally, reveals aspects of the problem: Iranian cinema has had commercial success at home and has won critical respect abroad; Iranian novels, however, lack both' (Azadibougar 2014: 1). It is partly because cinema has been given a special status with the Islamic Republic regime that it has been possible for it to have this national standing and to travel globally. Globally, the state heavily invested in it and saw it as a way to promote the country. It played an important role in public diplomacy: 'the Iranian authorities found in Iranian cinema an effective cultural diplomacy tool' (Salamati 2019: 107). It invested in it through funding as well as defined rules and censorship. Blake Atwood states:

> to refashion the cultural status of film required unprecedented state control of the industry . . . The project included both legal and extralegal policies that enabled state intervention in every aspect of the film industry, from the training of filmmakers and access to equipment to the oversight of scripts and control over exhibition, including imported films. (Atwood 2016: 3)

The Special Place of Cinema for the Regime

Early on at the beginning of the Islamic Republic regime, cinema took on a particular place in the cultural system. Since cinema was created in the west, Islamic thinkers have had an uneasy relationship with it. However, in 1979, Khomeini stated in a speech: 'Cinema is a modern invention that ought to be used for the sake of educating the people' (Khomeini and Algar 1981: 258). Agnès Devictor argues that the involvement of the state in cinema comes from three types of motivation: socio-political (the people need entertaining), ideological (cinema can convey Islamisation) and nationalist (it manifests the greatness of the country) (2004: 57).

The Sacred Defence cinema, which started just after the outbreak of the war with Iraq, helped in shaping Iranian cinema after the revolution: it received lots of financial support and interested people received training. The famous director Mohsen Makhmalbaf started as a director following the revolutionary ideals (Dabashi 2008: 64) and made a film on the war called *Two Blind Eyes*. It is only later on that he made controversial films, eventually deciding to leave the country (Naficy 2012: 40). A specificity of Iranian cinema after the revolution is the apparatus put in place to make sure cinema was conforming to Islamic norms. This specificity was shared with other cultural productions like literature, as I detailed in Chapter 3, but it encountered different challenges with the visual medium. Atwood argues:

> the government institutionalized filmmaking in 1982 and 1983, when it relocated all cinematic affairs to the newly established Ministry of Culture and Islamic Guidance . . . and established the Farabi Foundation . . . These two institutions implemented a series of policies that sought simultaneously to encourage and to limit filmmaking. (Atwood 2016: 12)

Cinema, as a representative of what the new Islamic codes should be, interestingly, blurred the distinction between the codes applied privately and in the public sphere, and the codes of the public sphere had to be applied, even in the representation of a private sphere like the home. Hamid Naficy calls post-revolutionary Iranian cinema 'Islamicate cinema', to insist on the fact that it is made in 'a predominantly Muslim country' while 'Islamic cinema' would be 'a cinema that is about the religion of Islam and its tenets, characters, and stories' (2012: 8). Michelle Langford explains this:

> While the majority of films produced in Iran since the revolution are not overtly about Islam, Iran's Islamicate cinema would necessarily conform to and in many cases promote Islamicate culture and values . . . [T]hese values include theocracy, monotheism, ethics and moralism, modesty, martyrdom

and purification, as well as political and economic independence. (Langford 2019: 74)

It is indeed important to keep in mind that the revolution, although a major break in the cultural history of Iran, did not erase previous values and builds up on forms and references that were current before it happened.

How Policies on Cinema have Influenced its Worldwide Circulation

Maybe an unintended consequence of the state's support of cinema is that it helped not only the governmental sector but also the independent sector. The films made in the independent sector are mostly the ones that are travelling abroad. It is important to remember that the independent sector in cinema is not equivalent to the independent one I have distinguished in the case of literature. There is not such a sharp divide between the two fields in cinema, as many independent filmmakers, including the ones being awarded international film festivals awards, receive some form of help from the state, since we are dealing with much larger budgets than that needed to write a book.

The state realised a few years into the war that it could not export its most ideological films and settled on the films that appealed to western audiences and acted as positive and intellectual representations of the country, as opposed to the image of an Iran stuck in the war and the revolution. It used them to present a different image of Iran, although those films might not have been the ones they preferred and were also, for a time, not the ones preferred by the Iranian audience. Azadeh Farahmand argues that the Iranian state's strategies on cinema led to the production and distribution of apolitical arthouse films, with filmmakers having to compromise with the state (2002: 87). Some Iranian critics have termed these arthouse films that avoid political content 'festival films' (*film-ha-ye jashnvareh-i*). After the 1990s, thanks to the diversification of distributors and digital technologies allowing filmmakers like Panahi to actively engage in the circulation of their own films, this category of 'festival films' becomes less relevant.[3] Despite these tensions, Iranian cinema is undoubtedly the cultural product that is most widely acknowledged and revered globally nowadays:

---

[3] Thanks to Mahsa Salamati for clarifying this point for me.

The politics put in place by the Islamic republic reveals an undisputable success of public power, even if only by the average number of films produced (60 feature films/year), despite some fragilities in the sector, such as the diffusion of cinema on the whole of the territory. The vitality of Iran's cinematographic industry, even if relative, makes it one of the main producing nations in the region, except India, and one of the most celebrated internationally. (Devictor 2004: 55)

This vitality cannot be seen in the literary field, apart from a few exceptions.

The Global Circulation of Visual Arts

Uneven Attention to the Visual Arts in the Past Forty Years

Shortly after the revolution, there was some interest from the government directed towards visual arts. Two institutions played important roles in promoting contemporary Iranian arts: the Tehran Museum of Contemporary Art (TMoCA), and the Centre of Plastic Arts of Iran (*Markaz-e honar-ha-ye tajassomi-ye keshvar*).

> The latter, which came under the control of the Deputy Minister of Culture and Islamic Guidance for Artistic Affairs, had been established in 1983, and was directed by the head of the TMoCA. Both the museum and centre have also supported visual arts through the establishment of organised programmes, including giving their biennials more comprehensive aims (and also involving the newly established artists' societies directly) and holding thematic exhibitions both of contemporary Iranian art and of contemporary European and American art (for example, on twentieth-century British sculpture in 2004 and contemporary Japanese art in 2005). (Keshmirshekan 2015b: 131–2)

Helia Darabi mentions the major international festival of Iranian art and culture in Düsseldorf, Germany, in 1991,

> with opening speeches from the Iranian Minister of Culture and Islamic Guidance, Mohammad Khatami, and the German Minister of Education. This was the largest festival of Iranian art and culture ever held outside the country, either before or after the Revolution up to that time. (Darabi 2015: 20)

She demonstrates clearly the different approaches to the museum by the state and how policies have changed more recently to encompass a broader definition of visual arts that is not only for governmental artists. In the 2000s and 2010s, the Ministry of Culture and Islamic Guidance organised art events as well as the annual and governmental Fajr International Festival of Visual Arts (*Jashnvareh-ye beinolmelali-ye honar-ha-ye tajassomi-ye Fajr*).

> These exhibitions are conventionally held in public art centres and museums under the control of the ministry or the Iranian Academy of the Arts – in particular the Tehran Museum of Contemporary Art, the Niavaran Cultural Centre and the Saba Cultural and Artistic Centre. (Keshmirshekan 2015b: 116)

With the conservative governments of Ahmadinejad, the TMoCA exhibited more governmental painters, but the movements started during the early decade could not be stopped (Darabi 2015: 238–9).

A Recent Move to the Independent Sector

The most globally oriented approaches are coming, perhaps unsurprisingly, from the independent sector. Whereas most of the art supported by the government had to follow Islamic norms, the support from the independent sector means that artists have to redefine their sense of identity and negotiate both global discourses on art and their sense of being Iranian without subjugating to self-orientalising discourses (Keshmirshekan 2015b: 129). Commercial galleries and art centres were created in the 2010s, as well as the Tehran Annual Auction, established in 2011 (Keshmirshekan 2015a: 144). This move to the independent sector is particularly interesting as it follows the interest in Middle Eastern art, spurred on after the mid-2000s with international fairs like Art Dubai (created in 2007) and the opening of Christie's in Dubai in 2006. Just a few years later, the independent art sector became more prominent in Iran itself and intensified its links with regional actors, especially in the United Arab Emirates. Just like cinema, it is the independent sector in visual arts that has been able to reach out to international audiences. With some support from the state, even if only at the start, it has the potential to become more globalised.

In the last section of this chapter, I argue that there is a historical change in the dominance of cultural products in Iran. I begin this section by discussing the forms central to the Persian cultural system, arguing for an evolution from poetry to visual arts. There is a prevailing divide between prose and poetry in Iran. Poetry is the most highly revered form due to a long poetical tradition, while prose, more specifically the genre of the novel, faces several issues, due to factors like the mimicry of western genres and a high reliance on translations of foreign prose texts, which I discussed earlier in the book. While prose is increasingly more central to the literary system in the twenty-first century than it was mid-twentieth century, it still suffers from less cultural capital than poetry. I hereby analyse and explain the dominance of poetry in the Iranian literary field, based on the Jakobsonian idea of the dominant (Jakobson *et al.* 1987). I also assess the challenges faced by prose in recent decades and argue that the literary is losing its place of dominance in the Persian cultural system, to be replaced by visual media.

The Divide between Prose and Poetry

Poetry at the Centre of the Persian Cultural System

> At the center of the Persian literary system, since its origins around mid-9th century of the Christian era, poetry, or more exactly versified forms (*nazm*) constitute the axis of reference. This system is the product of a common construction on ancient Iranian heritage and Arab cultural contribution (mainly formal). (Balaÿ 2017: 10)

Christophe Balaÿ demonstrates that Persian poetical forms became the language of cultural power to counter the conquest of Iran by Muslim Arabs, while prose was used mostly for sciences, philosophy and Qur'anic exegesis, among other disciplines (Balaÿ 2017: 11). Other scholars have commented on this aspect. Dick Davis, who translated the poet Hafez, uses the Jakobsonian idea of the dominant when he says that different cultures put their energies into different arts at different times and that Iran has put its energy into poetry (Davis 2013). Jakobson argues:

> We may seek a dominant not only in the poetic work of an individual artist and not only in the poetic canon, the set of norms of a given poetic school,

but also in the art of a given epoch, viewed as a particular whole. For example, it is evident that in Renaissance art such a dominant, such an acme of the aesthetic criteria of the time; was represented by the visual arts. Other arts oriented themselves toward the visual arts and were valued according to the degree of their closeness to the latter. On the other hand, in Romantic art the supreme value was assigned to music. (Jakobson *et al.* 1987: 42)

For centuries, poetry was at the centre of the Persian literary system. The consensus, although it is starting to be challenged, among literary scholars is to establish a link between the Persian poetical language and Iranian identity, which started at a time when the sense of being Iranian was being constructed in opposition to the sense of being Arab. A scholar like Abdolhossein Zarrinkoub delves into this opposition, focusing on the two centuries after the conquest of Iran by Arabs, when Persians went 'silent' and had to build up their strength to regain control of their identity and destiny (Zarrinkub and Sprachman 2017). Setrag Manoukian has analysed the role played by poetry in how Iranians define themselves in the post-revolutionary era. Along with history, poetry is a dominant mode of discourse and form of knowledge (Manoukian 2012).

The cliché that poetry is the soul of Iranian culture therefore has a deeply rooted basis. Iran is a nation that defines itself through poetry: many people write and recite poems, regardless of their social class; visits to the tombs of poets, especially Hafez, the poet of love, are a favourite journey for families and lovers of all backgrounds; people use poetry as a reference in everyday life to understand the world around them. *Fal-e Hafez*, a tradition where one picks a line from Hafez's *Divan*, the most canonical of all collections of poems, and interprets it to determine the course of action or what the future might hold, is commonly practised. What is perhaps surprising to non-Iranians is that Persian poetry, especially classical poetry, is philosophical, dense, and often linked to mysticism.

The positive role of poetry comes with a counterpart for some thinkers, who see it as impeding innovation and the development of new forms. In *The Poetic Persian Soul*, the philosopher Dariush Shayegan refers to this cultural identity linked to poetry and warns: 'this famous cultural identity is double-edged. Since the other aspect of this infallible identity and fidelity is the difficulty to free oneself from this long procession of the tradition that follows you like a shadow' (2017: 14). It 'deprives us of the liberty to rebel, to go against the grain, to doubt' (Shayegan 2017: 15). Omid Azadibougar also mentions poetry as a way to avoid confronting forms like the novel and sees it as an 'exit strategy' (Azadibougar 2014: 70). But we could also see this over-reliance on poetry as an Iranian strategy to maintain its identity. In *Culture and Imperialism*, Edward Said argues that the genre of the novel is central to imperialism: 'I have looked especially at cultural forms as the novel, which I believe were immensely important in the formation of imperial attitudes, references, and experiences' (Said 1993: xii). It is interesting, in the context of post-revolutionary Iran as an anti-imperialist country on the periphery of the world, to notice that the form of poetry is the preferred mode of literature. While countries like India, dominated by the British Empire with the whole education system in English, have excelled in the form of the novel in the twentieth century, Iran still focuses its literary strength on poetical forms. Can we see this, even though unconsciously, as part of its anti-imperial struggle? It is certainly not a direction taken in criticism by scholars based in Iran, who have not analysed the novel in those terms as postcolonial theory is scarcely used and even less so when referring to the Iranian context (Vafa 2020: 334).

It is indeed very striking to notice, when one browses bookstores in Iran and spends some time listening to readers, that those who are looking for poetry mostly turn to their national poets, while they turn to foreign writers when they look for fiction. I recall countless instances of such discussions between readers/buyers and sellers over my years of fieldwork in Iran. The exception is the popular novels, mostly romances, discussed in Chapter 1, which are bestsellers but do not benefit from high cultural capital and are not discussed by critics. It might be that, in the terms of Itamar Even-Zohar, Persian literature considers itself a poetic tradition and, therefore, does not need the poetry of other nations (Even-Zohar 1990: 47). Reuven Snir uses a similar argument when he discusses Arabic poetry in the Abbassid period. Whereas Greek texts in most other fields including philosophy, medicine and astronomy were translated at the time, Greek epic poetry was not translated, so Homer for example was only translated into Arabic in the twentieth century. Snir argues that it is because Arabic poetry did not need Greek poetry at this stage and was self-sufficient (Snir 2018: 25–6). Similarly, the Persian cultural system seems to feel self-sufficient in terms of poetry, but not in terms of prose – or more precisely in terms of novels.

A Literary Crisis?

> [I]f you look back at the modern Iranian literature from the Constitutional Revolution onwards, you can put together a thick collection of short stories by various authors that can rub shoulders with some of the greatest stories of the century, while in terms of novels, we lag far behind the rest of the world. (Ahmadi Arian 2014)

Amir Ahmadi Arian's argument represents a common discourse on the novel. An idea often advanced for the supposed deficiencies of contemporary novels, testified by the fact that contemporary readers read foreign novels but not many Persian ones apart from romances, is that the Iranian novel mimics the west too much and has not been able to find its native voice. A reason for this mimicry can be found in the history of modern Persian prose, which is closely linked to the influence of translations from European languages, especially French and English, on Persian culture at the end of the nineteenth century and beginning of the twentieth (Nanquette 2013a, Chapter 3; Balaÿ 1998, 2017). Balaÿ has argued that translations, especially from French novels at the end of the nineteenth century, were crucial in the development of the genre of the Persian novel in the beginning of the twentieth century and that the genre took some time to gain its independence from the mimicry of western texts (Balaÿ 1998). However, he affirms that, just like Arabic helped the spread of a new culture with the Muslim conquest, Persian culture was struggling at the end of the nineteenth century and, with the encounter with the Europeans, took up a new vitality:

> In this movement towards modernity, the contact with foreign languages and the importation of these to Persian, through translation, contributed to a profound transforming (similar to the one that happened ten centuries earlier) of Persian language and literature, as well as of Iranian culture. (Balaÿ 2017: 37)

It is a common argument among scholars of Persian literature and among literary critics: 'The failure of the Persian novel to gain international recognition was in fact a central theme at the first conference on the Persian novel held at Tehran in 1994' (Yazdi and Mozafari 2019: 40); and also: 'Unsurprisingly, a study on the pathology of Persian fiction reached its sixth reprint in 2015' (Yazdi and Mozafari 2019: 41).

In contrast, Mehdi Khorrami is critical of those who assert that the genre of the novel and of the short story were imported from the west: 'Most studies on the history of Persian prose fiction begin with the apparently-accepted myth that the Persian novel and short story were imported to Iran from the West' (Khorrami 2003: 5). For him, this is an orientalist reading of the process. He insists on the fact that Persian stories existed before the arrival of the European novel, and that modern European-inspired texts grafted themselves onto this long tradition. It is true that scholars writing in Persian, like Jamal Mirsadeghi, try hard to emphasise the link with the English tradition of the short story and the novel, and that it sometimes seems forced and obfuscates the Persian literary tradition. However, I believe it is important to distinguish between fiction and the genres of the novel and the short story when dealing with this argument, as well as to remember the complexity of the processes of influence. It is not a question of importation versus nativism. Khorrami reminds us that in the debate, it is important to bring back literary elements and to stop using political elements, as these are not helpful to evaluate literary forms (Khorrami 2003: 23).

Balaÿ proposes such a nuanced argument when it comes to the short story (*dastan-e kutah*), and he does make the distinction between genres, linking the short story to the long tradition of short forms in classical Persian literature like *qesseh*, *dastan* and *hekayat* (Balaÿ and Cuypers 1983). He argues that ancient forms were integrated into a new frame with the first Persian short-story writers. This was helped with the vitality of the press and of the many literary magazines. One of his examples is Ali Akbar Dehkhoda who, in *Charand o parand* (Dehkhoda 2016), uses narrative techniques borrowed from the west, like destructing the illusory relation between writer and reader by negating novelistic realism (Balaÿ and Cuypers 1983: 100). With Mohammad-Ali Jamalzadeh and his *Once Upon a Time* (*Yeki bud, yeki nabud*), widely considered as the first short story collection in Persian, there is a conscious decision, clearly expressed in the preface, to blend European techniques and 'Persian spirit' together. Interestingly, Jamalzadeh's short story *Persian is Sugar* (*Farsi shekar ast*) was actually first published in the Berlin magazine *Kaveh*, outside of Iran, before being published in Iran in the collection *Once Upon a Time* (Balaÿ 2017: 158). With Sadegh Hedayat and his *Buried Alive* (*Zendeh be gur*), this experimentation really comes together, argues Balaÿ, and the homage to the classical forms of short fictions almost disappear to fully bloom into a solid modern Persian short story (Balaÿ 2017: 159). Omid Azadibougar also insists that it is important to differentiate between fiction or prose and the form of the novel:

> The introduction of the novel into Persian implies two authority shifts: one is a shift away from poetry, the backbone of Persian literary heritage, and the other a shift of class. Classical Persian literariness is produced and determined by the elites. (Azadibougar 2014: 48)

To him, the shift has not been successful when it comes to the novel (Azadibougar 2014: 54).

These analyses resonate with my study of contemporary Iranian texts as literary forms as well as with my experiences of the Iranian literary field. It is, however, important to remember that the issue of the novel as 'a sign of integration in world culture' (Omri 2007: 8) is vexed. Omri advises us:

> Consider how much interest has been invested in determining the first novel in any particular community's literary tradition. What is being talked about in fact is nothing short of a symbolic pinning down of the point of entry into Western modernity and – by extension – into nationhood. (Omri 2007: 319–20)

The novel should not be seen as the pinnacle of literature. It is especially the case in Iran where the cultural heritage is strong and widely recognised. In a way, writers do not have much problem with the idea that the genre of the novel would not be local or indigenous since there are so many indigenous productions. Additionally, as Eric Hayot argues, the problem with such narratives of literary progress and innovation is that we will always write a literary history where the non-west is behind and needs to catch up. He suggests we think of literary movements and genres as modes, not as historical moments, the idea being to break up the periodical hierarchy (Hayot 2012).

Even if we take into account the problem mentioned above with the novel being seen as a pinnacle of literary form, I believe there is a general crisis of the literary, which explains the shift from literature to visual arts. This shift is more important to explain the general crisis with the literary than the issue of mimicry of the Iranian novel. It is a shift that is happening on the general level of the literary.

The Replacement of the Literary in the Persian Cultural System?

Scholars like Christophe Balaÿ have recently argued that prose, which he uses as a shorthand for fiction, has become as central as poetry in the Persian literary system:

> The status of prose has, if not overcome, the one of poetry, at least caught up with it, and this in a short time. This phenomenon can be analysed in terms of duration and of rapidity. If it needed one century to appear and develop, it needed only a few decades to succeed. (Balaÿ 2017: 484)

It is true that the number of novels and short stories published might be as high as those of poetic texts, but the cultural capital conferred upon the novel is still less than the one bestowed on poetry. Balaÿ concedes that

> the role of poetry is still essential: quotidian reference to the poets of the past is strong. Persian poetry keeps its symbolic charge (in Iran and outside) but at the same time, the loss of its hegemonic power is sign of the decline of the literary at the centre of the cultural system. (Balaÿ 2017: 14)

This is indeed where the main issue is to be located: the replacement is not so much of poetry by prose, but of the literary as a whole by different media and arts. There is a peripheralisation of the literary in the Persian cultural system. The literary has become less dominant. It does not mean it is being replaced entirely, but it is less dominant and it is more interlinked with other arts than it ever was. The international success of Iranian cinema comes to confirm and maybe accelerate this process. Iran is not by any means exceptional in the replacement of the verbal form of communication by the visual. Jan Baetens argues that 'Contemporary culture is a visual culture or, more precisely, a culture marked by the visual turn, the transition from a culture dominated by the model of writing to a culture dominated by a model of the image' (2005: 43). However, it might be a quicker acceleration of the process than in other parts of the world, because the Islamic Republic regime has invested a lot of effort and means into the visual medium as an effective tool to promote its ideology, and not as much into literature, except children's literature and some forms of governmental literature.

Khatereh Sheibani argues that poetry, which was the dominant form of cultural expression in Iran, has been replaced by film since the revolution:

> I argue that Iranian culture has changed over time, both by looking back to its past, examining other cultures and philosophies and bringing to the fore elements once considered secondary or peripheral. In this shifting of the dominants, poetry did not disappear, but lost its key role within Persian culture. (Sheibani 2011: 3)

She quotes the critic Dariush Ashuri in his famous essay *Modernity and Us*, who says that the visual culture put an end to the prevalence of permanence, 'based on a belief in an unchanging and transcendent ideal of beauty', and that it was replaced by ideas of change and novelty (Ashuri 1987: 1). In the Persian literary tradition, like in other traditions, this ideal of unchanging beauty is linked to poetry, as Franco Moretti reminds us when he analyses the distinction between verse and prose:

> Verse, *versus*: there is a pattern that turns around and comes back: there is a symmetry, and symmetry always suggests permanence, that's why monuments are symmetrical. But prose is not symmetrical, and this immediately creates a sense of im-permanence and irreversibility: prose, *pro-vorsa*: forward-looking. (Moretti 2008: 112)

Persian poetry was versified for most of its history, until the arrival of New Poetry in the 1920s (*She'r-e now*) with Nima Yushij who broke the regularity of the classical Persian metres (Ahmed 2009), and even more so with Ahmad Shamlou in the 1950s with White Poetry (*She'r-e sepid*) and its free verse. This 'literary revolution' has been well-documented and I will not discuss it again here (Karimi-Hakkak 1995, chapter 3; Browne 1914, translator's preface; Ghanoonparvar 1984, chapters 1 and 4). Suffice to say that from that time onwards, the ideal of classical beauty linked to the permanence of the verse started to lose ground. The new ideal of prose as forward-looking, uneven, oriented toward novelty, replaces it, and is taken up by media like cinema. This does not obstruct Iranian cinema from being deeply linked to the tradition of classical poetry. Sheibani says on this: 'This literary heritage lends itself to a symbolical cinema that favours ambiguity over precision. The element of ambiguity in Iranian art films is a deliberate choice stemming from Persian cultural values with highly mystical potential' (2011: 177). Another way to read this infusion of Iranian cinema by literary tropes is to refer to Langford's study of 'the cinematic ghazal' (2019). The cinematic ghazal might be looked at as a projection of a literary technique onto the new arising cultural medium of cinema. It is a way for the Persian cultural system to maintain its tradition and link these two media. Langford studies its occurrence in Makhmalbaf's films, which present us 'with a kind of formal, modernist exploration of the possibilities of the cinematic *ghazal,*' and in Majid Majidi's films, with 'its more traditional spiritual and mystical tendencies' (Langford 2019: 136). Cinema uses literary tropes, literary forms and literary techniques, and heavily links itself to the Persian poetical tradition. This evolution from poetical to visual, and this increased interlinking of literature to other arts, is an important evolution in the post-revolutionary Iranian context.

Conclusion

In this chapter, reflections on the global circulation of post-revolutinary Iranian literature, both in the Persian cultural system and in the world, led me to make comparisons with other Persian art forms, cinema and visual arts. In the context of post-revolutionary Iran, Persian literature, including its cherished form of poetry, is being replaced and more interlinked to visual arts in the Persian cultural system both within Iran and abroad. We are thus confronted with a major shift in the history of Persian culture. While this is not a radical break, since this is more an interlinking of media than a replacement of the literary entirely, it is an important evolution to consider the production and circulation of Iranian literature nationally and globally. In this concluding chapter, I have attempted to think about the cultural field as a whole, and to compare the literary field to other arts, in this case to cinema and visual arts. While the rest of the book was dedicated to the minute details of some of the production and circulation aspects of Iranian literature, my aim in this chapter was to take a step back and give some perspective to some of the debates that take place on the role of the Persian novel or the circulation of contemporary Iranian literature globally.

Afterword

While classical Persian literature is widely considered to be rich and multi-layered, and has a long tradition of scholarship devoted to it, my aim throughout this book has been to offer insights into the comparatively understudied contemporary Iranian literary field; insights, that would demonstrate its richness, its paradoxes, its negotiations and its evolutions. By paying close attention to such narratives as the Sacred Defence texts dicussed in Chapter 1, the literary blogs featured in Chapter 2, the children's literature explored in Chapter 5, and those works by diasporic writers which occupy the second part of the book, my aim was to analyse the relation of the contemporary Iranian literary field to its social, economic and political contexts. This has in turn made it possible to unpack some of the literary relationships forged between Iran and its large diaspora, as well as with non-Iranians through the medium of translated texts.

I would like to conclude by reiterating how much I value the assistance of all the people in Iran and in the US, the UK, France and Australia who have helped me capture the picture of the Iranian literary field presented in this book. For a book based on interviews, participant observation and fieldwork, human encounters have not only been essential to my task, but also deeply enriching on many levels. Of course, although I have tried to give an encompassing view of the Iranian literary field, there remain aspects of it that are still largely unexplored by scholarship, including the country's literary circles and institutions – significant dimensions of the Iranian literary field that I hope to explore in the future.

Some readers may find my conclusions regarding the enclosure of the literary field bleak. Post-revolutionary Iranian literature within Iran suffers profound constraints, particularly those imposed as a result of sanctions from the US government and the European Union. My intention has been to confront the problems this situation has created over several decades. Issues pertaining to censorship and the internal divisions of the Iranian literary field are also inescapable: although the literary field within Iran continues to be occupied by competing governmental, independent and underground practitioners, it is important to keep in mind that these categories are not immutable and are still evolving, thanks to the efforts of literary practitioners. Negotiation is a day-to-day exercise for Iranian literary practitioners, and these divisions remain an impediment to the expansion of the literary field nationally. Such divisions also partly explain the relative absence of contemporary Persian literature from the global marketplace, with the notable exception of children's fiction – which has been recognised both nationally and internationally. Contrary to other artistic forms like cinema and the visual arts, contemporary Persian literature produced in Iran does not circulate widely on a global scale. Equally, literature produced in the diaspora does not tend to penetrate Iran beyond a small underground circulation.

One of the conclusions I least expected to come to concerns the relations between literary Iran and the diaspora. When I started this project several years ago, I had hoped to break through the boundary that exists between the studies of the Iranian diaspora and the study of Iran. Lulled by the Tehrangeles music that played in shared taxis as I travelled through different cities in Iran, I wondered whether similar cultural and artistic exchanges might exist in the literary field. However, my findings have largely underscored the divide between Iran and the diaspora when it comes to literary production and circulation. Because Iran is so isolated it can be difficult to bypass national borders. As I have argued, the Iranian diaspora is far-ranging and is otherwise well-connected to the motherland, but not so much when it comes to literary exchange. The literary fields within Iran and the diaspora function as parallel spaces, where literary exchanges are the exception rather than the rule – a phenomenon reflected in the book's division into two parts. Even with the advantages of our new digital landscape, it is not yet easy to envision a globally integrated Iranian literary sphere; one in which Iranian writers and publishers living in different countries could together facilitate literary exchange, promote texts for international publication, serve on literary juries for major prizes, and generally work towards gaining international recognition for Iranian literature of all kinds. This is in part because Iranian literary fields in different countries have their own particularities and are far from homogenous, a development that is particularly evident in my analysis of the texts written by Iranians in Australia and how strongly they differ from the texts of Iranian-Americans. What is striking – and consistent – is the enclosure of each of these literary spaces within their own national borders.

This enclosure, however, works against any impulse to fetishise diasporic formations. I see the diversity of diasporic literature as a sign of Iranians' deep commitment to their new homes, and of their self-reflective understanding of how they are positioned within their new society's culture and literature. This is perhaps surprising at first, given that Iranians tend to connect intensely with the national and cultural identity of their homeland. However, it became evident to me that Iranian patriotism is not antithetical to a strong relationship to the national literatures of their adopted countries. As Shu-mei Shi has shown to be true in the case of the Chinese diaspora, there is no inherently positive aspect of being diasporic. I have reached a similar conclusion regarding the Iranian literary diaspora. While there may be little exchange across national borders, Iranian diasporic literatures are well integrated into the various national literary fields to which they contribute, and diasporic Iranian writers tend to be invested in their local cultures. Although my conclusions go against the grain of some of the current thinking in the fields of postcolonial and World Literature regarding increasing transnational exchanges and the disappearance of national borders, these findings could not have been reached without studying the Iranian literary field with this global lens in mind. If post-revolutionary Iranian literature is on the margins of the world system, it nevertheless plays a part in several national systems: not only the Iranian one, but also in a constellation of imagined Iranian communities.

This dispersal is a departure from the more concentrated Persian culture that existed up until two centuries ago, and it is important to insist on this essential change. Recent studies have analysed the transregional influence of Persian culture in what is commonly referred to as the Persianate world (Amanat and Ashraf 2018; Green 2019). From the fifteenth century until the end of the nineteenth, Persian was a *lingua franca* in a vast space ranging from Turkey to parts of Central Asia and India. During the reign of the Qajars, who started the slow construction of Iran as a nation state, and later the Pahlavis, who carried out this project with force, the influence of Persian across the region diminished. For example, Kevin Schwartz has argued that the genre of the biographical anthology (*tazkireh*), which had once crossed borders relatively freely, began to become localised and restricted to the capital of Qajar Iran during the nineteenth century (Schwartz 2018). Although the *tazkireh* was only one of many genres, and Persian continued to have an impact through other forms – particularly in newspapers that were published across the Persianate world – the process of enclosure had begun. The Qajars had made great efforts to link literature and culture to the state, and with the end of their rule the scope and influence of the Persian language began to shrink, whilst Persian texts and practices became less interlinked throughout a vast territory and more enclosed to a particular country. This process continued throughout the twentieth century and, in the decades following the revolution, it is possible to chart how an earlier focus on the Persian language comes to be replaced by an insistence on Iran as an imagined community and a space of belonging. Literatures produced by Iranians around the world thus generate separate and often separated Iranian microcosms outside of the country's borders which can nonetheless thrive in Persian as well as in other local languages.

References

Abdelsadek, Nafisa (2011), 'The Effects of Social and Political Dislocation on Persianate Children's Literature: Change and Continuity', PhD thesis, University of South Africa.
Abdoh, Salar (2000), *The Poet Game*, New York: Picador USA.
Abdoh, Salar (2014a), *Tehran at Twilight*, Brooklyn: Akashic Books.
Abdoh, Salar (2014b), *Tehran Noir, Akashic Noir Series*, Brooklyn: Akashic Books.
Abdollahyan, Hamid, Mehdi Semati and Mohammad Ahmadi (2013), 'An Analysis of Second-Level Digital Divide in Iran', in Massimo Ragnedda and Glenn W. Muschert (eds), *The Digital Divide: the Internet and Social Inequality in International Perspective*, New York: Routledge.
Abrahamsen, Eric (2015), 'The Real Censors of China', *The New York Times*, 16 June 2015.
Adelkhah, Fariba (2016), *The Thousand and One Borders of Iran: Travel and Identity*, London: Routledge.
Adibi, Hossein (1998), 'Iranians in Australia: Proceedings of the Seminar in Persian Studies', in Garry Trompf and Morteza Honari (eds), *Mehregan: Iranians in Australia*, Sydney: School of Studies in Religion, University of Sydney, pp. 104–30.
Afshar, Iraj (2009), 'Publishing in Iran after the Revolution', in J. T. P. de Bruijn (ed.), *General Introduction to Persian Literature*, London: I. B. Tauris.
Afshari Behbahanizadeh, Zardosht, and Farrindokht Zahedi (2013), 'Analysis of Migrant Dramatic Literature of an Iranian in Australia: Postcolonial Analysis of a Mammad Aidani's Play: "In the Mirror"', *Sociology of Art and Literature (Jame'eh shenasi-ye honar va adabiyyat)* 5, no. 1: 147–64.
Ahmadi Arian, Amir (2014), 'Creating a territory between the Iranian and Western

literature', *IBNA*, 15 June, http://www.ibna.ir/en/doc/naghli/201390/creating-a-territory-between-the-iranian-and-western-literature (last accessed 28 June 2014).

Ahmed, Amr Taher (2009), 'The *Literary Revolution*: A Study of the Influence of French Poetry on the Modernization of Persian Poetic Forms since the Beginning of the 20th Century' ('La révolution littéraire. Étude de l'influence de la poésie française sur la modernisation des formes poétiques persanes au début du XXe siècle'), PhD thesis, Université Sorbonne Nouvelle-Paris 3.

Ahmed, Amr Taher (2012), *La 'Révolution littéraire': étude de l'influence de la poésie française sur la modernisation des formes poétiques persanes au début du XXe siècle*, Vienna: Verlag der Österreichischen Akademie der Wissenschaften.

Aidani, Mammad (1993), *Into the Dark Skin*, Upper Ferntree Gully, VIC: Papyrus Publishing.

Aidani, Mammad (1995), *Better Not to Explain: Poems*, Upper Ferntree Gully, VIC: Papyrus Publishing.

Aidani, Mammad (1996), *An Idiot Amongst Us*, self-published.

Aidani, Mammad (1997), *A Picture out of Frame*, North Fitzroy, VIC: Black Pepper.

Aidani, Mammad (2010), *Welcoming the Stranger: Narratives of Identity and Belonging in an Iranian Diaspora*, Altona, VIC: Common Ground.

Aidani, Mammad (2014), *Narrative and Violence: Ways of Suffering Amongst Iranian Men in Diaspora*, Farnham: Ashgate.

Akhavan, Niki (2011), 'Exclusionary Cartographies: Gender Liberation and the Iranian Blogosphere', in Roksana Bahramitash and Eric Hooglund (eds), *Gender in Contemporary Iran: Pushing the Boundaries*, New York: Routledge, pp. 62–82.

Akhavan, Niki (2013), *Electronic Iran: The Cultural Politics of an Online Evolution*, New Brunswick, NJ: Rutgers University Press.

Akhavan, Niki (2016), '"Neither Eastern nor Western": Economic and Cultural Policies in Post-Revolutionary Iran', in Kennan Ferguson and Patrice Petro (eds), *After Capitalism: Horizons of Finance, Culture, and Citizenship*, New Brunswick, NJ: Rutgers University Press, pp. 183–95.

Alavi, Nasrin (2005), *We are Iran*, Brooklyn: Soft Skull Press.

Alexanian, Janet (2008), 'Poetry and Polemics: Iranian Literary Expression in the Digital Age', *MELUS* 33, no. 2.

Alizadeh, Ali (2002), *eliXir: A Story in Poetry*, Melbourne: Grendon Press.

Alizadeh, Ali (2006), *Eyes in Times of War*, Cambridge: Salt.

Alizadeh, Ali (2010), *Iran: My Grandfather*, Yarraville: Transit Lounge Publishing.

Alizadeh, Ali (2011), *Ashes in the Air*, St Lucia: University of Queensland Press.

Alizadeh, Ali (2017), *The Last Days of Jeanne d'Arc*, Artarmon: Giramondo.
Alizadeh, Farahnaz (2013a), 'I Am Waiting to Understand the Flash Fiction' ('Montazer-e daryaft-e dastanak-ha hastam'), *A Window to Stories and Criticism (Daricheh-i be dastan va naqd)*, 1 October, http://f-alizadeh.mihanblog.com/post/960 (last accessed 6 October 2015).
Alizadeh, Farahnaz (2013b), *Story of Revelation (Dastan-e mokashefeh)*, Tehran: Ghatreh.
Allen, Esther (2007), *To Be Translated or Not to Be*, Barcelona: Institut Ramon Llull.
Amanat, Abbas, and Assef Ashraf (2018), *The Persianate World: Rethinking a Shared Sphere*, Leiden: Brill.
Amini, Iradj (1995), *Napoléon et la Perse. Les relations franco-persanes sous le premier Empire dans le contexte des rivalités entre la France, l'Angleterre et la Russie*, Paris: Éditions de la Fondation Napoléon.
Amiri, Mahdis (2014), 'The Fake Colonel in the Market' ('Kolonel-e taqalobi dar bazar'), *BBC Persian*, 4 August, http://www.bbc.com/persian/arts/2014/08/140804_l51_colonel_book_publication (last accessed 4 September 2014).
Amrein, Roshanak (2010), *One Million Flights: Poetry*, Berlin: Gardoon.
Amrein, Roshanak (2012), *Songs from a Far Island*, Berlin: Gardoon.
Anderson, Benedict (1983), *Imagined Communities: Reflections on the Origin and Spread of Nationalism*, London: Verso.
Anderson, Benedict (1992), *Long-Distance Nationalism: World Capitalism and the Rise of Identity Politics*, Wertheim Lecture, Amsterdam: Centre for Asian Studies Amsterdam.
Ansari, Ali (2005), '"Persia" in the Western Imagination', in Vanessa Martin (ed.), *Anglo-Iranian Relations*, New York: Routledge.
Arasteh, Reza (1962), 'The Education of Iranian Leaders in Europe and America', *International Review of Education* 8, no. 3/4: 444–50.
Arbabzadah, Nushin (2007), *From Outside In: An Anthology of Writings by Refugees on Britain and Britishness*, London: Arcadia Books.
Ashcroft, Bill (2001), *Post-colonial Transformation*, London: Routledge.
Ashuri, Dariush (1987), *Modernity and Us (Ma va modernniyat)*, Tehran: Serat.
Atwood, Blake (2012), 'Sense and Censorship in the Islamic Republic of Iran', *World Literature Today* 86, no. 3 (May/June): 38–41.
Atwood, Blake (2016), *Reform Cinema in Iran: Film and Political Change in the Islamic Republic*, New York: Columbia University Press.
Ayman, L. (2011), 'Children's Literature', in Ehsan Yarshater (ed.), *Encyclopedia*

Iranica, last modified 17 October 2011, https://iranicaonline.org/articles/children-vii (last accessed 28 March 2019).

Azadibougar, Omid (2014), *The Persian Novel: Ideology, Fiction and Form in the Periphery*, Amsterdam: Rodopi.

Azadibougar, Omid, and Esmaeil Haddadian-Moghaddam (2019), 'The Persian Tradition', in Yves Gambier and Ubaldo Stecconi (eds), *World Atlas of Translation*, Amsterdam: John Benjamins.

Azadibougar, Omid, and Simon Patton (2015), 'Coleman Barks' Versions of Rumi in the USA', *Translation and Literature* 24: 172–89.

Azali, MohammadReza (2017a), 'Infographic: Instagram Usage Statistics in Iran', *TechRasa*, 21 June, http://techrasa.com/2017/06/21/infographic-instagram-usage-statistics-iran/ (last accessed 28 March 2019).

Azali, MohammadReza (2017b), 'There are 48 Million Smartphones in Iran', *TechRasa*, 19 July, http://techrasa.com/2017/07/19/48-million-smartphones-iran/ (last accessed 28 December 2019).

Azarang, Abdolhossein, and Ali Dehbashi (2014), *Oral History of Iranian Publishing (Tarikh-e shafahi-ye nashr-e Iran)*, Tehran: Qoqnoos.

Baetens, Jan (2005), 'Novelization, a Contaminated Genre?', *Critical Inquiry* 32, no. 1: 43–60.

Baharloo, Mohammad (1998), 'The Iranian Short Story: 23 stories from Iranian Writers' ('Dastan-e kutah-e irani: 23 dastan az 23 nevisandeh-ye irani'), *Hamshahri*, 5 August, https://bit.ly/2zrWg2A (last accessed 6 October 2015).

Bajoghli, Narges (2019), *Iran Reframed: Anxieties of Power in the Islamic Republic*, Stanford: Stanford University Press.

Bajoghli, Narges, and Mana Kharrazi (2015), 'Iranian Alliances Across Borders', in Heinrich Böll Foundation and Transparency for Iran (eds), *Identity and Exile. The Iranian Diaspora between Solidarity and Difference*, Berlin: Heinrich Böll Foundation, pp. 132–42.

Balaÿ, Christophe (1998), *The Genesis of the Modern Persian Novel* (*La genèse du roman persan moderne*), Tehran: Institut français de recherche en Iran.

Balaÿ, Christophe (2017), *The Crisis of Iranian Consciousness: History of Modern Persian Prose (1800–1980)* (*La crise de la conscience iranienne: histoire de la prose persane moderne (1800–1980)*), Paris: L'Harmattan.

Balaÿ, Christophe, and Michel Cuypers (1983), *Aux sources de la nouvelle persane*, Paris: Éditions Recherche sur les Civilisations.

Bani-Etemad, Rakhshan, and Mojtaba Mir-Tahmasb (2018), *Lady Touran* (*Touran Khanum*), Kara Film Studio.

Baqer Sakhaei, Seyyed (2016), 'Saadi Foundation, Motives and Plans' ('Bonyad-e Saadi, angizeh-ha va barnameh-ha'), *Tabnak*, 18 June, shorturl.at/brP24 (last accessed 9 February 2018).

Barzegar, Laleh (2014), *Ali Dehbashi, my Bukhara* (*Ali Dehbashi, Bukhara-ye man*), https://www.youtube.com/watch?v=tOfSRfsZoNQ (last accessed 7 August 2019).

Basmenji, Kaveh (ed.) (2005), *Afsaneh: Short Stories by Iranian Women*, London: Saqi.

BBC Persian (2013), 'Opposition to Granting Censorship Role to Publishers Themselves in Iran', *BBC Persian*, 20 August 2013, http://www.bbc.com/persian/iran/2013/08/130820_l38_book_ershad (last accessed 28 December 2019).

Beard, Michael (1998), 'Translations of Modern Persian Literature', in Ehsan Yarshater (ed.), *Encyclopedia Iranica*, last modified 15 December 2011, http://www.iranicaonline.org/articles/english-4-translation-modern (last accessed 28 December 2014).

Beecroft, Alexander (2015), *An Ecology of World Literature: from Antiquity to the Present Day*, New York: Verso

Behnoud, Masoud (2011), *Robin Hood of the Desert*, London: Candle & Fog.

Bjerre Christensen, Janne (2016), *Guests or Trash: Iran's Precarious Policies Towards the Afghan Refugees in the Wake of Sanctions and Regional Wars*, Copenhagen: Danish Institute for International Studies.

Bledstein, Max (2019), 'Certified Copy: Transnational Exchange in Fereydoun Jeyrani's *Parkway*', *Australasian Universities Languages & Literature Association Conference, University of Wollongong, 10 December 2019*.

Bode, Katherine (2018), *A World of Fiction: Digital Collections and the Future of Literary History*, Ann Arbor: University of Michigan Press.

Bokobza, Anaïs (2004), 'Translating Literature: From Romanticized Representations to the Dominance of a Commercial Logic: The Publication of Italian Novels in France (1982–2001)', PhD thesis, European University Institute, Florence.

Boochani, Behrouz (2015), 'Becoming MEG45', *Mascara*, http://mascarareview.com/behrouz-boochani/ (last accessed 28 October 2015).

Boochani, Behrouz (2018), *No Friend but the Mountains: Writing from Manus Prison*, London: Picador.

Bourdieu, Pierre, and Randal Johnson (1993), *The Field of Cultural Production: Essays on Art and Literature, European Perspectives*, New York: Columbia University Press.

Bradshaw, Tom, and Bonnie Nichols (2004), *Reading at Risk: A Survey of Literary Reading in America*, Washington, DC: National Endowment for the Arts.

Brouillette, Sarah (2007), *Postcolonial Writers in the Global Literary Marketplace*, New York: Palgrave Macmillan.

Brouillette, Sarah (2014), 'UNESCO and the Book in the Developing World', *Representations* 127, no. 1: 33–54.

Browne, Edward Granville (1914), *The Press and Poetry of Modern Persia: Partly Based on the Manuscript Work of Mirza Muhammad Ali Khan*, Cambridge: Cambridge University Press.

Büchler, Alexandra, and Alice Guthrie (2011), *Literary Translation from Arabic into English in the United Kingdom and Ireland, 1990–2010*, Report, Aberystwyth University, UK.

Bullock Jenkins, William (2016), 'Bonyads as Agents and Vehicles of the Islamic Republic's Soft Power', in Shahram Akbarzadeh and Dara Conduit (eds), *Iran in the World: President Rouhani's Foreign Policy*, London: Palgrave Macmillan.

Buzelin, Hélène (2005), 'Unexpected Allies', *The Translator* 11, no. 2: 193–218.

Cardon, Dominique (2010), *Internet Democacry, Promises and Limits (La démocratie Internet, promesses et limites)*, Paris: Seuil.

Census Explorer, http://www.sbs.com.au/censusexplorer (last accessed 2 June 2015).

Chan, Felicia (2011), 'The International Film Festival and the Making of a National Cinema', *Screen* 52, no. 2: 253–60.

Chapman, Cameron (2011), 'A Brief History of Blogging', *WebdesignerDepot*, 14 March, http://www.webdesignerdepot.com/2011/03/a-brief-history-of-blogging/ (last accessed 22 September 2015).

Chehabi, Houchang (2018), *Culture Wars and Dual Society in Iran*, Amsterdam: International Institute of Social History.

Chow, Rey (1993), 'Against the Lures of Diaspora: Minority Discourse, Chinese Women, and Intellectual Hegemony', in Rey Chow, *Writing Diaspora*, Bloomington: Indiana University Press, pp. 99–119.

Cohen, Robin (1997), *Global Diasporas: An Introduction*, Seattle: University of Washington Press.

Coser, Lewis A. (1982), *Books: The Culture and Commerce of Publishing*, New York: Basic Books.

Dabashi, Hamid (2008), *Makhmalbaf at Large: the Making of a Rebel Filmmaker*, London: I. B. Tauris.

Dabashi, Hamid (2012), *The World of Persian Literary Humanism*, Cambridge, MA: Harvard University Press.

Daghighi, Mojdeh (2005), 'On the Innocence of Iranian Women: An Interview with Parinoush Saniee' ('Revayat-e ma'sumiyat-e zan-e Irani: Goftegu ba Parinoush Saniee'), *Zanan*, 18 February, http://zananmag.org/spip.php?article44 (last accessed 5 August 2014).

Damrosch, David (2003), *What is World Literature?* Princeton, NJ: Princeton University Press.

Daneshvar, Esfaindyar (2018), *Franco-Persian Transcultural Literature. A Literary Evolution Since the 1980s (La littérature transculturelle franco-persane. Une évolution littéraire depuis les années 80)*, Leiden: Brill.

Daneshvar, Simin (1969), *Suvashun*, Tehran: Kharazmi.

Darab, Hamed (2015), 'Interview with Kaveh Mirabbasi: After 150 Years the First Persian Detective Fiction is Published', *Book City*, 21 February 2015, http://www.bookcity.org/news-5779.aspx (last accessed 28 August 2019).

Darabi, Helia (2015), 'Tehran Museum of Contemporary Art as a Microcosm of the State's Cultural Agenda', in Hamid Keshmirshekan (ed.), *Contemporary Art from the Middle East: Regional Interactions with Global Art Discourses*, London: I. B. Tauris.

Daralshafaei, Bahman (2013), 'The Children's Book Council Turned 50' ('Shora-ye ketab-e kudak panjah saleh shod'), *BBC Persian*, 26 February 2013, http://www.bbc.com/persian/arts/2013/02/130224_l17_children_book_council.shtml.

Daryaee, Touraj, and Kourosh Beigpour (2016), *50th Anniversary of Kanun*, Brentford: H&S Media.

Darznik, Jasmin (2008), 'The Perils and Seductions of Home: Return Narratives of the Iranian Diaspora', *MELUS* 33, no. 2: 55–71.

Davis, Dick (2013), 'Faces of Love and Poetry in Iranian Culture', *Public Broadcasting Service*, 24 December, https://www.youtube.com/watch?v=JCXA0vx1Zps.

Dehbashi, Ali (2012), 'The Story Behind the Book Two Centuries of Silence' ('Majara-ye ketab-e do qarn sokut'), *Bukhara* no. 9, 1999.

Dehkhoda, Ali Akbar (2016), *Charand-o parand: Revolutionary Satire from Iran, 1907–1909*, trans. Janet Afary and John R. Perry, New Haven: Yale University Press.

Delfani, Mahmoud (ed.) (2009), *L'Iran et la France malgré les apparences*, Paris: Europerse.

Démy-Geroe, Anne (2020), *Iranian National Cinema: The Interaction of Policy, Genre, Funding, and Reception*, London: Routledge.

Department of Immigration and Citizenship, Australian Government (2014), 'Immigration Detention Statistics Summary', 30 April 2014, http://www.immi.

gov.au/managing-australias-borders/detention/_pdf/immigration-detention-statistics-apr2014.pdf (last accessed 17 April 2016).

Department of Social Services, Australian Government (2014), 'The Iran-born Community', https://www.dss.gov.au/our-responsibilities/settlement-and-multicultural-affairs/programs-policy/a-multicultural-australia/programs-and-publications/community-information-summaries/the-iran-born-community (last accessed 29 April 2016).

Devictor, Agnès (2004), *Politics of Iranian Cinema: From Ayatollah Khomeini to President Khatami* (*Politique du cinéma iranien: de l'âyatollâh Khomeyni au Président Khâtami*), Paris: CNRS.

Devictor, Agnès (2014), 'Iranian Film Policy in a Global Context', in Peter Decherney and Blake Atwood (eds), *Iranian Cinema in a Global Context: Policy, Politics, and Form*, London: Routledge, pp. 13–32.

Donya-ye eqtesad (2018), 'Tracing subsidies in the publication cycle' ('*Masiryabi yaraneh dar charkheh-ye nashr*'), *Donya-ye eqtesad*, 9 April, https://donya-e-eqtesad.com/بخش-فرهنگ-هنر-32/1113792-مسیریابی-یارانه-در-چرخه-نشر (last accessed 10 May 2018).

Doostdar, Alireza (2004), '"The Vulgar Spirit of Blogging": On Language, Culture, and Power in Persian Weblogestan', *American Anthropologist* 106, no. 4: 651–62.

Doostdar, Alireza (2010), 'Weblogs', in Ehsan Yarshater (ed.), *Encyclopedia Iranica*, last modified 15 March 2010, http://www.iranicaonline.org/articles/weblogs (last accessed 14 April 2014).

Doostdar, Alireza (2019), 'Haunted Ramadan: Ghosts, Devils, and the Soul of Iranian Television', *Ajam Media Collective*, https://ajammc.com/2019/10/20/haunted-ramadan/ (last accessed 25 November 2019).

Ebtekar, Masoumeh (2007–17), *Persian Paradox*, http://ebtekarm.blogspot.com.au/ (last accessed 17 April 2010).

Ehsani, Kaveh (2015), 'The Cultural Politics of Public Space in Tehran's Book Fair', in Houchang Chehabi, Peyman Jafari and Maral Jefroudi (eds), *Iran in the Middle East: Transnational Encounters and Social History*, London: I. B. Tauris, pp. 213–34.

Ehsani, Kaveh (2017), 'War and Resentment: Critical Reflections on the Legacies of the Iran-Iraq War', *Middle East Critique* 26, no. 1: 5–24.

Ekhtesari, Fatemeh (2011–14), *Online Writing Workshop*, http://www.havakesh14.blogfa.com/ (last accessed 10 April 2018).

El Hamamsy, Walid, and Mounira Soliman (2013), *Popular Culture in the Middle East and North Africa: A Postcolonial Outlook*, New York: Routledge.

English, James F. (2005), *The Economy of Prestige: Prizes, Awards, and the Circulation of Cultural Value*, Cambridge, MA: Harvard University Press.

Etehad, Melissa (2017), 'Telegram was the App where Iranians Talked Politics. Then the Government Caught On', *Los Angeles Times*, 13 March, http://beta.latimes.com/business/la-fi-telegram-iran-20170313-story.html (last accessed 12 October 2017).

Etemadi, Akhtar, and Ali Dehbashi (2004–5), 'Conversation with Parinoush Saniee', *Bukhara*, no. 39–40: 257–72.

Even-Zohar, Itamar (1990), 'The Position of Translated Literature within the Literary Polysystem', *Poetics Today* 11, no. 1: 45–51.

Faiq, Said (2004), 'The Cultural Encounter in Translating from Arabic', in Said Faiq (ed.), *Cultural Encounters in Translation from Arabic*, Clevedon: Multilingual Matters, pp. 1–13.

Falasiri, Arash, and Nazanin Ghanavizi (2015), 'The Persian Blogosphere in Dissent', in Babak Rahimi and David M. Faris (eds), *Social Media in Iran: Politics and Society after 2009*, Albany: SUNY Press.

Farahmand, Azadeh (2002), 'Perspectives on Recent (International Acclaim for) Iranian Cinema', in Richard Tapper (ed.), *The New Iranian Cinema: Politics, Representation and Identity*, London: I. B. Tauris.

Farsight (2015), 'Iranian Refugees: Irregular Migration to Australia', *Seefar*, http://seefar.org/research/iranian-refugees-irregular-migration-to-australia/ (last accessed 2 May 2016).

Farzad, Narguess (2007), 'Qeysar Aminpur and the Persian Poetry of Sacred Defence', *British Journal of Middle Eastern Studies* 34, no. 3: 351–74.

Fassaie, Saeed (2015), *Rising from the Shadows: A Memoir: Revolution, War and the Journey that Made Me*, Balmain, NSW: Richmond Ventures.

Fathi, Nazila (2005), 'Women Writing Novels Emerge as Stars in Iran', *New York Times*, 29 June 2005, https://www.nytimes.com/2005/06/29/books/women-writing-novels-emerge-as-stars-in-iran.html (last accessed 20 April 2014).

Fetveit, Anne-Marie (1987), 'Support to Book Publishing and Distribution, and Reading Habits in Norway', *Poetics* 16: 227–36.

Fotouhi, Sanaz (2015), *The Literature of the Iranian Diaspora: Meaning and Identity Since the Islamic Revolution*, London: I. B. Tauris.

Fotouhi, Sanaz (2016), 'Commodification of Censorship in Iranian Writing in English', *Sanglap* 2, no. 2: 98–126.

Fotouhi, Sanaz (2017), 'Iranians in Australia: An Analysis of Cultural and Creative

Events', in Mohsen Mobasher (ed.), *The Iranian Diaspora: Challenges, Negotiations, and Transformations*, Austin: University of Texas Press.

Franssen, Thomas, and Giselinde Kuipers (2013), 'Coping with Uncertainty, Abundance and Strife: Decision-Making Processes of Dutch Acquisition Editors in the Global Market for Translations', *Poetics* 41, no. 1: 48–74.

Friedl, Erika, and Mary Elaine Hegland (2004), 'Guest Editors' Introduction', *Iranian Studies* 37, no. 4: 569–73.

Frow, John (2014), *Genre*, New York: Routledge.

Gelder, Ken (2004), *Popular Fiction: The Logics and Practices of a Literary Field*, New York: Routledge.

Ghaeni, Zohreh (2006), 'Children's Literature in Iran: From Tradition to Modernism', *Barnboken* 29, no. 1.

Ghahramani, Zarah, and Robert Hillman (2008), *My Life as a Traitor*, New York: Farrar, Straus and Giroux.

Ghanoonparvar, M. R. (1984), *Prophets of Doom: Literature as a Socio-Political Phenomenon in Modern Iran*, Lanham: University Press of America.

Gharehgozlou, Bahareh (2018), 'A Study of Persian-English Literary Translation Flows: Texts and Paratexts in Three Historical Contexts', PhD thesis, Kent State University, Kent.

Ghods, Saideh, and Sara Phillips (2012), *Kimya Khatun. The Mystic and the Dove*, London: Candle & Fog.

Gholami Jaliseh, Majid (2016/1394), *Statistics of Book Publications in Iran: 1980–2015*, Tehran: Iran Book House.

Gholami, Reza (2015), *Secularism and Identity: Non-Islamiosity in the Iranian Diaspora*, London: Routledge.

Gholamshahi, Soheyla Masoumeh (2009), 'Emerging Communities From East to West: Case Study of the Iranian Community in Sydney, Australia', PhD thesis, University of Technology, Sydney.

Ghorashi, Halleh (2009), 'The "Iranian Diaspora" and the New Media: From Political Action to Humanitarian Help', *Development and Change* 40: 667–91.

Giacobino, Laurent, Arash Abadpour, Collin Anderson, Fred Petrossian and Caroline Nellemann (2014), *Whither Blogestan: Evaluating Shifts in Persian Cyberspace*, Philadelphia: Iran Media Program, Center for Global Communication Studies at Annenberg School for Communication, University of Pennsylvania.

Gonsalves, Roanna (2016), 'Writers vs. Money: Negotiating the Field of Indian Literature in English', PhD thesis, University of New South Wales.

Green, Nile (2019), *The Persianate World: The Frontiers of a Eurasian Lingua Franca*, Los Angeles: University of California Press.

Habibi, Mariam (2004), *L'interface France-Iran, 1907–1938: Une diplomatie voilée*, Paris: L'Harmattan.

Hadidi, Javad, and Dominique Carnoy (1994), *De Sa'di à Aragon: l'accueil fait en France à la littérature persane (1600–1982)*, Tehran: Éditions Internationales Alhoda.

Haj Seyed Javadi, Fattaneh (1995), *The Morning After* (*Bamdad-e khomar*), Tehran: Alborz.

Hakimzadeh, Shirin, and David Dixon (2006), 'Spotlight on the Iranian Foreign Born', *Migration Policy Institute*, 1 June, http://www.migrationinformation.org/USFocus/display.cfm?ID=404#8 (last accessed 17 March 2012).

Hamdhaidari, Shokrollah, Hossein Agahi and Abdulhamid Papzan (2008), 'Higher Education During the Islamic Government of Iran (1979–2004)', *International Journal of Educational Development* 28: 231–45.

Harris, Kevan (2017), *A Social Revolution: Politics and the Welfare State in Iran*, Berkeley: University of California Press.

Hayot, Eric (2012), *On Literary Worlds*, Oxford: Oxford University Press.

Heilbron, Johan (1999), 'Towards a Sociology of Translation: Book Translations as a Cultural World-System', *European Journal of Social Theory* 2, no. 4: 429–44.

Heinrich Böll Foundation and Transparency for Iran (2015), *Identity and Exile. The Iranian Diaspora between Solidarity and Difference*, Berlin: Heinrich Böll Foundation.

Hejazi, Arash (2011), 'You don't deserve to be published', *Article 19*, 17 August.

Held, David (1999), *Global Transformations: Politics, Economics and Culture*, Cambridge: Polity Press.

Helgesson, Stefan, and Pieter Vermeulen (eds) (2016), *Institutions of World Literature: Writing, Translation, Markets*, New York: Routledge.

Hellot-Bellier, Florence (2007), *France-Iran, Quatre cent ans de dialogue*, Leuven: Peeters Press.

Hemmasi, Farzaneh (2020), *Tehrangeles Dreaming: Intimacy and Imagination in Southern California's Iranian Pop Music*, Durham: Duke University Press.

Hirsch, Marianne (2012), *The Generation of Postmemory: Writing and Visual Culture after the Holocaust*, New York: Columbia University Press.

Hmeid, Saleh (2018), 'Rouhani Criticizes Khamenei's Large Budget Meant to "Islamize" Science', *Al Arabiya.net*, 25 February.

Hodgson, Marshall G. S. (1977), *The Venture of Islam 2: The Expansion of Islam in the Middle Periods*, Chicago: University of Chicago Press.

Hojvani, Mehdi (2001), 'A Survey of Iranian Children and Young Adults' Literature after the Revolution' ('Seyri dar adabiyat-e kudak va nowjavan-e Iran pas az enqelab (1379–1389)'), *Periodical on Children and Young Adults' Literature* (*Pazhuheshnameh-ye adabiyat-e kudak va nowjavan*), 20: 19–38.

Huggan, Graham (2007), *Australian Literature: Postcolonialism, Racism, Transnationalism*, Oxford: Oxford University Press.

IBNA (Iran's Book News Agency) (2015), 'The Publisher Candle & Fog will be at the 28th Bookfair with Thirty Books' ('Entesharat-e Sham' va Meh ba 30 Onvan Ketab be namayeshgah-e bist va hashtom miravad'), *IBNA*, 3 May 2015, https://tinyurl.com/tq2n97e (last accessed 3 June 2015).

Idjadi, S. (2012), *Iranienfr.com*, http://aveciraniensenfrance.com/index.php?action=accueil.

Ilam Today (2006), 'A Brief Look at the Life and Work of Abdul Jabbar Kakaei, The Poet from Ilam', *Ilam Today*, 11 June, https://www.ilamtoday.com/article/article.asp?n=140 (last accessed 7 September 2015).

ILNA (2017), 'A Seven-Hour Long Queue for Book Lovers Under Rain and Hail' ('Saf-e haft sa'ateh alaqemandan-e ketab zir-e baran va tagrag'), *ILNA*, 26 April, https://www.ilna.ir/بخش-هنر-فرهنگ-6/482428-صف-هفت-ساعته-علاقه-مندان-کتاب-باران-تگرگ-قهوه-سرد-آقای-نویسنده-رکورددار-شد (last accessed 28 January 2018).

International Campaign for Human Rights in Iran (2015), 'Two Poets Sentenced to Flogging and Nine and Eleven Years in Prison', *Centre for Human Rights in Iran*, 14 October 2015, https://www.iranhumanrights.org/2015/10/two-poets-sentenced/ (last accessed 29 May 2017).

Irani, Bamdad (2008), 'Khabgard is More than a Weblog' ('Khabgard yek fara-weblog ast'), *Bamdadi*, 14 June, http://bamdadi.com/tag/خوابگرد-وبلاگ/ (last accessed 28 January 2018).

IRIB (Islamic Republic of Iran Broadcasting) (2017), 'Mirbaqeri in conversation with Eqtesad Radio' ('Mirbaqeri dar goftegu ba radio Eqtesad'), *IRIB*, 9 December, http://radio.irib.ir/ChannelNewsDetails/?m=202020&n=166392 (last accessed 13 December 2017).

Islamic Republic of Iran (2014), *Constitution of the Islamic Republic of Iran*, http://www.wipo.int/edocs/lexdocs/laws/en/ir/ir001en.pdf (last accessed 7 August 2020).

ISNA (Iranian Students News Agency) (2006a), 'Economy Council Decided to

Eliminate Paper Subsidies from Next Year' ('Ba tasmim-e showra-ye eqtesad yaraneh-ye kaghaz az sal-e ayandeh hazf mishavad'), *ISNA*, 23 August, https://www.isna.ir/news/8506-00460/آینده-سال-از-کاغذ-یارانه-اقتصاد-شورای-تصمیم-با-شود-می-حذف (last accessed 20 August 2007).

ISNA (Iranian Students News Agency) (2006b), 'Report on Best-Selling Iranian Novels in the last Fourteen Years' ('Gozaresh az roman-ha-ye porforush-e Iran dar 14 sale gozashteh'), *Iranian Student's News Agency*, 25 August 2006.

ISNA (Iranian Students News Agency) (2015), 'The Results of the Latest Youth Survey Have Been Published', *ISNA*, https://www.isna.ir/news/93061710204/نتایج-جدیدترین-نظرسنجی-از-جوانان-اعلام-شد (last accessed 12 November 2019).

ISNA (Iranian Students News Agency) (2018), 'Best-selling Iranian Novels of the Last 5 Decades', *ISNA*, 30 November, https://www.isna.ir/news/97090904004/پرفروش-رمان-ترین-های-ایرانی-در-۵-دهه-اخیر (last accessed 23 September 2019).

Jafari Aghdam, Majid (2012), 'POL Literary and Translation Agency', *POL*, http://www.pol-ir.com/html/eng/index.html (last accessed 20 August 2019).

Jakobson, Roman, Krystyna Pomorska and Stephen Rudy (1987), *Language in Literature*, Cambridge, MA: Belknap Press.

Jazeini, Mohamad Javad (2011), *Dastanak, Flash Fiction, Introduction to the Different Genres of Short Fiction*, Tehran: Hezareh Qoqnoos.

Kakaei, Abdul Jabbar (2007–present), *Sal-ha-ye takonun*, http://jabbarkakaei.blogfa.com/ (last accessed 20 January 2018).

Kakaei, Abdul Jabbar (2007), 'Interview with Shahrvand: I Do Not Agree With Any Red Line', *Sal-ha-ye takonun*, 14 August, http://www.jabbarkakaei.blogfa.com/post-30.aspx (last accessed 28 January 2018).

Kakaei, Abdul Jabbar (2009), 'For My Son Who Has Been Slapped Today for No Reason', *Sal-ha-ye takonun*, 10 July, http://jabbarkakaei.blogfa.com/post-112.aspx (last accessed 28 January 2018).

Kalb, Zep (2017), 'Neither Dowlati nor Khosusi: Islam, Education and Civil Society in Contemporary Iran', *Iranian Studies* 50, no. 4: 575–600.

Kamali Dehghan, Saeed (2015), 'Digital Age Poses a New Challenge to Iran's Relentless Book Censors', *The Guardian*, 15 May 2015, https://www.theguardian.com/world/2015/may/15/digital-age-poses-a-new-challenge-to-irans-relentless-book-censors (last accessed 27 May 2016).

Kamali Sarvestani, Arash, and Behrouz Boochani (2017), *Chauka, Please Tell Us the Time*, (Documentary), Netherlands/Australia.

Kamalinejad, Maryam (2015), 'Flash Fiction: ("*Dastanak*")', http://mkamali.mihanblog.com/ (last accessed 8 October 2015).

Karim, Persis M. (2006), *Let Me Tell You Where I've Been: New Writing by Women of the Iranian Diaspora*, Fayetteville: University of Arkansas Press.

Karim, Persis (ed.) (2015), 'Writing Beyond Iran: Four Voices in Exile', Special issue, *World Literature Today*, March, https://www.worldliteraturetoday.org/2015/march (last accessed 27 May 2016).

Karim, Persis M., and Mohammad Mehdi Khorrami (1999), *A World Between: Poems, Short Stories, and Essays by Iranian Americans*, New York: George Braziller.

Karim, Persis, and Nasrin Rahimieh (2008), 'Special Issue: Iranian American Literature', *Journal of the Society for the Study of the Multi-Ethnic Literature of the United States* 33, no. 2.

Karimi, Kooshyar (2012), *I Confess: Revelations in Exile*, Elsternwick: Insight Publications.

Karimi, Kooshyar (2015), *Leila's Secret*, Scoresby: Penguin Group Australia.

Karimi-Hakak, Mahmood (2003), 'Exiled to Freedom: A Memoir of Censorship in Iran', *The Drama Review* 47, no. 4: 17–50.

Karimi-Hakkak, Ahmad (1985), 'Protest and Perish: A History of the Writers' Association of Iran', *Iranian Studies* 18, no. 2: 189–229.

Karimi-Hakkak, Ahmad (1995), *Recasting Persian Poetry: Scenarios of Poetic Modernity in Iran*, Salt Lake City: University of Utah Press.

Kazemi, Zoha (2017), *The Human-Wearing Earth* (*Khak-e adampush*), Tehran: Qoqnoos.

Kelly, John, and Bruce Etling (2008), *Mapping Iran's Online Public: Politics and Culture in the Persian Blogosphere*, Cambridge, MA: Berkman Center for Internet & Society at Harvard University.

Keshavarz, Fatemeh (2007), *Jasmine and Stars. Reading More Than Lolita in Tehran*, Chapel Hill: University of North Carolina Press.

Keshmirshekan, Hamid (2015a), 'The Contemporary Art Scene of Iran: Cultural Policy, Infrastructure, Dissemination and Exchange', in Nick Wadham-Smith and Danny Whitehead (eds), *Didgah: New Perspectives on UK-Iran Cultural Relations*, London: British Council.

Keshmirshekan, Hamid (2015b), 'The Crisis of Belonging: on the Politics of Art Practice in Contemporary Iran', in Hamid Keshmirshekan (ed.), *Contemporary Art from the Middle East: Regional Interactions with Global Art Discourses*, London: I. B. Tauris.

Khaledian, Naser (2015), 'Weblog: A Quick Chronology', *Khabgard*, 4 March, http://khabgard.com/?id=1123386575 (last accessed 28 January 2018).

Khazaei Farid, Ali, and Nasrin Ashrafi (2013), 'A Descriptive Glance into the Status of Translated and Original Literary Publications in Iran from 2001 until 2010', *Language and Translation Studies* 8: 19–41.

Khiabany, Gholam (2007), 'Iranian Media: The Paradox of Modernity', *Social Semiotics* 17, no. 4: 479–501.

Khiabany, Gholam (2010), *Iranian Media: The Paradox of Modernity*, London: Routledge.

Khoei, Effat, Anna Whelan and Jeffery Cohen (2008), 'Sharing Beliefs: What Sexuality means to Muslim Iranian Women living in Australia', *Culture, Health & Sexuality* 20, no. 3: 237–48.

Khomeini, Ruhollah, and Hamid Algar (1981), *Islam and Revolution: Writings and Declarations of Imam Khomeini*, Berkeley: Mizan.

Khorrami, Mohammad Mehdi (2003), *Modern Reflections of Classical Traditions in Persian Fiction*, New York: The Edwin Mellen Press.

Khosravi, Bahareh (2016), 'Dialogue with Amir Ahmadi Arian', *Zeitoon*, 14 November.

Khosravi, Shahram (2010), *'Illegal' Traveller: An Auto-ethnography of Borders*, New York: Palgrave Macmillan.

Khosravi, Shahram (2017), 'A Fragmented Diaspora: Iranians in Sweden', *Nordic Journal of Migration Research*, https://doi.org/10.1515/njmr-2018-0013.

Khosravi Yeganeh, Elaheh (2014), 'We Make Things Happen, We Don't Shout Beautiful Slogans: Story of the President of the Union of Tehran Publishers and Booksellers on the State of the Publishing Industry', *KhabarOnline*, 21 December, http://www.khabaronline.ir/detail/391209/culture/literature (last accessed 12 January 2015).

Khosrokhavar, Fahrad, and Olivier Roy (1999), *Iran: How to Get Out of a Religious Revolution* (*Iran: Comment sortir d'une révolution religieuse*), Paris: Seuil.

Kouchaki Dehshali, Yadollah (no date), http://www.y-k-shali.com (last accessed 24 August 2014).

Kryzhanouski, Yauheni (2017), 'Gouverner la dissidence. Sociologie de la censure sous régime autoritaire: le cas du rock contestataire biélorusse', *Critique internationale* 3, no. 76: 123–45.

Langford, Michelle (2019), *Allegory in Iranian Cinema: The Aesthetics of Poetry and Resistance*, London: Bloomsbury.

Lavasani, Masoud (2013), 'Thirty Years of Book Censorship, Old Stuff, New Stuff' ('Si sal momayezi-ye ketab; harf-ha-ye kohneh, harf-ha-ye now'), *BBC Persian*, 21 October 2013, http://www.bbc.com/persian/arts/2013/08/130821_l41_book_ershad_new_decision_review (last accessed 12 December 2014).

Lefevere, André (1992), *Translation, Rewriting, and the Manipulation of Literary Fame*, London: Routledge.

Levett, Connie (2007), 'Free at last . . .', *Sydney Morning Herald*, 7 July, https://www.smh.com.au/national/free-at-last-20070907-gdr1yf.html (last accessed 12 December 2008).

Lobato, Ramon (2012), *Shadow Economies of Cinema: Mapping Informal Film Distribution*, London: Palgrave Macmillan.

Lydon, Christopher (2009), 'Shahriar Mandanipour: The "Love" Cure for Iran', *Radio Open Source*, 24 July 2009.

Mahdi, Ali Akbar (1998), 'Ethnic Identity among Second-Generation Iranians in the United States', *Iranian Studies* 31, no. 1: 77–95.

Malek, Amy (2011), 'Public Performances of Identity Negotiation in the Iranian Diaspora: The New York Persian Day Parade', *Comparative Studies of South Asia, Africa and the Middle East* 31, no. 2: 388–410.

Malek, Amy (2015), 'Displaced, Re-rooted, Transnational Considerations in Theory and Practice of Being an Iranian outside Iran', in Heinrich Böll Foundation and Transparency for Iran (eds), *Identity and Exile. The Iranian Diaspora between Solidarity and Difference*, Berlin: Heinrich Böll Foundation, pp. 24–31.

Malek, Amy (2019a), 'Subjunctive Nostalgia of Postmemorial Art: Remediated Family Archives in the Iranian Diaspora', *Memory Studies* (online): 1–19.

Malek, Amy (2019b), 'Mobile Subjects, Multiple Fields: Iranian Diaspora Studies as Transnational Inquiry', in *40 Years & More International Conference on Iranian Diaspora Studies, San Francisco State University, March 29*, https://www.youtube.com/watch?v=pjRfyD-jTJM (last accessed 30 June 2019).

Malekzadeh, Shervin (2016), 'Paranoia and Perspective, or How I Learned to Stop Worrying and Start Loving Research in the Islamic Republic of Iran', *Social Science Quarterly* 97, no. 4: 862–74.

Mandanipour, Shahriar (2009), *Censoring an Iranian Love Story*, trans. Sara Khalili, New York: Knopf.

Manoukian, Setrag (2012), *City of Knowledge in Twentieth Century Iran: Shiraz, History and Poetry*, New York: Routledge.

Marchant, James (2015), *Writer's Block: The Story of Censorship in Iran*, Small Media Publication.

Mardani, Mostafa (2009), 'Interview with Leila Sadeghi', *Green Word* (*Kalameh-ye sabz*), 27 May, http://leilasadeghi.com/leila-sadeghis-work/interview/463-interview-mardani.html (last accessed 28 January 2018).

Mardomak (2010), 'Censorship of Literary Texts on the Eve of the Tehran

International Bookfair', *Mardomak*, 20 May, http://www.mardomak.org/story/censorship_books_exabition/ (last accessed 28 August 2014).

Masoudi, Faramarz (1998), 'Production and Distribution of Published Books Across the Country: Introduction to Iran Book House' (*Tolid va tozi'-e ettela'at-e ketab-ha-ye montasher shodeh-ye keshvar; ashnaei ba khaneh-ye ketab-e Iran*), interview by Hamidreza Nowrouzpour, *Ketab-e mah-e koliyat*, 11 October 1998.

Matin-Asgari, Afshin (1991), 'The Iranian Student Movement Abroad: The Confederation of Iranian Students, National Union', in Asghar Fathi (ed.), *Iranian Refugees and Exiles Since Khomeini*, Costa Mesa: Mazda Publishers.

McAuliffe, Cameron (2007), 'A Home Far Away? Religious Identity and Transnational Relations in the Iranian Diaspora', *Global Networks* 7, no. 3: 307–27.

McAuliffe, Cameron (2008a), 'Challenging "the Problem" between Two Nations: The Second Generation in the Iranian Diaspora', in Helen Lee (ed.), *Ties to the Homeland: Second Generation Transnationalism*, Newcastle: Cambridge Scholars, pp. 126–50.

McAuliffe, Cameron (2008b), 'Transnationalism Within: Internal Diversity in the Iranian Diaspora', *Australian Geographer* 39, no. 1: 63–80.

McDonald, Peter D. (2009), *The Literature Police: Apartheid Censorship and its Cultural Consequences*, Oxford: Oxford University Press.

Megerdoomian, Karine (2008), *Analysis of Farsi Weblogs: A Survey of the Literature*, MITRE.

Mehr News (2016), 'Interview with the director of Qoqnoos', *Mehr News*, 11 December, https://www.mehrnews.com/news/3839077/مدیریت-خانوادگی-در-حوزه-نشر-ایامی-که-صف-کتاب-تشکیل-می-شد (last accessed 13 June 2019).

Mehr News (2019), 'The French Experienced Iranian Theatre' (*Faransavi-ha teatr-e Iran ra tajrobeh kardand*), *Mehr News*, 18 February, https://www.mehrnews.com/news/4544761/فرانسوی-ها-تئاتر-ایران-را-تجربه-کردند-رویارویی-با-کارگردان-اثر.

Mehtari, Ebrahim (2012), 'Interview with Tinoush Nazmjou, Manager of Naakojaa Publisher', *Roozonline*, 7 March, http://www.roozonline.com/persian/news/newsitem/article/-cb82957990.html.

Milani, Farzaneh (1985), 'Power, Prudence and Print: Censorship and Simin Danashvar', *Iranian Studies* 18, no. 2–4: 325–47.

Milani, Farzaneh (2011), *Words, Not Swords: Iranian Women Writers and the Freedom of Movement*, Syracuse: Syracuse University Press.

Mina, Nima (2007), *Blogs, Cyber-Literature and Virtual Culture in Iran*, George C. Marshall Center for Security Studies, online (December).

Mina, Nima (2019), *Freydoun Farokhzad: Another Season, Andere Jahreszeit. A Bilingual Edition with Critical Introduction, Annotations and Archival Material*, London: Mehri Publication.

Ministry of Culture and Islamic Guidance (2019), 'Foundation of Iranian Poetry and Fiction Literature. List of Registered Associations', *Ministry of Culture and Islamic Guidance*, https://www.hlclubs.ir/list (last accessed 10 July 2020).

Mir-Hosseini, Ziba (2006), 'Muslim Women's Quest for Equality: Between Islamic Law and Feminism', *Critical Inquiry* 32, no. 4: 629–45.

Mirabeidini, Hassan (2007), *One Hundred Years of Story Writing in Iran* (*Sad sal-e dastan nevisi-ye Iran*), Tehran: Cheshmeh.

Mirsadeghi, Jamal (2008), *Fiction Literature (Tales, Romances, Shorts Stories, Novels)* (*Adabiyat-e dastani (Qesseh, romans, dastan-e kutah, roman)*), Tehran: Sokhan.

Missaghi, Poupeh (2015), '34 Animal Farms: Literary Translation and Copyright in Iran', *Asymptote*, 13 July, https://www.asymptotejournal.com/blog/?s=34+Animal+Farms (last accessed 18 July 2015).

Moghadam, Amin (2015), '"Being Persian" au pays des Arabes. Représentations et hiérarchies sociales parmi les Iraniens de Dubaï', *Hommes et Migrations* 4, no. 1312: 23–30.

Moghadam, Amin, and Serge Weber (2016a), 'Circulating by Default: Yerevan and Erbil, the Backyards of Iranian Mobility', in Leïla Vignal (ed.), *The Transnational Middle East: People, Places, Borders*, pp. 164–81.

Moghadam, Amin, and Serge Weber (2016b), 'Iranians Abroad: An Essential Component of Iranian Society', *Hommes et migrations* 4, no. 1312: 7–11.

Moghadam, Fatemeh (2010), 'Discussion with Mehdi Moussavi, poet of the postmodern ghazal', 12 July, http://fatemehmoghadam.blogfa.com/post-21.aspx (last accessed 28 August 2019).

Moghaddari, Sonja (2015), 'Engaging with Social Inequalities: The Stakes of Social Relations among Iranian Migrants', in Heinrich Böll Foundation and Transparency for Iran (eds), *Identity and Exile: The Iranian Diaspora between Solidarity and Difference*, Berlin: Heinrich Böll Foundation.

Mohafez, Sudabeh (no date), 'The Absolute Mouthpiece of Sudabeh Mohafez' ('Das absolut einzige Mundartstück von Sudabeh Mohafez'), http://www.sudabehmohafez.de (last accessed 28 August 2015).

Mohafez, Sudabeh (2007–13), 'Ten Lines. Eukapirates tries the Small Form' ('Zehn Zeilen. Eukapirates versucht sich an der kleinen form'), http://eukapi.twoday.net (last accessed 28 August 2015).

Mokhtari, Tara (2013), *Anxiety Soup: A Collection of Poetry*, Braidwood, NSW: Finlay Lloyd.
Moosavi, Amir (2015), 'How to Write Death: Resignifying Martyrdom in Two Novels of the Iran-Iraq War', *Alif* 35: 9–31.
Moosavi, Amir (2016), 'Stepping Back from the Front. A Glance at Home Front Narratives of the Iran-Iraq War in Persian and Arabic Fiction', in Arta Khakpour, Mohammad Mehdi Khorrami and Shouleh Vatanabadi (eds), *Moments of Silence: Authenticity in the Cultural Expressions of the Iran-Iraq War, 1980–1988*, New York: New York University Press.
Moosavi, Amir (2017), 'Dark Corners and the Limits of Ahmad Dehqan's War Front Fiction', *Middle East Critique* 26, no. 1: 45–59.
Moradi Kermani, Houshang (2014), *The Water Urn*, London: Candle & Fog.
Moretti, Franco (2008), 'The Novel: History and Theory'. *New Left Review* 52: 111–24.
Morozov, Evgeny (2011), *The Net Delusion: How Not to Liberate the World*, London: Allen Lane.
Motlagh, Amy (2008), 'Towards a Theory of Iranian American Life Writing', *MELUS* 33, no. 2.
Mousavi, Najmeh (2013), *Éclats de vie: histoires persanes*, Paris: L'Harmattan.
Naeej, Elham (2018), 'The Literary Heritage of Contemporary Iranian Romance Novels', in *Iranica Conference: Mirrors of Iran, Unveiling Iranian Literary Heritage*, Sydney: State Library of NSW.
Naeej, Elham (2020), 'The Female Body in Contemporary Iranian Romance Novels: Repression and Resistance', PhD thesis, University of New South Wales.
Naficy, Hamid (2012), *A Social History of Iranian Cinema, vol. 4*, Durham, NC: Duke University Press.
Naghibi, Nima (2016), *Women Write Iran: Nostalgia and Human Rights from the Diaspora*, Minneapolis: University of Minnesota Press.
Nahapétian, Naïri (2009), *Qui a tué l'Ayatollah Kanuni?* Paris: Liana Levi.
Nahapétian, Naïri (2012), *Dernier refrain à Ispahan*, Paris: Liana Levi.
Nahapétian, Naïri (2013), *Qui a tué l'Ayatollah Kanuni*, Paris: Points.
Nahapétian, Naïri (2014), *Dernier refrain à Ispahan*, Paris: Points.
Nahapétian, Naïri (2015), *Un agent nommé Parviz*, La Tour-d'Aigues: Éditions de l'Aube.
Nahapétian, Naïri (2016), *Un agent nommé Parviz*, La Tour-d'Aigues: Éditions de l'Aube.

Nahapétian, Naïri (2017a), *Jadis, Romina Wagner*, La Tour-d'Aigues: Éditions de l'Aube.

Nahapétian, Naïri (2017b), *Le mage de l'Hôtel Royal*, La Tour-d'Aigues: Éditions de l'Aube.

Najafian, Ahoo (2018), 'Poetic Nation: Iranian Soul and Historical Continuity', PhD thesis, Stanford University.

Najmabadi, Afsaneh (2004), 'The Morning After: Travail of Sexuality and Love in Modern Iran', *International Journal of Middle East Studies* 36: 367–85.

Nanquette, Laetitia (2013a), *Orientalism versus Occidentalism: Literary and Cultural Imaging between France and Iran Since the Islamic Revolution*, London: I. B. Tauris.

Nanquette, Laetitia (2013b), 'An Iranian Woman's Memoir on the Iran–Iraq War: The Production and Reception of *Da*', *Iranian Studies* 46, no. 6: 943–57.

Nanquette, Laetitia (2014a), 'Iranian Exilic Poetry in Australia: Reinventing the Third Space', *Antipodes* 28, no. 2: 393–403.

Nanquette, Laetitia (2014b), 'Refugee Life Writing in Australia: Testimonios by Iranians', *Postcolonial Text* 9, no. 2.

Nanquette, Laetitia (2016), 'The Global Circulation of an Iranian Bestseller', *Interventions* 19, no. 1: 56–72.

Nanquette, Laetitia (2017a), 'The Circulation of Iranian Texts around the World: The Appearance of a Transnational Iranian Publishing Industry?', *Australian Humanities Review* 62.

Nanquette, Laetitia (2017b), 'The Translations of Modern Persian Literature in the United States: 1979–2011', *The Translator* 23: 49–66.

Nanquette, Laetitia, and Ali Alizadeh (eds) (2017), 'Persian Passages', *Southerly* 76.

Nassehy-Behnam, Vida (2000), 'Persian Community in France', in Ehsan Yarshater (ed.) *Encyclopedia Iranica*, online.

Nateq, Homa (1994), *Report on Western Culture in Iran: 1837–1921 (Karnameh-e farhangi-ye farangi dar Iran: 1837–1921)*, Paris: Khavaran.

Nemat, Marina (2008), *Prisoner of Tehran: A Memoir*, London: John Murray.

Nilsson, Louise, David Damrosch, and Theo d'Haen (eds) (2017), *Crime Fiction as World Literature*, New York: Bloomsbury.

Olszewska, Zuzanna (2015), *The Pearl of Dari: Poetry and Personhood among Young Afghans in Iran, Public Cultures of the Middle East and North Africa*, Bloomington: Indiana University Press.

Omri, Mohamed-Salah (2007), 'Guest Editor's Introduction', *Comparative Critical Studies* 4, no. 3: 317–28.

Palm, Christian (2017), Exile and Construction of Identity on the Literature of Exiled Authors of German Language, the Case of SAID and Rapithwin (*Exil und Identitätskonstruktion in deutschsprachiger Literatur exilierter Autoren: Das Beispiel SAID und Rapithwin*), Heidelberg: Universitätsverlag Winter.

Parham, Angel Adams (2004), 'Diaspora, Community and Communication: Internet Use in Transnational Haiti', *Global Networks* 4, no. 3: 199–217.

Parrinder, Patrick (2008), *Nation and Novel: The English Novel from its Origins to the Present Day*, Oxford: Oxford University Press.

Partovi, Pedram (2017), *Popular Iranian Cinema Before the Revolution: Family and Nation in Filmfarsi*, New York: Routledge.

Parviz, Mohsen (2018), 'Transformation in the Area of Children and Young Adults' Fiction after the Islamic Revolution' ('*Tahavvol dar adabiyat-e dastani-ye kudakan va nowjavanan pas az enqelab-e eslami*'), 19 April, http://www.imam-khomeini.ir/fa/n127942/ (last accessed 20 April 2019).

Portal of Imam Khomeini (2017), 'Ruhollah Story Festival' ('*Jashnvareh-ye dastan-e Ruhollah*'), 17 March, http://www.imamkhomeini.ir/fa/n116295/مهلت_آخرین_ارسال_آثار_به_اولین_دوره_جشنواره_داستان_روح_الله_تا_بیستم_فروردین96_تمدید_شد) (last accessed 28 August 2019).

Pym, Anthony (1996), 'Venuti's Visibility', *Target: International Journal of Translation Studies* 8, no. 1: 165–77.

Qiasi, Nasser (2014), '"Lolita", From Writing to Translating and Publishing into Persian in Afghanistan' ('*"Lolita", az neveshtan ta tarjomeh va enteshar be Farsi dar Afghanestan*'), *BBC Persian*, 10 January, http://www.bbc.com/persian/arts/2014/07/140705_l41_book_lolita_akramnia_afghanistan (last accessed 12 December 2015).

Quayson, Ato, and Girish Daswani (2013), *A Companion to Diaspora and Transnationalism*, Hoboken, NJ: Wiley-Blackwell.

Rafiei, Mehran (2017), *A Persian Odyssey: A Memoir of an Iranian Migrant*, Queensland: Brookfield.

Rahbaran, Shiva, and Maryam Mohajer (2016), *Iranian Cinema Uncensored: Contemporary Film-makers Since the Islamic Revolution*, London: I. B. Tauris.

Rahimi, Babak (2003), 'Cyberdissent: The Internet in Revolutionary Iran', *Middle East Review of International Affairs* 7, no. 3.

Rahimi, Babak, and David M. Faris (2015), *Social Media in Iran: Politics and Society After 2009*, Albany: SUNY Press.

Rahimieh, Nasrin, and Persis Karim (2008), 'Iranian American Literature', *Multi-Ethnic Literature of the United States* 33, no. 3.

Rahnama, Ali, and Farhad Nomani (1990), *The Secular Miracle: Religion, Politics and Economic Policy in Iran*, London: Zed.

Rajabzadeh, Ahmad (2002), *Book Censorship: Research into 1400 Documents on Censored Books in 1997 (Momayezi-ye ketab: pazhuheshi dar 1400 sanad-e momayezi-ye ketab dar sal-e 1375)*, Tehran: Kavir.

Ramazan Shirazi, Davood (2012), 'A Quick Look at the History of the Union', http://www.nasheran.org/index.php/2012-05-21-07-33-31/history (last accessed 12 December 2013).

Rastegar, Kamran (2016), 'Treacherous Memory: Bashu the Little Stranger and the Sacred Defense', in Arta Khakpour, Mohammad Mehdi Khorrami and Shouleh Vatanabadi (eds), *Moments of Silence: Authenticity in the Cultural Expressions of the Iran-Iraq War, 1980–1988*, New York: New York University Press.

Razavi, Reza (2009), 'The Cultural Revolution in Iran, with Close Regard to the Universities, and its Impact on the Student Movement', *Middle Eastern Studies* 45, no. 1: 1–17.

Rendy, Leila Samadi (2017), *Iranian Diaspora Literature of Women*, Freiburg im Breisgau: Klaus Schwarz Verlag.

Robertson, Bronwen, and James Marchant (eds) (2014), *Revolution Decoded: Iran's Digital Landscape*, Small Media, https://smallmedia.org.uk/revolutiondecoded/a/RevolutionDecoded.pdf (last accessed 9 January 2015).

Rose, Jacqueline (1984), *The Case of Peter Pan, or, The Impossibility of Children's Fiction*, London: Palgrave Macmillan.

Rucker, Robert E. (1991), 'Trends in Post-Revolutionary Iranian Education', *Journal of Contemporary Asia* 21, no. 4: 455–68.

Saadi Foundation (2010), 'Constitution of the Saadi Foundation', 25 November, Saadi Foundation, http://saadifoundation.ir/fa/contents/aboutus/History_SaadiFoundation1/بنیاد.اساسنامه.html (last accessed 4 November 2016).

Sadat Hosseini, Shahimeh, and Dariush Matlabi (2013), 'A Review on the Status of Copyright in Iran's Publication Industry: Studying Tehran Publishers' View', *Middle-East Journal of Scientific Research* 16, no. 3: 383–91.

Sadeghi, Sahar (2015), 'Boundaries of Belonging: Iranian Immigrants and their Adult Children in the US and Germany', in Heinrich Böll Foundation and Transparency for Iran (eds), *Identity and Exile: The Iranian Diaspora between Solidarity and Difference*, Berlin: Heinrich Böll Foundation.

Sadr, Hamid Reza (2002), 'Children in Contemporary Iranian Cinema: When We Were Children', in Richard Tapper (ed.), *The New Iranian Cinema: Politics, Representation and Identity*, London: I. B. Tauris, pp. 227–37.

Saeedi, Samira (2019), 'The Role of Translators in Contemporary Iran: New Perspectives on Collaboration, Retranslation, and Visibility', PhD thesis, University of Melbourne.

Safran, William Spring (1991), 'Diasporas in Modern Societies: Myths of Homeland and Return', *Diaspora: A Journal of Transnational Studies* 1, no. 1: 83–99.

Said, Edward W. (1993), *Culture and Imperialism*. London: Chatto & Windus.

Sakurai, Keiko (2004), 'University Entrance Examination and the Making of an Islamic Society in Iran: A Study of the Post-Revolutionary Iranian Approach to "Konkur"', *Iranian Studies* 37, no. 3: 393–4.

Salamati, Mahsa (2016), 'Non-formal Film Circulation: Technology, Transnational Copyright Regimes and the Iranian State', in *Conference: Worlding Iran: Contemporary Iranian Culture and the World*, 8–9 December, University of New South Wales.

Salamati, Mahsa (2019), 'Transnational Film Circulation in the Iranian Context: From Conjunctural Crisis to Discursive Heterotopia', PhD thesis, University of New South Wales.

Salami, Shahnaz (2014), 'Politics of Intellectual Property in Iran: Internal Contradictions and International Treaties' ('Politique de la propriété intellectuelle en Iran: contradictions internes et traités internationaux'), in *Congrès mondial de science politique, 21 July, Université de Lyon, Institut d'Étude Politique*.

Sami, Osamah (2015), *Good Muslim Boy*, Melbourne: Hardie Grant Books.

Saniee, Parinoush (2013), *The Book of Fate*, trans Sara Khalili, London: Little, Brown.

Sapiro, Gisèle (2003), 'The Literary Field between the State and the Market', *Poetics* 31: 441–64.

Sapiro, Gisèle (2010), 'Globalization and Cultural Diversity in the Book Market: The Case of Literary Translations in the US and in France', *Poetics* 38: 419–39.

Sapiro, Gisèle (2015), 'Translation and Symbolic Capital in the Era of Globalization: French Literature in the United States', *Cultural Sociology* 9, no. 3: 1–27.

Sarvas, Mark (2014), 'TEV 2.0 – Volume 1, Number 1: THE DOG, Beha, Plesko and "Life Gets in the Way"', *The Elegant Variation*, 16 October, http://tinyletter.com/elegvar/letters/tev-2-0-volume-1-number-1-the-dog-beha-plesko-and-life-gets-in-the-way (last accessed 5 December 2015).

Schirasi, Ali (2004–15), *Website of the German-Iranian Writer Ali Schirasi* (*Website des Deutsch-Iranischen Schriftstellers Ali Schirasi*), http://www.alischirasi.de (last accessed 24 August 2014).

Schwartz, Kevin (2018), 'Mapping a Persian Literary Sphere, 1500–1900', Library of Congress, https://www.youtube.com/watch?v=CJyydV1pqWE (last accessed 20 August 2020).

Scott, Rosie, and Thomas Keneally (eds) (2007), *Another Country*, Broadway: Sydney PEN & Halstead Press.

Sekaf (2002–4), https://3kkk.wordpress.com/ (last accessed 7 October 2015).

Selim, Samah (2009), 'Nation and Translation in the Middle East', *The Translator* 15, no. 1: 1–13.

Sepanlou, Mohammad Ali (2002), *A History of the Writers' Association of Iran (Sargozasht-e kanun-e nevisandegan-e Iran)*, Spanga: Baran.

Sepehri, Abazar (1988), 'Contemporary Non-Serial Persian Publishing in Exile', *MELA Notes* 45: 6–22.

Serov, Banafsheh (2008), *Under a Starless Sky: A Family's Escape from Iran*, Sydney: Hachette Australia.

Seyed-Gohrab, Asghar (2012), 'Martyrdom as Piety: Mysticism and National Identity in Iran-Iraq War Poetry', *Der Islam: Journal of the History and Culture of the Middle East* 87, no. 1–2, https://doi.org/10.1515/islam-2011-0031.

Seyedabadi, Aliasghar (2004), 'Collective Weblogs, Opening the Circles to Dialogue', *BBC Persian*, 14 November, http://www.bbc.com/persian/iran/story/2004/11/041114_mj-asa-iran-web-logs-anniv.shtml (last accessed 7 September 2015).

Shahid, Mohammad Reza (2017), 'Interview with Tinouche Nazmjou', *YouTube*.

Shahrestani, Mohammad Ali (2004), 'Review of The Book of Fate', *Bukhara* 37 (August): 381–9.

Shahsavari, Mohammad Hassan (2013), 'Interview with Mohammad Hassan Shahsavari about "Dear M."', by Davoud Atashbeik, *Our Literature: The Voice of the New Generation of Iranian Literature*, http://www.adabiatema.com/index.php/2013-03-02-20-02-43/2013-03-20-17-06-42/241-1392/1198-2013-03-20-12-51-13 (last accessed 4 June 2015).

Shams, Fatemeh (2015a), 'Literature, Art, and Ideology under the Islamic Republic. An Extended History of the Center for Islamic Arts and Thoughts', in Kamran Talattof (ed.), *Persian Language, Literature and Culture: New Leaves, Fresh Looks*, Abingdon: Routledge.

Shams, Fatemeh (2015b), 'Official Voices of a Revolution: A Social History of Islamic Republican Poetry', PhD thesis, University of Oxford.

Shams, Fatemeh (2016), 'Ideology of Warfare and the Islamic Republic's Poetry of War', *International Journal of Persian Literature* 1, no. 1: 5–58.

Shams, Fatemeh (2020), *A Revolution in Rhyme: Poetic Co-option Under the Islamic Republic*, Oxford: Oxford University Press.

Shayegan, Darius (2017), *The Poetic Persian Soul* (*L'âme poétique persane: Ferdowsî, Khayyâm, Rûmî, Sa'dî, Hâfez*), Paris: Albin Michel.

Sheibani, Khatereh (2011), *Poetics of Iranian Cinema: Aesthetics, Modernity and Film After the Revolution*, London: I. B. Tauris.

Shih, Shu-mei (2010), 'Against Diaspora: The Sinophone as Places of Cultural Production', in Jing Tsu and David Der-wei Wang (eds), *Global Chinese Literature*, Leiden: Brill.

Shojaei, Seyyed Mehdi (1986), *The Berthed Ship* (*Kashti-ye pahlu gerefteh*), Tehran: Madresseh.

Shojaei, Seyyed Mehdi (2013), *Father, Love and Son* (*Pedar, eshq va pesar*), Tehran: Neyestan.

Shokrollahi, Reza (2010), 'Linking Khabgard to other Weblogs', *Khabgard*, 31 January, http://khabgard.com/?id=-1871374833 (last accessed 6 October 2018).

Shokrollahi, Reza (2015), 'The Personal History of Blogging: This is a Weblog Game, Serious and a Bit Tough', *Khabgard*, 1 March, http://khabgard.com/?id=1745262891 (last accessed 6 October 2018).

Shokrollahi, Reza (2019), 'A Billion Dollar Deal to Censor 13 Million Books Pages', *Radio Farda*, 13 August, https://www.radiofarda.com/a/contract-between-the-ministry-of-guidance-and-a-private-company/30109820.html (last accessed 9 October 2019).

Siamdoust, Nahid (2017), *Soundtrack of the Revolution: The Politics of Music in Iran*, Stanford: Stanford University Press.

Siavoshi, Sussan (1997), 'Cultural Policies and the Islamic Republic: Cinema and Book Publication', *International Journal of Middle Eastern Studies* 29: 509–30.

Sifry, David (2007), *Technorati, State of the Blogosphere*, http://www.sifry.com/alerts/2007/04/the-state-of-the-live-web-april-2007 (last accessed 6 October 2014).

Small Media (2015a), *Writer's Block: The Story of Censorship in Iran*, https://smallmedia.org.uk/work/writers-block-the-story-of-censorship-in-iran (last accessed 28 August 2019).

Small Media (2015b), *Iranian Internet Infrastructure and Policy Report*, July, http://www.smallmedia.org.uk/sites/default/files/u8/IIIP_JULY15.pdf (last accessed 9 October 2015).

Smith, David (2016), 'Iranian Americans Dismayed by Discrimination in New Visa Regulations', *The Guardian*, 16 January, http://www.theguardian.com/us-news/2016/jan/15/iranian-americans-visa-regulations-waiver-programme-us-immigration (last accessed 6 October 2018).

Snir, Reuven (2018), *Modern Arabic Literature: A Theoretical Framework*, Edinburgh: Edinburgh University Press.

Sobhe, Khosrow (1982), 'Education in Revolution: Is Iran Duplicating the Chinese Cultural Revolution?', *Comparative Education* 18, no. 3: 271–80.

Soleimani, Sajadeh (2016), 'Deputy for International Affairs of the Saadi Foundation: The Number of Persian Language Courses Have Declined' ('Moaven-e beynol-melali-ye bonyad-e saadi: kors-ha-ye zaban-e Farsi kam shodeh'), *Iran Students Correspondents Association*, 9 July, http://www.iscanews.ir/news/660097/ فارسی-زبان-های-کرسی-گذشته-سال-درصد:سعدی-بنیاد-الملل-بین-معاون (last accessed 9 February 2018).

Soltany Zand, Mohsen (2010), *Inside Out*, Armidale: Kardoorair Press.

Sprachman, Paul (2017), 'State-Sponsored Serial Murder in Film and Fiction Banned in Iran', in Faridoun Farrokh (ed.), *Bright Diversities of Day: Essays on Persian Literature and Culture in Honor of M. R. Ghanoonparvar*, Costa Mesa: Mazda.

Sreberny, Annabelle, and Reza Gholami (2016), *Iranian Communities in Britain*, London: SOAS London Middle East Institute.

Sreberny, Annabelle, and Gholam Khiabany (2010), *Blogistan: The Internet and Politics in Iran*, London: I. B. Tauris.

Supreme Council of the Cultural Revolution (1988), *Objectives, Policies and Rules for the Publication of Books*, Office for the Development of Books and Book Reading, 10 May.

Tabriznia, Mojtaba, and Esmaeil Afghahi (2017), *The Statistics of Books in Iran: Statistical Data of Book Publishing in Iran from 1979 to 2016*, Tehran: Iran Book House.

TAFE NSW Outreach –(2007), 'Afghan and Iranian Program: A collaborative project to develop an educational program for the Farsi speaking community', Sydney: Northern Sydney Institute Hornsby College.

Taheri, Zahra (1990), *Milad*, Berkeley: Study Group on Iran, UC Berkeley.

Taheri, Zahra (1997), *Primal Dawn (Pegah-e Nakhostin)*, Langley Park, MD: Langley Printing.

Tangestani, Mohammad (2017), 'Interview with Tinouche Nazmjou', *IranWire*, 27 October, https://iranwire.com/fa/blogs/838/23717 (last accessed 12 December 2018).

Taraqi, Goli (2013), *The Pomegranate Lady and Her Sons*, trans. Sara Khalili, New York: W. W. Norton & Company.

Tasnim News (2018), 'Qadyani: Non-Professional but Wealthy Publishers Have Seized the Children's Book Market' (*'Qadyani: Nasheran-e gheir-e herfeh-i amma puldar bazar-e ketab-e kudak ra qebzeh kardehand'*), *Tasnim News*, 1 January, https://www.tasnimnews.com/fa/news/1396/10/11/1616097/-قدیانی-ناشران اند-کرده-قبضه-را-کودک-کتاب-بازار-پولدار-اما-ای-حرفه-غیر (last accessed 6 October 2018).

Tenty, Tiffany Amber, and Christopher Housten (2013), 'The Iranian Diaspora in Sydney: Migration Experience of Recent Iranian Immigrants', *Iranian Studies* 46, no. 4: 625–40.

Three Percent: A Resource for International Literature at the University of Rochester, http://www.rochester.edu/College/translation/threepercent/ (last accessed 15 March 2012).

Tompkins, Ptolemy (2002), 'Rumi Rules!', *Time*, 29 October, http://content.time.com/time/magazine/article/0,9171,356133,00.html#ixzz2sIvCIX00Time (last accessed 6 October 2011).

Türkkan, Sevinç (2012), 'Orhan Pamuk's Kara Kitap (the Black Book): A Double Life in English', in Mehnaz Mona Afridi and David M. Buyze (eds), *Global Perspectives on Orhan Pamuk: Existentialism and Politics*, Basingstoke: Palgrave Macmillan, pp. 159–76.

UNESCO (no date), 'Table 21: Historic Data (1995–1999): Book Production', *UIS. stat*, http://stats.uis.unesco.org/unesco/TableViewer/tableView.aspx?ReportId=5594.

UNESCO (2012a), 'Top 10 Authors translated for a given original language: Farsi', *Index Translationum*, online.

UNESCO (2012b), 'TOP 10 Countries publishing translations from a given original language', *Index Translationum*, online.

UNESCO (2012c), 'Top 10 Publishers publishing translations in a given country', *Index Translationum*, 26 March, http://www.unesco.org/xtrans/bsstatlist.aspx?m=12.

Vafa, Amir (2020), 'Lost in Paradise: On the "Coloniality" of English Literary Studies in Iran', *International Journal of Middle East Studies* 52: 334–9.

Vahabi, Nader (2011), *Iranian Migration in Belgium, a Diaspora by Default* (*La migration iranienne en Belgique, une diaspora par défaut*), Paris: L'Harmattan.

Vahabi, Nader (2015), 'La diaspora iranienne en France: profil démographique et socioéconomique', *Migrations Société* 27, no. 158: 19–39.

Van den Bos, Matthijs (2012), '"European Islam" in the Iranian Ettehadiyeh', in Lloyd V. J. Ridgeon (ed.), *Shi'i Islam and Identity: Religion, Politics and Change in the Global Muslim Community*, London: I. B. Tauris.

Vanzan, Anna (2009), *Daughters of Sheherazad: Iranian Women Writers From the 19th Century Until Today* (*Figlie di Shahrazād: scrittrici iraniane dal XIX secolo a oggi*), Milan: B. Mondadori.

Varzi, Roxanne (2006), *Warring Souls: Youth, Media, and Martyrdom in Post-Revolution Iran*, Durham, NC: Duke University Press.

Venuti, Lawrence (1995), *The Translator's Invisibility: A History of Translation*, London: Routledge.

Venuti, Lawrence (1998), *The Scandals of Translation: Towards an Ethics of Difference*, New York: Routledge.

Wake, Caroline (2010), 'Performing Witness. Testimonial Theatre in the Age of Asylum, Australia 2000–2005', PhD thesis, University of New South Wales.

Walkowitz, Rebecca (2015), *Born Translated: The Contemporary Novel in an Age of World Literature*, New York: Columbia University Press.

Wallerstein, Immanuel Maurice (1974), *The Modern World-System: Studies in Social Discontinuity*, New York: Academic Press.

Whitlock, Gillian (2007), *Soft Weapons: Autobiography in Transit*, Chicago: University of Chicago Press.

Yasrebi, Chista (2016), *The Postman* (*Postchi*), Instagram.

Yazdi, Hamid Rezaei, and Arshavez Mozafari (2019), *Persian Literature and Modernity: Production and Reception*, London: Routledge.

Zanganeh, Lila (2007), 'Goli Taraqi and José Manuel Prieto: Freedom Above All' ('Goli Taraqi et José Manuel Prieto: la liberté par-dessus tout'), *Le Monde des Livres*, 25 May.

Zarrinkub, Abdolhossein, and Paul Sprachman (2017), *Two Centuries of Silence: An Account of Events and Conditions in Iran During the First Two Hundred Years of Islam, from the Arab Invasion to the Rise of the Tahirid Dynasty*, Costa Mesa: Mazda.

Zendehru, Mohammad (2014), 'Self-publishing, constraint or evolution?' ('*Khod-nasheri, asib ya tahavol?*'), *Book of the Week* (*Ketab-e hafteh*), 23 November.

Zia-Ebrahimi, Reza (2016), 'Better a Warm Hug than a Cold Bath: Nationalist Memory and the Failures of Iranian Historiography', *Iranian Studies* 49, no. 5: 837–54.

Zimbler, Jarad (2009), 'For Neither Love nor Money: The Place of Political Art in Pierre Bourdieu's Literary Field', *Textual Practice* 23, no. 4: 599–620.

Index

Page numbers in italics refer to illustrations; t indicates tables,
m indicates maps, n indicates notes

Abad, Masoumeh, 'Heroines of Iran' ('*Shir zanan-e Iran*'), 42
Abdelsadek, Nafisa, 140, 141–2, 145
Abdoh, Salar, 32, 33, 205
Academy of Persian Language and Literature, 105
Act of Union 1958, 108
Adelkhah, Fariba, 13, 158
Afghahi, Esmaeil, *The Statistics of Books in Iran: Statistical Data of Book Publishing in Iran from 1979 to 2016*, 113–37
Afghanistan
  The Colonel, 100
  Lolita, 99
Afghans, in Australia, 4, 218
Afsaneh: Short Stories by Iranian Women, 190n
Afshari, Zardosht, 216
Aftab, 203
The Age, 217
Ahmadi, Ahmadreza, 70
Ahmadi Arian, Amir, 248
  The Disappearance of Danyal (Ghiyab-e Danyal), 99
Ahmadinejad, President, 81, 120–1, 127, 129–30, 171, 235, 244
Aidani, Mammad, 208, 212, 216, 221, 222
  A Picture Out of Frame, 216
Akhavan, Niki, 4–5, 53, 58, 102–3
  Electronic Iran, 166
Akhtar, 167
Aknoon Cultural Centre, 223, 225, 227

Al-e Ahmad, Jalal, 192, 197
  Westruckness, 193–4
Alhoda International Publishing Group, 239
Ali, Imam, 42, 43
Alinejad, Masih, 52–3
Alizadeh, Ali, 216, 221
Alizadeh, Farahnaz, 59
Allameh Tabatabai University, 105
Alliance Française, 103
Al-Mustafa University, 77, 105
Amazon
  Candle & Fog, 175, 176
  Ghahramani, Zarah, 220, 220n
  Naakojaa, 172
  reviews, 232
  sanctions in Iran, 66, 94
  translations, 183
Amini, Bahman, 170
Aminpur, Qeysar, 40
Amraei, Asadollah, 59
Amrein, Roshanak, 221
Anderson, Benedict, 6, 177–8
  'imagined community', 5
Anh Do, *The Happiest Refugee*, 215
Another Country, 216–17
Ansari, Noushafarin, 144
Anushiravani, Alireza, 183
Arabic language, 166
  translations from, 195–6
Arabs, and Iranian identity, 246
Araghi, Alireza Taheri, 'Persian translated', 118

Arash: A Persian Monthly of Culture and Social Affairs, 204, 223
Arasteh, Reza, 201
Arbabzadeh, Nushin, 214
Armenia, Iranians in, 158
Art Dubai, 244
Ashrafi, Nasrin, 129
Ashuri, Dariush, *Modernity and Us*, 252
Assassin's Creed series, 28
Association of Iranian American Writers (AIAW), 186
Association of Writers for Children and Youth (*Anjoman-e nevisandegan-e kudakan va nowjavanan*), 145
Assyrians, in Australia, 210
Astrid Lingren Award, 151
asylum seekers, 209, 215n; *see also* refugees
Atwood, Blake, 84, 240
Australia
  Afghans in, 4, 218
  Baha'i migration, 161
  Iranians in, 161, 181, 208–14
  Iranian institutions in, 225–7
  Iranian texts in, 214–24
  Iranian writers in, 109–12, 157, 207–28
  Iraqi writers in, 218
  Jews in, 210
  Lebanon-born community in, 210
  literary production, 214–16
  poetry writers in, 221–2
  religious affiliation of Iranians in, *211*
  texts in English, 216–22
  texts in Persian, 222–4
  universities, 226
  see also New South Wales; Sydney
Australian Book Review, ABR Behrouz Boochani Fellowship, 218
Australian Bureau of Statistics, 210
Australian Department of Immigration, 209, 226
Australian National University, Canberra, 107, 222
Avini, Morteza, 'Chivalrous Warriors' ('*Darya delan-e saf shekan*'), 42
Ayati, Ata, *Iran in Transition (L'Iran en transition)*, 204
Ayla Drama Group, 225
Azadibougar, Omid
  censorship, 79
  cinema, 240
  copyright, 93
  genre, 27
  novels, 250
  poetry, 247
  Rumi, 182
Azar, Shokoofeh, *The Enlightenment of the Greengage Tree*, 220
Azar Yazdi, Mehdi
  Good Stories for Good Children (Qesseh-ha-ye khub baraye bache-ha-ye khub), 141
  UNESCO award, 141
Azeris, 158

Back Window (Panjereh-ye poshti), 56, 66
Baetens, Jan, 251
Baha'is, 161, 165–6, 209, 210
Bahmani, Kazem, 70
Bahram Sadeghi Prize, 55, 63
Bajoghli, Narges, 2, 41, 110
Balaÿ, Christophe, 167, 197–8, 245, 248–9, 250, 251
Bamdad, 223–4
Bani-Asadi, Mohammad-Ali, 150
Bani-Etemad, Rakhshan, 147
banned books, 100–1, 135
Baran, 174
Basijis, 57
Basmenji, Kaveh, 194
Beecroft, Alexander, 4
Behbahani, Simin, 60, 197
Behnoud, Masoud, *Robin Hood of the Desert*, 175
Belarus, censorship, 90
Berlin
  Gardoon, 174
  Kaveh, 167, 250
Berne Convention, 92, 149, 174–5
Beyzai, Bahram, *Bashu, Little Stranger*, 142
biographical anthology (*tazkireh*), 168, 258
black market, 74, 91, 97–102
blasphemy, 60
Blogfa, 'Literature and poetry', 49–51
blogger.com, 47
blogs, 45–6, 173
  China, 51–2
  'ultra-weblog', 55
  women, 52–3
  'the year of blogs' 2004, 47
  see also literary blogs
'blogspeak', 61
Boccaccio prize, 236
Bo'd-e haftom Science Fiction Club, 29
Bokartus, 174
Bologna Children's Book Fair, 150

INDEX | 289

Bombay, *The Blind Owl*, 167
Boochani, Behrouz, 217–18
　No Friend but the Mountains, 218
Book City (*Shahr-e Ketab*), 36–7
　creative writing workshops, 31
　Flying Turtle Award (*Lakposht-e parandeh*), 151
　Khabgard, 56, 66
　khosulati, 96
　Short Story Award, 56
book fairs, 149, 175
　Bologna Children's Book Fair, 150
　Frankfurt Book Fair, 177
　International Belgrade Book Fair 2016, 104n
　see also Tehran International Book Fair
Book Garden (*Bagh-e ketab*), 138, 139
Book of the Month (*Ketab-e mah*), 56, 115
Book of the Week (*Ketab-e hafteh*), 56, 115
Book of the Year Awards, 115
book production, 113–37
　categories of books published, 125
　centralisation of, 130–2
　number of titles per year, 122, 123
　number of titles per year per production location, 131
　number of titles per year per type, 128
　number of titles per city for the year 2012, 132t
　number of books versus number of copies, 121
　number of publishers per type, 134
　'Objectives, policies and rules for the publication of books', 81–2
　paper supplies versus support of the final book product, 90–1
　percentage according to genres, 25t
　poetry, 25
　policies on, 78–83
　proportion of publishers by activity, 189
　ties to governments, 118–21
Bourdieu, Pierre, 9, 181
British Empire, 247
Brouillette, Sarah, 9
'building up of books' (*ketabsazi*), 127, 129–30, 137
Bukhara, 235

Calcutta, *Hablo al-matin*, 167
California, Iranian-American community, 190
Candle & Fog, 43, 105, 156, 174–7, 178
canonical literature, 25–6
Cartoon Biennial of Tehran, 150
censorship, 78–97, 112
　allegorical techniques, 142
　banned books, 100–1, 135
　child characters in film, 142, 145–6
　circumvention tools (*filtershekan*), 64–5
　crime stories, 31–2
　erotic fiction, 61
　internet, 49n, 50–1
　Iranian intranet, 45–6
　Kakaei, Abdul Jabbar, 57–8
　Kanun, 143
　literary blogs, 48–9, 53–5, 67
　online publishing, 74
　and open society, 166–7
　privatisation of, 96
　romances, 34
　Shokrollahi, Seyed Reza, 64
　state-filtering, 53–4
　Union of Tehran Publishers and Booksellers, 109
　and women, 86–7
　see also self-censorship
Census Explorer 2011, 210–11
Center for Iranian Diaspora Studies, 165
Center for Islamic Arts and Thoughts (*Howzeh-ye honari-ye sazeman-e tablighat-e eslami*), 57
Central Bank of Iran, 121
Centre for Iranian Documentation and Research, 203–4
Centre for Islamic Arts and Thought, 39–40, 84–5, 135
Centre for the Intellectual Development of Children and Young People (*Kanun-e parvaresh-e fekri-ye kudakan va nowjavanan*), 43, 142–4, 146, 147, 149, 151
Centre for the Organisation of the Translation and Publication of Islamic Studies and Humanities Abroad, 238
Centre National du Livre, 173
Centre of Plastic Arts of Iran (*Markaz-e honar-ha-ye tajassomi-ye keshvar*), 243–4
Chamlou, Nadereh, 159
Chan, Felicia, 239
charitable foundations (*owqaf*), 238
Chehabi, Houchang, 167
Cheshmeh
　crime stories, 31
　Kiayan, Said Hassan, 109

Cheshmeh (cont.)
  literary blogs, 56
  Rouhani, President Hassan, 121, 136
  Shokrollahi, Seyed Reza, 55
  Tehran International Book Fair, 72, 85
Children's Book Council (CBC) (Shora-ye ketab-e kudak), 142–5, 147
children's literature, 125, 138–53, 222, 238–9
Children's Literature Studies Periodical, 151
China
  blogging, 51–2
  state intranet, 45
  universities, 76–7
Chinese Cultural Revolution, 76–8
Chinese diaspora, 156, 257
  in Australia, 210, 213–14
Christie's, Dubai, 244
cinema, 240–3
  allegorical techniques, 142
  censorship, 85
  child characters in, 142, 145–6
  Iranian New Wave, 142
  'Islamicate cinema', 241–2
  Kanun, 142
  Moussavi, Granaz, 222
  Sheibani, Khatereh, 252–3
  'social issues films', 82–3
'cinematic ghazal', 253
circles (dowrehs), 11n, 111–12
Cohen, Robin, 14–15, 157
Commission to Determine the Instances of Criminal Content, 49
Committee Charged with Determining Offensive Content, 49
Confederation of Iranian Students, 202
Confucius Institute, 103
Constitutional Revolution 1907, 14
Contemporary Art Museum, Tehran, 'Children's Book Illustrators in Iran', 150
copyright, 92–3
Coser, Lewis, 190
Cotsen Children's Library archive, 140
Council for the Dissemination of Persian Language (Shora-ye gostaresh-e zaban-e Farsi), 107
Council of Guardian (Shora-ye negahban), 80
Courses to Increase Knowledge (Dowreh-ha-ye danesh afzaei), 105
creative writing workshops, 226

crime stories, 30–3, 205
  noir banned, 31–2
Croskery, Caroline, 43, 194n
Cultural Centre of the Islamic Republic, 203
cultural dominance, 184–5
Cultural Institute for Women Publishers (Anjoman-e farhangi-ye zanan-e nasher), 126
Curtin Immigration Detention Centre, 217
Cyber Army, 49
Cyber Police, 49
'cyberutopians', 48

Da, 26, 38, 41, 72
Damrosch, David, 12
Daneshvar, Simin, 87–8, 194
  Savushun, 26, 193, 233
Danestani-ha, 223
Dar al-Fonun, 201
Darabi, Helia, 243–4
Darbandi, Seyyed Mohammad Reza, 101n, 105
  Observed by the Moon (Zir-e negah-e mah), 42–3
Darznik, Jasmine, 161
Dastyari, Elaheh Manafi, 223
Davis, Dick, 245
Dehkhoda, Ali Akbar, 167
  Charand o parand, 249
Dehqan, Ahmad, 40, 85, 186n
Démy-Geroe, Anne, 82–3
Dena, 174
Derakhshan, Hossein (Hoder) see Hoder
Devictor, Agnès, 85, 102, 241
diaspora, 13–16, 157–62
  in Armenia, 158
  in Australia, 109–12, 157, 161, 181, 207–28, 211, 212m
  California, 190
  community networks, 213–14
  connectedness of, 162–7
  divisions between Iran and, 155–79
  in England, 202
  in France, 157, 159, 161, 205
  in Germany, 161, 162–3, 201–2
  in Iraq, 158
  in Italy, 161
  in Japan, 158
  Jews in Australia, 210
  Jews in US, 161

literary blogs, 177–8
  in Malaysia, 158
  in Middle East, 158
  Muslims in UK, 160
  in Sweden, 158–9, 160, 164
  in Turkey, 158
  in UK, 159, 202
  in United Arab Emirates (UAE), 158
  in US, 157, 158, 159, 161, 163, 165
'diaspora brokers', 160
'diaspora by default', 163–4
digital literature, 45–71
  digital humanities, 116–18
'digital Orientalism', 48, 58
Domain of Children Literature (Qalamrow-e adabiyyat-e kudakan), 144
Doostdar, Alireza, 63, 64
Dowlatabadi, Mahmoud, 83, 111
  The Colonel, 198n
  The Disappearance of the Colonel, 100
  Kelidar, 197
dystopian fiction, 29

Ebadi, Shirin, 235
Ebtekar, Massoumeh, 53
Ecole Polytechnique, 201
education
  children's literature, 146
  French Catholic missions, 201
  high school students, 42–3
  higher education, 133
  Montessori, 144–5
Ehsani, Kaveh, 37, 41
Ekhtesari, Fatemeh, 60, 70, *70*, 178
electronic publications, 169, 172
The Encyclopedia for Young People, 144–5, 147
The Encyclopedia Iranica, 140
Endowed Foundations (*bonyads*), 102–3
Enghelab area, Tehran, 98, 99, 101
English
  crime stories written in, 33
  translations, 126–7, 166
Entesharat-e roshangaran, 126
Erfan, Ali, 205
erotic fiction, 61, 69–70
erotic poetry, 69–70
Ershad *see* Ministry of Culture and Islamic Guidance
Esfahan, 130, 132
Esfahani, Homa Pur, 63
  It Wasn't Meant To Be (Qarar nabud), 69

Eshtehardi, Mohammad, 'Summary of Lessons' (*'Kholaseh-ye danesh-ha'*), 42
E'temad Daily, 56
E'tesami, Parvin, 223
E'tesami Literary Prize, 176
European Union, 93–4
Even-Zohar, Itamar, 247
Exbrayat, Charles, 30
exile
  in Australia, 216
  diaspora, 13–15, 157
  in France, 204–5
  Paris, 201
  politicians in, 167
  women in France, 205
  see also asylum seekers; diaspora; refugees

Facebook, 45, 53–4, 67, 177
Faiq, Said, 195
Fajr (Film and Theatre) festivals, 43
Fajr International Festival of Visual Arts (*Jashnvareh-ye beinolmelali-ye honar-ha-ye tajassomi-ye Fajr*), 244
Fajr International Poetry Festival, 57, 58
Falasiri, Arash, 47, 54
Fal-e Hafez, 246
Fantasy Academy, 29
fantasy fiction, 29
Fanus, 104
Farahmand, Azadeh, 242
Faraji, Mehdi, 70
Fardi, Amir Hossein, 144
Farid, Ali Khazaei, 129
Faris, David, 48
Farrar, Straus and Giroux, 219, 224
Farrokhzad, Forough, 62, 86–7, 193
Farzad, Narguess, 40
Fassaie, Saeed, 221
Fassih, Esmaeil, *Sorraya in a Coma*, 204
Fatahi, Hossein, 144
Fatemeh Zahra, 42–3
Fatemi, 104
Fathi, Nazila, 85, 125
feminism, Islamic, 235–6
Ferdowsi University, Mashhad, 107
'festival films' (*film-ha-ye jashnvareh-i*), 242
Fidibo, 66
film festivals, 239
  Iranian and Persian, 165
Filmfarsi, 34
filtered sites (*filter shod*), 65

Finglish (transliteration of Persian words in English), 60
First Asian Biennial of the Works of Illustrators of Children's Books in Tehran, 150
flash fiction (*dastan-e nagahani*), 59–60
Flashes of Life, Persian Stories (Éclats de vie, histoires persanes), 205
Flying Turtle Award (*Lakposht-e parandeh*), 151
folktales, 143
foreign fiction, 129
'foreignization', 195
Forough, 174
Fotouhi, Sanaz, 161, 205–6, 208, 212–13, 225–6
Fowler, Alastair, 27
France
    Centre National du Livre, 91
    Iranian texts in, 200–6
    Iranian women in, 205
    Iranian writers in, 157, 161
    Iranians in, 159
    literary blogs, 178
    literary critics, 26n
    Muslims, 160
    Naakojaa, 170–4
    online publishing, 66
    Persian language classes, 203
    Saadi Foundation, 106–7
    Sufi brotherhoods, 160
    translations, 94, 126, 197–8
Frankfurt Book Fair, 177
French
    crime stories written in, 33
    language, 186–7
    Persian prose, 248
'French cultural exception', 94
Frow, John, 27
Frye, Northrop, 27
Funak, 223–4

Gaj, 133
Gardoon, 100, 174
Garmaroodi, Mousavi, 'In the Shade of the Palm of Sanctity' ('*Dar sayeh sar-e nakhl-e velayat*'), 42
Gazelle literary agency, 176, 239
Gelder, Ken, 28
genre, 23–44, 25t
    translations, 196–7
genre literature (*adabiyyat-e zhanr*), 26

German, Pirzad, Zoya, 198n
Germany
    Iranian writers in, 161
    Iranians in, 162–3, 201–2
    Kouchaki Dehshali, Yadollah 178
    Najafi, Shahin, 68
    translations, 185
Ghahramani, Zarah, 219–20, 220n, 224
Ghanavizi, Nazanin, 47, 54
Ghanooparvar, Mohammad, 187, 190
Gharehgozlou, Bahareh, 192
Ghasemi, Abbasali, 223
Ghassemi, Reza, 63
    Davat, Literary Journal, 178
Ghatreh, 68
ghayr-e maktabi (not in line with the Islamic values presented by the Islamic republic), 75
Ghazanfari, Ameneh, *The Bold Halo of Sorrow*, 89
Ghods, Saideh, *Kimya Khatun*, 175–6
Gholam Hossein, 180
Gholami, Reza, 160, 165
Gholamshahi, Soheyla, 211
globalisation, 12–13, 230–40
    crime stories, 33
Goethe Institute, 103
Goethe Institute, Tehran, 111
Golrouee, Yaghma, 68, 71
Golshiri, 56
Goodreads, 11, 94, 183, 232
Google, 172
'governmental' (*dowlati*) publishers, 7–8, 36–44, 72–112, 133–5
Green Movement, 60
The Guardian, 220
The Guardian (Australia), 217

H&S Media, 66, 173–4
Hablo al-matin, 167
Haddad Adel, Gholam-Ali, 103–4, 106, 107
Haddadian-Moghaddam, 79, 93
Hafez, 245
    Divan, 246
Haitian diaspora, 162
Haj Seyyed Javadi, Fattaneh, 12
    The Morning After (Bamdad-e khomar), 194, 194n
Hamshahri, 59, 118
Hamyar Centre, 223
Hans Christian Andersen Medal, 150–1

Harlequin romantic fiction, 35, 219
Harris, Kevan, 75, 103, 105
Hassanpour, Houman, 109
Hassanzadeh, Farhad, 151
Hayeri Yazdi, Lili, 149–50
Hayot, Eric, 250
Heavenly Circle (Halqeh-ye malakut), 62
Hedayat, Sadegh, 26, 135, 182
  The Blind Owl, 98, 101, 167–8
  Buried Alive (Zendeh be gur), 250
Heilbron, Johan, 184
Held, David, 12
Hemmasi, Farzaneh, 15
Hemmat, Parsa, 69–70
Hermes, 37
Hillman, Robert, 219
Hirsch, Marianne, 'postmemory', 15
Hockx, Michel, 52
Hoder, 47, 52, 63
Hodgson, Marshall, 5
Hojvai, Mehdi, 144
'homeness', 164
horror genre, 29
Hossein Sanat'izadeh Kermani, Abdol, 29
'hostage narrative', 219
House of Anansi, 236
Housten, Christopher, 210
Huggan, Graham, 215
Hushang Golshiri Prize, 85

Ibex, 174
illustrations, 148–52
'imagined community', 5, 177–8
Imen, Leyli, 144
'immorality', 86–7
Imperial Award for Book of the Year, 141
'independent' (*khosusi*) publishers, 8, 36–44, 72–112, 133–5
India, literary agents, 238–9
indigenisation *(bumi sazi)*, 129–30
INSEE (National Institute of Statistics and Economic Studies), 202n
Instagram, 45–6, 54, 65, 67, 67–71, 70, 178
Institute for Research on the History of Children's Literature in Iran (*Daftar-e ta'lif-e farhangnameh-ye kudakan va nowjavanan*), 144
Institute for the Compilation and Publication of Imam Khomeini's Works (*Moasseseh-ye tanzim va nashr-e asar-e Imam Khomeini*), 146–7

Institute for Translation and Publication of Books (*Bongah-e tarjomeh va nashr-e ketab*), 141–2
International Alliance of Independent Publishers, France, 11
International Belgrade Book Fair 2016, 104n
International Board on Books for Young People, 144
International Federation of Translators, 238
internet
  censorship, 49n, 50–1
  and nationalism, 4–5
intranet, censorship, 45–6
Iran Book House report, 119, 123, 124, 128, 131, 132t, 134
Iran Book House, Tehran, 1, 24–5, 56, 113–37
Iran Book News Agency, 2
Iran Cultural Fairs (*Moasseseh-ye namayeshgah-ha-ye farhangi*), 151
Iran newspaper, 30
Iranian Academy of Persian Language and Literature, 104
Iranian Alliances Across Border, 165
Iranian Constitution, Article 24, 79
Iranian Constitutional Revolution, 202
Iranian Cultural Association, Sydney (*Anjoman-e farhang va honar*), 225–6
Iranian Embassies, 107
Iranian Illustrators Society (*Anjoman-e tasvirgaran-e Iran*), 151
Iranian Society for the Promotion of Persian Language and Literature (*Anjoman-e tarvij-e zaban va adab-e Farsi-ye Iran*), 107
Iranian Student's News Agency, 125–6
Iranian Studies, 10
Iranian Welfare Association (*Sazman-e hamyari-ye Iranian*), 226
Iranian Writers' Association (*Kanun-e nevisandegan-e Iran*), 110–11
Iranian.com, 173
'Iranianness', 161, 163, 194–5
Iran–Iraq war
  Aidani, Mammad, 216
  book production, 118
  Da, 26
  flash fiction (*dastan-e nagahani*), 59
  Kakaei, Abdul Jabbar, 57
  paper market, 90
  Sacred Defence cinema, 241

Iran–Iraq war (*cont.*)
   Sacred Defence literature, 25, 37–41, 186n
   Sorraya in a Coma, 204
   victim diaspora, 157
Iraq, Iranians in, 158
Iraqi, writers in Australia, 218
IRIB, 32–3, 55
ISBN, 114, 115, 203
Islamic Azad University, 105
Islamic Culture and Relations Organisation (*Sazman-e farhang va ertebatat-e eslami*), 186, 186n
Islamic feminism, 235–6
'Islamicate cinema', 241–2
Islamisation, 241
   of science, 77
   universities, 146
ISSN, 203
Istanbul, *Akhtar*, 167
Italian, *The Book of Fate (Sahm-e man)*, 236
Italy
   Aidani, Mammad, 216
   Iranian writers in, 161

Jadiri, Sepideh, 172
   Blue is the Warmest Colour, 172
Jafari, Ali, 30, 223
Jahan-e Ketab, 30
Jakobson, Roman, 245–6
Jalal Al-e Ahmad Literary Prize, 115
Jamalzadeh, Mohammad-Ali
   Once Upon a Time (Yeki bud, yeki nabud), 181, 183, 249–50
   Persian is Sugar (Farsi shekar ast), 167, 250
Jami, *Baharestan*, 59
Japan, Iranians in, 158
Japanese
   cartoons, 148
   literature translations into English, 182–3
Jenkins, Bullock, 103
Jews
   Iranians in Australia, 210
   Iranians in US, 161
   Karimi, Kooshyar, 220
journals, 223–4

Karaj, 132
Kakaei, Abdul Jabbar, 56–8
Kalb, Zep, 77
Kalilah va Dimnah, 140
Kanoon-e Towhid, London, 160

Karim, Persis, 161, 165, 186
Karimi, Kooshyar, 220
Karimi-Hakak, Mahmood, 85
Kaur, Rupi, *Milk and Honey*, 68
Kaveh, 167, 250
Kazemi, Zoha, *Khak-e adampush (The Human-Wearing Earth)*, 29
Kermani, Mirza Agha Khan, 167
Ketab Corp, 170
Khabgard, 55–6, 63, 65–6
Khalili, Bijan, 170
Khalili, Sara, 190–1n, 194, 230, 231n, 234, 236, 236–7
Khamenei, President, 80
Khamenei, Supreme Leader Ali, 104, 118–20
   poetry nights, 2
Khan, Malkam, 167
Khansari, Hadi, 60
Khatami, President, 80–1, 118, 120, 137, 234
Khavaran, 170–1, 173, 174
Khiabany, Gholam, 1
Khomeini, Ayatollah, 14, 43–4, 57, 74–5, 80, 109, 240–1
Khorrami, Mehdi, 27, 249
Khorshid, 172
Khorshidfar, Amir Hossein, 68
   The Tehranis (Tehrani-ha), 83
Khosravi, Shahram, 13, 157, 160, 164
Khosrokhavar, Fahrad, 1–2
Khosrow, Nasser, 42
khosulati, 95–6
Kia Literary agency, 149
Kiarostami, Abbas, *Where is the Friend's House*, 142
Kiayan, Said Hassan, 109
Kirkus, 233
Knopf, 191–2, 230, 231n, 232
Kouchaki Dehshali, Yadollah, 178
Kryzhanouski, Yauheni, 90
Kurds, borders, 158

Lahiji, Shahla, 126
Langeroodi, Shams, 227
Langford, Michelle, 142, 241–2, 253
Law Enforcement Force (*Niru-ye entezami*), 32–3
Law for the Protection of Authors, Composers and Artists Rights, 92
Lebanon-born community, in Australia, 210

legitimacy, 156
Librairie Utopian, 171–2
Library of Congress, 117, 183
literary agents, 238–9
 children's literature, 149, 151–2
 Gazelle literary agency, 176
 Hayeri Yazdi, Lili, 10
 POL, 175
 role of translator in US, 191
 Susijn, Laura, 236
literary blogs, 46–54, 58–67, 156
 diasporic, 177–8
 France, 178
 see also blogs
Literature of Resistance (*adabiyyat-e paydari*), 38, 39
Little, Brown, 231n, 236
'local' (*bumi*) texts, 237
Los Angeles, Ketab Corp, 170
Lydon, Christopher, 233

Mafan, Masoud, 174
magazines, children's literature, 140–1
Mahoutchi-Hosaini, Nasrin, 222, 226
Mahshid, N. D., *Silk and Roses*, 175
Makhmalbaf, Mohsen, 241, 253
maktabi (followers of the school of Islam), 75
Malakut, 62
Malaysia, Iranians in, 158
Malek, Amy, 157, 162, 165
Malekzadeh, Shervin, 10
 school curriculum, 76–7
Mandanipour, Shahriar
 Censoring an Iranian Love Story, 180, 230, 230–4, 231n, 232t
 Khalili, Sara, 194
 literary agent and translator, 191
 Persian Library in Sydney, 227
 Violet Orient (Sharq-e banafsheh), 180
Manoukian, Setrag, 246
Markaz, 93, 109
market
 external restrictions to, 93–4
 lack of integration, 92–3
 and politics, 94–7
 UK, 224
 UNESCO, 8
 US, 184–6, 224
 volume, 119
Maroufi, Abbas, 100
'martyr', 75–6

Maryland, Ibex, 174
Mascara, 217
Mashad, 130–2
Masjed-Jamei, Ahmad, 120
Massoud, 202
Mastoor, Mostafa, 'Malakeh Elizabeth', 65–6
McDonald, Peter, 88
Meftah-al-Molk, Mirza Mahmud Khan, *Disciplining Children (Ta'dib al-atfal)*, 140
Mehrjui, Dariush, 155
memoirs, 218–21
Mesghali, Farshid, 150
Michael TV series, 32
Middle East, Iranians in, 158
Milani, Farzaneh, 87–8, 126, 219
Mina, Nima, 161
Ministry of Commerce, 91
Ministry of Culture and Islamic Guidance, 79
 Ahmadi Arian, Amir, 99
 book distribution, 114, 115
 The Book of Fate (Sahm-e man), 234
 censorship, 74, 49, 84, 101
 Contemporary Art Museum, Tehran, 150
 Council for the Dissemination of Persian Language (*Shora-ye gostaresh-e zaban-e Farsi*), 107
 Domain of Children Literature (Qalamrow-e adbiyyat-e kudakan), 144
 Dowlatabadi, Mahmoud, 100
 independent publishers, 176–7
 Kanun, 143
 literary associations, 11n
 paper market, 90
 permission to print (*Parvaneh-ye nashr*), 80–3, 136
 Rouhani, President Hassan, 109
 Sacred Defence literature, 38
 Sureh Mehr, 40
 'Translation & Publication Grant Program', 151
 visual arts, 243–4
Ministry of Youth and Sports, 64–5
Mirabbasi, Kaveh, 30
 S like Sudabeh (Sin mesl-e sudabeh), 30
Mirabeidini, Hassan, 39, 166
Mirhadi, Touran, 144–5, 147
Mir-Hosseini, Ziba, 235
Mirsadeghi, Jamal, 27, 249
Mirza, Iraj, 61

Mirzay, Mohammad Said, 60
Missaghi, Poupeh, 92–3
Mobtakeran, 133
Modarressi, Taqi, 197
  Adab-e ziarat, 197
  The Pilgrim's Rules of Etiquette, 197
Moebali, Mahsa, *Don't Worry (Negaran nabash)*, 29
Moein, Roozbeh, *The Cold Coffee of Mr Writer (Qahveh-ye sard-e aqa-ye nevisandeh)*, 69
Moghadam, Amin, 97, 158, 164
Moghaddam, Cyrus, 32
Moghaddari, Sonja, 163
Mohafez, Sudabeh, 178
Mohaghegh, Mehdi, 107
Mohammad Ali, Mohammad, 227
Mohammadi, Ali, 109
Mohammadi Ardahali, Ali, 109
Mokhtari, Tara, 221
Monir, Alexandra, *The Final Six*, 29
Moosavi, Amir, 40
Morad, Mehrdad, 30
Moradi Kermani, Houshang, 143
  Iranology (Iran shenasi), 105
  The Water Urn (Khomreh), 105, 175, 176, 176n
Moretti, Franco, 252
The Morning After (Bamdad-e khomar), 34–5
Morozov, Evgeny, 48
Mortezaei, Mehran, 225
Mosallah, 72
Motlagh, Amy, 161
Moussavi, Granaz, 222
  Red Memories, 224
Moussavi, Seyed Mehdi, 60, 178
Mujahedin-e khalq, 202
Munro, Alice, 59
Museum of Sacred Defence, 138n
Muslims
  extremists, US, 160
  in France, 160
  in UK, 160
My Tehran for Sale, 222

Naakojaa
  Candle & Fog and, 177
  divisions between Iran and diaspora, 156, 169, 170–4, 178, 200
  France, 66, 205
  online presence, 204
Nabokov, Vladimir, *Lolita*, 99

Naeej, Elham, 35, 113
Naficy, Hamid, 241
Nafisi, Azar, *Reading Lolita in Tehran*, 156, 195–6, 220, 230, 231–2, 232t
Naghibi, Nima, 219
Nahapétian, Naïri, 33, 205
Najafi, Shahin, 60, 68
Naji Honar, 32–3
Najmabadi, Afsaneh, 34
Nam Le, *The Boat*, 215
Namjoo, Mohsen, *Toranj*, 40
Nanquette, Laetitia
  Censoring an Iranian Love Story, 231
  Da, 26, 38, 41
  Franco-Iranians, 203
  global cultural exchanges, 13
  Iranian migration, 161
  Iranians in Australia, 212, 222
  memoirs, 219
  Naakojaa, 172–3
  'Other', 204
  refugees, 215, 217
  Southerly, 221
  translations, 127, 248
Nashr-e sokhan, 101
Nasrabadi, Manijeh, 186
Nassehy-Behnam, Vida, 159
National Endowment for the Arts, 184
National Information Network (*Shabakeh-ye melli-ye ettela'at*), 45–71
National Iranian American Council (NIAC), 159
National Library, 115, 138n
Nazmjou, Tinouche, 171–3
Negarestani, Reza, *Cyclonopedia*, 29
Nemat, Marina, *Prisoner of Tehran*, 220
Nevertheless (Hanuz), 62
New Horizon Award, 150
New Poetry (*She'r-e now*), 252
New South Wales, Iranians in, 210–11
The New York Review of Books, 231, 233
The New York Times, 180, 220
The New Yorker, 231, 233
New Zealand, Boochani, Behrouz, 218
Newbery, John, 140
Ney, 173
Neyestan, 43
Nezami, 42
Nia, Akram Pedram, 99
Nimatullahi Sufi Center, Sydney, 160
Nobel Prize in Literature, 59, 185
Nogaam, 66, 173–4

Nojoumian, Amir-Ali, 37
Nomani, Farhad, 74–5, 76
Nooraninejad, Setayesh, 226n
Norton, W. W., 190–1n
Norton Anthology of World Literature, 198
Norway, Cultural Council, 91
'not ourselves' (*gheyr-e khodis*), 110
Novin, 68
Nowruz Literary Agency, 239
NSW Premier's Literary Awards, Multicultural Prize, 221
Nuraei, Saman, *Pines are Upside Down (Kajha varunehand)*, 31

Office for the Development of Books and Book Reading (*Daftar-e tose'eh-ye ketab va ketabkhani*), 81–2
official (*rasmi*), 74
offset (*ofset*), 97
Ofoq, 30, 55, 93
OFPRA (French Office for the Protection of Refugees and Stateless People), 202n
oil industry, 208
Olszewska, Zuzanna, 9, 111
Omri, Mohamed-Salah, 250
Once Upon a Time (Yeki bud, yeki nabud), 167
online communication, 162
  democratic online communities, 61–4
online publishing, 65–6, 169, 172
  censorship, 74
  France, 66
  readers' comments, 70–1
  UK, 66
'open doors', 120
Organization for Researching and Composing University Textbooks in the Humanities (*Sazman-e motale'e va tadvin-e kotob-e olum-e ensani-ye daneshgah-ha*), 75
Orientalism, 195
  'digital Orientalism', 48, 58
'Other', 156, 204, 218
Our Literature (Adabiyyat-e ma), 66
'ours' (*khodis*), 110
Overland, 217
Oziran, 223

Pacific Solution 1 and 2, 215n, 217
page-turner (*Pavaraqi*), 68–9
Pahlavi, Empress Farah, 99, 142, 202
Pahlavi period, 202, 258

Palm, Christian, 161
Pamuk, Orhan, 185, 198
  My Name is Red, 198
Panahi, 242
paper market 90–1
Papua New Guinea, asylum seekers, 209
'parallel space', 74
Paris
  exile, 201
  Hedayat, Sadegh, 167–8
  Khavaran, 174
  Naakojaa, 170
Park-e shahr, 144
Parramatta Council, 227
Parsipour, Shahrnush, 231, 233
Parvin E'tesami Literary Prize, 115
patronage, 186
Patton, Simon, 182
Payam-e hamyar, 223
Payam-e Noor University, 105
PEN International, 172
People's Mujahedin, 213
permission to print (*Parvaneh-ye nashr*), 79; *see also* publishing permit
Persian Constitutional Revolution 1905-11, 164–5, 167
Persian cultural system, 229–254
Persian Gulf, 166
The Persian Herald, 224
Persian language, 2–3, 5–6, 166, 168–9, 176, 257–8
Persian Language and Literature Olympiad, 107
Persian Language Centre, Belgrade, 104
Persian Library in Sydney, 226–7
Persian New Year (*Nowruz*), 165, 226, 227
Persian Publishers Network, 11
'Persianate literature', 5–6
Persianblog.ir, 47
Peyk-e hamyar, 223–4
Phillips, Sara, 176
Pirzad, Zoya, 197–8, 198n
  I Turn Off the Lights, 198n
  Things We Left Unsaid, 198n
'poet of the revolution' (*Sha'er-e enqelab*), 57
Poeticas Magazine, 68
poetry
  book production, 25
  Candle & Fog, 175
  divide between prose and poetry, 245–3
  erotic, 69–70

Index Translationum, 182
Iranian writers in Australia, 221–2
Jadiri, Sepideh, 172
Persian cultural system, 6–7, 245–8, 251–2
Schirasi, Ali, 178
translations, 129, 196–7
POL, 175, 239
pop music, 15
The Postman (Postchi), 68–9
'postmodern *ghazal*', 60
PourEsfahani, Homa, *Bitter Chocolate (Shokolat-e talkh)*, 71
Pouya Cultural Centre, 203
pre-publication permit (*Mojavez-e pish az enteshar-e ketab*), 79–80; *see also* publishing permit
Prosecutor General of Iran, 49
Public Affairs Alliance of Iranian Americans (PAAIA), 159
publishers
  per type, *134*
  proportion by activity, *189*
  across borders, 169–70
  by region, *191*
publishing permit, 79–80, 99–101, 136

Qabbani, Nizar Tawfiq, 'Dawn' ('*Sepideh dam*'), 42
Qajars, 168, 201–2, 258
Qalibaf, Mohammad Baqer, 138n
Qazvini, Mohammad, 201
Qom, 96, 130–2
Qoqnoos, 30–1, 30–1n, 66
quatrain forms *roba'i*/*do-beyti*, 59

Rafiei, Mehran, 221
Rafsanjani, President Hashemi, 120
Rahbaran, Shiva, 155
Rahimi, Babak, 48
Rahnama, Ali, 74–5, 76
Rajabzadeh, Ahmad, 85–7, 89
Rajavi, Maryam, 202
Rasht, 132
Rastegar, Kamran, 39
Ravanipour, Moniru, 54
Razaghipoor, Sirous, 226n, 227
refugees, 212–13, 214–15, 215n
  in Britain, 214
  stories and plays, 216–18
  see also asylum seekers
religious authors, 182

religious figures, literary texts on, 41–4
religious literature, 25, 125, 130–2, 186
religious minorities, 210
Rendy, Leila Samadi, 161
Research Centre for Written Heritage (*Markaz-e pazhuheshi-ye miras-e maktub*), 238
Revolution Square, Tehran, 1, 98
Rey Chow, 'Against the Lures of the Diaspora', 156
romances, 25, 33–6
  circulation of, 230
  female characters in, 35–6
  gender stereotypes, 35–6
  Harlequin romantic fiction, 35, 219
  readers' comments, 63
  translations, 194
Rose, Jacqueline, 'The Impossibility of Children's Fiction', 140
Roshan Initiative in Persian Digital Humanities, 117
Rouhani, President Hassan, 77, 109, 120–1, 136–7
Rousseau, Jean-Jacques, 140
Roy, Olivier, 1–2
Rumi, 182, 197
Rushdie, Salman, 177

Saadi Foundation, 102–8
  Candle & Fog and, 176
  constitution Article 13, 106
  cultural institutions, 101–2
  Darbandi, Seyyed Mohammad Reza, 42–3, 101n
  translations, 186
Sabuhi, Nasrolah, 109
Sacred Defence Book of the Year, 57
Sacred Defence cinema, 241
Sacred Defence literature, 2, 25, 37–8, 38–41, 186n
Sadeghi, Leila, 62–3
Sa'di, 61
  Golestan, 59
Sadr, Abolhassan Bani, 202
Sadr, Hamid Reza, 142
Sadr, Musa, 42
Sahamizadeh, Nazanin, *Manus*, 217
Said, Edward, *Culture and Imperialism*, 247
Sakurai, Keiko, 76
Salamati, Mahsa, 92, 96, 162
Salami, Shahnaz, 96–7
Sameni, Nasrin, *The Grey Nights*, 89

Sami, Osamah, *Good Muslim Boy*, 221
San Francisco State University, 'Forty Years & More', 165
Saniee, Parinoush
  The Book of Fate (Sahm-e man), 183, 190–1n, 194, 230, 231–2, 232t, 234–7
  My Fate (Sahm-e man), 81
Sapiro, Gisèle, 73, 78, 112, 126
Saqi, 190n
Satrapi, Marjane, *Persepolis*, 156
Sayeh, 223
Schirasi, Ali, 178
School of Oriental and African Studies, 107
Schwartz, Kevin, 168, 258
science fiction, 29
self-censorship, 34–6, 74, 87–8; *see also* censorship
Selim, Samah, 199
Serbia
  International Belgrade Book Fair 2016, 104n
  Soleimani, Mohsen, 104
Serov, Banafsheh, 221
Seyedabadi, Aliasghar, 62
Seyed-Ghorab, Asghar, 40
Shafaei, Shahin, *Refugitive*, 217
Shah, Ahmad, 201
Shah, Mohammad Ali, 201
Shah, Mohammad Reza, 78
Shahnameh, 30, 111, 140
Shahneh Tabar, Afshin, 174–7
Shahr-e Ketab (Book City), 36–7
  creative writing workshops, 31
  Flying Turtle Award (*Lakposht-e parandeh*), 151
  Khabgard, 56, 66
  khosulati, 96
  Short Story Award, 56
Shahrokhi, Mahmoud, 'The Brave Men of Iran' ('*Deliran va Mardan-e Iran Zamin*'), 42
Shahrvand, 58
Shahsavari, Mohammad Hasan, 31, 56
  Crazy Mordad (Mordad-e divaneh), 31
  Dear M., 66
Shamlou, Ahmad, 197, 252
Shams, Fatemeh, 7–8, 25, 39–40, 40, 57
Sharjah International Book Fair Translation Grant Fund, 236
Shayegan, Dariush, *The Poetic Persian Soul*, 246–7
Shegeftzar journal, 29

Sheibani, Khatereh, 252, 253
'she'rgraphy', 70, *70*
Shih, Shu-Mei, 164, 257
  'Against Diaspora', 156
Shiism, 37–8, 40, 41–2, 210
Shiraz, 130, 132
Shojaei, Seyyed Mehdi, 43
Shojaiyan, Fahimeh, 223
Shokrollahi, Seyed Reza, 55–6, 63–4
short story (*dastan-e kutah*), 205, 249–50
short story (hekayat), 59
Siamdoust, Nahid, 169
Siavoshi, Sussan, 79
Simenon, Georges, 30
Sirjani, Sa'idi, 135
Sleepwalker (Khabgard), 47
Small Media, 174
  report, *119*, *122*
  Writer's Block: The Story of Censorship in Iran, 115–37
smartphones, 54
smuggled (*qachaq*), 97, 99
Snir, Reuven, 247
social media, 53–4
  democratic online communities, 61–4
  Facebook, 45, 53–4, 67, 177
  Instagram, 45–6, 54, 65, 67–71, *70*, 178
  Telegram, 45, 67, 178
'Soft war' (*Jang-e narm*), 2
Soleimani, Mohsen, 104
Soroush, 77
South Africa, apartheid, 88, 90
Southerly, 221, 222
Soviet Union, children's literature, 139–40
Spectator Index 2016, 2
Sprachman, Paul, 186n
Sreberny, Annabelle, 165
story (*dastan*), 129
Story Writing Workshop for Gypsies (*Kargah-e dastan nevisi-ye koli-ha*), 54
Sufi brotherhoods, 160–1
'Sufi cool', 161
Supreme Council of Cyberspace, 49
Supreme Council of the Cultural Revolution, 79–82
Sureh Mehr, 1, 7, 39–40, 72, 85, 135
Susijn, Laura, 236
Sweden
  Bokartus and Baran, 174
  Iranians in, 158–9, 160, 164

Sydney
  Iranians in, 211, 212m
  journals, 223
Sydney PEN, 217, 222
Sydney Persian Library, 223, 225–6
Sydney Writers Festival, 217
Syndicate of Paper and Paperboard Manufacturers, 90–1

Tabriz, 132
Taghdis, Sousan, 144
Taheri, Zahra, 222
Tamass, 239
Taraqi, Goli, 87, 89
  'The Encounter', 87
  The Pomegranate Lady and Her Sons, 190–1n
Tat Shahdust, Fereshteh , 63
Tehran Annual Auction, 244
Tehran International Book Fair
  Cheshmeh, 85
  children's literature, 138
  illustrations, 151
  independent versus governmental publishers, 72, 112
  Sacred Defence literature and popular literature, 37
  Uncensored Tehran Book Fair, 174
  Union for Cooperative Publishers of Iran (*Etehadiyeh-ye sherkat-ha-ye ta'avoni-ye nasheran-e Iran*), 108
Tehran Museum of Contemporary Art (TMoCA), 243–4
Tehrani, Abdolah Vaez, 109
Telegram, 45, 67, 178
television, 29, 84–5, 148
  crime stories, 31, 32–3
  satellite, 148
Tenty, Tiffany Amber, 210
'testimonio', 215
TEXT, 222
text mining, 117–18
'textgraphy', 70
3kkk.wordpress.com, 61
Three Percent website, 184n
Tirgan Festival, Stockholm, 164
Tofighian, Omid, 218
translations
  Amazon, 183
  from Arabic language, 195–6
  Australia, 214–24
  children's literature, 140–2

crime stories, 61
diversity and, 197–8
English, 126–7, 166
European languages, 174–5, 248
Finglish (transliteration of Persian words in English), 60
France, 94, 126, 157, 161, 180–206, 248
genre, 196–7
Germany, 185
Japanese literature into English, 182–3
of modern Persian literature in the US, 181–200
number of texts per author, 193
versus original, 126–30
poetry, 129, 196–7
from politics to the market, 94–5
and reception in the US and France
retranslations, 92–3
romances, 194
Russia, 185
Saadi Foundation, 186
Turkish, 185, 198
UNESCO, 185n
US, 94, 180–206, 224
Translator (Motarjem), 95
translators
  ethnic origin of, 187
  primary activity of, 188
Turkey, Iranians in, 158
Turkish, translations, 185, 198
Two Blind Eyes, 241

UK
  Candle & Fog, 174–7
  Iranian Muslims, 160
  Iranians in, 159
  market, 224
  online publishing, 66
  Saadi Foundation, 107
UN Security Council, 93–4
Uncensored Tehran Book Fair, 174
underground (*zirzamini*), 97
underground literary space, 1, 97–102
  and self-publishing, 135–6
UNESCO
  Index Translationum, 126–7, 182, 183
  literacy rates, 11
  market, 8
  translations, 185n
UNHCR, 209

Union for Cooperative Publishers of Iran (*Etehadiyeh-ye sherkat-ha-ye ta'avoni-ye nasheran-e Iran*), 108
Union of Islamic Students Association, UK, 160
Union of Tehran Publishers and Booksellers, 1, 90–1, 101–2, 101n, 108–12, 136
United Arab Emirates (UAE)
  Iranians in, 158
  visual arts, 244
Universal Copyright Convention, 92, 171–2
universities
  Australia, 226
  independent versus governmental publishers, 74–7, 133
  Islamisation, 75–7, 146
University of Maryland, 117
University of Melbourne, 212
University of Strasbourg, 106–7
University of Tehran, 98
  Hamshahri collection, 118
University of Texas, 187
University of Texas Press, 190
US
  hostage crisis 1979, 77, 93
  Iranian Jews, 161
  Iranian writers in, 157, 161
  Iranian-American community, 158, 159, 163, 165
  Iranian-Americans in California, 190
  literary agents as translators in, 191
  literary critics, 26n
  Muslim extremists, 160
  sanctions, 93–4
  translations, 94, 184–6, 224
US State Department, 159, 159n
US Terrorist Travel Prevention Act 2015, 159n
US Visa Waiver Program, 159, 159n

Vafi, Fariba, 197–8
Vahabi, Nader, 163–4, 202n
Vambakhsh, Djamileh, 226
  Periodical of Poetry and Stories from Aknoon (Gahnameh-ye she'r va dastan-e Aknoon), 223
Vanzan, Anna, 161
Varzi, Roxanne, 160–1
Venuti, Lawrence, 95, 182–3, 194–5, 198, 199

verification (*momayezi*), 48–9, 78–9
very short story (*dastanak*), 59–60
Victorian Premier's Prize for Nonfiction, 218
Victorian Prize for Literature, 218
Vietnamese, refugees, 215
visual arts, 243–5
'vulgarity debate', 63–4

Wallerstein, Immanuel, centre-periphery model, 12
white cover (*jeld-e sefid*), 97
White Poetry (*She'r-e sepid*), 252
Wild Dingo, 220
women
  blogging, 52–3
  and censorship, 86–7
  in French exile, 205
  as literary practitioners, 125–6
World Intellectual Property Organization, 92
World Literature Today, 236
World Values Survey 2011 poll, 5

xeroxed (*ziraks*), 97

Yaghmaee, Pirayeh, 222, 226
Yarshater, Ehsan, 141–2
Yasrebi, Chista, 68–9
Years to Today (Sal-ha-ye takonun), 56–8
young adult fiction, 69, 125, 141–2
Youshij, Nima, 175
YouTube, 65
Yushij, Nima, 252

Zakani, Obeid, 61
Zand, Mohsen Soltany, 221
Zareh, Laleh
  Without Coffin (Bitabut), 31
  Young Skull (Jomjomeh-ye javan), 31
Zarrinkelk, Noureddin, 149
Zarrinkoub, Abdolhossein, 246
  Two Centuries of Silence (Do qarn sokut), 100–1
Zaryab, 99
Zendehru, Mohamad, 136
Zia-Ebrahimi, Reza, 101
Zibakalam, Sadegh, 77
Zimbler, Jarad, 90
Zulma, 197–8

EU representative:
Easy Access System Europe
Mustamäe tee 50, 10621 Tallinn, Estonia
Gpsr.requests@easproject.com

www.ingramcontent.com/pod-product-compliance
Lightning Source LLC
Chambersburg PA
CBHW051601230426
43668CB00013B/1931